John Locke and Natural Philosophy

Peter R. Anstey presents a thorough and innovative study of John Locke's views on the method and content of natural philosophy. Focusing on Locke's *Essay concerning Human Understanding*, but also drawing extensively from his other writings and manuscript remains, Anstey argues that Locke was an advocate of the Experimental Philosophy: the new approach to natural philosophy championed by Robert Boyle and the early Royal Society who were opposed to speculative philosophy.

On the question of method, Anstey shows how Locke's pessimism about the prospects for a demonstrative science of nature led him, in the *Essay*, to promote Francis Bacon's method of natural history, and to downplay the value of hypotheses and analogical reasoning in science. But, according to Anstey, Locke never abandoned the ideal of a demonstrative natural philosophy, for he believed that if we could discover the primary qualities of the tiny corpuscles that constitute material bodies, we could then establish a kind of corpuscular metric that would allow us a genuine science of nature. It was only after the publication of the *Essay*, however, that Locke came to realize that Newton's *Principia* provided a model for the role of demonstrative reasoning in science based on principles established upon observation, and this led him to make significant revisions to his views in the 1690s.

On the content of Locke's natural philosophy, it is argued that even though Locke adhered to the Experimental Philosophy, he was not averse to speculation about the corpuscular nature of matter. Anstey takes us into new terrain and new interpretations of Locke's thought, by exploring his mercurialist transmutational chymistry, his theory of generation by seminal principles, and his conventionalism about species.

Peter R. Anstey is an ARC Future Fellow in the Department of Philosophy at the University of Sydney.

John Locke and Natural Philosophy

Peter R. Anstey

UNIVERSITY PRESS

OXFORD
UNIVERSITY PRESS

Great Clarendon Street, Oxford OX2 6DP

Oxford University Press is a department of the University of Oxford.
It furthers the University's objective of excellence in research, scholarship,
and education by publishing worldwide. Oxford is a registered trade mark of
Oxford University Press in the UK and in certain other countries

© Peter R. Anstey 2011

The moral rights of the author have been asserted

First published 2011
First published in paperback 2013

All rights reserved. No part of this publication may be reproduced,
stored in a retrieval system, or transmitted, in any form or by any means,
without the prior permission in writing of Oxford University Press,
or as expressly permitted by law, by licence or under terms agreed with the appropriate
reprographics rights organization. Enquiries concerning reproduction
outside the scope of the above should be sent to the Rights Department,
Oxford University Press, at the address above

You must not circulate this work in any other form
and you must impose this same condition on any acquirer

British Library Cataloguing in Publication Data
Data available

Library of Congress Cataloging in Publication Data
Data available

ISBN 978-0-19-958977-7 (Hbk)
ISBN 978-0-19-967952-2 (Pbk)

For D. M. A.

Contents

Acknowledgments	viii
Preface	ix
Abbreviations	xi
Introduction	1
1. Natural philosophy and the aims of the *Essay*	12
2. Corpuscular pessimism	31
3. Natural history	46
4. Hypotheses and analogy	70
5. Vortices, the deluge, and cohesion	90
6. Mathematics	110
7. Demonstration	136
8. Explanation	153
9. Iatrochemistry	169
10. Generation	188
11. Species	204
Conclusion	219
List of manuscripts	226
Bibliography	228
Index	243

Acknowledgments

The author would like to acknowledge permission to reproduce the following copyright material:

Chapter 3 derives from 'Locke, Bacon and natural history', *Early Science and Medicine*, 7, 2002, pp. 65–92: copyright Brill.

Chapter 4 derives from 'Locke on method in natural philosophy', in *The Philosophy of John Locke: New Perspectives*, ed. Peter R. Anstey, London: Routledge, 2003, pp. 26–42: copyright Routledge.

Chapter 9 derives from 'John Locke and Helmontian medicine', in *The Body as Object and Instrument of Knowledge: Embodied Empiricism in Early Modern Science*, eds Charles Wolfe and Ofer Gal, Dordrecht: Springer, 2010, pp. 93–117: copyright Springer.

Figure 5.2 (cross-section of a vortex) is reprinted with permission of Open Court Publishing Company, a division of Carus Publishing Company, Chicago, IL from *The Principles of Descartes' Philosophy* by Benedictus de Spinoza, transl. H. H. Britan, 1974: copyright Open Court Publishing.

Jacket illustration: the 'Science and Philosophy' window of the Great Hall at the University of Sydney picturing (from left to right) Robert Boyle, Sir Isaac Newton, and John Locke. The window was executed by Clayton and Bell and photographed by Raymond de Berquelle on behalf of the University of Sydney. Reproduced with permission of the University of Sydney Archives.

Preface

The long period of gestation that this book has enjoyed has coincided with the very rewarding process of editing (with Lawrence Principe) John Locke's writings on natural philosophy and medicine for the Clarendon edition of Locke's *Works*. The book is, in a sense, an opinionated commentary on those writings and their relation to Locke's *Essay concerning Human Understanding*. Most of Locke's writings on natural philosophy and medicine are available in print; however, a significant amount remains unpublished amongst Locke's notebooks and papers. The challenge of editing and interpreting the rich array of material to be found among Locke's manuscript remains, which pertains to natural philosophy, has led me to produce a variety of ancillary studies. These studies are not included in the present book, but they have established a crucial platform of scholarship on which a number of the central claims presented here are based. These studies have also led me to draw on the expertise of others, and in this regard I owe a significant debt to the following people. First, I should like to thank Stephen Harris of the Department of Plant Sciences at Oxford University for his assistance in the analysis of the material that relates to Locke's botanical interests. Second, I have drawn on the expertise of John Burrows of the University of Newcastle, NSW, Australia in order to determine the authorship of some of Locke's early medical essays. Burrows, a pioneer of the method of computational stylistics, has become a long-distance friend through his good humour and brutally honest assessment of my work. Ours has been a thoroughly enjoyable and stimulating collaboration.

I have also profited greatly from my collaboration with Michael Hunter on matters relating to Locke and Robert Boyle among Locke's papers in the Bodleian Library and among the Boyle Papers at the Royal Society in London. I also owe a large debt to J. R. Milton of King's College London for all that he has taught me about Locke's manuscript remains in the Lovelace Collection in the Bodleian Library and about the materials found among the Shaftesbury Papers in the National Archives at Kew. Finally, Lawrence Principe was an invaluable guide to me as I worked my way through Locke's chymical notebooks and papers.

The book has been a decade in the making, and during its writing I have accrued many debts. Earlier versions were used as the texts for postgraduate courses at the University of Sydney and at the University of Otago, and I profited from numerous insightful comments and criticisms made by students. In addition, Jack MacIntosh graciously read much of an advanced draft and gave detailed comments, as did three anonymous readers for the Press. John Rogers kindly provided a part of his transcription of Draft C of Locke's *Essay*. Among the many others who have contributed through advice, reflection, comment, and encouragement are the following: Julia

Anstey, David Armstrong, David Braddon-Mitchell, Daniel Carey, Philip Catton, Antonio Clericuzio, Sorana Corneanu, Angus Dingwell, Mihnea Dobre, Lisa Downing, Ofer Gal, Stephen Gaukroger, Rod Girle, Juan Manuel Gomez, Bill Harper, Colin Harris, Peter Harrison, Sara Hilder, David Howard, Dana Jalobeanu, Donald Kerr, Fred Kroon, Jo Macdonald, Noel Malcolm, Julia Mant, Peter Millican, Clemency Montelle, Alan Musgrave, Bill Newman, Victor Nuovo, Josh Parsons, Charles Pigden, Greg Radick, John Schuster, Alan Shapiro, Richard Serjeantson, George Smith, M. A. Stewart, Alberto Vanzo, J. C. Walmsley, Rob Wilson, and Charles Wolfe.

Earlier versions of Chapters 3 and 4 were read at a symposium on 'New work on the philosophy of John Locke' held at the University of Sydney in 2001. This symposium, and my research from 2000 to 2003, were generously funded by a U2000 Postdoctoral Fellowship at the University of Sydney. Chapter 7, on demonstration, was read at the AAPNZ conference at the University of Canterbury in December 2008 and at the University of Otago. Chapter 8, on explanation, was first read at the University of Bucharest in May 2007. It was also read at the inaugural Otago/Sydney Early Modern Seminar in October 2007 at the University of Otago. Chapter 9 derives from a paper entitled 'John Locke and Helmontian medicine', which was presented to the 'Embodied empiricism' workshop at the University of Sydney, where I am an Honorary Professor, in February 2009. An earlier version of Chapter 10, on generation, was read at the John Locke Tercentenary conference in Oxford in April 2004 and has been available online since 2007. Earlier versions of Chapter 11 were read at the universities of Leeds, Oxford, Otago, Paris X Nanterre, and Sydney in 2005.

Abbreviations

Abrégé	John Locke (1688) 'Extrait d'un livre Anglois qui n'est pas encore publié, intitulé *Essai philosophique concernant l'entendement, où l'on montre quelle est l'étendue de nos connoissances certaines, & la maniere dont nous y parvenons*. Communique par Monsieur Locke', *Bibliothèque universelle et historique de l'année*, Tome 8, pp. 49–142.
Bacon Works	Francis Bacon (1996–) *The Oxford Francis Bacon*, 15 vols, ed. Graham Rees et al., Oxford: Clarendon Press.
Bodl.	Bodleian Library.
BP	Royal Society Boyle Papers.
Boyle Correspondence	Robert Boyle (2001) *The Correspondence of Robert Boyle*, 6 vols, ed. M. Hunter, A. Clericuzio, and L. M. Principe, London: Pickering and Chatto.
Boyle Works	Robert Boyle (1999–2000) *The Works of Robert Boyle*, 14 vols, ed. M. Hunter and E. B. Davis, London: Pickering and Chatto.
Conduct	John Locke (1823) *Of the Conduct of the Understanding*, in *Locke Works*, Vol. 3, pp. 205–89.
Correspondence	John Locke (1976–) *The Correspondence of John Locke*, 9 vols, ed. E. S. de Beer, Oxford: Clarendon Press.
Essay	John Locke (1975) *An Essay concerning Human Understanding* [1690], 4th edn, ed. P. H. Nidditch, Oxford: Clarendon Press.
Locke Works	John Locke (1823) *The Works of John Locke*, 10 vols, 12th edn, London: Thomas Tegg.
Library of John Locke	J. Harrison and P. Laslett (1971), *The Library of John Locke*, 2nd edn, Oxford: Clarendon Press.
LL	Locke's Library—introducing entry numbers from *Library of John Locke*.
Oldenburg Correspondence	Henry Oldenburg (1965–86) *The Correspondence of Henry Oldenburg*, 13 vols, ed. A. R. Hall and M. B. Hall, Madison, Milwaukee, and London: University of Wisconsin Press, Mansell, and Taylor & Francis.
PRO	Public Record Office.
Second Reply	John Locke (1823) *Mr. Locke's Reply to the Bishop of Worchester's Answer to his Second Letter*, in *Locke Works*, Vol. 4, pp. 193–498.
STCE	John Locke (1989) *Some Thoughts concerning Education* [1693], 3rd edn, ed. J. W. Yolton and J. S. Yolton, Oxford: Clarendon Press.
TNA	The National Archives.

A note on citations

References to passages in the *Essay* are given as *E*, followed by book number, chapter number, section number; e.g. *E* IV. xii. 1.

References to quotations from the *Essay* are given as *E*, followed by book number, chapter number, section number, and page number; e.g. *E* IV. xii. 10, p. 645.

References to quotations from editions of the *Essay* other than the 4th, which is listed here, are marked by adding an ordinal subscript to *E*. All such quotations derive from the critical apparatus of the 1975 Nidditch edition of the *Essay* and the page numbers of the quotations reflect this; e.g. E_1 IV. iii. 18, p. 549.

References to Draft A and Draft B of the *Essay* are from John Locke (1990) *Drafts for the* Essay *concerning Human Understanding and Other Philosophical Writings*, Vol. 1: *Drafts A and B*, ed. P. H. Nidditch and G. A. J. Rogers, Oxford: Clarendon Press.

References to passages in Draft A and Draft B are given by draft, section number, page number; e.g. Draft A, §11, p. 22.

Quotes from manuscript sources have been silently corrected and contractions expanded.

The solidus (/) is used in references to printed works to indicate facing-page translations.

The solidus is used in references to manuscripts to indicate continuous entries that occur on non-sequential pages.

Introduction

> I had much rather the speculative and quick-sighted should complain of my being in some parts tedious, than that any one, not accustomed to abstract Speculations, or prepossessed with different Notions, should mistake, or not comprehend my meaning.
>
> John Locke[1]

John Locke was not a natural philosopher, and yet what he had to say about our knowledge of the natural world has been enormously influential from his day until our own. This study is an attempt to look anew at Locke's writings on natural philosophy, with special reference to his *Essay concerning Human Understanding*, and to present a fresh analysis of Locke's philosophical contribution to what we now call the philosophy of science. As such, it is a study in the history of philosophy rather than a study in the history of science. This is not to say that the history of science does not inform and set parameters on the enquiry. Rather, the study aims throughout to be sensitive to Locke's historical, intellectual and social contexts. Yet the central questions asked and the key issues addressed will be of most interest to historians of philosophy, and it is hoped that this study will offer new leads and suggest new lines of inquiry for historians of philosophy in general and for Locke scholars in particular.

Locke retained an active interest in natural philosophy for over four decades: he wrote on the subject; he knew many of the leading English natural philosophers of his day and some continental ones as well; he was a member of the Royal Society from November 1668[2] and contributed to the *Philosophical Transactions* of the Society; he read widely in the field; he dabbled in experiments and was a keen observer of nature. As early as 1666, Robert Boyle could call him a virtuoso,[3] and by the last decade of his

---

[1] 'Epistle to the Reader', *Essay*, p. 9.
[2] Locke was elected as a Fellow on 26 November 1668 and served on the Council in 1669 and 1672. See Hunter 1994, pp. 184–5.
[3] Boyle to Locke, 2 June 1666, *Correspondence*, Vol. 1, p. 279.

life Locke had acquired such a reputation for his knowledge in natural philosophy that in August 1694 Hans Sloane, then Secretary of the Royal Society, writing to Locke to report on a whirlwind in Northamptonshire, could say: 'All philosophic occurrences are so well known to you that I am sure you might inform me, better than I, you . . . '.[4]

It is my contention that the writings of John Locke on natural philosophy have in many cases been poorly interpreted and that a new approach is required. To this end, I have undertaken a broad and thorough survey of Locke's extant writings on the subject, including his reading notes, his unpublished reflections, his correspondence, and his published works. Such a survey has raised a number of issues over and above those of interpretation, which are not unique to Locke, but which are comparatively rare in early modern scholarship. They arise from the vast quantity of material from Locke's archive that has survived, coupled with the almost obsessive nature of Locke's note taking and recording of his thoughts. Pierre Coste certainly had Locke's measure when he reflected that 'Mr. Locke above all things, loved Order; and he had got the way of observing it in every thing, with wonderful exactness'.[5]

The issues that one confronts when dealing with Locke's writings are the following. First, there is the question of his intellectual development. It is well known that Locke was influenced by those leading natural philosophers and physicians with whom he associated, but the problem of reconstructing his relationships with the likes of Boyle, Thomas Sydenham, Isaac Newton, and William Molyneux, and of establishing sources of influence, is a complex one, which has not always been handled well by Locke scholars. Furthermore, many significant developments within natural philosophy occurred during the period of Locke's interest in the subject—for instance the establishment of the first scientific institutions, the widespread discussion of natural philosophical methodology, and the publication of seminal works like Robert Boyle's *New Experiments Physico-Mechanicall, Touching the Spring of the Air and its Effects* (1660, LL 462, 2nd edn 1662; hereafter *Spring of the Air*). Not surprisingly, Locke's writings reflect these developments, and at times he had to make adjustments to opinions he had expressed in print. It is also important to point out that Locke's views on natural philosophy played a role in other aspects of his thought, in particular in those concerned with the nature of knowledge and belief.

Second, we know that there are gaps in the manuscript materials available today. Some of Locke's notebooks have not survived, and it is likely that we cannot identify all of Locke's writings, even though some may still be extant. For example, we know that Locke wrote a number of reviews for the *Bibliothèque universelle et historique*; and yet, to date, only two have been positively identified: these are reviews of the Latin edition of Boyle's *Specific Medicines* (*De specificiorum remediorum cum corpusculari*

---

[4] *Correspondence*, Vol. 5, p. 114. See also Philipp van Limborch to Joannes Georgius Graevius, 21 November/1 December 1684, ibid., Vol. 2, p. 653: 'Locke [...] is a most scholarly gentleman, [...] in knowledge of the humanities, of theology, medicine, and natural philosophy he has few equals'.

[5] 'The character of Mr. Locke', in Locke 1720, p. xvi.

philosophia concordia, 1686) and Newton's *Mathematical Principles of Natural Philosophy* (*Philosophiae naturalis principia mathematica*, 1687, LL 2083).[6] Third, until recently, some of the more important material has not been easily accessible to scholars; and, out of the material from Locke's manuscripts that has been published, some is not in a reliable form, whereas in other cases the provenance of the material has not been correctly understood. For example, until recently, the only available version of Locke's early essay on the use of respiration, 'Respirationis usus', was seriously defective because it follows the pagination of the manuscript which has been misbound.[7] The upshot of all of these considerations is that a fresh and thorough analysis of all of Locke's extant writings on natural philosophy needs to be undertaken.

Early modern philosophy

Early modern disciplinary boundaries differed markedly from those of the twenty-first century. In fact the period is characterized by a degree of fluidity in the manner in which the various disciplines of knowledge were divided up, and even Locke's own writings contain a number of different maps of knowledge. Overall, the most widespread view of philosophy was that it is most naturally divided into moral philosophy and natural philosophy. Turning to natural philosophy, the most important frame of reference for understanding early modern English specimens of it is that of the distinction between speculative and experimental natural philosophy. From the early 1660s on, natural philosophy was increasingly understood as being polarized around these two different methodologies. The distinction is well expressed in John Dunton's *The Young-Students-Library*, which appeared just after the publication of Locke's *Essay*:

Philosophy may be consider'd under these two Heads, Natural and Moral: The first of which, by Reason of the strange Alterations that have been made in it, may be again Subdivided into *Speculative* and *Experimental*.[8]

Or, again, it is formulated by Locke's adversary John Sergeant, who claims:

The METHODS which I pitch upon to examine, shall be of two sorts, viz. that of *Speculative*, and that of *Experimental* Philosophers; The Former of which pretend to proceed by *Reason* and *Principles*; the Later by *Induction*; and both of them aim at advancing *Science*.[9]

---

[6] Locke's friend Jean Le Clerc claimed that '[h]e [Locke] made me likewise several Extracts of Books, as that of Mr. *Boyle concerning Specifique Remedies*, which is in the same Tome, and some others that are in the following', Le Clerc 1706, p. 14. For further discussion, see J. R. Milton 2011.

[7] See Dewhurst 1960. The correct pagination is given in Milton 1994, p. 33 n. 13. For a new translation, see Walmsley and Meyer 2009. A critical edition of the Latin, with an English translation, will appear in *John Locke: Writings on Natural Philosophy and Medicine*, ed. Peter Anstey and Lawrence Principe, Oxford: Clarendon Press.

[8] Dunton 1692, p. vi.

[9] Sergeant 1696 (LL 2627), Preface [Sig. b.6r–v], underlining added. See also John Baron to Locke, 12 September 1698, *Correspondence*, Vol. 6, p. 475: 'Science or Knowledge is either *Speculative* [...] or *Practicall* [...]'.

This distinction provided some of the fundamental terms of reference for anyone practising natural philosophy or reflecting on the nature of natural philosophical method in Britain. The experimental philosophy was characterized by a commitment to observation and experiment. It was also characterized by either opposition to, or at best a very cautious application of, hypotheses in natural philosophy. The speculative philosophy, by contrast, was characterized by the development of speculative hypotheses without recourse to experiment or observation, or, at best, by a kind of *post hoc* concession to experiment or by an attempt to save the phenomena. Speculative philosophers were renowned for proceeding from first principles to the development of full-blown natural philosophical systems. By the late seventeenth century, Descartes' vortex theory of planetary motions had come to be regarded as the archetypal speculative system.[10] It is my contention that this distinction between experimental and speculative philosophy is absolutely essential for understanding Locke's involvement in natural philosophy both as a part-time practitioner and as a philosopher. The experimental and speculative methodologies were not simply empty rhetoric; rather they were actively applied. For example, Robert Boyle's very detailed prescriptions for the correct method of experimental natural philosophy, which Boyle developed in the mid-1660s, were applied by Boyle in almost all of his subsequent publications in natural philosophy.[11]

Now the experimental philosophers' commitment to observation and experiment took a very specific form in the first decades of the life of the Royal Society. Experimental philosophy was largely practised through the application of the Baconian method of natural history. The content and structure of such histories is spelt out in Chapter 3 below. The major proponents of this method were all associates of Locke. It is somewhat harder, however, to single out the proponents of the speculative philosophy from the latter half of the seventeenth century, and there is no doubt that, once the experimental approach attained ascendency, the speculative philosopher became something of a straw man—although, throughout the period his schools or leading systems were evident. These leading systems or hypotheses of speculative philosophers were the Cartesian, the Epicurean, and the Aristotelian. In some instances the chymists, who followed Paracelsus or Joan Baptista van Helmont, were also regarded as putting forward speculative systems.

The new experimental philosophy constituted not just the experimental method practised along natural historical lines. Ironically, it also spawned a new speculative hypothesis of its own: the corpuscularian hypothesis, as articulated and championed by Boyle. This state of affairs requires some explanation. Two mitigating factors rendered the development of the corpuscularian hypothesis a legitimate speculative theory in the

---

[10] For a detailed treatment of the experimental/speculative distinction in natural philosophy, see Anstey 2005.
[11] For a detailed treatment of Boyle's natural philosophical method, see Anstey and Hunter 2008. For Boyle's prescriptions, see Boyle 2008.

eyes of the experimental philosophers. First, it was specifically developed as a *via media* or generic hypothesis, which was neutral on the question of the divisibility of matter. The experimentalists regarded the disputes about the infinite divisibility of material substance as a purely philosophical inquiry (given the limits of our senses)—an issue that was independent of observation and therefore not one that could be settled by natural philosophers, who were prepared to examine nature itself. This rendered the corpuscularian hypothesis superior to its main rivals, insofar as it avoided a purely speculative dispute.

Second, and this is of significance for Locke's philosophy, most leading experimentalists did not preclude speculation altogether, but believed that it should only be undertaken once the project of natural history is complete or nearing completion. Of particular importance here, again, is Robert Boyle, who repeatedly stressed the mutual benefit that experimental and speculative philosophers offer each other. To that end, Boyle wrote a number of essays, no longer extant, on the theme 'Of Usefulnes of Speculative & Experimental Philosophy to one another'.[12] Boyle himself carefully crafted his own speculative writings so that they would dovetail with his 'historical' writings, and he did this with a view to making them lend mutual support to each other. Following Bacon, he also recommended that natural philosophers familiarize themselves with a summary of the leading speculative theories of the day, though here he stressed the danger of prepossession. It was quite in keeping with the experimental philosophy, then, that one should develop speculative theory. There was an important constraint, however: such speculation should only proceed on the foundation of extensive observational evidence.

Throughout the late seventeenth century, methodological reflection on the practice of natural philosophy did not remain static. And a crucial development took place on the experimental side of the experimental–speculative divide. From the late 1680s it came to be believed that Newton, in his *Principia*, had developed and applied a new mathematical form of the experimental philosophy. This radically different and enormously powerful experimental method eventually displaced the Baconian method of natural history. To be sure, people still paid lip service to Francis Bacon as the progenitor of the experimental philosophy and to Boyle as his leading protégé, yet the Baconian method of natural history (as distinct from traditional natural history, which involved cataloguing nature) was eventually eclipsed. The Newtonian method became the dominant way in which natural philosophy was supposed to be practised. The method championed by the early Royal Society had been supplanted. This transition was too late for Boyle, who died in 1691, but it was to have a lasting effect on Locke after the publication of the first edition of his *Essay*—or so I shall argue in the pages that follow.

---

[12] *Boyle Works*, Vol. 14, p. 342, Vol. 11, p. 413. See also Sargent 1995, p. 164 (from BP 9, fol. 30v, overlapping with BP 10, fol. 12) and BP 9, fols 26 and 59. This is also the subject of one of the chapter headings for Boyle's *Paralipomena*: see Hunter 2007b, p. 190.

Natural philosophy and medicine

A second issue involved in Locke's understanding of natural philosophy concerns its relation to medicine. Locke was a physician. He first became interested in medicine in the late 1650s, and this interest continued uninterruptedly, although through periods of varying intensity, until very near the end of his life.[13] Some of the claims that Locke makes in his medical writings are also found in his writings on natural philosophy and recur in the *Essay*. The most important example is the corpuscular pessimism exhibited in Locke's early medical essay 'Anatomia'—a pessimism which is prominent in his *Essay*.[14] It is crucial therefore to point out that Locke conceived the relation between natural philosophy and medicine to be a relatively seamless one.

In Italian universities of the late Renaissance, medicine was regarded as subaltern to natural philosophy in the division of the sciences. Yet natural philosophy and logic were considered the most useful subjects for medical students to study. The precedent for this state of things is found in Aristotle's comments on the close relation between medicine and natural philosophy in the *De sensu*.[15] The widely used catch-phrase 'Where the natural philosopher finishes, there begins the physician'[16] summed up the close relationship between natural philosopher and physician during the Renaissance.[17]

By the beginning of the seventeenth century, there were strident calls for a reform of medicine, and it was only natural that these calls were closely aligned, in some quarters, with the need to reform natural philosophy. The calls came from the followers of Paracelsus and from Francis Bacon, who regarded the renovation of medicine as part of his all-encompassing great instauration of knowledge.[18] Bacon's programme for a new natural philosophy, under which medicine was effectively subsumed, was taken up by the early Royal Society, and physicians played a major role in the emergence of the new experimental natural philosophy, in Baconian style, of the Society.[19] The connection between medicine and natural philosophy in the late 1650s and early 1660s, a crucial period in Locke's intellectual formation, was quite intimate. Thus for example the physician Thomas Willis, whose lectures on 'physic' were attended by Locke,[20] was appointed Sedleian Professor of Natural Philosophy at Oxford in 1660.

---

[13] On 11 September 1697 Locke told William Molyneux that 'having now wholly laid by the study of physick, I know not what comes out new, or worth reading, in that faculty': *Correspondence*, Vol. 6, p. 190. However, Locke was still giving Henry Fletcher medical advice for his wife in April 1701 (ibid., Vol. 8, pp. 441–3).

[14] On the authorship of 'Anatomia', see Anstey and Burrows 2009.

[15] *De sensu* 436^{a}18–^{b}2, in Aristotle 1984, Vol. 1, p. 693.

[16] *Ubi desinit physicus, ibi medicus incipit.*

[17] For further discussion, see Schmitt 1985 and Maclean 2002, pp. 80–4.

[18] On the importance of Paracelsianism for medical reform, see Pagel 1982, ch. 5; Debus 1991 and 2001, ch. 1. On Bacon and medical reform, see Webster 2002.

[19] For Boyle's Baconianism, see Anstey and Hunter 2008. For physicians and Baconian method, see Cook 1990 and Frank 1979.

[20] Locke's copy of Richard Lower's notes on Willis' lectures survive and are reproduced in Dewhurst 1980.

Conversely, some of Locke's contemporaries who were natural philosophers maintained an active interest in medicine. The likes of Boyle and Hooke were central to the exciting experimental work of the 'Oxford physiologists', alongside the physicians Richard Lower, John Mayow, and Ralph Bathurst.[21]

Furthermore, some of those pressing for the reform of medicine appealed explicitly to the changes that were taking place within natural philosophy, taking it as a model for the advancement of the medical arts. Marchamont Nedham, in his *Medela medicinæ*, construed medical reform in Baconian terms and stressed the need for changes that paralleled those which characterized the new natural philosophy. He explicitly appealed to the authority of Thomas Willis and Robert Boyle, quoting Boyle's claim that

till men have a righter Knowledg of the Principles of Natural Philosophy, without which 'tis hard to arive at a more comprehensive Theorie of the various possible Causes of Diseases, [...] the Method which supposes this knowledge should be other than in many things defective.[22]

In fact, so intertwined were the experimental investigations of physicians and natural philosophers into anatomy, physiology, and chymistry at this time that it comes as no surprise to find Boyle claiming that medicine is really 'a *Part* or *Application* of natural philosophy'.[23] In his *Specific Medicines*, which incidentally Boyle advertises as a 'Speculative discourse' rather than an historical one, Boyle delineates their relation more clearly. He says: 'it must often happen, that the Medicinal Art and this Science [natural philosophy] will be conversant about the same subject, tho' in differing ways, and with differing scopes'.[24] For Boyle, the former aims at cures and the latter aims at the discovery of truth. Locke seems to have held a similar view, for in his review of this very book, in 1686, he speaks of the enormous range of speculations about the nature of the corpuscles that constitute the observable bodies by saying:

[t]here have been an infinite number of Conjectures made upon these little Bodies, and some have made it their endeavour to draw hence Consequences, not only for Natural and Experimental Philosophy, but also for Medicine.[25]

That Locke and his contemporaries saw the implications of corpuscular conjectures not only for natural philosophy, but also for medicine is indicative of the way in which developments in medical methodology in the latter half of the seventeenth century in many respects mirrored those in natural philosophy. Thus medicine could be practised

---

[21] See Frank 1980. Boyle received an honorary MD from Oxford in 1665.
[22] Nedham 1665, p. 209; see *Boyle Works*, Vol. 3, p. 458. For a reference to Willis, see Nedham 1665, pp. 237–8. Note, too, William Simpson's comments on medicine as natural philosophy in his preface to *Hydrologia Chymica*, 1669 (LL 2684), 'To the Reader', sig. A5–6.
[23] *Boyle Works*, Vol. 11, p. 398, quoted in Hunter 2000b, p. 157. Thomas Sprat paraphrases Aristotle by saying 'Where the Natural Philosopher ends, the Physitian must begin' (Sprat 1667, p. 33), and William Petty declared: 'The Physician must be a Philosopher' (Petty 1647, p. 12).
[24] Boyle, *Specific Medicines*, in *Boyle Works*, Vol. 10, p. 353.
[25] Quoting the translation in Dunton 1692, p. 184.

by using experiment or observation, as the chymical physicians stressed, or by appeal to speculative systems such as Galenism. In fact, it is Locke's medical writings that best exemplify the rhetoric of the experimental philosophy against speculation. Locke clearly identified himself with the chymical physicians in the 1660s and retained an interest in iatrochemistry for the remainder of his life. Furthermore, like natural philosophy, medicine had its competing hypotheses. Naturally, Galenism was the hegemonic theory of the day, but Helmontian medicine, with its ontological conception of disease, was widely accepted in England (see Chapter 9 below), and Boyle and other Helmontians developed corpuscular explanations of disease and of the operations of medicines. It is also not surprising that the Baconian method of natural history was promoted as a more efficacious approach to the study and treatment of disease, and (as we shall see in Chapter 3 below) that Locke was intimately involved in this development. But it is less well known that Locke also pursued mercurialist transmutational chymistry for much of his adult life; and this entailed a commitment to the Philosophical Mercury, which was believed to be an essential ingredient in the preparation of the Philosopher's Stone.[26] Finally, while it is beyond the scope of this study, a methodological shift away from the natural history of disease to a mathematical medicine—a shift that parallels developments in natural philosophy—is in evidence from the late 1690s in Britain in the work of Archibald Pitcairne and others.[27] Thus, while there are some aspects of the development of English medicine that do not find parallels in that of natural philosophy, such as the role of the College of Physicians in regulating the professional status of physicians, overall developments within medical methodology roughly parallel those in natural philosophy.

The main theses of this study

Where, then, does John Locke fit into all of this? Locke's precise relation to the natural philosophy of his day is somewhat complex and has proven difficult to interpret in a consistent and clear way. I believe that at least part of the reason is that he has often been interpreted by using the wrong terms of reference. The aim of the present study is to interpret Locke's writings and their bearing on natural philosophy in the light of four theses. It is my firm view that these four theses go a long way to explaining Locke's ambiguous attitude to speculative natural philosophy and to resolving the tension one finds in his writings that relate to the subject. The four theses about Locke and natural philosophy are the following:

1. Locke emphasized the utility of experimental natural philosophy and remained sceptical as to the epistemic status of speculative natural philosophical systems.

---

[26] See Chapter 9 below and Principe 1998, pp. 175–9.
[27] See Guerrini 1987 and Schaffer 1989.

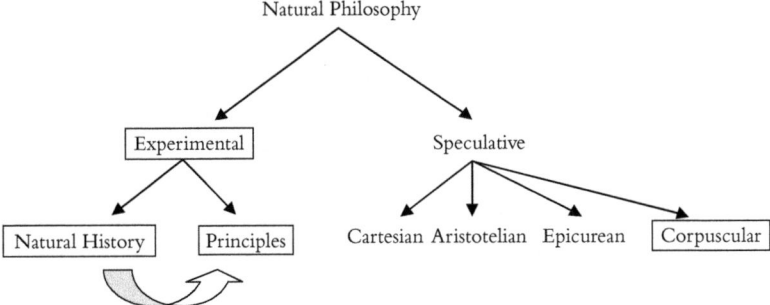

Figure 0.1. Locke's position on the natural philosophy of his day

2. Locke believed that a demonstrative science of natural philosophy is out of our reach and that the development of Baconian natural histories was the most efficacious method of natural philosophy.
3. Locke, like Boyle and Hooke, engaged in speculative natural philosophy and, like Boyle, he favoured the corpuscularian hypothesis and mercurialist transmutational chymistry.[28]
4. Locke was affected by the efficacy of the mathematical experimental method of Newton's *Principia*, and especially by Newton's principles of natural philosophy, and this is reflected in changes to his views in the 1690s.

Figure 0.1 represents Locke's main affiliations and commitments with regard to the changing nature of the natural philosophy of his day. The boxed words indicate that he was committed to the experimental philosophy; that he initially promoted and practised the method of natural history, but during the 1690s he came to see the efficacy of the Newtonian mathematical method of natural philosophy and the foundational nature of Newton's principles of natural philosophy; and that he adhered to a form of the corpuscularian hypothesis about the nature of matter and about the efficacy of mechanical explanations in terms of the shape, size, and motion of the constituent corpuscles of substances.

Overview

One aim of the present study is to establish each of these four theses. The arguments for them will be extended, cumulative, and not confined to any particular chapter. For the chapters that follow, each has its own focus and contains far more than what pertains to these four broader themes. Chapter 1 is concerned with Locke's aims in writing the *Essay*. The dominant view amongst Locke's interpreters over the last forty years has

---

[28] The term 'chymistry' is now commonly used to designate a cluster of theories and practices which were combined in the seventeenth century, but which later came to be separated out into chemistry and alchemy. See Newman and Principe 1998 and 2001.

been that he penned the *Essay* as a defence or as a philosophical counterpart to the mechanical or corpuscular philosophy of his day. However, through an examination of Locke's statements of aim in the *Essay* and elsewhere, I argue that this interpretation misses the mark, and I suggest that it is far more natural to regard Locke as writing the *Essay* in sympathy with the experimental philosophy (Thesis 1). I show how Locke's early writings in moral philosophy deployed a distinction between speculative and practical principles that is analogous to the experimental/speculative distinction with which he was familiar from natural philosophy. Furthermore, I show how his preference for experimental philosophy is expressed as a corollary of his strictures against the epistemic status of speculative natural philosophical systems in the *Essay* and in *Some Thoughts concerning Education*.

Chapter 2 deals with the problem of corpuscular pessimism—the problem of acquiring knowledge of the sub-microscopic corpuscles that Locke believed to make up every material body. After sketching the contours of the general problem as it appears in Locke's philosophy, the chapter examines his early discussions of it in his medical writings of the late 1660s and in the drafts of the *Essay* composed in 1671. As it happens, the problem of our lack of epistemic access to the inner constitutions of material bodies provides the backdrop to many of the positive theses that Locke develops in his discussions of natural philosophy. One thesis adumbrated in the early writings is the claim that our lack of knowledge of the inner natures of things forces us to resort to the method of natural history.

Chapter 3 takes up the subject of Locke and natural history in greater detail, examining his exposure to and involvement in natural philosophical and medical projects that applied this neo-Baconian method. This and the subsequent chapter, on his views on hypotheses and analogy, combine to provide strong historical and philosophical evidence for Thesis 2—the claim that Locke was committed to the method of natural history as the most efficacious manner of advancing natural philosophy. In fact Chapter 4 surveys Locke's rather negative views on the utility and role of hypotheses and analogical reasoning in natural philosophy, views that are representative of the experimental philosophy of his day (Thesis 1). The one concrete example of Locke's critical view of speculative hypotheses that is discussed in this chapter is the acid and alkali hypothesis, advocated by François André and others. But this is far from being the only speculative hypothesis that Locke considered. Chapter 5 examines others, which Locke dealt with in various writings, and thus serves to reinforce the argument of Chapter 4. The hypotheses discussed in Chapter 5 are: the Cartesian vortex theory; the accounts of the deluge in the writings of Thomas Burnet and William Whiston; and Jakob Bernoulli's ether theory of cohesion.

Locke provides a careful summary of Newton's argument against the vortex theory in his 1688 review of Newton's *Principia*; this almost certainly marked the beginning of a long process by which he slowly came to grips with the Newtonian achievement—an achievement which applied a new mathematical method, not the method of natural history. Chapters 6 and 7 combine to lay out the manner in which Locke was able to accommodate the mathematical method to views that he already held about the role of mathematics, and of demonstrative reasoning in general, in an ideal natural philosophy of very small bodies. Locke's conception of what I call a corpuscular metric is in evidence from the early drafts of the *Essay*, and this already gave pride of place to mathematical reasoning. Moreover, I show that the theory of demonstration that Locke develops in the *Essay* itself is, according to him, exactly the form of reasoning that Newton himself used in his 'incomparable book'. Yet grafting Newton's method onto his idealized corpuscular metric would have required significant adjustments to Locke's views as published in the *Essay*. I argue in Chapter 7 that over the 1690s Locke began to backtrack on his strident attack on metaphysical maxims and principles as foundations of the science of nature, because he had come to realize that Newton had in fact discovered and used foundational principles in the *Principia*—principles that matters of fact justify, such as that all bodies gravitate to one another (Thesis 4).

One might expect that another adjustment, which was incumbent on Locke as a result of his coming to grips with Newton's celestial dynamics, was to provide a more central role for laws of nature in his account of explanation in natural philosophy. This, however, is not the case. In Chapter 8 I argue that Locke was committed to a number of the explanatory principles and explanatory constraints, but had a surprisingly minor role for nomological explanation. The explanatory principles that he does adopt are typical of the proponents of the corpuscular hypothesis, not least Robert Boyle, and it is these explanatory principles that direct and constrain Locke's own speculative natural philosophy. I also argue that Newton's principles of natural philosophy provided him with the resources for resolving a fundamental tension in his views on the possibility that some qualities might be superadded to matter, yet Locke never fully incorporated these principles into his theory of knowledge.

Chapters 9 and 10 spell out two important aspects of the content of Locke's own speculative views (Thesis 3). Chapter 9 surveys the manuscript evidence for his long-standing commitment to mercurialist transmutational chymistry and to the Helmontian theory of salts, seminal principles, and the alkahest. Chapter 10 examines his views, deriving from this Helmonto-Boylean legacy, on generation by seminal principles. Interestingly, Locke's views on seminal principles have implications not simply for certain theological doctrines such as that of resurrection, but also for his view on the nature of species. This is the subject of the final chapter, which provides a new interpretation of Locke's ideas on species. I argue that here Locke was a conventionalist, but his was a constrained and convergent conventionalism, predicated not on species nominalism, but on a robust realism about species in nature—a realism informed by natural philosophy.

1

Natural philosophy and the aims of the *Essay*

> 'Tis of great use to the Sailor to know the length of his Line, though he cannot with it fathom all the depths of the Ocean. 'Tis well he knows, that it is long enough to reach the bottom, at such Places, as are necessary to direct his Voyage, and caution him against running upon Shoals, that may ruin him.
>
> John Locke[1]

This chapter reviews the recent history of interpretation of Locke's *Essay* on the question of the relation between natural philosophy and the aims of the *Essay*, and then presents a new interpretation which, it is hoped, will be established throughout the remainder of the book. I argue that, rather than being composed with a special reference to the mechanical philosophy, Locke's *Essay* is an attempt to give an account of human understanding in broad conformity with the new *experimental philosophy*. In fact I aim to show that the *Essay* is not a philosophical defence of mechanism or an exploration of the consequences of mechanism for an account of the faculty of the understanding. Rather, one of the consequences of its 'Historical, plain Method'—the method of the experimental philosophy—is that the *Essay* set methodological prescriptions for how to proceed in natural philosophy that, when applied, were antithetical to some forms of the mechanical philosophy. Furthermore, not only were these prescriptions set within an innovative approach to the study of the understanding, but they were also, or so Locke claimed, applied in that very investigation itself.

Introduction

What place did natural philosophy have in Locke's aims for the *Essay*? Unhappily, the evidence on this question is somewhat ambiguous. On the one hand, the under-labourer passage in the opening 'Epistle to the Reader' suggests that Locke saw the

[1] *E* I. i. 6, p. 46.

Essay as having some sort of subsidiary role to the work of the great Master-Builders. Locke famously says:

> The Commonwealth of Learning, is not at this time without Master-Builders, whose mighty Designs, in advancing the Sciences, will leave lasting Monuments to the Admiration of Posterity; But every one must not hope to be a *Boyle*, or a *Sydenham*; and in an Age that produces such Masters, as the Great—*Huygenius*, and the incomparable Mr. *Newton*, with some other of that Strain; 'tis Ambition enough to be employed as an Under-Labourer in clearing Ground a little, and removing some of the Rubbish, that lies in the way to Knowledge [...][2]

Locke's construal of his role as an under-labourer to the likes of Boyle and Newton seems, at first sight, to tie his own aspirations for the *Essay* to the new natural philosophy. And, to be sure, some early readers of the *Essay* saw its connections with the new philosophy. John Evelyn, in writing to Samuel Pepys, claimed that it '[c]elebrates the stupendous operations of Algebra, Mechanical Arts, and Experimental Philosophy'.[3] The fact that the work was dedicated to the Earl of Pembroke, who was President of the Royal Society in 1690, may have encouraged the popular conception that the work was at least of interest to the Society's members. Furthermore, throughout the eighteenth century Locke was commonly associated with Newton and Boyle. A nice illustration of this is the erection by Queen Caroline in 1732 of a bust of Locke to stand with busts of Boyle (who was given pride of place), Newton, Samuel Clarke, and William Wollaston in The Hermitage in Richmond Gardens.[4]

On the other hand, none of Locke's statements of aim in the *Essay* and in its drafts, nor his comments on this work in his correspondence, suggest either that he intended to make any contribution to natural philosophy or that his book stood in some special relation to the discipline itself. Moreover, in the *Essay*, Locke expresses scepticism about our ability to know the nature of material body and its qualities, as well as a deep pessimism about the prospects of natural philosophy as a science. In spite of this, however, modern commentators have almost universally affirmed some version of the view that amongst Locke's aims in penning the *Essay* was that it should stand in a very positive relation to the new natural philosophy of his day.

Locke and mechanism: An historical sketch

The first wave of concerted interest in Locke's relations with the new science amongst historians of philosophy and philosophers in general began in earnest with the publi-

---

[2] *Essay*, pp. 9–10. For earlier uses of these tropes, see Glanvill 1668, p. 91: '*true* knowledge of *general Nature*, [...] must proceed *slowly*, by degrees almost *insensible*: and what *one* Age can do in so *immense* an Undertaking as *that*, wherein all the generations of Men are concerned, can be little *more* than to remove the *Rubbish*, lay in *Materials*, and *put* things in *order* for the *Building*'; see also Power 1664 (LL 2380), p. 192, who claims that 'all the old Rubbish must be thrown away'.
[3] De la Bédoyère 2005, p. 214.
[4] See Colton 1976.

cation of two books in 1964. One was Maurice Mandelbaum's *Philosophy, Science, and Sense Perception* and the other was Rom Harré's *Matter and Method*. Both of these books, in their own way, highlighted the manner in which the natural philosophy of Locke's intellectual milieu bore, in crucial ways, on our interpretation of the *Essay*. In his opening essay, 'Locke's realism', Mandelbaum argued that Locke was a realist about the external world and that the particular form of realism he adopted was atomism. According to Mandelbaum, Locke's real essences are identical to the internal *atomic* constitution of bodies. Furthermore, he claimed that, for Locke, the smallest particles of matter are unobservable in principle. Throughout this essay, Boyle's 'atomism' is portrayed as the model from which Locke's theory of matter and its qualities developed.[5]

Harré's work was not equally influential, but it reinforced the view that there is an intimate connection between Locke's philosophical programme and the new science. Like Mandelbaum, Harré also gave prominence to the views of Robert Boyle. Harré saw Locke's agenda in the following terms: 'Locke set himself the task of developing in a coherent, systematic and rational way what he took to be the fundamental tenets of the corpuscularian philosophy'.[6] Following these books came an influential article by Larry Laudan, entitled 'The nature and sources of Locke's view on hypotheses', in 1967. In this paper Laudan sought to 'build upon Mandelbaum's analysis by looking carefully at the theory of scientific method implicit in the *Essay*'.[7] The point of dialectical engagement for Laudan was the same as for Mandelbaum, namely an attack on an earlier paper by Robert Yost, entitled 'Locke's rejection of hypotheses about sub-microscopic events' (1951), which had down-played the importance of hypotheses, and therefore of the mechanical philosophy, in Locke's thought. Roger Woolhouse's *Locke's Philosophy of Science and Knowledge* (1971), which purported to be 'a critical account of what Locke said about knowledge, belief, and opinion in the specific context of the natural sciences', acquiesced in Mandelbaum's and Laudan's rejection of Yost's thesis.[8]

John Yolton's *John Locke and the Compass of Human Understanding*, of 1970, in one sense confirmed the trend, arguing again for an intimate connection between Locke's epistemological project and the prevailing natural philosophy of the day. But at the same time Yolton's book complicated matters, for he was more partial to the views of Yost, so fiercely criticized by Mandelbaum and Laudan, and he introduced a complementary thesis adumbrated by Yost, namely that the salient point at which the new

---

[5] Mandelbaum 1964, ch. 1, pp. 1–60. For a critique of the attribution of atomism to Locke, see Hill 2005.

[6] Harré 1964, p. 93. See the claim, also made in the same year by Hans Aarsleff, that 'the *Essay* was, as it were, intended as a manual in the epistemology of the Royal Society, whose aim was the promotion of natural knowledge': Aarsleff 1964, p. 178. It should be pointed out that Aarsleff's discussion of Locke's aims in writing the *Essay* is more historically sensitive than those of Mandelbaum or Harré.

[7] Laudan 1967. Laudan's article was subsequently reworked and published as ch. 5 of his *Science and Hypothesis* (1981), and this latter version should be used when analysing his view.

[8] Woolhouse 1971, pp. 113–14.

philosophy bears upon the *Essay* is Locke's emphasis on the importance of the construction of Baconian natural histories. For Yolton, 'Locke's main objective [is] not to extend our knowledge of things but to show us some of the ways of doing so, even to explain how Boyle, Newton, Sydenham were extending human knowledge'; and again, 'Locke sought to elaborate an account of human understanding which would make sense of the new science of nature'.[9] Yolton's work was widely read, but, with the exception of Neal Wood's *The Politics of Locke's Philosophy* (1983), his main theses were not widely accepted.

By the late 1970s and early 1980s, the claims began to become more focused, moving from the general thesis that in the *Essay* Locke was promoting or defending the new natural philosophy to the more specific claim that Locke sought to promote some form of *mechanism*. This soon became the orthodox view,[10] and a new derivative debate arose as to the purity of that mechanism. Margaret Wilson argued, in the light of Locke's statements about God superadding properties to matter, that Locke's mechanism was decidedly impure (in so far as it contains non-mechanical causes) and inconsistent.[11] Edwin McCann agreed with the charge of impurity, but argued that it was entirely consistent.[12] Michael Ayers on the other hand argued, in a number of writings, that Locke's mechanism was both pure and consistent.[13] Furthermore, the orthodoxy spawned its own minor controversies—such as discussions as to whether Lockean corpuscles are in principle unobservable.[14] By the time of the publication of *The Cambridge Companion to Locke* (Chappell 1994), Edwin McCann could claim unreservedly that 'one of Locke's main aims in the *Essay* was to promote the corpuscularian version of mechanism over the Cartesian one, and to eliminate the Aristotelian–Scholastic obstacles to the acceptance of mechanism'.[15]

Another line of approach was further to explore the relations between Locke's mechanism and that of Robert Boyle. Peter Alexander's book *Ideas, Qualities and Corpuscles: Locke and Boyle on the External World* (1985) argues that Locke's mechanism is almost a carbon copy of Boyle's, and that this relation is the key to understanding the *Essay*. Alexander considers that the under-labourer passage 'suggests that Locke saw himself as helping to make natural philosophy, the views of scientists, more accessible to the intelligent layman [...] he saw himself as a popularizer, in the best sense, of current scientific ideas and controversies'.[16] And the best scientific theory was Boyle's

---

[9] J. W. Yolton 1970, p. 16. Yolton's thesis regarding Locke's endorsement of Bacon-style histories, first developed in Yolton 1969a, is discussed in Chapter 3 below. Schouls 1980 appears to misunderstand Locke's 'Historical, plain Method', as he takes 'historical' to refer to the sequence or order of that which presents itself to the mind as the latter seeks out the nature of the understanding; see pp. 155–7.

[10] See Davidson and Hornstein 1984, p. 281: 'As everyone now agrees, Locke was attempting to provide a philosophical *foundation* for English corpuscularianism'. See also Soles 1985, who claims that Locke took on 'the self-appointed task of providing epistemological foundations for the emerging empirical sciences' (p. 339).

[11] M. D. Wilson 1979.   [12] McCann 1985.   [13] Ayers 1981a, 1991.
[14] See Downing 1992.   [15] McCann 1994, p. 85.   [16] Alexander 1985, p. 6.

corpuscularianism: 'A sympathetic reading of the *Essay* as a whole, in conjunction with the relevant works of Boyle, seems to me to put it beyond doubt that the "lasting monument" of the Master-Builders that most impressed Locke was the corpuscular philosophy'.[17]

Finally, it is worth summarizing the variety of the claims made by the proponents of both the older and more recent orthodox views, for they do not all hold the same interpretation. Some, like Mandelbaum and Alexander, maintained that Boyle's corpuscularianism is an interpretative key to the *Essay*, and they used it to establish their own interpretations. Harré claimed that Locke was actually developing the corpuscular philosophy in his *Essay*. Others, like Yolton, claimed that Locke was providing a supplement or epistemological sub-structure to the new science of nature. He claimed of Locke that '[h]e gave a philosophical foundation for the new science'; and Aarsleff claimed that the *Essay* is a manual of the epistemology of the Royal Society.[18] McCann claimed that Locke was defending Boyle's corpuscularianism against its opponents. So we have the *Essay* as an interpretative key, as a development of corpuscularianism, as a philosophical foundation or epistemological manual, and as a defence. Four quite different claims, but all having the unifying theme that Locke saw a positive and intimate relation between his *Essay* and the new science.

Locke and mechanism: A reassessment

There were some early dissenters to the later orthodoxy concerning mechanism, notably Patrick Romanell, Margaret Atherton, and, to a lesser extent, J. R. Milton.[19] Atherton had claimed as early as 1991 that 'it is surprisingly difficult, in the light of the frequency with which the claim is made, to find any textual support for the notion that what Locke was setting out to do in the *Essay* was to defend mechanism'.[20] But their views were far out-weighed by the overwhelming majority view that the writing of the *Essay* was in some positive way intimately related to the status of the mechanical philosophy. It was only in the latter years of the 1990s that a third wave of scholarly reflection on Locke and natural philosophy began to erode the view that Locke was in some sense a champion of the mechanical philosophy. The case for this claim was set out in two important articles in 1998. Lisa Downing's 'The status of mechanism in Locke's *Essay*' argued that Locke does not assume the truth of corpuscularianism and

---

[17] Alexander 1985, p. 7.
[18] J. W. Yolton 1970, p. 75 and Aarsleff 1964, p. 178 (= Aarsleff 1982, p. 57). John and Jean Yolton also claim that the *Essay* 'is in large measure a defence of proper experimental science', *STCE*, p. 248, n. 94. See also Osler 1970, p. 10: 'The philosophy of John Locke was a major step in the formation of a new philosophy of science [...] his theory of knowledge represents an effort to fill the epistemological void left by Boyle's and Newton's rejection of the Cartesian ideal of certainty in natural philosophy'.
[19] See Romanell 1983, 1984; Milton 1985, and 1994, p. 40; and Atherton 1991.
[20] Atherton 1991, p. 48, n. 6.

does not use it as a starting point in his philosophy. He does, however, according to Downing, regard it as a uniquely natural and clear account of body, which has such explanatory potential that it can be put to use to illustrate certain notions in Locke's broader philosophical project.[21] Matthew Stuart's 'Locke on superaddition and mechanism' took an even more deflationary line, arguing that Locke's attitude to mechanism is ultimately non-committal and that his view of the manner in which God can superadd powers to bodies was not compatible with the sort of mechanical philosophy espoused by Boyle or Descartes.[22]

This third wave of scholarship has been reinforced by the careful study of Locke's philosophical development as revealed by his medical notebooks. For example, in 2001 J. R. Milton pointed out that Locke's early natural philosophical inclinations as found in the 1660s were more eclectic than those of the *Essay* and that, amidst the thousands of pages of Locke's published and unpublished writings, there is only a handful of references to problems in mechanics or to the laws of motion, problems that were central to the concerns of the mechanical philosophers.[23] However, one of the most telling factors against the 'Locke and mechanism' thesis is the revisionist historiography of early modern matter theories and its consequences for our understanding of the mechanical philosophy itself.

For much of the debate over Locke and mechanism, the interpretation of mechanism that has been in view is that of R. S. Westfall and A. R. Hall: a theory of natural phenomena that considers all matter to be completely inert; change in nature, both qualitative and quantitative to be brought about through collisions between parcels of this inert matter; matter to have the primary qualities of shape, size, motion, and texture; and this ontology to be all that is needed to explain all natural phenomena. Explanations of natural events and of the functioning of macroscopical bodies, as well as of the functioning of microscopical bodies, are to be reached by analogy with explanations of the functioning of machines such as levers, scales, and clocks.[24] However, recent work on the matter theories of the leading proponents of the mechanical philosophy has shown that many of the mechanical philosophers admitted some sorts of powers or forces to material bodies, many of which do not fit with the traditional paradigm.[25] Furthermore, recent research on early modern matter theory has revealed that the popular tripartite division of theories into atomist, continuist, and *minima naturalia* theories is also too simplistic, and that a more generic form of corpuscular theory, which could remain neutral on the issue of divisibility but appropriated some atomist and *minima naturalia* terminology, was prevalent in the period and

---

[21] Downing 1998, p. 413.
[22] Stuart 1998.
[23] Milton 2001, p. 221. This is not to claim that Locke did not read works which contained discussions of problems in mechanics.
[24] See for example Westfall 1971, Hall 1983, and Deason 1986.
[25] See for example Henry 1986, Schaffer 1987, Anstey 2000 and 2002c.

held by 'mechanists' and 'non-mechanists alike'.[26] In short, the contours of early modern mechanical philosophies have been redrawn, and many of the discussions of Locke's commitment to mechanism, particularly the early ones, provide rather outmoded reading in the light of recent research. For example, Mandelbaum's discussion of Boyle and Locke as atomists, believers in uncuttable particles, misses entirely the point that what was constitutive of Boyle's corpuscularianism was the fact that it was neutral on the issue of the divisibility of matter.[27]

What is important however, in the light of this revisionist work on early modern matter theories, is to give as precise definitions of 'mechanism' (or 'mechanical philosophy') and of 'corpuscular philosophy' as is possible. For, while they are often used interchangeably, they are not co-extensive, and a degree of precision here will help to untangle a number of issues that otherwise are susceptible of conflation. By 'mechanism', then, we mean a theory of explanation of material phenomena that proceeds by analogy to an explanation of the functioning of machines. Mechanical explanations are reductive in so far as one phenomenon or quality is explained in terms of the rather sparse ontology that is available. A paradigm case is heat is the motion of corpuscles.

By contrast, the phrase 'corpuscularian philosophy', coined by Boyle, connotes an explanation of the qualities of bodies by appeal to invisible corpuscles, which are postulated as the constituents of all material bodies and whose properties and structural arrangements are thought to give rise to the sorts of powers and qualities that these bodies possess. It is the building block view of material things, and, in Boyle's version— the one that Locke was quite familiar with—it is neutral on the issue of the divisibility of matter. Corpuscularianism plays on the intuitively plausible notion that all visible objects are made up of invisible parts and that the only mode of composition is mereological.

Mechanism, therefore, emphasizes the machine analogy, whereas corpuscularianism emphasizes matter theory and the theory of qualities. The point of significant overlap between the mechanical philosophy and the corpuscularian philosophy lies in the central *explanans* deployed both by mechanists and by corpuscularians. This is the cluster of 'mechanical affections', shape, size, motion, and texture, which are appealed to in explanations by analogy with those of machines and are thought to be the basis of any explanations of qualities that bodies have. Thus there are some contexts in which it would not be appropriate to substitute one term for the other. To complicate matters, it should also be pointed out that not all of those who held a corpuscular matter theory were mechanical philosophers. Daniel Sennert, for example, whose corpuscular theory exerted a strong influence on Boyle, was most definitely not a mechanical philosopher and not an adherent of the corpuscularian philosophy.[28] Moreover, not all

---

[26] See Clericuzio 1990; Lüthy et al. 2001, pp. 1–38 (Introduction); Newman 2006.
[27] See Boyle's 'Some Specimens', in *Certain Physiological Essays, Boyle Works*, Vol. 2, p. 87.
[28] See Newman 2006, ch. 6.

of the adherents of the experimental philosophy were mechanical philosophers or corpuscularians.

Natural philosophy and the aims of the *Essay*

Armed then with these definitions of 'mechanism' and 'corpuscularianism', we can now turn to the evidence for and against the claim that Locke regarded his *Essay* as standing in some positive relation to the new natural philosophy of his day. Three types of evidence can be adduced to argue the case for a positive relation. First, as we have seen, there is the under-labourer passage. We will return to this theme below. Second, there is a number of passages in the *Essay* where Locke tacitly accepts the truth of the corpuscularian hypothesis in order to make a point with regard to his broader philosophical concerns. A nice example is in *E* II. viii. 22, where his development of the primary and secondary quality distinction is articulated in terms of a corpuscular theory of matter. Locke's primary qualities of matter overlap almost exactly with Boyle's mechanical or catholic affections of matter and with those of Descartes.[29] Passages like these naturally create a presumption that Locke believed in corpuscular matter theory and that this is why he saw fit to mobilize it in developing such a crucial distinction among the qualities of bodies. This evidence can be reinforced by occasional remarks made by Locke, which are found in writings other than the *Essay*. For instance, in his posthumously published *Elements of Natural Philosophy*, he concludes by claiming: 'By the figure, bulk, texture, and motion, of these small and insensible corpuscles, all the phenomena of bodies may be explained'.[30] Indeed, recent work by Downing and Walmsley has revealed the developmental stages by which corpuscularian ideas entered into Locke's drafts of the *Essay*.[31]

Third, not only does Locke tacitly assume the truth of a form of corpuscular matter theory in the *Essay*, but he adopts some of the central explanatory principles of the mechanical philosophy both implicitly and explicitly. The most obvious example is his appeal, in the first three editions of the *Essay*, to the principle that bodies operate one upon another '*by impulse*, and nothing else. It being impossible to conceive, that Body should operate on what it does not touch'.[32] This is rightly seen as adherence to a central tenet of mechanism, although Locke slightly modified his view in the fourth edition of the *Essay* once he had grasped the implications of Newton's theory of gravity, which appeared to be a case of action at a distance.[33] It is hardly surprising, then, that at a number of points in the *Essay* Locke quite unselfconsciously speaks in

---

[29] See also *E* II. xxi. 73, quoted above. For Boyle's mechanical affections, see Anstey 2000, chs 1 and 2; for Descartes, see for example *Principles of Philosophy*, I, §§49 and 69–70; Descartes 1985, pp. 209 and 217–18.
[30] *Locke Works*, Vol. 3, p. 330.
[31] Downing 2001; Walmsley 2004, 2006a, and 2006b.
[32] *E* II. viii. 11, p. 135.
[33] In fact the evidence here is ambiguous because, while Locke did weaken the claim at II. viii. 11, he made a countervailing change at IV. x. 19. For further discussion, see Chapter 8.

mechanical terms about various phenomena and occasionally uses familiar tropes of the mechanical philosophers: in speaking of sensitive plants, he supposes that the best account of their behaviour is that it 'is all bare mechanism',[34] and he uses Boylean terminology in referring to the insensible 'mechanical affections' of objects.[35]

This evidence for a positive relation between the *Essay* and both corpuscular matter theory and the mechanical philosophy has provided the ballast for the case that Locke was defending, popularizing, or even providing a philosophical sub-structure for the new natural philosophy of his day. However, a careful perusal of the work reveals a substantial body of counterevidence to this reading of Locke's aims. The natural place to start is with an examination of Locke's explicit statements about his purpose in composing the work. Locke gives us an insight into the original stimulus for the *Essay* in the 'Epistle to the Reader'. There he describes his reaction to unresolved issues arising in a meeting with some friends in his chamber in 1671, which, Locke tells us, proved to be the catalyst for the early drafts of the *Essay*:

> it came into my Thoughts, that we took a wrong course; and that, before we set our selves upon Enquiries of that Nature, it was necessary to examine our own Abilities, and see, what Objects our Understandings were, or were not fitted to deal with.[36]

It is clear from this statement that Locke's long-term *desideratum* had been to discover the appropriate objects of human understanding, to sort out just what things the understanding could and could not deal with. When we turn to the body of the *Essay*, we find numerous, similar statements of the aim of the work, most of which find their first expression in Draft B. Thus the work begins with a very positive general statement of its aim:

> This, therefore, being my *Purpose*, to enquire into the Original, Certainty, and Extent of humane Knowledge; together with the Grounds and Degrees of Belief, Opinion, and Assent.[37]

And it continues with a list of what falls outside this aim:

> I shall not at present meddle with the Physical Consideration of the Mind; or trouble my self to examine, wherein its Essence consists, or by what Motions of our Spirits, or Alterations of our Bodies, we come to have any Sensation by our Organs, or any *Ideas* in our Understandings; and whether those *Ideas* do in their Formation, any, or all of them, depend on Matter or no. These are Speculations, which, however curious and entertaining, I shall decline, as lying out of my Way, in the Design I am now upon.[38]

---

[34] *E* II. ix. 11, p. 147. Locke's herbarium contains a specimen of *Herba mimosa sive sensibilis* (*Mimosa pudica*): Bodl. MS Locke b. 7, fol. 151.

[35] *E* IV. iii. 25 *bis*, 26 and 28.

[36] *E*, p. 7.

[37] *E* I. i. 2 (= Draft B, §2). In Draft A, §1, p. 4 Locke characterizes his inquiry as being designed to 'make any discovery what knowledg our understandings are capable of of things abstracted from words & well destinguish between the understanding of words & the knowledg of things'.

[38] *E* I. i. 2, p. 43 (=Draft B, §2).

Locke excludes discussions of the nature of mind and mind/body interaction, both of which, he later tells us, come under the subject of natural philosophy broadly conceived (*E* IV. xxi. 2). Locke is also concerned to demarcate just what it is about which we can and cannot have knowledge.

> It shall suffice to my present Purpose, to consider the discerning Faculties of a Man, as they are employ'd about the Objects, which they have to do with: and I shall imagine I have not wholly misemploy'd my self in the Thoughts I shall have on this Occasion, if, in this Historical, plain Method, I can give any Account of the Ways, whereby our Understandings come to attain those Notions of Things we have, and can set down any Measures of the Certainty of our Knowledge, or the Grounds of those Perswasions, which are to be found amongst men, so various, different, and wholly contradictory; and yet asserted some where or other with such Assurance, and Confidence, that he that shall take a view of the Opinions of Mankind, observe their Opposition, and at the same time, consider the Fondness, and devotion wherewith they are embrac'd; the Resolution, and Eagerness, wherewith they are maintain'd, may perhaps have Reason to suspect, That either there is no such thing as Truth at all; or that Mankind hath no sufficient Means to attain a certain Knowledge of it.[39]

> It is therefore worth while to search out the *Bounds* between Opinion and Knowledge; and examine by what Measures, in things, whereof we have no certain Knowledge, we ought to regulate our Assent, and moderate our Perswasions. In Order whereunto, I shall pursue this following Method.[40]

> If by this Enquiry into the Nature of the Understanding, I can discover the Powers thereof; *how far* they reach; to what things they are in any Degree proportionate; and where they fail us, I suppose it may be of use, to prevail with the busy Mind of Man, to be more cautious in meddling with things exceeding its Comprehension; to stop, when it is at the utmost Extent of its Tether; and to sit down in a quiet Ignorance of those Things, which, upon Examination, are found to be beyond the reach of our Capacities. We should not then perhaps be so forward, out of an Affectation of an universal Knowledge, to raise Questions, and perplex our selves and others with Disputes about Things, to which our Understandings are not suited; and of which we cannot frame in our Minds any clear or distinct Perceptions, or whereof (as it has perhaps too often happen'd) we have not any Notions at all. If we can find out, how far the Understanding can extend its view; how far it has Faculties to attain Certainty; and in what Cases it can only judge and guess, we may learn to content our selves with what is attainable by us in this State.[41]

Locke's programmatic demarcation is primarily aimed at epistemic hygiene, at having a sober estimate of our understanding in order to avoid wasteful, futile disputes over subjects about which we cannot have knowledge. This theme of epistemic demarcation is absolutely fundamental to the agenda and structure of the *Essay* and to its drafts. It recurs often.[42] Locke believes that we have a faculty called the understanding; that

---

[39] *E* I. i. 2, pp. 43–4 (=Draft B, §2).
[40] *E* I. i. 3, p. 44 (=Draft B, §2).
[41] *E* I. i. 4, pp. 44–5.
[42] See for example *E* II. xxiii. 12–13; IV. iv. For the doctrine of the limits of reason in Boyle, see for example *A Discourse of Things above Reason. Inquiring Whether a Philosopher Should Admit There are Any Such* (LL 457; hereafter *Things above Reason*), *Boyle Works*, Vol. 9, pp. 370–1.

this faculty has certain limited powers; that these limits were placed on it by God; and that an appreciation of the limits of these powers will enable us to thank God for what powers we do have, to avoid unproductive disputes about things beyond our powers, and to focus on what is within our powers, which will issue in right conduct.

Our Business here is not to know all things, but those which concern our Conduct. If we can find out those Measures, whereby a rational Creature put in that State, which man is in, in this World, may, and ought to govern his Opinions, and Actions depending thereon, we need not to be troubled, that some other things escape our Knowledge.[43]

This was that which gave the first *Rise* to this Essay concerning the Understanding. For I thought that the first Step towards satisfying several Enquiries, the Mind of Man was very apt to run into, was, to take a Survey of our own Understandings, examine our own Powers, and see to what Things they were adapted. Till that was done I suspected we began at the wrong end, and in vain sought for Satisfaction in a quiet and sure Possession of Truths, that most concern'd us [...][44]

Thus there is a threefold normative aim for the *Essay*: first, to avoid idle speculations; second, to be thankful to God for what powers we do have; and, third, to conduct ourselves rightly. We should not underestimate these normative aims, for they too dictate portions of the *Essay's* content and structure. There are further statements of Locke's aims in later passages,[45] but this sampling is sufficient to grasp his stated objectives. Notice that none of these statements makes any mention, implicit or explicit, of the mechanical philosophy. They are all concerned with a rather self-contained epistemological project, of mapping the powers of the faculty of understanding and of demarcating the scope of the understanding in the broader context of some normative objectives. Of course, the *Essay* is a rambling work, 'written by incoherent parcels',[46] which does not follow Locke's stated intentions to the letter, and it is evident that, when Locke digresses, other agendas intrude. But at least it is clear that his stated aims do not so much as allude to natural philosophy. It is also worth considering the following reference to the aim of the *Essay* in Book Two:

I shall not, contrary to the Design of this Essay, set my self to enquire philosophically into the peculiar Constitution of Bodies, and the Configuration of Parts, whereby they have the power to produce in us the *Ideas* of their sensible Qualities: I shall not enter any further into that Disquisition; it sufficing to my purpose to observe, That Gold, or Saffron, has a power to produce in us the *Idea* of Yellow; and Snow, or Milk, the *Idea* of White; which we can only have by our Sight, without examining the Texture of the Parts of those Bodies, or the particular Figures, or Motion of the Particles, which rebound from them, to cause in us that particular

---

[43] *E* I. i. 6, p. 46.
[44] *E* I. i. 7, pp. 46–7.
[45] See for example *E* IV. xii. 11. For a recent study of the normative dimensions to Locke's study of the understanding, see Corneanu 2011.
[46] *Essay*, 'Epistle to the Reader', p. 7. See also Locke's letter to Edward Clarke, 22 December 1684, *Correspondence*, Vol. 2, p. 671.

Sensation: though when we go beyond the bare *Ideas* in our Minds, and would inquire into their Causes, we cannot conceive any thing else, to be in any sensible Object, whereby it produces different *Ideas* in us, but the different Bulk, Figure, Number, Texture, and Motion of its insensible Parts.[47]

Far from indicating a connection with the subject of natural philosophy, here is a statement of aim which explicitly distances the *Essay* from the domain of that discipline. Yet at the same time this passage implies a commitment to the explanatory value of corpuscularianism.

A similar picture emerges from the early drafts of the *Essay*. In Draft A, §27 Locke tells us

[t]o bring all therefor to our present purpose & consider what is the extent of humane understanding & what it is capable of. I thinke from what hath been said it is evident [...][48]

This statement is one of the few in Draft A that explicitly mentions the purpose of Locke's inquiry. It is clearly more general than Locke's central statement of aim in *E* I. i. 2, and the context is different, though there are some verbal parallels. In Draft B, however, we find that Locke has now not only articulated his aim clearly, but has placed it at the beginning of the text (§§1–3), and that this is in fact a fuller statement than that of the *Essay* itself. Thus, for example, we find an extension of the opening section of the *Essay* to include the claim that a study of the understanding will shape

their enquiry where tis fit makeing us content to sit downe in a quiet ignorance of those things which upon examination we shall finde to lie beyond the reach of our capacitys. & not out of an affectation of universall knowledg raise questions & perplex our selves and others with disputes about things to which our understandings are not suited, & of which we can not frame in our mindes any cleare or destinct conceptions [...][49]

Locke's statement of the scope of the understanding is also fuller and less guarded. He adds to the central statement of purpose that opinion, belief, persuasion, or assent are 'all those things which are the objects of our thoughts, and all the ways wherein our Understandings can be imploid about them' (§2). In neither draft is there any mention of, or allusion to, natural philosophy in their statements of aim or purpose. This should hardly surprise us, if James Tyrrell's comments are to be taken at face value when he said, of that first meeting in Locke's chamber in 1671, that 'the discourse began about the principles of morality and reveal'd religion'.[50] Finally, in his letter to Pembroke of 28 November 1684, Locke claims of the *Essay* that he is composing it 'to give some account of the weaknesse and shortnesse of humane understanding'.[51]

It is clear then, that, apart from the under-labourer passage, natural philosophy does *not* feature in Locke's explicit aims in composing the *Essay*. But even the

---

[47] *E* II. xxi. 73, p. 287.   [48] Draft A, §27, p. 42. See also §31, p. 58.
[49] Draft B, §1, p. 101.   [50] Quoted from Locke 1936, p. xii.
[51] *Correspondence*, Vol. 2, p. 665.

under-labourer passage is problematic for those who have interpreted Locke as aiming to defend the mechanical philosophy; for one of the Master-Builders, Thomas Sydenham, was definitely *not* a mechanical philosopher. Indeed, the inclusion of Thomas Sydenham with the Master-Builders certainly does not sit well with the view that Locke, in the *Essay*, sought to defend the mechanical philosophy. Sydenham was neither a philosopher nor a natural philosopher, but a physician.[52]

Furthermore, as many scholars have pointed out, in the *Essay* and elsewhere Locke develops an account of knowledge that renders it highly unlikely that we will ever come to know the real nature of material bodies, and he articulates with great ingenuity serious objections to the coherence of mechanical and corpuscular explanations of the qualities of bodies. For example he attacks various mechanical accounts of the nature of cohesion, and he proffers a voluntaristic account of the relation between the primary qualities of bodies and the secondary qualities that are said to arise from them. The upshot is that, at various points in the *Essay* and elsewhere, Locke expresses a deep pessimism about the prospects of natural philosophy ever becoming a science. Perhaps the most poignant expression of this is at *E* IV. xii. 10 (p. 645) where he claims:

> I deny not, but a Man accustomed to rational and regular Experiments shall be able to see further into the Nature of Bodies, and guess righter at their yet unknown Properties, than one, that is a Stranger to them: But yet, as I have said, this is but Judgment and Opinion, not Knowledge and Certainty. This *way* of getting, and *improving our knowledge in Substances only by Experience* and History, which is all that the weakness of our Faculties in this State of *Mediocrity*, which we are in in this World, can attain to, makes me suspect, that natural Philosophy is not capable of being made a Science.[53]

It seems then that we are at an impasse. How do we resolve the tension in the evidence for the claim that Locke regarded the *Essay* as standing in some positive relation to the new natural philosophy of his day? How can Locke see himself as an under-labourer to natural philosophy while at the same time expressing highly sceptical doubts about its content and prospects? I believe that there is a very natural and persuasive explanation of this apparent tension. The tension is only apparent because what Locke is committed to as an under-labourer is not natural philosophy *per se*, and not the mechanical philosophy or the corpuscular hypothesis in particular; rather, Locke is committed to the *experimental* philosophy. That is, he is committed to the experimental philosophy as distinct from the speculative philosophy—as a distinctive and new approach to the acquisition of knowledge about the world.

---

[52] In his *Methodus curandi febres* (1666), Sydenham says: 'For my own part, I am not ambitious of the name of a Philosopher, and those who think themselves so, may, perhaps, consider me blameable on the score of my not having attempted to pierce into these mysteries', Sydenham 1987, p. 101.

[53] See also *E* IV. iii. 26 and 29.

Locke and experimental natural philosophy

Let us consider how the apparent tension in Locke's attitude to the natural philosophy of his day can be resolved if we take him to be committed to the experimental philosophy. A first step in resolving this tension is to show that, from his earliest known philosophical writings, Locke deployed a distinction analogous to the experimental/speculative one.

In his *Essays on the Law of Nature*, written in 1664, Locke deploys a distinction between speculative versus practical principles. At the end of the third essay he claims:

> If the law of nature were written in our hearts, it would have to be inferred that speculative as well as practical principles are inscribed.[54]

He goes on to give, as an example of a speculative principle, the proposition 'that it is impossible that the same thing should at the same time both be and not be'.[55] The very same distinction is found in his *An Essay concerning Toleration*, written a few years later, in 1667, where he speaks of the way in which people's opinions bear on the issue of toleration:

> Let us next consider the opinions & actions of men, which in reference to toleration divide them selves into 3 sorts
>
> 1. Are all such opinions & actions as in them selves concerne not government or society at all, & such are all puerly speculative opinions, & Divine worship
> 2. Are such as in their owne nature are neither good nor bad but yet concerne society & mens conversations one with an other, & these are all practicall opinions & actions in matters of indifferency
> 3. Are such too as concerne society, but are also good or bad in their owne nature & these are morall virtues & vices
>
> 1 I say that the first sort only viz. speculative opinions & Divine worship are those things alone which have an absolute & universall right to toleration. 1st Puerly speculative opinions as the beleife of the trinity, purgatory transsubstantion, Antipodes, Christs personall reigne on earth, &c, & that in these every man has unlimited freedom appears.[56]

It is clear, then, that by the mid-1660s Locke is not only familiar with the distinction between speculative and practical opinions in moral philosophy, but that this distinction plays an important role in the manner in which he demarcates moral from non-moral principles. In the *Essay concerning Toleration* the speculative opinions listed are all theological doctrines, but we have already seen that in the *Essays on the Law of Nature* speculative opinions also include general metaphysical principles.

Now, contemporaneously with these writings in moral philosophy, Locke was engaged in a very focused and intense project of equipping himself as a physician.

---

[54] Locke 1954, p. 145. [55] Ibid. [56] Locke 2006, p. 271.

This involved extensive reading of medical and natural philosophical texts; the practice of chymistry; and close involvement with the exciting physiological research that was taking place in Oxford in the mid-1660s. His exposure to the new natural philosophy and to some of the leading virtuosi themselves naturally led him to encounter the new methodological emphasis, amongst English natural philosophers, on experimental natural philosophy over the speculative or theoretical approach to the knowledge of nature. Not surprisingly, Locke's reading notes show that, from the early to the middle 1660s, he was fully apprised of this development. For example, an otherwise unexceptional excerpt on bees from Henry Power's *Experimental Philosophy* (1664) speaks of 'our English *Butler* an Experimental & not theoricall writer on that subject. Power Exp: phil: p. 4'.[57] Again, Locke shows his awareness of the distaste for speculative systems when he excerpts Boyle's comment, in *Certain Physiological Essays, Written at Distant Times, and on Several Occasions* (1661, LL 439; hereafter *Certain Physiological Essays*), on speculative philosophers like Campanella and Aristotle:

> I am apt to impute many of the deficiencys [...] chiefly to this thing, that they have too hastily, & either upon a few observations, or at least without a competent number of experiments, presumed to Establish principles & deliver axioms.[58]

It is little wonder, then, that in early 1669, after the most intense period of involvement in 'hands-on' medicine that Locke was to experience in his life, he should compose a short essay on the need for reform in the art of physic and that in this work he should deploy this new methodological emphasis opposing speculative hypotheses. Thus we find that 'De arte medica' is replete with anti-speculative rhetoric, makes seven references to useless and empty speculations, and places a strong emphasis on the need for direct observation (for further discussion, see Chapter 2).

Meanwhile Locke continued to use the distinction between speculative and practical principles as it was adumbrated in his early moral writings, in the second draft of the *Essay* written in 1671. In Draft B, sections 4 to 16 are taken up with elaborating the point of the final paragraph of the third essay in the *Essays on the Law of Nature*, namely that there are no innate, 'κοιναὶ ἔννοιαι first principles in which all man kinde doe universally agree'. Locke opposes those who assert such innate 'practicall as well as speculative' principles.[59] And, of course, these sections were reworked and appeared as Book One of the *Essay*, where the case against innate principles is developed first for speculative principles and then for practical ones. Thus we find the deployment of the distinction between speculative and practical opinion alongside Locke's express preference for the experimental approach to natural philosophy over the speculative.

---

[57] Bodl. MS Locke d. 11, fol. 3v (copied from Bodl. MS Locke f. 14, p. 76). See Power 1664, p. 4. Locke's original entry was made in 1664.

[58] Bodl. MS Locke f. 14, p. 23, quoting *Boyle Works*, Vol. 2, p. 13. Locke used this notebook between c. 1659 and c. 1667.

[59] Draft B, §5, p. 104. Draft A, §27 discusses innate principles, but not in terms of the speculative/practical distinction.

Just how this preference is expressed in the *Essay* itself will be the concern of later chapters, but it is important here to address a potential objection to Locke's endorsement of the experimental over the speculative in natural philosophy; and this objection arises from his very own definition of 'natural philosophy' at the end of the *Essay*.

In the very last chapter of the *Essay*, Locke describes natural philosophy as a speculative science. It is worth quoting him in full.

> The Knowledge of Things, as they are in their own proper Beings, their Constitutions, Properties, and Operations, whereby I mean not only Matter, and Body, but Spirits also, which have their proper Natures, Constitutions, and Operations as well as Bodies. This in a little more enlarged Sense of the Word, I call φυσική, or *natural Philosophy*. The end of this, is bare speculative Truth, and whatsoever can afford the Mind of Man any such, falls under this branch, whether it be God himself, Angels, Spirits, Bodies, or any of their Affections, as Number, and Figure, *etc.*[60]

Here Locke defines 'natural philosophy' so as to make it include the study of God and spirits. Locke uses this 'enlarged Sense of the Word' here because he is attempting to give a comprehensive tripartite division to all those things about which we can have knowledge. However, the semantic range of 'natural philosophy' here is somewhat wider than in Locke's normal use of the phrase, and wider, too, than it will be in this study. On the whole, when Locke speaks of 'natural philosophy' in the *Essay* and elsewhere, he restricts this name to the study of material bodies. For example, in *Some Thoughts concerning Education*, Locke also introduces natural philosophy using this broader sense:

> *Natural Philosophy* being the Knowledge of the Principles, Properties, and Operations of Things, as they are in Themselves, I imagine that there are Two Parts of it, one comprehending Spirits with their Nature and Qualities; and the other *Bodies*. The first of these is usually referr'd to *Metaphysicks*: But under what Title soever the consideration of *Spirits* comes, I think it ought to go before the study of Matter, and Body, not as a Science that can be methodized into a System.[61]

But two sections later Locke tells us that the study of the doctrine of the Scriptures, that is, the study of spirits, should precede the study of '*Natural Philosophy*' because 'Matter being a thing, that all our Senses are constantly conversant with, it is so apt to possess the Mind, and exclude all other Beings'.[61a] Here 'natural philosophy' clearly refers to the study of material bodies, and this narrower sense continues in the ensuing discussion.

It is also important to clarify just what Locke means by the term 'science' here. In the seventeenth century, 'science' could refer to a general domain of knowledge or a discipline, but it also had a more technical meaning, associated with the Aristotelian conception of a system of knowledge. Thus 'science' often referred to a system of

---

[60] *E* IV. xxi. 2, p. 720.   [61] STCE, §190, p. 245.   [61a] STCE, §192, p. 246.

knowledge derived by demonstration from first principles. This Aristotelian sense of 'science' was equivalent in meaning to the Latin term *scientia* which was commonly used in the seventeenth century, and it is the sense that Locke has in mind when he speaks of the science of natural philosophy.[62]

Returning to the *Essay*, what is important for us to clarify here is the import of Locke's claim that the end of natural philosophy is 'bare speculative Truth'. First, it must be stressed that, in the study of immaterial entities such as God and spirits, all reflection (over and above revelation) must be speculative, because there is no observational evidence that can be brought to bear on these matters. We have already seen how, in the *Essay concerning Toleration*, Locke listed such doctrines as trinitarianism and transubstantiation as speculative. Second, when it comes to philosophical systems which account for the nature of material bodies and of their affections—that is, their qualities—here too we can only hope for speculative truth. But, in the case of our speculations about material bodies, Locke's message in the *Essay* is that these are to be based, as far as possible, upon experiment and observation. At least that is what will be argued in the ensuing chapters of this study. To be sure, the study of immaterial entities is speculative in so far as it does not rely on revelation. And speculative hypotheses such as corpuscularianism are, in a sense, the end point of all natural philosophical reflection. However, it will be argued below that, for Locke, the centre of gravity or, better still, the burden of activity in the natural philosophical enterprise was not bare speculation, but the accumulation of facts through observation and experiment.[63] This goes some way to explaining why Locke's own speculative natural philosophy is largely absent from the *Essay*.

Locke's commitment to the experimental philosophy also provides a natural explanation for the occurrence of Sydenham's name on the list of Master-Builders. I have argued elsewhere that, by mid-1669, Sydenham was committed to the central tenets of the experimental philosophy: he was opposed to speculative systems and the use of hypotheses; he was opposed to the futile exploration for underlying causes of disease, which lay beyond the power of the senses; and he favoured the method of natural history in the investigation of diseases.[64] Sydenham was a Master-Builder just because of his adherence to the *experimental* philosophy.

Locke's commitment to the experimental philosophy also goes some way to explaining the reason for Locke's pessimism about the prospects of natural philosophy as a science. The business of the natural philosopher is to focus on observation and

---

[62] For further discussion see the Introduction to Sorell et al. 2010, pp. vii–xiii.

[63] John Yolton makes heavy weather of this passage in *E* IV. xxi. 2. In his *The Two Intellectual Worlds of John Locke*, he claims 'the inclusion of bodies as objects of speculative truth is rather odd' and that 'Natural philosophy is larger in scope than the science of nature he so carefully described earlier in the *Essay*; that science, an experimental science, is restricted to experience and does not allow for speculation' (J. W. Yolton 2004, pp. 46–7). Once we take into account the experimental/speculative distinction, however, it becomes clear that material bodies can be the objects of speculative natural philosophy, even if Locke is pessimistic about the epistemic status of those speculations.

[64] Anstey and Burrows 2009, pp. 19–23 and Anstey 2011b.

experiment, and only then to engage in speculative theory. However, the task of accumulating facts about nature is colossal and beyond the powers of any one individual, or even one generation. Thus it seems that a true speculative natural philosophy is a very long way off, if at all achievable. As Locke puts it in *Some Thoughts concerning Education*: 'Natural Philosophy, as a speculative Science, I imagin we have none, and perhaps, I may think I have reason to say, we never shall be able to make a Science of it'.[65]

In fact, it is often overlooked that *Some Thoughts concerning Education*, a work published just three years after the *Essay*, is concerned with the status of speculative systems of natural philosophy. There Locke says:

> But to return to the study of *Natural Philosophy*, though the World be full of Systems of it, yet I cannot say, I know any one which can be taught a Young Man as a Science, wherein he may be sure to find Truth and Certainty, which is, what all Sciences give an expectation of. I do not hence conclude that none of them are to be read: It is necessary for a Gentleman in this learned Age to look into some of them, to fit himself for Conversation. But whether that of *Des Cartes* be put into his Hands, as that which is most in Fashion; or it be thought fit to give him a short view of that and several other also, I think the Systems of *Natural Philosophy*, that have obtained in this part of the World, are to be read, more to know the *Hypotheses*, and to understand the Terms and Ways of Talking of the several Sects, than with hopes to gain thereby a comprehensive, scientifical, and satisfactory Knowledge of the Works of Nature.[66]

It is the *systems* of the speculative philosophers that Locke sees little value in. This sentiment is more cautious and pessimistic than that which characterized many proponents of the experimental philosophy. Boyle, for example, discussed at some length the role and value of familiarizing oneself with the current systems and hypotheses of speculative philosophers such as Descartes and Epicurus. Naturally, Locke regards the corpuscularian hypothesis as one of these speculative systems.

> Only this may be said, that the Modern *Corpuscularians* talk, in most Things, more intelligibly than the *Peripateticks*, who possessed the Schools immediately before them.[67]

This is a sentiment which he also expressed in the *Essay*.[68] Once the student has familiarized himself with the systems 'in Fashion', Locke recommends serious study of experimental natural philosophy. Not surprisingly, he recommends Boyle as an author who should be read.

> But I would not deterr any one from the study of Nature, because all the Knowledge we have, or possibly can have of it, cannot be brought into a Science. There are very many things in it, that are convenient and necessary to be known to a Gentleman: And a great many other, that will

---

[65] STCE, §190, pp. 244–5.
[66] STCE, §193, p. 247.
[67] STCE, §193, pp. 247–8.
[68] E IV. iii. 16.

abundantly reward the Pains of the Curious with Delight and Advantage. But these, I think, are rather to be found amongst such Writers, as have imploy'd themselves in making rational Experiments and Observations, than in starting barely speculative Systems. Such Writings therefore, as many of Mr. *Boyle's* are, with others, that have writ of *Husbandry, Planting, Gardening,* and the like, may be fit for a Gentleman, when he has a little acquainted himself with some of the Systems of the *Natural Philosophy* in Fashion.[69]

It is entirely natural then, given Locke's commitment to the experimental philosophy, that in the *Essay* he felt free to criticize the speculative mechanical accounts of cohesion and motion and could express his nescience about the very nature of matter and its qualities.

The real problem that the natural philosopher faces, however, is not the colossal task of accumulating observations and experiments, but the fact that one cannot gain access to the inner nature of things. As Locke puts it after a passage already cited:

Natural Philosophy, as a speculative Science, I imagin we have none, and perhaps, I may think I have reason to say, we never shall be able to make a Science of it. The Works of Nature are contrived by a Wisdom, and operate by ways too far surpassing our Faculties to discover, or Capacities to conceive, for us ever to be able to reduce them into a Science.[70]

James Tyrrell concurred with Locke on this point, claiming, in early 1691:

I perfectly agree with you: there is but one objection against natural experimental philosophy that I know of, and that you have given us in your booke, when you shew us, the reasons why it can never arrive to the perfection of a science: yet however even the very guesses at truth, are certainly the best and most instructive of all Romances.[71]

It is this problem, of epistemic access to the inner natures of things, that presented the main stumbling block to the development of sound speculative natural philosophical systems and at the same time provided the rationale for redirecting the natural philosopher to the task of accumulating, from observation and experiment, matters of fact about material bodies. Locke's early engagement with this problem is the subject of the next chapter.

---

[69] *STCE*, §193, p. 248. Locke had offered advice on planting and gardening to the Clarke family. See Locke to Edward Clarke, 27 January 1685, *Correspondence*, Vol. 2, pp. 683–5. Furthermore, Locke's own treatise on *Observations upon the Growth and Culture of Vines and Olives*, written for the First Earl of Shaftesbury (*Locke Works*, Vol. 10, pp. 323–56), provides an example of the sort of work that he has in mind here. For further background see Harris and Anstey 2009.

[70] *STCE*, §190, pp. 244–5.

[71] James Tyrrell to Locke, 19 March 1691, *Correspondence*, Vol. 4, p. 243. Interestingly, in this letter Tyrrell mentions Locke's 'designe of againe resumeing the study of natural things' (ibid.), which suggests that at this point Locke regarded himself as having left off natural philosophical concerns, perhaps because of his preoccupations with writings of the late 1680s.

2

Corpuscular pessimism

[T]he Perfection of Telescopes, and Microscopes, by which our Sense is so infinitely advanc'd, seems to be the only Way to penetrate into the most hidden Parts of Nature, and to make the most of the Creation.

Christopher Wren[1]

Corpuscular pessimism is the doctrine that it is unlikely in the extreme that we could ever have knowledge of the nature of the corpuscular sub-structure of material bodies. It is to be distinguished from the stronger doctrine of corpuscular scepticism,[2] which is the view that we cannot *in principle* have epistemic access to the corpuscular sub-structure of material bodies. The qualifier 'corpuscular' in the expression 'corpuscular pessimism' connotes a prior commitment both to the existence of unobservable corpuscles, which are the constituents of material objects, and to the intelligibility of corpuscular explanations of observable phenomena. And Locke is well aware that these, in themselves, are contested hypotheses about the nature of the unobserved. Thus corpuscular pessimism is not scepticism about the existence of corpuscles, but rather it is pessimism with regard to the possibility that we can have epistemic access to the determinate natures of the corpuscles that constitute the substances around us.

It is also important to distinguish corpuscular pessimism from scepticism about the existence of the external world, which threatens to arise from a commitment to the view that ideas are the immediate objects of perception.[3] Locke certainly believed in the 'veil of perception', but as early as Draft B of the *Essay* it is clear that he had no sceptical concerns about the existence of the external world: in this respect he was a realist.[4] Nor was Locke particularly concerned about the fallibility of the senses—a

---

[1] Christopher Wren, 'Inauguration Speech', Gresham College, 1657, in Wren 1750, pp. 204–5.
[2] I borrow the phrase 'corpuscular scepticism' from Garber 1982, though I use it in a more restricted sense than Garber.
[3] Garber 1982, pp. 174–5.
[4] Some scholars have denied that Locke held a representative theory of perception, most famously John Yolton. For a recent debate on this issue, see the special issue of *Pacific Philosophical Quarterly*, 85, 2004.

subject on which he declared his hand in a direct passage in Draft B, which was subsequently incorporated into the *Essay* itself.

[W]hen ever our senses doe actualy convey into our understandings any Idea. we have a certein undoubted knowledg that there doth some thing at that time realy exist without us which doth affect our senses & by them give notice of its self to our apprehensive facultys, & actualy produce that Idea which we then perceive.[5]

Furthermore, it is important to distinguish between corpuscular pessimism and the problem of justifying inferences from the observable world to the sub-microscopic, in order to construct a scientific image of the world. This latter problem, sometimes called 'the problem of transdiction' following Maurice Mandelbaum,[6] is clearly related, and intimately so, to the problem of corpuscular pessimism: if there were no grounds on which one could justify inferences from the observed to the sub-microscopic, and if the sub-microscopic is in principle unobservable, then corpuscular scepticism seems unavoidable. And in fact the problem of transdiction was one of the watershed issues that divided early modern advocates of the experimental philosophy from those who practised the speculative philosophy. However, our concern in this chapter is with corpuscular pessimism and with the way in which it set the terms of reference for Locke's framing of two natural philosophical problems that would concern him for many years.

The problem of corpuscular pessimism is central to Locke's discussions of natural philosophy. It is not too much to claim that it is the dominant philosophical problem that Locke confronted in his reflections on the nature of natural philosophy. From the time when he turned his mind to this discipline, this was the central problematic that determined his positive methodological prescriptions for it, the explanatory principles that he deployed, and his own speculative theory. His views on the usefulness of hypotheses and of analogical reasoning and on the distinctions between primary and secondary qualities and between real and nominal essences, as well as his nescience about the nature of matter and of its properties such as cohesion and motion—all are best interpreted as responses to the problem of corpuscular pessimism. Furthermore, the problem of corpuscular pessimism was, so far as we know, the first natural philosophical problem that Locke ever dealt with, even before the early drafts of the *Essay* in 1671.

This chapter first sets out the contours of the problem and then examines Locke's early discussion of corpuscular pessimism in his medical essays of the late 1660s. It then turns to the early drafts of the *Essay*, where we find that all of the problems addressed by Locke that pertain to natural philosophy are, at their core, problems stemming from our lack of epistemic access to the micro-structure of material things.

---

[5] Draft B, §40, pp. 147–8; §§39–40 = *E* IV. xi. 8–9.
[6] Mandelbaum 1964, pp. 61–117.

The contours of the problem of corpuscular pessimism

In line with the emphasis on observation and experiment in the new philosophy, Locke's early philosophical reflections accord observational evidence a very high epistemic status. Later, when he had worked out his full theory of ideas, he was to call the kind of knowledge that derives immediately from the senses sensitive knowledge;[7] but even in his early drafts of the *Essay* and in his earlier medical essays he regarded knowledge acquired through the senses as virtually certain. If the status of observational evidence is very high, then the fact that we lack epistemic access to the sub-microscopic level becomes particularly acute. For, if we cannot reason demonstratively from known premises to knowledge of the nature of the sub-microscopic, then we may not be able to have any knowledge of that realm at all. The foundational problem then is: How do we get knowledge of phenomena at the sub-microscopic level?

Compounding this problem is Locke's view that humankind experiences a form of imposed epistemic boundedness—a view we have encountered in his claims for the aims of the *Essay*. Locke is firmly of the belief that God has prescribed limits on our sensory capacities and that these limits are a guide to what our epistemic preoccupations should be: to live a morally upright life and to discover those conveniences that enable us to live well.[8]

Some commentators, such as Maurice Mandelbaum and Peter Alexander,[9] have gone even further, claiming that Locke was a corpuscular sceptic: that he was committed to the view that corpuscles are unobservable in principle. And indeed, in the early essay entitled 'Anatomia', Locke makes strong claims, which appear to imply in-principle unobservability. He says:

when we goe about to discover the curious artifice of nature & take a view of the instruments by which she works, we may with as much reason expect to have a sight of those very spirits by which we hope to see them, for I believe the one as far from the reach of our senses as the other.[10]

Should in-principle unobservability be in mind here, then there would be no prospect of ever having sensitive knowledge of the sub-microscopic realm; and this in turn would be seen as a stronger basis for Locke's pessimism with regard to our knowledge of the fundamental nature of reality. However, Lisa Downing rightly points out that there are countervailing passages in the *Essay*, such as the 'microscopical eyes' passage in Book II, which seem to imply that epistemic access to the properties of corpuscles is possible in spite of Locke's relatively pessimistic outlook on the prospects of extending the limits of our senses.[11] Furthermore, she has convincingly shown that there is no thesis in the *Essay* that entails any in-principle unobservability of corpuscles, hence those who

---

[7] *E* IV. ii. 14 and iii. 5.
[8] Draft B, §39, p. 147.
[9] Mandelbaum 1964, p. 18.
[10] 'Anatomia', TNA PRO 30/24/47/2, fol. 34r = Dewhurst 1966, p. 89.
[11] See *E* II. xxiii, 11–12, pp. 301–3.

claim that there is one are mistaken in their interpretations.[12] Corpuscles are not in principle unobservable for Locke.

A further doctrine, which is absent from Locke's mature writings but which many of his contemporaries (such as Robert Hooke) held, is the doctrine of epistemic impairment or fallen knowledge. This is the view that, at the Fall, when the powers of human senses were severely circumscribed, humankind lost the ability to perceive the inner natures of things. While Locke believed in the Fall, there appears to be only one allusion to this doctrine (to be discussed below) in all of his writings and no evidence that it played any role in his understanding of the problem.[13]

Another response to the problem, and one that Locke implicitly rejected, was to posit some sort of Platonic realm or to appeal to the existence of archetypes whose material correlates comprise the external world. His denial that there are universals or types that correspond to our general ideas implies that a Plato-style solution is firmly out of the question. Locke does in fact have a theory of archetypes, but it is largely cashed out in terms of his theory of ideas. (We will return to this in the discussion of mathematics in Chapter 6.)

It is perhaps most helpful to view Locke as considering two solutions to the problem of corpuscular pessimism and as rejecting the first and accepting the second. The first solution he discusses, to which he is firmly opposed, is that one should formulate a systematic theory about the nature of the sub-microscopic realm on the basis of speculative metaphysical principles. Locke has three objections to this way of proceeding. First, there are no innate speculative principles from which we can reason demonstratively to the inner nature of things. This claim occurs early in Draft A, but recedes into the background of his thought, as the critique of innatism takes on a life of its own and as the attack on maxims and principles takes a more generalized form in Book IV of the *Essay* and in the later correspondence with Stillingfleet (to be discussed in Chapter 8). Second, he rightly points out that speculative theories can be incompatible; it is observational evidence that will be the arbiter of the question which theory, if any, is correct. Third, he claims that speculative theories can be incoherent. The best illustration of this claim is found in his critique of the mechanical accounts of the cohesion of material bodies in Book II of the *Essay* (to be discussed in Chapter 5). The combined weight of these objections to the efficacy of speculative theory leads Locke to judge the epistemic status of theoretical knowledge to be very low, and to abandon speculative theory as a starting point in solving the problem of corpuscular pessimism. This, of course, is in keeping with the methodological views of the day, which decried the use of hypotheses and speculation and plumped for observation and experiment.

The second solution that Locke considers—and the one that, he believes, gives the natural philosopher greater purchase on the problem of corpuscular pessimism—is to attempt to close the gap between observation and speculative theory. This can be achieved both by extending sensory limits, though Locke is supremely pessimistic

---

[12] Downing 1992. See also Garber 1982, p. 177.
[13] For further discussion, see Harrison 2007.

about this, and by making use of analogical reasoning (to be discussed in Chapter 4). Now Locke is well aware of the point that analogical reasoning, which involves the use of hypotheses, is, in the final analysis, a form of speculation, and he is therefore very cautious in recommending its application to material things. Analogical reasoning is only to be pursued after all the facts that can be gleaned through experiment and observation have been accumulated by using the method of natural history.

Interestingly, however, simultaneously with these prescriptions for the method of natural philosophy, Locke himself engages in his own bridge-building doctrines in order to present an account of the origins and representative nature of our ideas and of their relations with the particular sorts of substances encountered in the external world and with their properties. It is by stipulation that some of our ideas resemble objectively existing qualities, and it is by bridge-building that Locke is able to establish both the distinction between primary and secondary qualities and the distinction between nominal and real essence. And, as many commentators have pointed out, the elaboration of these doctrines is made in terms of the sort of speculative theory which is itself to result from careful analogical reasoning and from speculation informed by natural history: that is, in terms of the corpuscular theory of matter.

Furthermore, it has been claimed that, for Locke, even if the method of natural history could eventually reveal the inner natures of substances and so dispel corpuscular pessimism, an insurmountable form of scepticism is in the wings to take its place. On the basis of Locke's comments that God might superadd certain qualities to matter independently of its nature, Matthew Stuart has argued that Locke is committed to the view that a science of nature is in principle out of our reach.[14] We will return in Chapter 8 to this claim—which amounts to saying that Locke was committed to a form of *natural philosophical scepticism*. However, as we round off the present overview of the problem of corpuscular pessimism, it should not be overlooked that Locke is adamantly of the opinion that this problem is not unique to bodies characterized by material qualities but applies equally to entities characterized by thought. That is, we are just as much in the dark about the nature of the mind or spirit as we are about the nature of matter.[15] It is this parity of reasoning across matter and mind that provides Locke with one of his key polemical moves against his critics and that, given the enlarged conception of natural philosophy he invokes at the end of the *Essay*, characterizes the basic epistemological dilemma for the science of bodies in general.

Background to Locke's early discussions of corpuscular pessimism

In the 1660s Locke was engaged in reading the central texts of the new natural philosophy. This reading included such works as Descartes' *Principles* and Boyle's

---

[14] Stuart 1996.   [15] See Draft A, §§ 1 and 2, pp. 2 and 7, Draft B, §19, pp. 129–30, *E* II. xxiii.

Certain Physiological Essays. Both the Cartesian and the Boylean natural philosophy appealed to unobservable entities and their qualities in order to explain observable phenomena. In particular, they appealed to what Boyle called the 'mechanical affections' of unobservable corpuscles—shape, size, motion, and texture—in order to explain observable phenomena for which the underlying causes were unknown. This mode of explanation had a long pedigree, which stretched back to the Greek atomists. However, there were two distinctive features of the revival of interest in micro-corpuscular explanations in the early to mid-seventeenth century which gave it a new impetus. The first, which we have already encountered in the previous chapter, was the manner in which it was believed that such explanations should be developed, namely by analogy with the functioning of machines. The second was the polemical context in which the new approach to corpuscular explanation was deployed. Micro-corpuscular explanations were based on a new theory of material qualities, supposedly superior to that of the dominant Aristotelian theory. In particular, Robert Boyle argued that all the qualities of bodies were derived from their mechanical affections—or, in Locke's terminology, from their primary qualities—and not from the Aristotelian-Galenic first qualities of hot, cold, wet, and dry.

The new mode of explanation required what we now call abductive inferences from the observable realm to the sub-microscopic realm. Boyle, for example, postulated that the mechanical affections of bodies that we perceive at the observable level are also properties of the constituents of bodies at the unobservable level. We will examine Locke's mature views on this form of explanation in Chapter 8 below. Our concern here, however, is to spell out the contours of the problem and to examine Locke's first engagement with it; for, as we have already noted, it was a problem which was to dominate much of his philosophical reflection on the nature of natural philosophy and on its prospects as a science.

By the 1650s many physicians and chymists in England, particularly those well disposed to the new philosophy, began to stress the need for observation and experiment and the futility of the search for underlying causes of disease. There was a number of aspects of this revisionist move in medicine. On the one hand, there was a critique of the natural philosophy that undergirded the Galenic *methodus medendi*. For example, the Galenists viewed disease as resulting from, and in, an imbalance of the four bodily humours: blood, phlegm, yellow bile, and back bile. Each humour was characterized as having a particular combination of the first qualities of hot, cold, wet, and dry. However, the theory of the *primae qualitates* was increasingly coming under attack from proponents of the mechanical philosophy and from the chymists.[16] Another aspect was a general scepticism about ancient authorities in physic, the curative part of medicine, and about the utility of a university education in physic, in preference to the practical training that chymists underwent for the preparation of medical remedies.

---

[16] See Anstey 2011a.

A third feature of the stress on observation and experiment and of the criticism of Galenic medicine was a critique of the usefulness of anatomy in physic.

There is some irony in this, because one of the champions of the need for first-hand observation was none other than William Harvey, the great English anatomist. It is almost certain that Harvey's methodological views on the importance of observation in anatomy were a stimulus to the calls for a more observational and experimentally based medicine. By the 1660s, however, anatomy was regarded by some chymical physicians—those who were skilled in the preparation of chymical remedies and practised medicine—as being of limited value, largely because it could not help with the search for knowledge of the cause of disease or for the prescription of efficacious chymical remedies.[17] As it happens, Locke read widely in medicine and took a keen interest in the protracted dispute between chymical and Galenic physicians, which was at its height in the 1660s. It is not surprising, therefore, that he penned his own views on the utility of anatomy in so far as it can contribute to the problem of gaining epistemic access to the underlying causes of diseases and their cures, and that this was probably part of a larger, projected (though not completed) work on the reform of physic, entitled 'De arte medica'. These two medical writings contain Locke's first discussion of the problem of corpuscular pessimism, and it is to them that we now turn.

Corpuscular pessimism in 'De arte medica' and 'Anatomia'

In the final weeks of 1668, Locke recorded his own views on the limits of anatomy for the physician in a short essay entitled 'Anatomia'. In it he spells out the limited uses of anatomy for the physician and stresses the inability of anatomical knowledge and inquiry to deliver knowledge of the nature of diseases or their cures. It is arguably the most philosophically sophisticated treatment of the subject that has survived from the period. The language that Locke uses is that of someone strongly disposed to the experimental philosophy. In his more rhetorical and programmatic essay entitled 'De arte medica', he reiterates the general point about our inability to find the underlying causes of disease and he provides a statement of the rationale for a reform of physic in keeping with the agenda of the chymical physicians, with whom he identified himself. Before examining the contents of these essays, however, it is important to summarize the case for the claim that they were composed by Locke.

Much has been made in the writings of previous commentators of the influence of the London physician Thomas Sydenham on these two essays and on Locke's thoughts about the futility of speculation on underlying causes and in favour of observation and

---

[17] For the critique of anatomy, see Wear 2000, pp. 442–8. This important background to 'Anatomia' is ignored by most commentators on this essay. D. E. Wolfe 1961 and Duchesneau 1973 are examples of early analyses which fail to mention the chymical physicians' critique of anatomy; see also and Walmsley 2008 for a recent example.

experiment.[18] A recent analysis of the contents of these essays, using computational stylistics, has established beyond reasonable doubt that Locke was their author; yet it has been claimed, even among those who favour his authorship, that Sydenham was a clear influence on the views that Locke expresses in them. It is important to point out, therefore, that all the methodological emphases within these essays were central to the views of the chymical physicians and virtuoso-physicians (Fellows of the College of Physicians who were sympathetic to the new philosophy) of the 1660s. Furthermore, Sydenham's only published work from this period, the *Methodus curandi febres* (1666), contains a highly speculative theory of fevers, which is just the sort of theory that Locke warns against in his medical essays. It is a work that shows little or no influence of the radical changes taking place in medical methodology during the 1660s. In fact, the highly speculative ebullition theory of fevers found in Sydenham's *Methodus* is presented in a far more muted form in his later work *Observationes medicae* (1676), and this change may well reflect the influence of Locke's methodological views as expressed in the 'Anatomia' and 'De arte medica'.[19]

When one turns to 'De arte medica', which Locke almost certainly wrote in early 1669, one is struck by the strongly anti-speculative tone of the essay. Again and again, Locke decries the use of hypotheses and speculation in medicine. After the opening statement concerning the unquestionable importance of finding a correct method for physic, Locke turns to the failings of both past and present writers on medicine. In fact, the essay contains hardly anything of positive doctrine, apart from the most general comments about the importance of observation—which, no doubt, was to be developed in the unfinished sections of the work. Instead, the essay contains a sustained critique of the speculative approach to medicine. Locke sees in humans a propensity 'to observe the operation of nature', and

the event of things is very inquisitive after their cause & very restlesse & unquiet till in those things which it is conversant about, it has framed to its self some hypothesis & laid a foundation whereon to establish all its reasonings.[20]

The mind then weaves 'all these phansies together fashioned to them selves systems & hypotheses'. The upshot is this:

those few hypothesis which had the long & elaborate discourses of the ancientts & sufferd not their enquirys to extend them selves any farther then how the phenomena of diseases might be explain'd by these doctrines & the rules of practise accomodated to the received principles has at last but confined & narrowed mens thoughts, amused their understanding with fine but uselesse speculations, & diverted their enquirys from the true & advantageous knowledg of things, the notions that have beene raised into mens heads by remote speculative principles.[21]

---

[18] See for example Walmsley 2004; 2006a, p. 420; and 2008.
[19] For further discussion, see Anstey and Burrows 2009.
[20] TNA PRO 30/24/47/2, fol. 50r = Dewhurst 1966, p. 80.
[21] TNA PRO 30/24/47/2, fol. 51r = Dewhurst 1966, pp. 80–1.

The anti-speculative rhetoric continues: 'These speculative theorems doe as little advantage the physick as food of men'. Locke has in mind here the theory of bodily humours, the fundamental physiological theory, which underlay the Galenic *methodus*. Locke's point is therefore methodological; and he is keen to stress the futility of our need to

> penetrate into the hidden causes of things lay downe principles & establish maximes to him self about the operations of nature, & then vainely expect that Nature or in truth god him self should proceede according to those laws his maximes had prescribed him.[22]

Interestingly, in an interpolated comment (referred to above), Locke claims that, as a result of this tendency 'man by desire to know more than was fit a second time lost the little remainder of knowledg that was left him'. It is likely that this passage contains an allusion to the Fall and Locke was appealing to the doctrine of epistemic impairment. It may, however, be inserted here more for rhetorical effect than as an expression of his considered opinion.[23]

Importantly for our purposes, Locke regards this inimical tendency to have worked its way right through natural philosophy:

> This vanity spread its self into many of usefull parts of naturall philosophy, & by how much the more it seemd subtile sublime or learned by soe much the more it proved pernicious & hurtfull, by hindering the growth of practicall knowledg.[24]

But, even worse, it is likely that 'the foundation of the mischief was first laid' in natural philosophy. Locke next sketches an outline of the subjects to be treated in the proposed work. He tells us that he will examine just how medicine has reached its current state; this will involve an analysis of:

> 1 Experience. 2 Method founded upon phylosophy & Hypothesis 3 Botaniques. 4 Chymistry. 5 Anatomy. In all which I shall indeavour to shew how much each hath contributed to the advanceing the art of Physick & wherein they came short of perfecting it.[25]

This list contains the main items on the agenda for the reform of physic as promoted by the chymical physicians. Of special importance, however, is the juxtaposition of experience with the 'Method Founded upon Phylosophy & Hypothesis'. Clearly Locke viewed the correct method in physic in terms of the experimental versus the speculative approach, and there are strong Baconian allusions in the text which leave the reader in no doubt as to Locke's own methodological predisposition.[26]

---

[22] TNA PRO 30/24/47/2, fols 52r–53r = Dewhurst 1966, pp. 81–2.
[23] This was suggested to me by Jo MacDonald.
[24] TNA PRO 30/24/47/2, fol. 53r = Dewhurst 1966, p. 82.
[25] TNA PRO 30/24/47/2, fol. 55r = Dewhurst 1966, p. 83.
[26] Locke's comment about the project of the reform of medicine being 'a business too large for any one mans comprehension and too great for his owne single endeavours' is a prominent Baconian allusion. The content of the pencilled reference to Bacon's *Novum organum* in this manuscript is apposite too (TNA PRO 30/24/47/2, fol. 55v). The passage to which Locke refers (§31) says: 'It is useless to expect great growth in the

Locke's fifth topic is anatomy, and it is reasonable to assume that his earlier essay entitled 'Anatomia' was to be drawn on, or even grafted into, the larger work on the reform of medicine. It is in 'Anatomia' that we find Locke's first serious engagement with the problem of corpuscular pessimism. The essay is concerned with the utility of anatomy for the cure of diseases. Interestingly, it was almost certainly written not long after the convalescence of Lord Ashley, who had undergone abdominal surgery to drain a large hydatid cyst above his liver. Locke, who had been resident in Ashley's household from April 1667, was intimately involved in the whole episode. The whole experience certainly provided sufficient grounds for Locke to reflect on the usefulness of anatomy in the cure of diseases. His conclusion, in keeping with the views of the chymical physicians, is that anatomy is of little or no use in discovering the causes and cures of diseases.

Locke begins his discussion with the claim that

it is certaine & beyond controversy that nature performs all her operations in the body by parts soe minute & insensible that I thinke noe body will ever have or pretend even by the assistance of glasses or any other invention to come to a sight of them.[27]

Here is, for the first time, Locke's statement of the problem of our lack of epistemic access to the sub-microscopic level. Importantly, he goes on to claim that, even if we were able to see the determinate shapes and sizes of particular parts of the relevant organs and bodily juices, this would be of no help in guiding the physician to the correct method of treatment.

For suppose anyone should have so sharp a knife & sight as to discover the secret & effective composure of any part, could he make an ocular demonstration that the pores of the perenchyma of the liver or kidnys were either round or square & that the parts of urin & gall separatd in those parts were in size & figure answerable to those pores. I ask how this would at all direct him in the cure either of the jaundice or stopage of urin what would this advantage his method or guid him to fit medicins.[28]

In this passage Locke is clearly speaking in corpuscular terms, though in neither essay does he use the term 'corpuscle'. The tone of this quotation and of the previous one is pessimistic about the prospects of ever discovering the causes and cures of disease. Indeed, much of Locke's treatment of the problem of corpuscular pessimism here is redolent of the later *Essay*.

---

sciences from the superinduction and grafting of new things on old; instead the instauration must be built up from the deepest foundations, unless we want to go round in circles forever, with progress little or pitiable', *Bacon Works*, Vol. 11, p. 77.

[27] TNA PRO 30/24/47/2, fol. 31r–v = Dewhurst 1966, pp. 85–6.
[28] TNA PRO 30/24/47/2, fol. 31v = Dewhurst 1966, p. 86.

Corpuscular pessimism in Draft A of the *Essay*

When we turn to Locke's first draft of the *Essay*, however, we find that the problem of our knowledge of, and of explanations in terms of, the sub-microscopic constituents of material bodies is far more muted. It appears in the framing of statements concerning our epistemic limits, although there is little by way of positive doctrine that addresses the problem. In fact, most of the allusions to natural philosophy in the early drafts are made in passing, and the interpreter has to go to some lengths to stitch together Locke's views on natural philosophy in 1671. To be sure, there are select passages wherein Locke reveals a commitment to some form of corpuscular account of the structure of material bodies and to the method of natural history. However, the content and method of natural philosophy are not discussed in any sustained way at all, and Draft A, unlike 'Anatomia' and 'De arte medica', apart from an attack on the notion of connate principles (§27), is not motivated by any overt polemical agenda. Instead the draft is concerned to develop a theory of ideas that accounts for the acquisition of knowledge of the external world as well as of mathematics and morality, and to develop an account of the relation between words and ideas.

Having said this, there are some sections in which corpuscular pessimism comes to the fore. Of special interest is §15, where Locke claims that we cannot have certain knowledge of 'universal propositions connecting causes and effects' because we lack knowledge both of 'the whole extent & efficacy of all possible agents to produce that effect' and of the powers of the passive subject which is acted upon. This kind of knowledge is 'out of the reach of humane understanding'. He then gives some concrete examples.

I see when I apply fire to gold it melts it; a load stone neare iron it moves it, that snow & salt put into a vessell of water in the inside hardens the water that touches it on the outside: but in many nay most of these I have noe knowledg of the *modus operandi*, the way how these effects are produced i.e. how these simple Ideas viz. **motion** in the iron, **fluidity** in the gold & **consistence** in the water are in those several subjects produced. because these alterations being made by particles soe small & minute that they come not within the observation of my senses I cannot get any knowledg how they operate [...] had we but senses that could discover to us the particles of water their figure site motion &c when it is fluid. And also the different postures of those very particles, or the addition or separation of some particles &c [...] we should as well know the very modus or way whereby cold produces hardness & consistency in water [...][29]

Then in §27, when pulling together the threads of the discussion so far, Locke states that, with regard to external objects, it is only knowledge of particular things derived from the senses that we can have with certainty; and he draws from this a lesson about the grounds of natural philosophy:

---

[29] Draft A, §15, pp. 30–1. See also §17, p. 32. For further discussion of corpuscularianism in Draft A, see Downing 2001, pp. 519–24 and Walmsley 2006a.

all a man can certainly know of things existing without him is only particular propositions, for which he hath demonstration by his senses the best ground of science he can have or expect.[30]

This is not yet the corpuscular pessimism that is so evident in his later writings, but it does indicate the direction of development of Locke's thoughts with regard to the foundations of natural philosophy; and this is reinforced by *obiter dicta* concerning the importance of natural history (discussed below).

Later in this section, Locke goes on to develop a speculative natural philosophical example at length. He contrasts the Cartesian plenist account of matter and space with the vacuist account. His point is that reasoning based on so-called connate principles—such as 'Whatever is, is'—will not determine which account is the correct one.

But yet though both of these propositions (as you see) may be equally demonstrated viz. That there may be a Vacuum, & that there cannot be a vacuum by these two certain principles [viz.] what is is, & the same thing cannot be & not be. yet neither of these principles or ways of demonstrations prove to us or can prove that Body doth exist or what it is as it exists. but for that we are left only to our senses to discover to us as far as they can.[31]

Particularly interesting here is, first, the way in which Locke brings the so-called connate principles to bear on the dispute about the nature of body. By the time of Draft B, these two issues have come apart, and, by the time the critique of innate principles is fully developed in the *Essay*, there is almost no trace of the original connection between these connate principles and Locke's concern with our knowledge of the nature of body. It is therefore important to note, concerning the earliest phase of Locke's thoughts about our knowledge of the nature of material body, that the connate principles are implicated in the speculative approach to natural philosophy. It is apparent, then, that the origins of the critique of innate principles in Book I of the *Essay* were tied to Locke's general critique of speculative natural philosophy, but that, once this critique was fully developed by Locke, it took on a life of its own and lost any overt ties to the critique of principles which appears in Book IV of the *Essay*.

A second, more pertinent point regarding this passage is Locke's claim that the conflicting hypotheses concerning the nature of matter have no bearing on the way things are in nature: they 'cannot discover or prove to us the least knowledg of the nature of things as they are framd & exist without us'. The question can only be settled by observation; for, with regard to the nature of matter and the possibility of the vacuum, he says: 'for that we are left to our senses to discover'.[32] The problem is that in the case of the sub-microscopic the senses are unable to perform the role of arbiter of truth.

Locke returns to this problem in §38, in the extended discussion of probability and certainty. With regard to opinions relying on observation and testimony, there are two sorts: the first concerning immaterial beings; and the second concerning 'the existence,

---

[30] Draft A, §27, p. 43.   [31] Draft A, §27, p. 46.   [32] Draft A, §27, p. 46.

modifications & manner of operation of insensible materiall things'. Unobservable things such as the effluvia of the loadstone 'comeing not within the scrutiny of humane senses cannot be examind or attested by our senses or any body useing them'; we can only form probable opinions concerning them. These opinions will be based upon their agreement with things we already believe, or 'as they doe beare analogie to our observations about sensible things'.[33] This passage was reworked and appears in the *Essay* at IV. xvi. 12 as the main discussion of the role of analogy in transdictive reasoning (see Chapter 4).

Finally, when summing up towards the end of the section, Locke reiterates that we can form propositions and we can reason demonstratively about metaphysics, divinity, and 'some sort of natural phylosophy', but we do not thereby gain any actual knowledge in these disciplines. He is referring to the speculative approach to natural philosophy, but little more is made of it here. The contrast comes up again, within a discussion of the meaning of the term 'Homo', where Locke comments parenthetically that the nature of people can only 'be knowne & made out by history & enquiry into particulars which is the foundation of knowledg of things & not definitions'.[34] This allusion to natural history and the earlier reference to speculative natural philosophy are clearly functioning as background terms of reference for Locke, but Draft A is certainly not concerned with natural philosophy in any direct way.

In short, Draft A provides something of a departure from the immediate concerns of Locke in 'Anatomia' and in 'De arte medica'. This is not to say that it is discontinuous with the issues raised in the earlier medical essays, for it is really a first attempt to lay out the groundwork for a theory of knowledge and language that will provide the resources for dealing with such problems as corpuscular pessimism, and much else besides. Instead, it has closer ties with his earlier *Essays on the Law of Nature*, particularly insofar as it picks up the critique of innate principles.

Corpuscular pessimism in Draft B of the *Essay*

The opening sections of Draft B develop the critique of innate principles in far greater depth than Draft A, deploying the speculative/practical distinction in the same way in which it appears later in the *Essay* (although in reverse order). Yet already in this extended treatment the link between innate speculative principles and our knowledge of the nature of body has been elided. Locke's discussion, from sections 4 to 16 of Draft B, does not contain the example of the vacuist versus plenist hypotheses concerning matter, but rather contains a fairly full version of a critique of innatism, which was to be reordered as Chapters 2 through to 4 of Book I of the *Essay*.

Draft B is also characterized by the fact that Locke's views on the nature of matter are underdeveloped. It is important in this regard to note, especially given his later

---

[33] Draft A, §38, p. 66. [34] Draft A, §29, p. 56.

criticisms of the notion of cohesion in the *Essay*, that in Draft B Locke considers cohesion, along with extension, to be clear and distinct. He speaks confidently of

the complex Idea which I call body being noething but these 2 simple Ideas Extension or cohæsion of parts

—noting that

Two primary qualitys or propertys of body. viz. Extension & cohæsion of parts we perfectly know & have destinct cleare Ideas of.[35]

In fact, he claims that all the qualities of material bodies are probably derived from extension and cohesion:

[F]or setting aside Extension and Cohæsion of parts, all other qualitys we observe in, or Ideas we receive from body as destinguishd from spirit [...] are probably but the results & modifications of these [extension and cohesion].[36]

By the time of the publication of the *Abrégé* in 1688, however, Locke had come to regard the notion of cohesion as deeply problematic and he drops it as a primary quality of body and uses it to define extension (for detailed discussion, see Chapter 5). Furthermore, Draft B does contain the kernel of Locke's later theory of sensible (or secondary) qualities:

[A]ll the other sensible qualitys in bodies as heate cold colours smels tasts & all the objects of sense & the Ideas thereof produced in us are probably in the bodys wherein we imagin they reside noe thing but different bulke & figure & in us those appearances or sensations of them are noe thing but the effects of various impulses made upon our organs by particles or little masses of bodys of different sise figure & motion.[37]

The key point here is that Locke has imbibed the Cartesian and Boylean doctrine that the sensible qualities have as their ontological ground the mechanical affections of constituents of the bodies in which they are thought to inhere. Locke provides no argument for this thesis, but seems to regard it as the most plausible explanation of the origin of the sensible qualities. It appears elsewhere in the draft in *obiter dicta*, such as Locke's comment on the kind of arrangement of particles which is required in order for the idea of the colour black to be caused (§58). And §15 of Draft A, which was discussed above, is recycled into a discussion of the causal relation, the salient point being that 'our organs faileing us in the discovery of those fine & insensible particles our understandings are unavoidably in the darke'.[38]

But there is no sustained treatment of the problem. Rather its presence is subterranean; it comes to the surface occasionally, when natural philosophical questions are alluded to or when he turns to our sensory limitations.

---

[35] Draft B, §80 and §94, pp. 188 and 210.   [36] Draft B, §94, p. 209.
[37] Draft B, §94, p. 209.   [38] Draft B, §137, p. 256.

All of this indicates general acquiescence in new explanatory categories and general adherence to a particulate view of matter rather than commitment to a developed form of corpuscularian philosophy. This is clearly illustrated in Locke's extensive discussion of the nature of species in Draft B; for there, unlike in the later treatment of species in the *Essay*, corpuscular pessimism does not provide the framework in which the nature of species is discussed. In particular, the discussion of species in Draft B pre-dates the distinction between nominal and real essences, which frames so much of the discussion in Book III of the *Essay*. To be sure, in Draft B Locke does consider the foundation of the collection of qualities by which we denominate particular species to be the constitution of the substance in question.[39] But he says very little about these constitutions, and the focus throughout is on the clusters of ideas we have of particular species rather than on their inner constitutions (or on what he will later call their real essences). The one place where Locke alludes to our lack of epistemic access to the inner natures of things is in his comments on our inability to demarcate the 'precise bounds' between species. Yet even here there is no mention of inner corpuscular structure, and the point is made in the most general form:

therefor though there be a foundation in nature for the divideing of things into sorts & tribes, yet because we seldom know the precise bounds where one ends & the other begins & where the destinction is made between them, [...] we devide them into species in respect of our selves.[40]

It is therefore clear that, by the early 1670s, when the drafts of the *Essay* were composed, Locke had not fully explored all of the implications of corpuscular pessimism for his 'De intellectu humano' project. But one desideratum of the quest for the knowledge of nature was already fixed in his mind, and that was the method of natural history. According to Draft B, this method is the proper business of the natural philosopher, who should make 'a laborious & exact scrutiny into the nature of the things & a searching out all their qualitys & propertys', and such 'a tolerable history of things is not to be made without long time & great industry'.[41] Indeed, Locke regarded his own inquiry into the understanding as itself being 'a short & I thinke a true history of the rise & originall of humane knowledge'[41a]—something he was to reaffirm in the Introduction to the *Essay*, which he claims was written according to 'this Historical, plain Method'. Just what he meant by the term 'history' is the subject of the next chapter.

---

[39] Draft B, §72 and §81. [40] Draft B, §75, p. 183.
[41] Draft B, §72, p. 176 and §85, p. 192. [41a] Draft B, §31, p. 140.

3

Natural history

> An important element in their [members of the Royal Society] design is the careful compilation of a Natural History such as our illustrious Bacon formerly proposed.
>
> Henry Oldenburg[1]

Introduction

In Book IV, chapter 12, §10 of the *Essay* Locke tells us that the way to improve our knowledge of the nature of bodies is

only by Experience and History, which is all that the weakness of our Faculties in this State of *Mediocrity*, which we are in in this World, can attain to. [...] Experiments and Historical Observations we may have, from which we may draw Advantages of Ease and Health, and thereby increase our stock of Conveniences for this Life: but beyond this, I fear our Talents reach not, nor are our Faculties, as I guess, able to advance.[2]

For Locke, natural philosophy proceeds only by 'Experiments and Historical Observations', that is, by the construction of natural histories. On the face of it this is not quite what one would expect, for there is no mention of the method of induction, or of hypotheses.[3] To be sure, Locke goes on to concede that hypotheses may have some role in natural philosophy (*E* IV. xii. 13), but the emphasis in his prescription for a method in natural philosophy appears to be on the construction of natural histories.

---

[1] Henry Oldenburg to René Sluse, 23 October 1667, *Oldenburg Correspondence*, Vol. 3, p. 537.
[2] *Essay*, p. 645. See also *E* IV. xii. 12, p. 647 and the Journal entry for 8 February 1677, where Locke claims that men 'need trouble their heads with noe thing but the history of nature, and an enquiry into the qualitys of the things in this mansion of the universe which hath fallen to their lott': Locke 1936, p. 86.
[3] In a discussion of Baconian method in natural philosophy, Bacon's early eighteenth-century editor Peter Shaw says: 'Mr. Locke appears to have designed a kind of familiar Explanation, and Illustration of many Aphorisms of the *first* Part of the *Novum Organum* [...] but he seems no where to have explained the *second* part of the *Novum Organum*; or the Art of Investigating Forms': Bacon 1733, Vol. 2, p. 568.

Now a new approach to the writing of natural histories was the foundation of Bacon's method for natural philosophy and became the desideratum of the experimental work carried out by many members of the early Royal Society. So it would appear that Locke's comments on method in natural philosophy, whatever their peculiarities, stand in a tradition stretching back to Bacon. Yet, surprisingly, many scholars have overlooked the influence of Francis Bacon on Locke. As long ago as 1917, J. P. Gibson claimed that '[o]f the work of Bacon there is not the slightest trace in the *Essay*'.[4] There are, however, some important exceptions to this in the secondary literature on Locke. Robert Yost's 'Locke's rejection of hypotheses about sub-microscopic events' of 1951, while not mentioning Bacon, stressed that, '[w]henever [Locke] spoke of the methods of increasing empirical knowledge, he recommended the "historical" method, not the "speculative" or "hypothetical" method'.[5] This view was enthusiastically embraced by John Yolton in his 1970 *Locke and the Compass of Human Understanding* and developed into the following claim:

> It was, however, the emphasis upon compiling natural histories of bodies, which was the chief aspect of the Royal Society's programme that attracted Locke, and from which we need to understand his science of nature.[6]

Yolton rightly emphasized the Baconian origin of the conception of the compilation of natural histories (1970, p. 55). Yet, surprisingly, his thesis seems to have had very little impact. While his book is frequently cited, the Bacon connection in Locke did not filter into the main stream of Locke studies.[7] An important exception is Neal Wood, who provided an analysis of the influence of Bacon on the *Essay* and whose second chapter, on 'Baconian natural history', in *The Politics of Locke's Philosophy* (1983) lays an important foundation for the argument of the present chapter.[8]

I want to argue that there is sufficient evidence to claim that Locke owed a significant debt to Bacon's conception of how natural philosophy should be done, even if that conception was largely mediated through the 'Baconianism' of those natural philosophers within his ambit. Here I am self-consciously attempting to revive Yolton's thesis and to extend the work of Wood through an examination of Locke's involvement in, and exposure to, natural philosophy, both of which were carried out in an explicitly Baconian manner. In short, I will provide a fresh analysis of Locke's exposure to the thought of Bacon and of Baconian practitioners in natural philosophy, which reveals that he was deeply involved in and committed to the construction of natural histories.

---

[4] Gibson 1917, p. 233. [5] Yost 1951, p. 127. [6] Yolton 1970, p. 6.

[7] Another seam to Locke scholarship from the 1960s to the mid-1980s has been the study of Locke's medical writings and interests. Two prominent researchers in this tradition have highlighted the Locke/Bacon connection, but their work has not, on the whole, been taken up by philosophical commentators on Locke. See Dewhurst 1963a and Romanell 1984.

[8] Richard Serjeantson drew my attention to Wood's important treatment of Locke's Baconianism. Unhappily, I had overlooked it when writing my 2002a and only cited Wood 1975 there.

Further, I will argue that this Baconian legacy is significant for interpreting Locke's comments on method in natural philosophy in the *Essay*. Far from being incidental or even irrelevant, the Baconian legacy is central to Locke's account of natural philosophical knowledge in the *Essay*. An exposition of Locke's account of natural philosophical method in the *Essay* will follow in the next chapter.

Locke's references to Bacon

It seems that we need first an inventory of the references to Bacon in Locke's published and unpublished works. This will show us if, when, and how Baconian ideas could have come to Locke's attention, and also the regard in which Locke held Bacon. Such an inventory was compiled in 1975 by Neal Wood,[9] who unfortunately missed the one reference to Bacon which, in all of Locke's published writings, is the most important element for establishing a close link between Bacon's and Locke's conception of the role of natural history. This reference occurs in Locke's 'Advertisement of the Publisher to the Reader' in Boyle's *General History of the Air, Designed and Begun by the Honourable Robert Boyle Esq.* (1692, LL 460; hereafter *General History of the Air*).[10] In addition to this passage, there are two references to Bacon in Locke's *Second Reply to the Bishop of Worcester*. In the first one—a passage reminiscent of the under-labourer passage—Locke says:

Are all the discoveries made by Galileo, my lord Bacon, Mr. Boyle, and Mr Newton, &c. to be rejected as false, because they teach us what the old philosophers never thought of? Mistake me not, my lord, in thinking that I have the vanity here to rank myself, on this occasion, with these great discoverers of truth, and advancers of knowledge.[11]

Then there are two other references to Bacon in Locke's posthumous works. The first one is the quotation of two passages from the *Instauratio magna* in section 1 of the work *Of the Conduct of the Understanding*.[12] The second one is a recommendation, made to a gentleman in his 'Some Thoughts concerning Reading and Studying for a Gentleman', first published in 1720, to read Bacon's *The Historie of the Raigne of King Henry the Seuenth*.[13] There are no references to Bacon in the *Essay*.[14] There are, however, many references to Bacon in Locke's notebooks that indicate which of Bacon's works he was reading at particular times. For example, on page 169 of the notebook Bodl. MS Locke f. 19, which was used by Locke between 1662 and 1669, Locke reveals that he was reading Bacon's *Sylva sylvarum*.[15] Again, there is a cross-reference to the 1640 edition

---

[9] Wood 1975, pp. 49–50; 1983, pp. 68–9.   [10] *Boyle Works*, Vol. 12, p. 6.
[11] *Second Reply*, pp. 402–3. The other reference is found at p. 427.
[12] *Conduct*, pp. 205–89, 206–7.
[13] See *STCE*, p. 325. The book is LL 162.
[14] Nidditch, however, finds a possible allusion to the *Novum organum*, I, 49 at *E* IV. xx. 12, p. 715.
[15] Locke writes: 'Telesius—who hath renewed the philosophy of Parmenides & of the best of the Novelists Bacon Nat. hist. ep 69.' The same entry is to be found in Bodl. MS Locke f. 14, p. 26. Locke has underlined the first letter of 'Telesius' in his copy of the 1664 edition of Bacon's *Sylva sylvarum*, marking the point at which this citation begins: LL 164, p. 19. Other references to Bacon's *Sylva sylvarum* can be found

of Bacon's *Advancement of Learning* (LL 166) in Bodl. MS Locke d. 11, fol. 3v. Finally, there is a quotation from Bacon in the unfinished tract on smallpox written by Sydenham and copied by Locke.[16]

As for books by Bacon in Locke's library, Peter Laslett has this to say: 'As might be expected, the work of the founder of the English scientific movement, Francis Bacon, was handsomely represented in the library [162–78ᵃ]. Locke held the *Novum Organum* [...], the *De Augmentis Scientiarum* [...], the *New Atlantis* [...], the *Sylva Sylvarum* [...], and several editions of the *Essays* [...]'.[17] Indeed, after Boyle, Bacon was the best represented writer in natural philosophy in Locke's library. So there is no doubt that Locke was familiar with the works of Bacon, and that he must have read some of them. They were not the only source that would have familiarized him with the nature and role of the new form of natural history espoused by the great Lord Chancellor, although, as we shall see, they were an important source.

What is a Baconian natural history?

What is a Baconian natural history? This needs to be spelt out in some detail if we are to understand the role that Locke has for such histories in his account of method in natural philosophy. Bacon sets out the nature of his natural histories in a number of works. Perhaps the most succinct account is in a short work appended to the *Novum organum*, the *Parasceve ad historiam naturalem, et experimentalem* (henceforth *Parasceve*), or 'Preparative toward a Natural and Experimental History'. It appears that this work is, in part, a summary version of the longer *Descriptio globi intellectualis* (henceforth *Descriptio*), which remained unpublished in Bacon's lifetime, though it was published in Isaac Gruter's edition of some of Bacon's posthumous writings, which was entitled *Scripta in naturali et universali philosophia* in 1653.[18] The *Parasceve* furnishes us with a 'description and delineation' of a natural and experimental history which serves as a foundation for natural philosophy. As such, natural history is indispensable, for 'this alone is the one

---

in Bodl. MS Locke f. 19, pp. 214 and 264. J. R. Milton has pointed out to me that there are notes from the *Novum organum* in Locke's copy of Blount's *Censura celebriorum authorum* (LL 358) dating from the 1690s. Further, it is worth noting that there is a reference in pencil to the *Novum organum* on a facing page of the manuscript 'De arte medica', which (contrary to what I claimed in Anstey 2002a) is in Locke's hand. See TNA PRO 30/24/47/2, fol. 55v. Locke also notes Glisson's summary of Bacon's kinetic theory of heat in the *Novum organum* at British Library Add. MS 32554, p. 38 (cited in Walmsley 1998, p. 49).

[16] Bodl. MS Locke f. 21, p. 16 = Sydenham 1991, p. 97. There are also occasional references to Bacon in Locke's correspondence. See for example Locke to Samuel Bold, 16 May 1699, in *Correspondence*, Vol. 6, p. 627.

[17] 'John Locke and his Books', in *Library of John Locke*, p. 24.

[18] For an example of numerous close textual parallels between the *Parasceve* and the *Descriptio* compare *Parasceve, Bacon Works*, Vol. 11, p. 454: 'Natura in triplici Statu ponitur, tanquam Regimen subit trinum. Aut enim libera est, & cursu suo ordinario se explicat; [...] Tractat enim aut Naturae *Libertatem*, aut *Errores*, aut *Vincula* [...]' with *Descriptio, Bacon Works*, Vol. 6, p. 100: 'Naturae, quae in triplici statu posita inveniatur, & tamquam regimen subit trinum. Aut enim *libera est* Natura ac sponte fusa, atque cursu consueto se explicans [...] Itaque tractat Historia Naturalis aut *libertatem* Naturae, aut *Errores* aut *Vincula*'.

thing needful for laying the foundations of a true and active philosophy'.[19] Natural histories are vast collections of facts about particular objects or qualities.[20] Any natural history is an undertaking of very great size and requires great labour and expense, involving many people in its execution. Indeed, 'the materials for the intellect are so widely spread out that they ought to be sought out and gathered in (as if by agents and merchants) from all sides'.[21] Baconian natural histories differ importantly from the popular type of history which was currently in use, which 'delights by the charm of its narratives [...] and which is admitted for the sake of such pleasure or profit'.[22] Bacon's histories are absolutely essential for human progress in science, for one

cannot make any headway in philosophy and the sciences worthy of the human race without a natural and experimental history.[23]

The scope of the subject of natural history is threefold, covering natural objects or species, aberrations of natural objects and the manipulation of nature by 'art and human agency'.[24] Bacon frequently refers to these three subjects as histories of generations, pretergenerations, and arts. The third of these, arts, is the subject of mechanical or experimental histories.

The use of natural history is twofold; first, as primary knowledge of particular things, and, second, as 'the primary matter of [natural] philosophy, and the basic stuff and raw material of true induction'.[25] Bacon believes that he is the first to appreciate this second use. He describes natural history as a nursing mother to infant philosophy.[26] Thus natural histories precede Baconian induction. The compiler of a natural history must 'seek out and collect the abundance and variety of things which alone will do for the constructing true axioms'.[27]

Bacon then gives some concrete guidelines for writing such a history; 'no more of antiquities, citations and differing opinions of authorities, or of squabbles and controversies, and, in short, everything philological'.[28] Never cite an author unless their credibility is in doubt; never introduce controversy; be brief and concise; avoid superfluity and superstition; and make sure that it is wide-ranging, that is, not restricted to a few instances or places. A natural history is not an end in itself, but a 'storehouse of things, not comfortable accommodation for staying or living in, but a place we go down to when we need to fetch out something useful'.[29]

---

[19] *Parasceve, Bacon Works*, Vol. 11, p. 453. See also *Great Instauration*, ibid., pp. 37–8 and *Novum organum*, Bk II, Aphorism X, ibid., p. 215.
[20] 'In Naturali Naturae res gestae & facinora memorantur' ('In Natural History the achievements and deeds of nature are recounted'), *Descriptio, Bacon Works*, Vol. 6, pp. 98–9.
[21] *Parasceve, Bacon Works*, Vol. 11, p. 451.
[22] *Descriptio, Bacon Works*, Vol. 6, p. 105.
[23] *Parasceve, Bacon Works*, Vol. 11, p. 453. For Boyle's similar dissatisfaction with current histories see his 'De Imperfectione Historiae Naturalis', *Boyle Works*, Vol. 13, pp. 358–61 and Boyle 2008, p. 11.
[24] *Parasceve, Bacon Works*, Vol. 11, p. 455 and *Descriptio*, ibid., Vol. 6, pp. 98–105.
[25] *Parasceve, Bacon Works*, Vol. 11, p. 455 and *Descriptio*, ibid., Vol. 6, pp. 104–7.
[26] *Parasceve, Bacon Works*, Vol. 11, p. 459.
[27] Ibid., p. 457.
[28] Ibid. and *Descriptio, Bacon Works*, Vol. 6, ch. 3, pp. 104–7.
[29] *Parasceve, Bacon Works*, Vol. 11, p. 459.

Then come the divisions. Of the three subjects, the first, natural objects or 'generations', can be divided into five categories: 1. Celestial; 2. Regions of the air; 3. Earth and sea; 4. The elements (meaning roughly those bodies that are very large such as mountains); 5. Species, that is, metals, plants, and animals. The history of arts can be divided into that of mechanical arts, of operative or liberal arts, and of miscellaneous crafts, which are not yet grown into an art. Interestingly, of the three subjects of natural history, the history of arts is the most useful one, because of its ability to remove 'the mask and veil from natural things'.[30] Then, after delivering more precepts, Bacon moves on to provide a catalogue of particular histories by title. He gives 130 titles, which are divided into the five categories of natural objects but also include some of the arts. The titles include:

14. History of air as a whole, or in relation to the configuration of the world

and

45. History of man's humours: blood, bile, sperm, etc.[31]

Of course few of these histories were ever begun by Bacon. But Bacon set the agenda for the Royal Society[32] and for its prominent members (such as Robert Boyle), and it is to Boyle's natural histories of the air and blood and to Locke's involvement in them that we now turn.

Locke and Boyle's natural histories

It is clear from Locke's medical notebooks that he was an avid reader of Boyle's natural philosophical works and that in the early to mid-1660s he read each publication. There are notes from the early 1660s on *Spring of the Air* (1660), *Certain Physiological Essays* (1661), and the first part of *Some Considerations of the Usefulness of Natural Philosophy* (1663, LL 465; hereafter *Usefulness of Natural Philosophy*), not to mention other works.[33] There are even what appears to be comments and corrections on a draft of Boyle's *Experiments and Considerations Touching Colours* (LL 469), which was published in 1664.[34] Among these works, *Certain Physiological Essays* is very significant in that, of all Boyle's early writings, it is in this work that he is most explicit about his Baconian agenda in natural philosophy. He says, echoing Bacon's strictures against the old style of history:

---

[30] Ibid., p. 463 and *Descriptio, Bacon Works*, Vol. 6, ch. 4, pp. 108–9.
[31] *Parasceve, Bacon Works*, Vol. 11, pp. 475 and 479.
[32] Oldenburg says, introducing Boyle's 'General Heads for a *Natural History* of a *Countrey*', that 'divers *Philosophers* aime, among other things, at the Composing of a good Natural History, to superstruct, in time, a *Solid* and *Useful* Philosophy upon', *Boyle Works*, Vol. 5, p. 508. See also the epigraph above and Boyle's posthumous *Appendix* to *The Christian Virtuoso, I, Boyle Works*, Vol. 12, pp. 415–16. For a discussion of the Baconianism of the early Royal Society, see Hunter and Wood 1989 and Anstey and Hunter 2008.
[33] For Locke's reading of Boyle, see Milton 1994, p. 37; Walmsley and Milton 1999, p. 98.
[34] See 'a Transcript of Dr Locks notes about light', Royal Society MS 186, fol. 172.

our design is only to inform Readers, not to delight or perswade them, Perspicuity ought to be esteem'd at least one of the best Qualifications of a style, and to affect needless Rhetorical Ornaments in setting down an Experiment [...] were little less improper than it were [...] to paint the Eye-glasses of a Telescope'.

And he continues:

I must inform you that many of the Particulars which we are now considering, were in my first Design collected in order to a Continuation of the Lord *Verulam's Sylva Sylvarum*, or Natural History.[35]

Locke cannot have missed this Baconian influence; for under four entries, each one entitled 'Baco[n]', in Bodl. MS Locke f. 14 pages 92, 93, and 196, he records a series of adulatory comments about Bacon that he found in Boyle, Henry Power, and others. He writes: 'Sir Francis Bacons novum Organum excellent books Boyle: Phys: Ess p6 That great & candid philosopher ib p 98 That profound Naturallist ib p 115', and quotes Power's remark that Bacon is the 'Patriark of experimentall philosophy'.[36] Moreover, it is important to note that Locke was also reading Bacon's *Sylva sylvarum*, which is itself a natural history, in the mid-1660s. Not only did he make some notes on it in a commonplace book (Bodl. MS Locke f. 19, p. 169), but he drew up an index of the book in his copy of the 1664 edition.[37] So it is clear that Locke's early reading in natural philosophy exposed him to an explicitly Baconian methodology.

Another work which Locke read carefully was *Spring of the Air* (1660). This was arguably Boyle's most important contribution to natural philosophy, containing as it did reports on his first round of experiments on the nature of air with the air-pump, and the digression on respiration. Both the nature of the air and the purpose of respiration were subjects about which Locke retained an interest for much of the rest of his life.[38] *Spring of the Air* was also the first instalment, on Boyle's part, of a long-term project to compile a Bacon-style history of the air, a project which at various times involved Locke. For Locke did more than simply read Boyle on the air; he actually aided him in his researches.

Part of Boyle's research into the atmosphere and into the nature of mines concerned a theory about epidemics, which he was exploring. Boyle was fascinated by the old

---

[35] *Certain Physiological Essays, Boyle Works*, Vol. 2, pp. 16 and 17. See also Ralph Cudworth's comment in a letter to Boyle: 'The writers of hypotheses, in Natural Philosophy will be confuting one another, a long time, before the world will agree, if ever it doe. But your pieces of Natural History are unconfutable. And will afford the best Grounds to build hypotheses upon. You have much outdone Sir Francis Bacon, in your Natural Experiments...', Cudworth to Boyle, 16 October 1684, *Boyle Correspondence*, Vol. 6, p. 48.

[36] Bodl. MS Locke f. 14, p. 92 quoting Boyle's *Certain Physiological Essays* (*Boyle Works*, Vol. 2, p. 13) and Power 1664, p. 82. See also Bodl. MS Locke f. 14, p. 122: 'Falkland and Bacon two incomparably learned persons'.

[37] See entry for LL 164 in *Library of John Locke*, p. 78. See also the 1679 entry in Bodl. MS Locke c. 29, fol. 57 and Bodl. MS Locke f. 22, pp. 44 and 54.

[38] Note the importance of *Spring of the Air* in Locke's posthumous *Elements of Natural Philosophy*, written sometime after 1697. See *Locke Works*, Vol. 3, pp. 311–13.

view that the air, in certain seasons and under certain conditions, carried morbific particles, which were responsible for the spread of disease and emanated from mines or subterranean regions. He wrote extensively on this theory[39] and pursued any avenue he could to acquire information on the nature of the airs in mines and on the relations between prevailing weather conditions and epidemics. That Boyle conceived of his project in natural historical terms is evident from his contributions to the *Philosophical Transactions* of 1666. In his 'General Heads for a Natural History of a *Countrey, Great or Small*', April 1666, Boyle lists as a head or title about the air of a country:

Especially, what Winds it is subject to; whether any of them be stated and ordinary, &c. What diseases are Epidemical, that are supposed to flow from the Air: What other diseases, wherein *that* hath a share, the Countrey is subject to; the Plague and Contagious sicknesses [...][40]

Then in the following November, in an article entitled 'Articles of Inquiries touching *Mines*' (which is, in effect, a continuation of the April article), he lists, as a topic of inquiry for the natural history, the question whether sudden changes in the weather may 'be imputed to the Mineral and Subterraneous Steams; and what they are'.[41]

It is not surprising, then, to learn that in the spring of 1666 Locke attempted to descend a mine in the Mendip hills in order to carry out some observations at Boyle's request. Boyle had sent him a barometer, which he hoped Locke would carry down a mine in order to measure the pressure of the air below the surface. Unhappily the expedition was a failure, the instrument being too cumbersome for the descent and the miners too suspicious to allow Locke to enter. He did, however, make some observations, by using the barometer to check the air pressure at the top and bottom of a nearby hill. A manuscript note records his barometric readings:

Aeris gravitas) 23 Apr 66. Hour inter 8 and 9 the matatin [sic.] the winde high & west. the day warme mercury in the house at the bottom of the hill 29 ⅛ at the top of the hill 28 ¾ & a little more at the bottom of the hill at my returne downe it wanted of ascending to its former height about ¹⁄₃₂ inch & rested at 29 ¹⁄₁₆. On the side of the hill going & comeing I found upon triall that mercury rose & fell proportionally as I was higher or lower. JL[42]

Locke wrote to Boyle about the abortive mission on the 5th of May 1666.[43] Boyle quickly replied to Locke to console him, and seems to have made note of his attempts in the

---

[39] See for example *Usefulness of Natural Philosophy, II, sect. I* (1663), *Boyle Works*, Vol. 3, p. 442; 'Cosmical Suspicions' (1670), ibid., Vol. 6, p. 310; 'Of Subterraneal Steames As they are capable of affecting the Aire', ibid., Vol. 13, pp. 405–23; and especially 'Of the Determinate Nature of Effluviums' (1673), ibid., Vol. 7, pp. 287–96; 'Some Suspicions about Some Hidden Qualities in the Air', ibid., Vol. 8, pp. 133ff., and 'An Experimental Discourse of some Unheeded Causes of the Insalubrity and Salubrity of the Air, &c', ibid., Vol. 10, pp. 303–49. For further discussion, see Keele 1974, and Kaplan 1993, pp. 106ff.

[40] *Boyle Works*, Vol. 5, p. 509.

[41] *Boyle Works*, Vol. 5, p. 530.

[42] Bodl. MS Locke d. 9, p. 41.

[43] Locke kept some notes on comments by a Mr Buckland, with whom he lodged, on the trip to the Mendip mine (British Library Add. MS 32554, p. 221). He subsequently incorporated these observations into his letter to Boyle. Locke's letter is published in *General History of the Air, Boyle Works*, Vol. 12, pp. 92–5. See also

A Continuation of New Experiments Physico-Mechanical, Touching the Spring and Weight of the Air, and their Effects (LL 414), published in 1669.[44] Within weeks, Locke had begun to take barometric readings at Oxford and to compile weather charts with a view to contributing to a history of the air. His first set of records span from June 1666 to June 1683. It appears that Locke followed Boyle's advice in constructing his register of atmospheric conditions. Boyle in the *Philosophical Transactions* of April 1666 directs virtuosi

> to set down in their Diarys not only the day of the month, and the hour of the day, when the *Mercuries* height is taken, but (in a distinct *Columne*) the weather, especially the Winds, both as to Quarters, whence they blow [...] and as to the Violence or Remisness, wherewith they blow.[45]

This is exactly the content and order of Locke's register beginning 24 June 1666.

Locke's medical notebooks and papers also reveal a continued interest in the nature of the air and its relation to disease.[46] In 1691 Locke began indeed another set of weather charts, very similar to the first, which continued for a decade. Some of these records were eventually published posthumously, in the *Philosophical Transactions* of 1705.[47]

These latter charts were most probably related to inquiries into the Boylean theory of morbific particles, for they coincided with another of Locke's projects.[48] In the early 1690s he and Dr Charles Goodall forwarded a questionnaire to a number of prominent physicians seeking information that might help them to correlate the occurrence of particular diseases with changes in the nature of the air. It was only natural that he and Locke should collaborate in this investigation into environmental medicine, for in the previous decade Locke had been involved in Goodall's natural history of Kinkina bark (quinine), sending him a leaf and receiving from him a set of queries for the history.[49]

Correspondence, Vol. 1, pp. 273–6. Mr Buckland is most likely the Somerset gentleman John Buckland, who had dealings with the early Royal Society. See *Oldenburg Correspondence*, Vol. 2, p. 24 and Hunter 1989, ch. 3.

[44] See Boyle to Locke, 2 June 1666, *Correspondence*, Vol. 1, p. 279.

[45] *Boyle Works*, Vol. 5, p. 506. Locke's early weather charts are to be found in *General History of the Air*, *Boyle Works*, Vol. 12, pp. 70–89.

[46] See for example the list of 'Preliminary Topicks or Articles of Inquiry in order to the history of Diseases', in the first part of Bodl. MS Locke c. 42 (first part), p. 98. The list is transcribed in Romanell 1984, pp. 102–3 and in Boyle 2005a, pp. 33–4, where it is collated with another copy of this list in British Library Sloane MS 2502, fols 1v–2. It is in the hand of Robin Bacon, one of Boyle's amanuenses, who worked for Boyle from the 1670s to the end of his life. This fact and the numerous parallels between the list's contents and Boyle's published works leave no doubt that Boyle is the author of this list. A number of points about this list are worth noting. First, being a list of titles for a history of diseases, it bears testimony to Locke's interest in and exposure to natural history and its application to medicine in particular. Second, the list begins with the inquiry 'What Climates are more Subject to give the Disease' which connects this list with the Boylean programme of investigation into the spread of morbific particles. See also TNA PRO/30/24/47/30, fol. 21v, which contains 'Mr Boyle's Scheme of Qualities'. The scheme dated 1668 contains, *inter alia*, the following two items: 'VIII. To the Cœlestiall Effluvia of the Aire belongs' and 'IX. To the Terrestriall Effluvia of the Aire belongs'.

[47] See the rear of Bodl. MS Locke d. 9 and Locke 1705. The published charts span from 9 December 1691 to 31 December 1692.

[48] Locke says of them to Sloane: 'I did not keep this register for my own sake alone', *Correspondence*, Vol. 7, p. 211.

[49] Goodall promised to acknowledge Locke's involvement in the history, but the work never materialised. See William Charleton to Locke, 12 April 1687, *Correspondence*, Vol. 3, p. 171. For Goodall's queries on Kinkina bark, see Goodall to Locke, c. 25 July 1687, ibid., pp. 232–3.

In fact, Locke had probably met Goodall through Sydenham, for Goodall had supported Sydenham in print in 1676, during the latter's embattled years with the medical fraternity in London,[50] and as a result they had become friends. Sydenham had dedicated his last book, *Schedula monitoria* (1686), to Goodall—a work which espouses the theory of 'constitutions' of the air.

It is apparent that Locke's and Goodall's questionnaire sought to test this theory; for the first two questions were:

1 What Bills of Mortality are kept in foreign Countreys, either as to the diseases of which persons dye or the Number who dye weekly, monthly or yearly in most Capitall Cities or Towns of Europe, or in other parts of the World, as Paris, Madrid [...]

2 The Aire of different Countreys with the temper and alteration of the same at the severall seasons of the year and the diseases these countreys are subject to, and the time when.[51]

Locke and Goodall received a number of replies, but Locke seems not to have taken the project further, apart from keeping his weather charts.[52] Goodall however, maintained an interest in the issue, for he wrote to Locke in April 1696 saying:

I shall likewise be glad to hear that you have made any farther observations about the influence of the aire in reference to acute or chronical diseases, as also Endemiall or Epidemical; what you meet with in travels or other books relating to that subject, be pleased to communicate to Dear Sir [Goodall].[53]

The theory of morbific particles, however, was only one facet of a wider research project that Boyle was undertaking on the nature of air. Manuscript fragments of a projected work survive from the 1660s. Boyle published some preliminary findings in his tract on 'Suspicions about Some Hidden Qualities in the Air' (1674), and the projected work is mentioned in a list of Boyle's writings as early as 1677.[54] In fact, a list of titles for a history of the air, clearly related to Boyle's ongoing project, is to be found in the first part of Bodl. MS Locke c. 42, pp. 16–17. It dates from 1682.[55] Toward the

---

[50] See Goodall 1676, pp. 34, 175–7 and 185. For an analysis of Goodall's support for and professional relations with Sydenham, see Anstey 2011b.

[51] Quoted from Dewhurst 1963a, p. 301.

[52] Two replies are extant. See the letters from Guenellon to Locke, *Correspondence*, Vol. 4, pp. 492–3 and 642–3 and the one from Dr Charles Willoughby to Goodall in Dewhurst 1956, pp. 370–81 (originally published in Wilde 1856). Locke maintained a long-term interest in bills of mortality and their relation to epidemics. For his journal references to these bills, see Dewhurst 1963a, *passim*.

[53] *Correspondence*, Vol. 5, p. 589. For further discussion, see Dewhurst 1963a, pp. 301–3, although this account contains some minor errors.

[54] See *Boyle Works*, Vol. 12, xiii and 'Oldenburg's lists of Boyle's papers, 26 March 1677', ibid., Vol. 14, p. 337. The Preface to 'Hidden Qualities' explicitly relates this work with a natural history of the air: ibid., Vol. 8, p. 119.

[55] *Boyle Works*, Vol. 12, xii and Dewhurst 1962, plate facing p. 203.

end of Boyle's life the project was still incomplete, and Boyle again requested Locke to help him. Locke was given responsibility for pulling together the materials which Boyle had assembled for a natural history of the air.[56] Locke fulfilled Boyle's wishes and the work was published soon after Boyle's death in 1691. The *General History of the Air* (1692) shows the imprint of Locke in its order and content. Locke's early weather charts are included,[57] as is his original letter to Boyle relating his unsuccessful attempts to descend the Mendip mine. However, the work is clearly that of Boyle, who tells us in the 'Preface' that it is far from complete and that he was 'not pretending to write the *History of the Air*, but only some Memoirs for it'.[58]

So, for at least twenty-five years, Locke was involved intermittently, though often intimately, in Boyle's ongoing researches into the nature of air. He read Boyle's works on the subject, he participated in at least one experiment, he kept his own weather charts, and he saw Boyle's last publication on the air through the press, while at the same time gathering information to confirm Boyle's theory of morbific particles. It is interesting, then, to note his comments on the *General History of the Air* in a letter of 26 December 1692 to his friend William Molyneux:

though left by him very imperfect, yet I think the very design of it will please you, and it is cast into a method that any one who pleases may add to it, under any of the several titles, as his reading or observation shall furnish him with matter of fact. If such men as you are, curious and knowing, would join to what Mr. Boyle had collected and prepared, what comes in their way, we might hope in some time to have *a* considerable history of the air, than which I scarce know any part of natural philosophy would yeild more variety and use; but it is a subject too large for the attempts of any one man, and will require the assistance of many hands to make it a history very short of compleat.[59]

Note here Locke's Baconian conception of Boyle's work, and also the several titles, the description of the project as a 'considerable history of the air', the claim that it is a subject too large for one person, the aim to make a history very short of complete. Clearly Locke conceives of Boyle's experimental programme on the air in Baconian terms, as he no doubt had done for quarter of a century or more. In fact, it is worth pointing out that Locke had his own copy of Boyle's *General History of the Air* interleaved, and he has included additional material from his reading of travel literature on pages facing p. 151 and p. 189. This material only serves to reinforce the impression

---

[56] It is worth noting that, around the time when Locke was preparing Boyle's *General History of the Air*, Boyle presented Locke with a copy of the second reissue of his *An Essay of the Great Effects of Even Languid and Unheeded Motion* (1690, LL 445), which contains the appended 'Salubrity of the Air'; and this is 'a Semplar or Specimen of what may be done upon the Heads of the design'd History', that is, of Boyle's 'Memorials for a Natural History of the Air', *Boyle Works*, Vol. 10, p. 305. Thus 'Salubrity of the Air' should be seen as a complement to the *General History of the Air*, which Locke was then preparing, and a most natural gift for Boyle to present at this time.

[57] *General History of the Air*, *Boyle Works*, Vol. 12, pp. 70–89.

[58] *Boyle Works*, Vol. 12, p. 10.

[59] *Correspondence*, Vol. 4, pp. 609–10, underlining added.

that Boyle's history was a work of provisional nature in Locke's conception—a point Locke had stressed in his 'Advertisement of the Publisher to the Reader', where he speaks as follows of Boyle's titles in the *General History*:

In that first Draught he followed my Lord *Bacon's* Advice, not to be over-curious or nice in making the first Set of Heads, but to take them as they occur.[60]

Boyle also followed Bacon's same advice in his listing of various titles in the first part of the *Memoirs for the Natural History of Humane Blood, Especially The Spirit of that Liquor* (1684, hereafter *Human Blood*). There, having referred to Bacon, he tells the reader that his titles are those which 'consist of such as occurr'd readily enough to my thoughts, upon the first deliberative view, or general Survey'.[61] Indeed, this work is a model of Baconian natural history from start to finish. Following the quotation from Bacon's *Historia naturalis et experimentalis ad condendam philosophiam* (1622) on the title page,[62] in the 'Preface Introductory' to *Memoirs for the Natural History of Humane Blood*, Boyle tells us that 'many years ago I propounded to some Ingenious Physicians a History of the Fluid parts of the Body, such as the Humours and other Juices [...]'.[63] This is Bacon's 'history of humours in man'. It was clearly begun in the 1660s, when Boyle was engaged in studying the blood on a number of fronts, in examining its role in respiration, in transfusion experiments, and the colouration of the blood.

In Part I of *Human Blood*, Boyle elaborates upon the nature of his history. He takes the Baconian schema further by breaking up the particular history into three classes of titles. Once again he refers to Bacon.[64] Boyle also refers us to his letter to Henry Oldenburg, in which he had outlined the way to construct a Baconian natural history, which letter contains the most important of Boyle's reflections on the natural historical method.[65] He then provides a list of some 30 titles.

In Part II he brings experimental evidence to bear on a number of these titles. This is clearly an example of Bacon's application of experimental observations by mechanical arts to the titles of a history. Boyle is also conscious that his history is only a partial one and that much work remains to be done; he echoes Bacon's claim that such histories require the labour of many people.[66] As we have seen, this is repeated by Locke in his 'Advertisement' to *General History of the Air*, where he claims that a history of the air is 'a Work too great for one single Man's Undertaking'.[67] Boyle's awareness of the

---

[60] *Boyle Works*, Vol. 12, p. 6.   [61] Ibid., Vol. 10, p. 9.
[62] Ibid., p. 3.   [63] Ibid., pp. 5–6.
[64] Ibid., p. 9. Note that the reference to Vespasian in *Human Blood* (ibid., p. 69) is also found in Bacon's *Parasceve*: *Bacon Works*, Vol. 11, p. 464/465.
[65] *Boyle Correspondence*, Vol. 3, pp. 170–5. For the correct ordering of this letter and for ancillary manuscript material, see Boyle 2008. For an exposition of Boyle's 'Designe about Natural History', see Anstey and Hunter 2008.
[66] In fact, almost as soon as it was published, Boyle set to work on collecting materials for a second edition, which, unhappily, never materialized. See Knight and Hunter 2007 and Boyle 2005b.
[67] *Boyle Works*, Vol. 12, p. 5.

Baconian structure of his project appears again in the postscript to the work, not least in his reference to additional experiments he would have liked to append—'to which 'tis probable our excellent *Verulam* would have given the Title of *Historia Designata*'.[68]

Now the relevant point here is not simply the parallels between the historical style of this work and that of the *General History of Air*, but the fact that *Human Blood* was written for, and apparently 'solicited' by, John Locke. While there is no record of the book in Locke's library, it is almost certain that he would have received or procured a copy. Boyle gave him a number of his works, and it would be remarkable if he had failed to give Locke a work dedicated to him, even though it came off the press while Locke was in exile in 1684. It is not surprising that Boyle would dedicate his book on blood to Locke, for the young Locke in the mid-1660s had been closely engaged in speculations and observations about the cause of changes in the colouration of the blood and about the role of air in these changes. Furthermore, Locke was an inquisitive and reflective onlooker to the exciting experimental programme of Lower, Hooke, and Boyle on the nature of respiration and its relation to air and blood.[69] Clearly, then, the researches on air, blood, and respiration were integrated in Locke's mind, just as they were for Boyle.

Thus we have two works by Boyle—one to which Locke contributed and which he saw through the press, another which was dedicated to Locke—both of which were explicitly cast as Bacon-style natural histories. Both works had a long gestation and were related to experimental work in which Locke was closely involved, either as a participant or through theoretical speculations. To this we should add the fact, noted above, that Locke owned more books by Boyle than any other single author. Now it is true that there is no necessary correlation between quantity of books owned and degree of influence. However, Locke was an avid reader of Boyle and we can safely conclude that he had a clear appreciation of Boyle's Baconian approach to the constructing of natural histories while he was writing the *Essay*. Thus, while there is something of a paucity of references to Bacon in Locke's published works, there are no grounds for the claim that Locke was unaware of the Baconian agenda for natural philosophy. He was a close associate of the leading exponent of that agenda and intimately associated with some of its published results. There cannot be any doubt, then, that Locke was *au fait* with the notion of a Baconian natural history as practised by members of the early Royal Society and with the means by which it was compiled and written up. Indeed, it is evident from the foregoing discussion that Locke's collaboration with Boyle's natural historical project on the blood, and particularly on the one on

---

[68] *Boyle Works*, Vol. 10, p. 96. Bacon refers to *Historia designata* in the *Historia naturalis et experimentalis*, that is, the work quoted on Boyle's title page. See *Bacon Works*, Vol. 12, p. 14/15.

[69] For details, see Frank 1980, pp. 186–8.

the air, was sustained over a long period of time and displays a striking continuity of interest on Locke's part.

Locke's books on travel and geography

Another strand of evidence for Locke's adherence to the theory and practice of the Baconian method of natural history, one that bears on Locke and his involvement in Boyle's *General History of the Air*, is Locke's use of travel literature. Those like Peter Laslett and Richard Ashcraft,[70] who have written about Locke's library, have categorized Locke's holdings under such heads as theology, natural science, economics, and so on. One well-represented category, containing 195 titles, is travel literature. Together with the eighty titles on geography, this was the fifth best represented subject in Locke's library, ahead of philosophy and natural science. Travel has traditionally been presented as an interest of Locke's, one he shared with many other assemblers of libraries of his time. It provided Locke with interesting illustrative material and anecdotes, and Laslett has pointed out the unexpected fact that all but one of the sixteen works quoted by Locke in Book I of the fifth edition of the *Essay* (1705) were culled from his collection of travel literature.[71]

However, as Daniel Carey has pointed out,[72] the citing of and quoting from travel literature is an integral part of the writing of natural history. If we take Locke at his word, that the *Essay* is a history of the faculty of the understanding,[73] then travel writers are exactly the sorts of sources we would expect to find in the *Essay*. Francis Bacon included testimonials from travel writers in his account of the construction of natural histories and he frequently quoted from them. Likewise, Boyle frequently has recourse to travel writers in his natural histories. Boyle is explicit about the role and importance of reports from travellers in his discussion of natural history in various works, including *Certain Physiological Essays* and *New Experiments and Observations Touching Cold* (LL 461ª, hereafter *Cold*).[74]

When we turn to Boyle's *General History of the Air*, the work with which Locke was so intimately involved, we find that numerous such authors are quoted. For example, Boyle refers to Piso's detailed weather records in his *Natural History of Brazil* and to de Acosta's account of the dryness of the air in Peru,[75] not to mention numerous first-hand interviews that Boyle carried out with travellers. Turning back to Locke's library,

---

[70] See *Library of John Locke*, pp. 27–9 and Ashcraft 1990.
[71] *Library of John Locke*, pp. 27–8.
[72] Carey 1996 and 1997. See also Carey 2006.
[73] *E* I. i. 2 and *Conduct*, §41, pp. 275–6.
[74] *Certain Physiological Essays*, *Boyle Works*, Vol. 2, p. 28 and *Cold*, ibid., Vol. 4, pp. 217–21. See also the Preface to the second edition of *Cold* (1683): ibid., p. 546; and Boyle to Oldenburg, 13 June 1666, *Boyle Correspondence*, Vol. 3, p. 171.
[75] *General History of the Air*, *Boyle Works*, Vol. 12, pp. 54 and 132.

we find that he held at least six of the works cited by Boyle.[76] Not every travel book mentioned by Boyle is in Locke's library, but most of them are. For Locke, travel literature should not be seen as a pastime or idle pursuit, but as integral to the study of natural philosophy itself.

The same can also be said of travellers' reports. Indeed this is illustrated by one of Locke's earliest publications: his short piece in the *Philosophical Transactions* of May 1675 entitled 'An Extract of a Letter, written to the Publisher by Mr. J. L. about poisonous Fish in one of the Bahama Islands'.[77] This brief item is an extract from a letter from Richard Lilburne to Locke, written on 6 August 1674. On 20 May 1675 Locke forwarded the extract to Oldenburg, who read it at a meeting of the Royal Society seven days later and subsequently published it in the Society's journal. Interestingly, Boyle called for just such reports in his 'General Heads for a *Natural History* of a Countrey', in the *Philosophical Transactions* of April 1666. There, under the head of 'Water', Boyle lists '*Fishes*, what kinds of them [...] are to be found in the Country; their Store, Bigness, Goodness, Seasons, Haunts, Peculiarities of any kind [...]'.[78] In fact, in early June 1676, while he was in France, 'divers shells and strange things' from the Bahamas arrived at Locke's London address, the house of the Earl of Shaftesbury. Shaftesbury forwarded them to Boyle, and they were soon before the Royal Society.[79]

It seems, therefore, that the study of travel literature and the study of natural philosophy are not discrete activities; for it is clear that, for the likes of Locke and Boyle, at times travel literature is, in effect, continuous with literature in natural philosophy. Interestingly, J. R. Milton has pointed out that some of Locke's travel books were placed under the heading 'philosophici', in a list of books Locke drew up

---

[76] The editions of works of travel literature and geography quoted or referred to in *General History of the Air* which are also in Locke's library are:

1. Job Ludolf, *Historia Aethiopica*, 1681, LL 1830, *Boyle Works*, Vol. 12, p. 61;
2. Jean de Thévenot, *Relation d'un voyage fait au Levant*, 1665, LL 2888, *Boyle Works*, Vol. 12, p. 44;
3. Gulielmus Piso, *Historia naturalis Brasiliae*, 1648, LL 2314, *Boyle Works*, Vol. 12, p. 54;
4. Pierre Belon, *Plurimarum singularium & memorabilium rerum in Graecia, Asia, Aegypto, Iudaea, Arabia...*, 1589 translation of French edn of 1553, LL 259, *Boyle Works*, Vol. 12, p. 106;
5. Joseph de Acosta, *The Natural and Moral History of the Indies*, 1604, LL 859, *Boyle Works*, Vol. 12, p. 132;
6. Samuel Purchas, *Pilgrimes*, 1625, LL 2409, *Boyle Works*, Vol. 12, p. 145.

Note also that Sir Paul Rycaut is mentioned in *General History of the Air* (*Boyle Works*, Vol. 12, p. 154). Locke had the French translation of his *The Present State of the Ottoman Empire*, 1668, LL 2479.

[77] Locke 1675, p. 312. See *Correspondence*, Vol. 1, pp. 406–7 and 423. Locke solicited more information on poisonous fish from Lilburne, which is found in the enclosure to Lilburne's letter to Locke of 12 August 1675: ibid., pp. 425–6.

[78] *Boyle Works*, Vol. 5, p. 509. Bacon's article 36 is 'History of fish and their parts and generation': *Parasceve*, *Bacon Works*, Vol. 11, p. 477. In Bodl. MS Locke c. 42 (first part), p. 248, Locke excerpts Hooke's Preface to Robert Knox's natural history of Ceylon (Knox 1681) with the following remark: 'A history of Groenland is lately writ in high Dutch by Dr Fogelius of Hamborough from the Information of Frederique Martin who had made severall voyages to that place, In the doeing of which he made use of the instructions given by the Royal Societie Hooke's pref. to Knox'. See Knox 1681, Sig. a3.

[79] Thomas Stringer to Locke, 5 June 1676, *Correspondence*, Vol. 1, p. 448. The specimens were sent by Isaac Rush; see Rush to Locke, 6 August 1675, ibid., p. 427.

around the time he left Oxford.[80] This is indicative of the way these works would be collected and read: namely with a view to their possible contribution to the construction of natural histories.[81] It is hardly surprising therefore to find Guenellon responding to Locke's and Goodall's question on the airs of different countries by saying 'et dans les descriptions des differents voyages en diverses contrées il poura recueillir ce quil demande'.[82] Far from being volumes reserved solely for times of leisure, travel books also furnished the reader with indispensable resources for natural philosophy. Of course this is consistent with the prominent role of human testimony, both written and oral, in Locke's theory of knowledge.

Locke's queries

Few travellers, however, were natural philosophers, and the vast quantities of knowledge and of specimens arriving from the new world needed to be organized, the inquiries of travellers needed to be directed towards specific ends. Moreover, natural histories themselves had to be ordered. To this end, members of the early Royal Society, following Francis Bacon's recommendations, deployed a new genre of natural philosophical writing, namely lists of queries or articles of inquiry. Of course, it is not as if the humble query had never been deployed in natural philosophy before. However, the early Royal Society followed Bacon in using such lists to structure the scope and depth of particular natural philosophical inquiries within a broadly Baconian agenda—the sort of agenda spelt out, for example, in Bacon's *Parasceve*. From the early 1660s on we find lists of queries for researching all sorts of phenomena, and some of the early issues of the *Philosophical Transactions*, which was first published in 1665, are dominated by such lists.

This is one instance in which the Royal Society seems to have influenced Boyle.[83] For in the mid-1660s lists of queries appear in his papers and publications, and articles of inquiry become central for his elaborate 'Designe about Natural History'. The first published evidence of this is in *Cold*, while at about this time there is plenty of manuscript evidence that Boyle developed lists of queries for a whole range of natural philosophical inquiries. Mention has already been made of Boyle's important 'General Heads for a *Natural History* of a *Countrey*'. But amongst his unpublished papers there are queries on elasticity, on tastes and odours, and on electrical bodies—to name just a few.[84] Likewise, the two natural historical works which related to Locke, *Human Blood* and *General History of the Air*, are organized around sets of queries. Of course, Locke, who from very early on had access to Boyle's papers, would have been privy to many of these lists, and in fact, after the Mendip episode, Boyle, seeking to encourage Locke's

---

[80] Milton 1994, pp. 45–6. [81] See Carey 1997, p. 286.
[82] *Correspondence*, Vol. 4, p. 492.   [83] As argued by Michael Hunter in Hunter 2007a.
[84] They are now published in Boyle 2005a.

interest in the nature of minerals, expressed a wish that 'I had time & conveniency to send you some sheets of Articles of Inquirys about Mines in generall'.[85]

It is hardly surprising, then, that we should find copies of sets of Boyle's queries among Locke's notes on natural philosophy and medicine. There is a set of fifty-one heads on flame and fire in Bodl. MS Locke c. 42 (first part), pp. 266–7, attributed to Boyle and dated 1682; then another twelve queries from 1682, on the history of diseases, in the same notebook (p. 98); and a set of queries for Boyle's *Cold* in Bodl. MS Locke c. 31 fol. 49v, copied in 1681. There is, however, an earlier set of queries relating to trials about human blood in Bodl. MS Locke f. 19, pp. 272–3 and 302–3, which is datable to 1665–7. Like the queries on the natural history of disease, these are not attributed to Boyle, but they almost certainly derive from him, as is evidenced if one compares them with the many other surviving lists of queries on human blood and other subjects surviving amongst Boyle's papers.[86] Not only is the list testimony to Locke's early exposure to the 'method of queries' by Boyle; it also constitutes the very sort of list that Locke himself was to construct some years later, when making inquiries about the poisonous fish in the Bahamas. A set of thirteen queries for Lilburne and Isaac Rush, dated 12 May 1675, is found in Bodl. MS Locke d. 9, pp. 87 and 236,[87] which nicely illustrate Locke's own appropriation of the query genre and are further evidence of his acquiescence in the method of natural history.

Finally, Locke's keen interest in the study of the natural history of the earth and of the theory of the deluge, which developed from the late 1680s on (see Chapter 5 below), reveals his continued exposure to the method of natural history. For not only did he lightly annotate his copy of John Woodward's *Natural History of the Earth* (1695, LL 3179), which explicitly endorses the Baconian method of natural history, but he also acquired Woodward's *Brief Instructions for Making Observations in All Parts of the World* (1696, LL 3180), which closely follows the genre of Boyle's earlier 'General Heads for a *Natural History* of a *Countrey*'. Interestingly, Woodward gives advice for the sending of seeds and plant parts from foreign lands, something that Locke himself had been actively engaged in throughout the 1680s.[88]

Locke and the natural history of disease

If Locke was exposed to the Baconian method of natural history through his involvement with Boyle, one would expect to find evidence of this in his early medical

---

[85] Boyle to Locke, 2 June 1666, *Correspondence*, Vol. 1, p. 279. The queries on mines were published in *Philosophical Transactions* in November of the same year. See *Boyle Works*, Vol. 5, pp. 508–11 and 529–40.

[86] All of Boyle's queries are transcribed in Boyle 2005b. Walmsley's (2007, p. 467) reasons for attributing the queries on blood to Locke are unconvincing. The extremely close parallels between Boyle's list of queries on blood in BP 18, fols 51–2 and the list in Locke's hand are compelling evidence that Locke's list derives from Boyle.

[87] See *Correspondence*, Vol. 8, pp. 428–9.

[88] Woodward 1696, p. 12. Locke probably received the *Brief Instructions* from Woodward himself. See *Correspondence*, Vol. 5, p. 506. For Locke's distribution of seeds and plant parts, see Harris and Anstey 2009.

writings; and indeed this is the case. In our discussion of corpuscular pessimism in the previous chapter, reference was made to the Baconian allusions in Locke's early essays on anatomy and on the reform of curative medicine. However, Locke's positive prescriptions for the correct method of proceeding in physic were not discussed. It should come as no surprise, then, that the method Locke advocates, particularly in 'Anatomia', as a replacement for speculative theories of disease, is the construction of histories of disease. Locke refers to the history of diseases in 'De arte medica' when he speaks in the following terms of the systems of the speculative physician:

if he hopes to bring men by such a system to the knowledg of the infirmities [of mens] bodys, the constitution nature signes changes & history of diseases with the safe & direct way of their cure, takes much what a like course with him that should walk up & downe in a thick wood over growne with briars & thornes with a designe to take a view & draw a map of the country.[89]

But it is possible that here he is simply referring to the traditional medical histories that were found in works such as those represented by the literature on fevers of the period. For example, it was common practice in the mid-seventeenth century to present a number of case histories in order to illustrate such things as the symptoms of fevers, the course of the various forms of fevers and the application of the physicians' *methodus* to the patient. These case histories either were derived from actual patients or were more general accounts of seasonal fevers or epidemics. Perhaps the most widely cited work on fevers in the 1660s was Thomas Willis' *De febribus*, the second part of his *Diatribae duae medico-philosophicae* (1659), which provides a number of clear examples of the use of these 'Histories and Observations'. For example, in his chapter on pestilential or malignant fevers Willis tells us:

That the figure, or Ideas of this malignant Feaver, may be painted to the life, very many observations or histories of sick people, are easily to be had; of the many examples of this Disease. I shall only mention a few [...][90]

The next chapter, on small pox and measles, uses the same format. After describing the disease and the *methodus*, Willis says:

It were easie to illustrate the afor-recited Doctrine, concerning the Small Pox, with Histories and Observations of the sick, because there is no Disease besides can supply with a greater plenty of Examples, or variety of Accidents: but of the great number of this kind, I shall only propose in this place a few Cases [...][91]

Then follows a chapter on women in child-birth which, likewise, 'may easily be illustrated with Histories and Observations'.[92]

Yet Willis' summary case histories were a far cry from what, for Boyle and others, would constitute a Baconian history of disease. Baconian natural histories would

---

[89] TNA PRO 30/24/47/2, fol. 52r = Dewhurst 1966, p. 81.
[90] Willis 1681, p. 136.   [91] Ibid., p. 145.   [92] Ibid., p. 158.

contain enormous numbers of facts about the occurrence, symptoms, and treatments of diseases, and these would be gleaned from the observations of many, made over long periods of time. Baconian disease histories were then to function as the foundation for theorizing about the causes, nature, and treatment of diseases. By contrast, traditional histories such as those of Willis were descriptive and illustrative, serving to confirm the efficacy of modes of treatment or of the description of typical symptoms.

In the essay 'Anatomia', however, the efficacy of histories of various diseases as a foundation for reflection on the nature and true method of treating these same diseases is positively endorsed. Locke claims that, if the physician wants to know

[h]ow regulate his dose, to mix his simples & to prescribe all in a due method, all this is only from *history & the advantage of a diligent observation* of these diseases, of their begining progresse & ways of cure. which a physitian may as well doe without a scrupulous enquiry into the anatomy of the parts.[93]

For Locke, it is the history and the diligent observation of a disease that enables one to develop the correct method for its treatment: history is that upon which the practice of physic is to be based.

It might be objected here that Locke does not use the phrase 'natural history', and therefore he may not be referring to anything other than the traditional histories found in the medical literature of his day. However, Locke and his contemporaries quite frequently used simply 'history' when referring to Baconian natural history. In the *Essay*, for example, Locke speaks of '*improving our Knowledge in Substances only by Experience* and History' and of 'Experiments and Historical Observations', where he is clearly referring to natural histories.[94]

The first reference in Locke's own hand to a particular, Bacon-style natural history of a disease occurs in his fair copy of Sydenham's essay on smallpox from July 1669, where Sydenham presents the work as follows:

This is the natural history of the small pox as comprehending the true & genuin Phaenomena belonging to them as they are in their owne nature [...][95]

Sydenham was clearly dissatisfied with his highly speculative theory of smallpox in his earlier *Methodus* because it was inadequately informed by observation.[96] Indeed his earlier treatment of smallpox bore little if any resemblance to a Baconian natural history, and it is quite possible that Sydenham began to acquiesce in the method of

---

[93] TNA PRO 30/24/47/2, fol. 31v = Dewhurst 1966, p. 86, emphasis added. See also fol. 35r (= Dewhurst 1966, p. 90): '[H]e that in a favor or any other malady is able to make advantage from his inspection into the urin, & by that takes any indication, & chooses time for purgeing bleeding or the giveing any medicin, doth not this one jot the better for knowing the structure of the veins ureters bladder &c, but by acquainting himself with the nature & history of the disease'.

[94] *E* IV. xii. 10, p. 645.

[95] Quoting the transcription of G. G. Meynell in Sydenham 1991, p. 74, which retains Locke's abbreviations. Locke's copy of the essay is in Bodl. MS Locke f. 21, pp. 3–17. For another example in Sydenham's writings, see *Epistolary Dissertation to Dr Cole*, in Sydenham 1848, Vol. 2, p. 85.

[96] Sydenham 1991, p. 96.

natural history as a result of his interactions with Locke and of his reading of Locke's 'Anatomia'.[97] Whatever the source of this influence on Sydenham's new conception of the importance of natural histories—and there could well have been a variety of sources—by the time of the publication of his *Observationes medicae* in 1676 he was fully committed to employing this method in his study of disease.

Importantly, near the end of the July 1669 essay on smallpox, Sydenham alludes to the distinction between the traditional notion and the newly advocated Baconian conception:

> I know to write the Hystory of a disease is comon, but so to doe it as not to deserve the just contempt expressed by that great Genius of rationall nature, the Lord Bacon, agaynst some undertakers of the like kind, is somewhat more difficult.[98]

This is followed by an extended Latin quotation from Bacon's *De augmentis scientiarum*, which spells out Bacon's account of the method of natural histories:

> For I well know that [this natural history of diseases] is extant, large in its bulk, pleasing in its variety, curious often in its diligence; but yet weed it of fables, antiquities, quotations, idle controversies, philology and ornaments (which are more fitted for table talk and the *noctes* of learned men than for the instauration of philosophy), and it will shrink into a small compass. Certainly it is very different from that kind of history which I have in view.[99]

Such a sentiment is common in Bacon's prescriptions to proceed with natural histories. The natural historical method could not be more explicitly Baconian, and the fair copy is in the hand of Locke.

Now it is important to note that this section of the smallpox fragment is incorporated into the preface to Sydenham's *Observationes Medicae*[100] and that in the 'Epistle Dedicatory' to that work Sydenham tells us:

> You know also how thoroughly an intimate and common friend, and one who has closely and exhaustively examined the question, agrees with me as to the method that I am speaking of; a man who, in the acuteness of his intellect, in the steadiness of his judgment, in the simplicity (and

---

[97] See Anstey and Burrows 2009 for an assessment of the mutual influence of Locke and Sydenham. Patrick Romanell was the first to stress that Sydenham most likely derived his mature medical methodology from Locke (though upon different grounds from those of the current author). See Romanell 1984, pp. 76–85.

[98] Sydenham 1991, p. 97.

[99] Sydenham 1991. In editing this text, Meynell claims that the 'quotation occurs twice in Bacon: *De augmentis scientiarum*, 2.iii, and *Descriptio globi intellectualis*, c.iii' (ibid., p. 188). However, the former passage is an abbreviation of the latter, and it is clear that what is being quoted is the abbreviated version from the *De augmentis scientiarum*. The quote, ignoring Locke's contractions, deviates occasionally from Bacon's text. I supply Spedding's translation of the passage, including Sydenham's insertion; see Bacon 1859, Vol. 4, p. 299. See also *Descriptio, Bacon Works*, Vol. 6, pp. 104/5–6/7.

[100] See Sydenham 1848, Vol. 1, p. 12. This was first pointed out by G. G. Meynell in his careful collation of the manuscripts relating to Sydenham's *Observationes*. See Sydenham 1991, p. 188.

by *simplicity* I mean *excellence*) of his manners, has, amongst the present generation, few equals and no superiors. This praise I may confidently attach to the name of JOHN LOCKE.[101]

Sydenham's nod towards Locke in this important methodological prolegomenon is not only further evidence of Locke's endorsement of the method of natural history in physic, but probably a tacit acknowledgement, on Sydenham's part, of Locke's influence on his own methodological views in medicine. Finally, Locke's continued endorsement of the natural historical method in physic and of Thomas Sydenham as one of its leading practitioners is evident throughout the rest of his life. Mention has already been made of his copy of Boyle's list of queries for the history of disease from 1682; a decade later we find him commending Sydenham's use of the method of natural history to Thomas Molyneux, in a letter of 1 November 1691:

That which I always thought of Dr. Sydenham living, I find the world allows him now he is dead, and that he deserved all that you say of him. I hope the age has many who will follow his example, and by the way of accurate practical observation, as he has so happily begun, enlarge the history of diseases, and improve the art of physick, and not by speculative hypotheses fill the world with useless, tho' pleasing visions.[102]

In fact, in *Of the Conduct of the Understanding*, begun in 1697, he is still speaking about developing the understanding of physic in terms of acquainting oneself with histories of diseases.[103]

Locke's division of the sciences

A final source of evidence on Locke's view of the centrality of natural history in natural philosophy is found in his discussions of the division of the 'sciences' (*scientiae*). J. R. Milton has rightly pointed out that, from the early 1670s on, Locke began to take a keen interest in the various divisions of human knowledge.[104] From this period until the publication of the *Essay* in 1690, there is a number of shifts in his groupings and

---

[101] Sydenham 1848, Vol. 1, p. 6. It is worth pointing out that Sydenham's *Tratactus de podagra et hydrope* (1683) contains on its title page another quotation from Bacon stressing a methodological maxim. This quotation reads: 'Non fingendum, aut excogitandum, sed inveniendum, quid Natura faciat, aut ferat, *Bacon*' ('What Nature would do or bring is not to be imagined or deduced, Bacon, but discovered'). It is from *Novum organum*, Book II, aphorism X and, not surprisingly, it concerns natural history. Together with its prefatory remark, it creates the following text: '[we must prepare a natural and experimental history, sufficient and good; and this is the foundation of all] for we are not to imagine or suppose, but to discover, what nature does or may be made to do'. Interestingly, Boyle uses the same quotation on the title page to *Experiments and Considerations Touching Colours* and *Cold*. See *Boyle Works*, Vol. 4, p. 3 and p. 203.

[102] *Correspondence*, Vol. 4, p. 563. See also Locke to Thomas Molyneux, 20 January 1692/3: 'I wonder that, after the pattern Dr. Sydenham has set them [physicians who start from speculative theories] of a better way, men should return again to that romance way of physick. But I see it is easier and more natural for men to build castles in the air of their own, than to survey well those that are to be found standing. Nicely to observe the history of diseases in all their changes and circumstances, is a work of time, accurateness, attention, and judgment [...]', ibid., pp. 628–9, underlining added.

[103] *Conduct*, §35, p. 270.

[104] Milton 1994, p. 46.

categorizations.[105] However, in spite of these differences, the general structure of some of Locke's divisions within the science of bodies is reminiscent of Bacon. The first part of Bacon's *Instauratio magna* concerned the division of the sciences. The general contours of Bacon's divisions, as spelt out in such works as *De augmentis scientiarum* or the *Parasceve*, can be found in some of Locke's own divisions. This is particularly evident if one compares the list of titles from the *Parasceve* with the heads for the science of bodies in the opening folios of the notebook 'Adversaria 1661' (c. 1670).[106] Almost every heading and sub-heading in Locke's table has a corresponding title in Bacon's (more extensive) list. This is not, however, to claim that Locke's divisions are derived from Bacon. It is merely to point out that his concern with divisions of knowledge and with the nature of the divisions themselves is indicative of the fact that Locke was conceiving of knowledge in natural philosophy within a broadly Baconian framework.

A more important feature of the Lockean divisions is the role of histories in the science of bodies. Under the heading of 'Corpus humanum: Medecina', the commonplace book 'Adversaria 1661' gives us the following subheadings: 'Anatomia sive hist. partium. Pathologia sive historia affectuum et Therapeutica sive hist. curationum'.[107] And, while the word 'history' does not occur in Locke's account of the division of the sciences in *E* IV. xxi, it is clear from the earlier discussion in IV. xii. 12 that the knowledge of bodies is got by 'Experience, Observation, and natural History'.[108] Furthermore, Locke's journal entry for 4 September 1677 lists, as the final heading for adversaria, *Historica Physica*—which is a 'natural history'. It is, namely,

the history of naturall causes and effects wherein it may be convenient in our reading to observe those severall propertys of bodys and the severall effects that severall bodys or their qualitys have one upon an other, and principally to remark those that may contribute either to the improvement of arts or give light into the nature of things which is that which I cald above philosophica [...][109]

Earlier that year, in his entry for 8 February, Locke commented that the business of mankind is, in part, 'the enjoyment of the things of nature' and claimed that

we need noe other knowledg for the atteinment of those ends but of the history and observation of the effects and operations of naturall bodys within our power [...][110]

---

[105] This can be observed by comparing the outline for the division of the sciences on the first few pages of the commonplace book commonly called 'Adversaria 1661', both with the list of headings and sub-headings for the writing of adversaria which is found in Locke's journal entry of 4 September 1677 and with the division of the sciences outlined at *E* IV. xxi. See Locke 1967, pp. 245–6; 1936, pp. 92–4; and *Essay*, pp. 720–1.

[106] Compare Locke 1967, p. 246 with *Bacon Works*, Vol. 11, pp. 474/5–84/5. For the dating of this table to c. 1670, see Milton 1998, pp. 108–10. Almost identical tables are found in 'Adversaria 1661', Bodl. MS Film 77, p. 291 (1681) and MS Locke c. 28, fol. 41r (1672).

[107] Bodl. MS Film 77, verso of second unpaginated leaf.

[108] Locke 1967, p. 246 and *Essay*, p. 647.   [109] Locke 1936, p. 94.   [110] Ibid., p. 88.

Natural history, then, is a fundamental notion in Locke's view of how knowledge is to be organized or demarcated. Important to note here is the fact that natural history is the way in which knowledge of bodies is characterized. It is not merely a methodological prescription, but a description of that branch of natural philosophy which concerns natural bodies. So, while for Locke natural philosophy also encompasses knowledge of spirits and of God, that which concerns natural bodies is to be understood in terms of natural history. This is the manner in which that branch of knowledge presents itself.

Conclusion

It is time now to take stock of all the evidence cited above and to determine whether Yolton was right in claiming that 'it was the emphasis upon compiling natural histories of bodies, which was the chief aspect of the Royal Society's programme, that attracted Locke, and from which we need to understand his science of nature'. Here is a summary of the evidence.

First, the two largest single author holdings of works pertaining to natural philosophy in Locke's library were those of Boyle and Bacon, both of whom were proponents of the natural historical method. Second, Locke was reading Bacon and Boyle on natural history in the 1660s and beyond. Third, Locke's reference to Bacon in Boyle's *General History of the Air* refers to Baconian histories. Fourth, the *General History of the Air* is itself a natural history, and it is this aspect of the work that Locke describes and endorses in his letter to William Molyneux. Fifth, Locke contributed to this natural history and saw it through the press after Boyle's death. Sixth, Boyle's work on human blood—which was dedicated to Locke, which explicitly mentioned Bacon on natural history, and for which manuscript material survives among Locke's papers—was a natural history. Seventh, Locke copied sets of Boyle's queries for natural histories and sought information on the poisonous fish of the Bahamas by using the method of queries. Eighth, from the late 1660s on Locke endorsed and promoted the natural history of disease as an essential constituent in a new medical *methodus*. Ninth, Sydenham's *Observationes*, which explicitly endorsed a natural historical approach to medicine, claimed that Locke wholeheartedly endorsed its author's medical method. Tenth, this is further confirmed in letters to Thomas Molyneux of 1692/3, some years after Sydenham's death. Eleventh and finally, Locke's discussions of the divisions of the sciences indicate that he conceived of the science of bodies in natural historical terms. To all this it is tempting to add, as evidence of Locke's interest in natural history, the fact that the works of many of the travel authors quoted by Boyle in the *General History of the Air* were in Locke's library. However, since it is argued above that Locke's interest in travel literature should be seen as deriving from his commitment to the method of natural history in natural philosophy, it would, strictly speaking, be begging the question to adduce this fact as evidence of Locke's interest in natural history.

While some of this evidence, taken on its own, may not appear to be of great consequence, the combined weight of all the pieces gives strong support to Yolton's thesis. Indeed, what is striking about all this evidence concerning Locke's connection with Bacon is that so much of it—virtually everything— concerns natural history and none of it touches on the inductive method, on Bacon's moral thought, or on anything else. In fact, Locke never even discusses Baconian induction.[111] The importance of natural history in natural philosophy emerges as one of the salient features of Locke's relations with Boyle and Sydenham and of his reading of Bacon and allusions to him. This brings us back, then, to the question of discovering which reading of Locke on method in natural philosophy is to be favoured: that of Yost and Yolton, or that of Mandelbaum and Laudan? Interestingly, in a postscript to his paper on Locke on hypothesis, Laudan sets up the dialectic as follows (quoting James Farr's summary):

The debate whether Locke is a natural historian of science or a hypotheticalist turns, then, on whether we place him in the tradition of Bacon or in the tradition of Boyle, respectively.[112]

However, if the argument of the present chapter is correct, this is a false dichotomy of traditions. Locke stands firmly in the Baconian tradition precisely because he was so heavily influenced by Boyle. I conclude, then, even before we embark upon an analysis of Locke's comments on natural philosophical method in the *Essay*, that Yolton's thesis appears to be substantially correct.

---

[111] There may be a vague allusion to it in section 13 of *Conduct*, p. 234. Interestingly, this (posthumously printed) passage contains the only use of 'induction' in the sense of 'inference' in Locke's published works, although by the 1690s the term was commonly used to describe the activity of experimental philosophers in contrast to that of speculative philosophers. See the quotation from Sergeant at p. 3.

[112] See Farr 1987, p. 53 and Laudan's 'Postscript: 1976' to 'Locke's views on hypothesis' in Tipton 1977, pp. 161–2.

4

Hypotheses and analogy

> He us'd to say too, that the knowledge of the Arts contained more true Philosophy, than all those fine learned Hypotheses, which having no relation to the nature of things, are fit for nothing at bottom, but to make men lose their time in inventing, or comprehending them.
>
> Pierre Coste[1]

There is a significant amount of historical and archival evidence to the effect that Locke conceived of the main task of natural philosophy in Baconian terms, as a compilation of natural histories. It is not surprising, therefore, when we turn to the *Essay concerning Human Understanding* to find that an important part of his prescription for the method of natural philosophy deals with the construction of natural histories. In his few sustained treatments of method in natural philosophy in the *Essay*, and in occasional *obiter dicta*, Locke appears to give pride of place to the construction of natural histories. For example, in *E* IV. xii. 10 Locke tells us that the way to improve our knowledge of the nature of bodies is '*only by Experience* and History',[2] that is, through the assembling of facts that constitute natural histories. Two sections later Locke says:

In the Knowledge of Bodies, we must be content to glean, what we can, from particular Experiments: since we cannot from a Discovery of their real Essences, grasp at a time whole Sheaves; and in bundles, comprehend the Nature and Properties of whole Species together. Where our Enquiry is concerning Co-existence, or Repugnancy to co-exist, which by Contemplation of our *Ideas*, we cannot discover; there Experience, Observation, and natural History,

---

[1] 'The Character of Mr Locke', Locke 1720, p. ix.
[2] For *obiter dicta*, see *E* III. xi. 24 and 25. See also *STCE*, §193, p. 248 and the Journal entry for 8 February 1677 in Locke 1936, p. 86.

must give us by our Senses, and by retail, an insight into corporeal Substances. The Knowledge of Bodies we must get by our Senses, warily employed in taking notice of their Qualities, and Operations on one another [...]³

In this chapter I will argue that, for Locke, given our lack of epistemic access to the real essences of bodies, the compilation of natural histories is that part of natural philosophy which holds the greatest prospect for the advancement of knowledge of the natural world, and that he regards hypotheses and analogical reasoning as having a minor and subservient role to that of these histories: they serve, namely, to augment and stimulate their construction and to provide aids to memory. This, however, is at odds with a widely held interpretation of Locke. For the trend seems to have been to follow Laudan in claiming that, for Locke, hypotheses lead the way in natural philosophy and Locke's talk of natural history is better regarded as an accretion not to be taken too seriously.⁴

Essay IV. xii. 9–12: Exegesis and paraphrase

Chapter 12 of Book IV is entitled 'Of the Improvement of Our Knowledge'. It begins by criticizing the scholastic view that knowledge is built upon maxims or principles. Locke's claim is that this is a dangerous approach to extending knowledge—and not only because the principles might be false. Knowledge of the certainty of principles, as of anything else, depends on the perception of agreement or disagreement between our ideas, and it is not blindly swallowing principles without reference to experience. The way to improve our knowledge is '*to get and fix in our Minds clear, distinct and complete Ideas, as far as they are to be had, and annex to them proper and constant Names*' (§6, p. 642).

Hence general and certain truths are found in the habitudes and relations of abstract ideas (§7). Moral principles may be shown to be demonstratively certain (§8). But what about our knowledge of substances—that is, ordinary objects? Locke tells us that in this case 'our want of *Ideas*, that are suitable to such a way of proceeding, obliges us to a quite different method' (§9). The method used to gain knowledge of principles does not work here. We need to turn from our own thoughts to the things themselves: '*Experience here must teach me*, what Reason cannot: and 'tis by trying alone, that I can certainly know, what other Qualities co-exist with those of my complex *Idea*' (§9, p. 644, underlining added). He then illustrates the point using the example of gold. As he rounds off section 9, Locke reiterates the idea that experience yields certain knowledge: 'I must apply my self to *Experience*; as far as that reaches, I may have certain Knowledge, but no farther' (p. 645).

---

³ *E* IV. xii. 12, p. 647, underlining added.
⁴ See Laudan 1967, Woolhouse 1971, Farr 1987, Wolterstorff, 1996, p. 34, Buchdahl 1969, pp. 211ff, and Soles 1985 and 2005. Soles initially claimed that, on the question of the status of hypotheses in Locke, 'Laudan has put the problem to rest' (1985, p. 361, n. 37), and recently he has vigorously reaffirmed this view (2005). It should be pointed out that the 2005 article contains a forthright attack on an earlier version of the present chapter (Anstey 2003a). A comparison with that earlier version will reveal that my view remains largely unchanged, in spite of Soles' criticisms. I respond to some of his claims in the notes of this and subsequent chapters.

We then come to section 10. Let me quote and paraphrase *E* IV. xii. 10–12 (p. 645) in order to get the flow of Locke's argument. He begins by saying:

§10. I deny not, but a Man accustomed to rational and regular Experiments shall be able to see farther into the Nature of Bodies, and guess righter at their yet unknown Properties, than one, that is a Stranger to them.

But such guessing still leads to judgement and opinion, not knowledge. Experience and history are the only ways of improving our certain knowledge of substances in our present condition, because we cannot have any general knowledge like that which we find in the other sciences.

We are able, I imagine, to reach very little general Knowledge concerning the Species of Bodies, and their several Properties. Experiments and <u>Historical Observations</u> we may have, from which we may draw Advantages of Ease and Health, and thereby increase our stock of Conveniences for this Life: but beyond this, I fear our Talents reach not, nor are our Faculties, as I guess, able to advance.[5]

This is because 'our Faculties are not fitted to penetrate into the internal Fabrick and real Essences of Bodies' (§11, p. 646). Rather they are fitted to 'discover to us the Being of a GOD, and the Knowledge of our selves, enough to lead us into a full and clear discovery of our Duty [. . .]' (ibid.). Therefore we should 'imploy those Faculties we have about what they are most adapted to, and follow the direction of Nature'. Locke would not, however, 'be thought to dis-esteem, or *dissuade the Study of Nature*' (§12). He would only say that 'we should not be too forwardly possessed with the Opinion, or Expectation of Knowledge, where it is not to be had'. What, then, of principles and hypotheses? He that shall consider

how little general Maxims, precarious Principles, and Hypotheses laid down at Pleasure, have promoted true Knowledge, or helped to satisfy the Enquiries of rational Men after real Improvements [. . .] towards the Knowledge of natural Philosophy, will think, we have Reason to thank those, who in this latter Age have taken another Course, and have trod out to us, though not an easier way to learned Ignorance, yet a surer way to profitable Knowledge.[6]

Of course, it is the likes of Boyle and others who have trod out this 'surer way to profitable Knowledge'. So ends the first half of the most important passage in the *Essay* on the method of natural philosophy.

In summary, then, experiment and observation, the two central components of both the experimental philosophy and natural history, yield the only certain knowledge we can have of bodies. Earlier in Book IV this sort of knowledge was characterized as sensitive knowledge (*E* IV. iii. 2–5, 21) and as experimental knowledge (*E* IV. iii. 29 and IV. vi. 7). It is particular and not general knowledge (*E* IV. iii. 5). Hypotheses, such as Cartesianism or corpuscularianism, are not forms of knowledge in natural

---

[5] *E* IV. xii. 10–12, p. 645, underlining added.   [6] *E* IV. xii. 12, p. 647.

philosophy; neither are forms of knowledge the guesses that good experimenters make about either unobservable qualities or the relations between such qualities.

Locke and hypotheses: *Essay* IV. xii. 13

Let us turn now to the crucial discussion of hypotheses in section 13, which follows directly from where we left off. The general direction of Locke's argument clearly indicates that the section on hypotheses is a concession, almost a digression, as it is sandwiched between two positive statements of method in natural philosophy. Note the following expressions in context: 'Not that we may not [...] make use of any probable *Hypothesis* whatsoever'; they are 'at least great helps to the Memory'; but we need to be very careful here, for a weakness of the mind is that 'the mind would always have Principles to rest on';[7] and 'most (I had almost said all) of the *Hypotheses* in natural Philosophy' (p. 648) are doubtful conjectures. Then follows the thought opened by an adversative: 'But [...] the *ways to enlarge our knowledge* [...] seem to me, in short, to be these two [...]' (§14, p. 648).

These are not the expressions of a positive, clearly articulated hypotheticalism in natural philosophical reasoning. They are not the 'way of hypothesis' or 'the method of hypothesis'; they are not an enunciation of the method implicit in the practice of the great Master-Builders of the 'Epistle to the Reader'. The central methodological thesis of section 12 is that one should proceed by compiling natural histories. In the Contents, this section is entitled 'But must beware of Hypotheses and wrong Principles'.[8] Section 13 then tells us that hypotheses may be helpful occasionally, but watch out: they have a very bad track record so far and that way of thinking reflects a form of intellectual laziness and leads to prepossession.[9] For the mind is wont to grasp principles without due wariness.

This interpretation, however, seems to fly in the face of those commentators—such as Laudan, Farr, and Soles—who have found a crucial role for hypotheses in Locke. Laudan claims that Locke 'insists that the enunciation of analogical hypotheses is the most productive and theoretically fertile method which the sciences possess'.[10] More recently, Soles has claimed that, for Locke, 'in the ideal case, explanations in natural philosophy will take the form of something like hypothetico-deductive explanations'.[11] In accounting for the negative evaluation of hypotheses in sections 12 and 13, Soles claims that 'Locke's targets are hypotheses laid down at pleasure, i.e. unfounded or unsupported hypotheses', and that Locke is not 'hostile to hypotheses per se'.[12] But, for Locke and for

---

[7] Note Bacon's similar sentiments in *Novum organum*, Book I, Aphorisms XIX and XX in *Bacon Works*, Vol. 11, p. 70/71.

[8] Soles (2005) ignores this section title.

[9] The danger of prepossession was a common Baconian trope of the period. For Locke's warnings on it, see Draft A, §42, pp. 70–1; *Conduct*, §§26, 42, pp. 254–5 and 278–81; and Locke to Thomas Molyneux (letter of 20 January 1693 quoted below).

[10] Laudan 1981, p. 63.   [11] Soles 2005, p. 21.   [12] Ibid., p. 12.

the experimental philosophers in general, the primary denotation of the term 'hypothesis' just is conjectures or speculations that are unfounded or assumed without recourse to observation and experiment. Let us examine the evidence for this claim, first by determining the meanings of the term in Locke's *Essay*, and then by referring to the use of the term within the wider context in which Locke's views were forged.

The term 'hypothesis' and its cognates appear no less than thirty-nine times in the *Essay* alone. Like the term 'idea', it seems to have a rather broad semantic range in Locke's writings. The first meaning of 'hypothesis', which is its primary referent in the *Essay*, is related to particular doctrines, which are nested in or implied by what we would call theories. The Bernoullian account of cohesion is such a hypothesis, deriving as it does from a speculative mechanico-corpuscular natural philosophy. Locke gives this hypothesis extended treatment in chapter 23 of Book II (see Chapter 5 below). Second, Locke, following the common usage of his day, also uses the term 'hypothesis' to refer not just to individual doctrines within a theory but to the cluster of doctrines that make up the speculative theory itself. Cartesianism, Epicureanism, and corpuscularianism are all hypotheses in this broader sense (*E* III. x. 14, p. 497 and IV. iii. 16, p. 547).[13]

As for the broader context in which Locke's views were formed, I supply here, in chronological order, a string of quotations many of which derive from leading figures associated with the Royal Society. First, in the early 1660s Sir Robert Moray, an important founding member of the Society, spoke of its agenda in these terms:

this Society will not own any Hypothesis, systeme, or doctrine of the principles of Naturall philosophy, proposed, or maintained by any Philosopher Aunceint or Moderne, nor the explication of any phaenomenon, where recourse must be had to Originall causes, [...] Nor dogmatically define, nor fixe Axiomes of Scientificall things, but will question and canvas all opinions[,] adopting nor adhering to none, till by mature debate & clear arguments, chiefly such as are deduced from legittimate experiments, the trueth of such positions be demonstrated invincibly.[14]

Joseph Glanvill, in his *Scepsis scientifica*, addressed the Royal Society in the following words:

Nor are these all the *advantages* upon the Account of which we owe *acknowledgments* to *Providence* for your *erection*; since from your *promising* and *generous endeavours*, we may hopefully expect a considerable inlargement of the *History* of *Nature*, without which our *Hypotheseis* are but *Dreams* and *Romances*, and our *Science* meer *conjecture* and *opinion*. For while we frame *Scheames* of things without consulting the *Phænomena*, we do but *build* in the *Air*, and describe an *Imaginary World* of our *own making*; that is but little a kin to the *real* one that *God made*. And [']tis possible that all the *Hypotheseis* that yet have been contrived, were built upon too narrow an *inspection* of things, and the phasies of the *Universe*.[15]

---

[13] For the same use of 'hypotheses' in Boyle, see for example Boyle to Oldenburg, 13 June 1666, *Boyle Correspondence*, Vol. 3, p. 171, and his 'The Requisites of a Good Hypothesis breefely Consider'd in a Dialogue', *Boyle Works*, Vol. 13, p. 271.
[14] Quoted in Hunter 1995b, p. 173.   [15] Glanvill 1665, Sig. b4r–v.

Likewise, Samuel Parker, who became a fellow of the Society in 1666, claimed:

> The chief reason therefore, why I prefer the Mechanical and Experimental Philosophie before the *Aristotelean*, is not so much because of its so much greater certainty, but because it puts inquisitive men into a method to attain it, whereas the other serves only to obstruct their industry by amusing them with empty and insignificant Notions. And therefore we may rationally expect a greater Improvement of Natural Philosophie from the *Royal Society*, (if they pursue their design) then it has had in all former ages; for they having discarded all particular *Hypotheses*, and wholly addicted themselves to exact Experiments and Observations, they may not only furnish the World with a compleat *History of Nature*, (which is the most useful part of *Physiologie*) but also laye firm and solid foundations to erect *Hypotheses* upon, (though perhaps that must be the work of future Ages:) at least we shall see whether it be possible to frame any certain *Hypotheses* or no, which is the thing I most doubt of, because, though the *Experiments* be exact and certain, yet their Appliction to any *Hypotheses* is doubtful and uncertain; so that though the *Hypothesis* may have a firm *Basis* to bottome upon, yet it can be fastned and cemented to it no other way, but by conjecture and uncertaine (though probable) applications, and therefore I doubt not but we must at last rest satisfied with true and exact Histories of Nature for use and practice; and with the handsomest and most probable *Hypotheses* for delight and Ornament.[16]

Then, after the publication of the *Essay*, we find William Wotton expressing the same sentiments, but with specific hypothetical systems in mind:

> I do not here reckon the several *Hypotheses* of *Des Cartes, Gassendi*, or *Hobbes*, as Acquisitions to real Knowledge, since they may only be Chimæra's and amusing Notions, fit to entertain working Heads. I only alledge such Doctrines as are raised upon faithful Experiments, and nice Observations; and such Consequences as are the immediate Results of, and manifest Corollaries drawn from, these Experiments and Observations.[17]

Finally, after Locke's death, we find Newton claiming that 'the word Hypothesis is here used by me to signify only such a Proposition as is not a Phænomenon nor deduced from any Phænomena but assumed or supposed without any experimental proof'.[18] And this view of hypotheses persisted through Newton's influence, as is witnessed in the claim of James Jurin, the Secretary of the Society at the time of Newton's death:

> [T]he Royal Society are much more desirous of accounts of new Experiments & new Observations, than of long reasonings, which generally contain either what is commonly known, or use uncertain Hypotheses & Speculations. Sir Isaac Newton has taught us, that the right & indeed the only way to advance real knowledge, is to lay aside all Hypotheses, & to reason only from matter of fact. By this means Philosophy will go forwards by degrees though the steps are slow, but by the other Method no natural truths ever were, or ever will be discover'd.[19]

This view was still prevalent in the late eighteenth century, as is evidenced by the philosopher Thomas Reid's comment: 'I have, ever since I was acquainted with

---

[16] Parker 1666, pp. 45–6.   [17] Wotton 1694, p. 244.   [18] Newton 1959–77, Vol. 5, p. 397.
[19] Jurin to Thomas Dereham, 7 August 1727, Jurin 1996, p. 366.

Bacon & Newton, thought that this Doctrine [the mistrust of hypotheses] is the very Key to Natural Philosophy, & the Touchstone by which every thing that is Legitimate & Solid in that Science, is to be distinguished from what is Spurious and Hollow'.[20] It is this view of hypotheses that predominates in Locke's *Essay*, and in particular in the section entitled 'But must beware of Hypotheses and wrong Principles'.

Hypotheses and analogical reasoning

There is another passage which is commonly adduced as evidence that Locke prescribed a method of hypothesis in natural philosophy. This is the discussion of analogical reasoning in *E* IV. xvi. 12. Laudan deals with the passage from *E* IV. xvi. 12 as if it were continuous with the earlier section on hypotheses (*E* IV. xii. 13).[21] It is my contention, however, that the two are different and that the distinction between them is important.

By contrast with 'hypothesis', the term 'analogy' and its cognates, which only appear nine times in the *Essay*,[22] normally refer to a type of reasoning rather than a particular doctrine or cluster of doctrines. In the context of Locke's theory of knowledge, 'analogy' consists in reasoning from effects to causes, on the basis of resemblances, or in reasoning from relations between qualities in observable objects to relations between qualities in unobservable objects. In modern terms, this is a form of inference to the best explanation—what some philosophers call ampliative inference or abduction.

Locke gives some examples of analogical reasoning in *E* IV. xvi. 12. It is to them that we now turn. The first one is this:

> observing that the bare rubbing of two Bodies violently one upon another, produces heat, and very often fire it self, we have reason to think, that what we call Heat and Fire, consists in a violent agitation of the imperceptible minute parts of the burning matter [...][23]

Locke could be characterized here as reasoning from the analogical principle of 'same effect, same cause'. This principle would then be an instance of what he calls the 'rule of analogy'. Of course, there was an important precedent for this type of reasoning in Newton's Hypothesis II in the first edition of the *Principia*, which claimed: 'The causes assigned to natural effects of the same kind must be, so far as possible, the same'.[24] Locke is then assuming the existence of insensible particles and inferring that the quality of heat at the unobservable level is analogous to the quality of heat at the observable level; that is, it is caused by motion. The second example concerns the

---

[20] Reid to Lord Kames, 16 December 1780, Reid 2002, p. 140.
[21] Laudan 1981, p. 63.
[22] See also Locke's Journal entry for 26 June 1681 (Locke 1936, pp. 117–18) for an early reference to analogical reasoning.
[23] *E* IV. xvi. 12, pp. 665–6.
[24] Newton 1999, p. 795. Hypothesis 2 of the first edition is identical to Rule 2 of the second and third editions.

refraction of light, and is very similar to the first. The third example, however, is rather different. Locke claims that among observable creatures there is a 'gradual connexion of one with another, without any great or discernable gaps between'—gaps, that is, of rationality and perceptivity. He continues:

Observing, I say, such gradual and gentle descents downwards in those parts of Creation, that are beneath Man, the rule of Analogy may make it probable, that it is so also in Things above us, and our Observation; and that there are several ranks of intelligent Beings, excelling us in several degrees of Perfection [...][25]

This example also offers an application of analogy in natural philosophy. It differs from the first two in that it does not appeal to resemblance between effects and causes. Locke argues that the sequential and incremental variation of a quality across observable particulars suggests the same variation across unobservable particulars. It is a kind of 'great chain of being' argument.[26] Thus Locke's talk here of the 'rule of Analogy' suggests that his conception of analogical reasoning is very broad indeed, encompassing as it does the two very different types of examples he uses.

Now Locke does not use the term 'hypothesis' in connection with this discussion of analogy, except at the end of the passage where he claims that analogy is the best 'rise of Hypothesis' (E IV. xvi. 12, p. 666). In what sense does Locke consider analogy to be the best rise of hypotheses? Hypotheses and analogical reasoning are often closely related. The corpuscular hypothesis is derived from analogical reasoning, and corpuscular explanations proceed by analogical reasoning on a case-by-case basis. Individual cases of analogy serve to confirm or to extend the hypothesis. This is what Locke is referring to when he says that analogy gives rise to hypotheses. But of course many hypotheses are not derived from analogical reasoning at all. Indeed many corpuscularians regarded this fact as a weakness of such hypotheses as substantial forms. Locke's view is that those hypotheses, such as corpuscularianism, that arise from analogical reasoning are superior to the ones that do not.

Now some corpuscularians, like Boyle and the later Newton, maintained that to explicate an unobservable quality is just to explain it by appeal to qualities that are already clearly understood, or with which we are already familiar. Thus not only was their corpuscularian hypothesis derived from analogical reasoning, but any further determinable or determinate explanation of unobserved qualities must, for them, conform to this 'familiarity condition'. We know that Locke regarded the corpuscular hypothesis as the most intelligible one we have. It may even be that part of its attraction to him lay in the manner in which it derived from analogical reasoning. Indeed, Locke's claim that analogy is the *only* help we have when it comes to unobservable qualities, if strictly interpreted, implies that Locke accepted the Familiarity Condition

---

[25] E IV. xvi. 12, p. 666.
[26] So Hesse 1962, p. 125 and Buchdahl 1969, p. 214. For a similar argument, see E II. ii. 3, p. 120.

(see Chapter 8 below).²⁷ If this line of reasoning is correct, we can then flesh out the sense in which Locke regarded the corpuscular hypothesis as uniquely intelligible. It is the most intelligible precisely because it explains unknown qualities in terms of known ones.

Uses of analogical reasoning and of hypotheses in natural philosophy

Locke furnishes us with a range of uses for hypotheses. The first one is this: hypotheses, 'if they are well made, are at least great helps to the Memory' (*E* IV. xii. 13, p. 648). There are grounds for believing that Locke regarded this use of hypotheses as the most important one. As early as his 'Anatomia', written in late 1668, Locke speaks of how anatomy

> may too in many cases satisfie a physitian in the effects he finds producd by his method or medicins & though it give him not a full account of the causes or their ways of operation yet may serve him in the frameing of a probable hypothesis give him some light in the observations he shall make in the history of deseases & and the ideas he shall frame of them which though not perhaps true in its self yet some of them will be a great help to his memory & a guid to his practise.²⁸

Here the term 'hypothesis' is deleted, but clearly the thought had occurred to Locke that hypotheses were of use to memory. Then, in a series of 'bullet' points on a folio that appears to be related to Sydenham's aborted work on smallpox, Locke speaks of

> Hypothesies serveing after the thing is discovered very well for helps to our memory but very seldom are sound & sure enough without experience to warrant our practise or lead us into the right way of operation.²⁹

This use of hypotheses seems rather strange to our ears, particularly if one follows Laudan in believing that, for Locke, analogical hypotheses are the best method for advancing the sciences. But Locke has already claimed, in this very chapter, that helping the memory is also a function of principles in general. He tells us that principles and general rules 'disburden the Memory of the cumbersome load of Particulars' (*E* IV. xii. 3 p. 640).

The idea seems to be best illustrated by a medical example. A hypothesis might be wildly speculative, but it may help the physician to order the symptoms of a disease in his memory, or to memorize the regimen in the treatment of a particular ailment. Happily Locke's medical notebooks do provide us with a concrete example of this usage. Locke's entry on 'Apoplexia' in Bodl. MS Locke d. 9, pp. 61 and 278, is derived

---

[27] See R. A. Wilson 2002, pp. 207–10.
[28] TNA PRO 30/24/47/2, fol. 31r. It should be noted that other deletions and interlineations in the text have been omitted here.
[29] TNA PRO 30/24/47/2, fol. 49r = Romanell 1984, p. 71.

from Sydenham's discussion of two forms of apoplexy in Sydenham's 'Medical Observations', as found in Royal College of Physicians MS 572. What is interesting about Locke's version of the Sydenham material is the manner in which he has broken it up and marked the different components of the discussion. What, for Sydenham, was one continuous description of the disease and of its treatment is divided by Locke into Dispositiones, Occasiones, Descripsio, Prognosis, Methodus, and—most importantly for our interests—Hypothesis. Locke extracts as follows Sydenham's speculative hypothesis about the cause of apoplexy:

Hypothesis. This sort is caused by extravasation of bloud upon the brain as is often found by dissection in those that die there of.

Perhaps Locke thought that this particular hypothesis might be of use in the treatment of that condition.

Finally, looking beyond the publication of the first edition of the *Essay*, we find a letter to Thomas Molyneux of 20 January 1693 in which Locke says:

[u]pon such grounds as are the establish'd history of diseases hypotheses might with less danger be erected, which I think are so far useful, as they serve as an art of memory to direct the physician in particular cases, but not to be rely'd on as foundations of reasoning, or verities to be contended for; they being, I think I may say all of them, suppositions taken up gratis, and will so remain, till we can discover how the natural functions of the body are perform'd [. . .][30]

The idea is that a physician may entertain distinct and even incompatible hypotheses about diseases because of their practical utility as 'distinct arts of memory in those cases'. As such, they are 'artificial helps to a physician, and not as philosophical truths to a naturalist'.[31] Interestingly, William Wotton makes a similar claim for medical theories in his *Reflections upon Ancient and Modern Learning*:

[A] Man's Prescriptions may be very valuable, because founded upon repeated Observations of the Phænomena of all Diseases. And he may form Secondary Theories, which, like *Ptolemee's Eccentricks* and *Epicycles*, shall be good Guides to Practice; not by giving a certain Insight into the first Causes, and several Steps, by which the Disease first began, and was afterwards carried on; but by enabling the Physician to make lucky Conjectures at proper Courses, and fit Medicines, whereby to relieve or cure his Patient.[32]

---

[30] *Correspondence*, Vol. 4, p. 629.
[31] Ibid., p. 630. See also Locke's Journal 22 July 1678: 'I have no doubts that to cure each species of disease a fixed method or specific remedies are necessary. Once these are ascertained, then the Rules which the dogmatists have built up out of their hypotheses of the humors, plethora, etc., may be very useful in applying the method or the remedies, modifying them according to the patient's particular constitution' (quoting the translation of Romanell 1984, p. 139). Locke appears to have written to Dr William Cole on the subject of hypotheses in 1690, but, frustratingly, the letter is no longer extant. For Cole's view of hypotheses in medicine, which probably echoes that of Locke, see Cole to Locke, 11 June 1690, *Correspondence*, Vol. 4, p. 91.
[32] Wotton 1694, p. 291.

The second use of hypotheses in natural philosophy derives from the fact that they 'often direct us to new discoveries' (*E* IV. xii. 13). Once again, Locke does not give any examples, but rather is concerned in this passage to caution us about their use. There are, however, some very clear examples in works of natural philosophy that Locke read. Take for instance Boyle's assessment of Linus' funicular hypothesis, namely that an invisible string held up the column of mercury in the Torricellian apparatus.[33]

As for uses of analogy in matters such as the cause of magnetism, generation, and movement in animals, '*Analogy* in these matters is the only help we have, and 'tis from that alone that we draw our grounds of Probability'. Locke concludes his discussion by saying:

[t]his sort of Probability [i.e. analogy], which is the best conduct of rational Experiments, and the rise of Hypothesis, has also its Use and Influence; and a wary Reasoning from Analogy leads us often into the discovery of Truths, and useful Productions, which would otherwise lie concealed.[34]

Like hypotheses, then, analogical reasoning can lead us to the discovery of new truths. By a 'discovery of new truths' Locke can only mean new matters of fact derived from experiment and observation. Locke also adds that analogy can give rise to hypotheses and lead to new productions, by which he seems to mean new phenomena in nature. Such may be a new chemical reaction or the creation of a partial vacuum in an air-pump. Furthermore, in the letter to Thomas Molyneux mentioned above, Locke speaks of the importance of observation for the physician who can, then, 'by analogy argue to like cases, and thence make himself rules of practice'. The idea seems to be that in, say, therapeutics a rule of thumb can be established on the basis of resemblance between symptoms, which are to be treated in similar ways. But throughout Locke is clear that the use of analogical reasoning is often little more than a directed form of guesswork.[35]

In summary, then, hypotheses aid the memory and direct us to new discoveries, while analogy gives rise to hypotheses and leads to the discovery of new truths, to novel phenomena, and to procedural rules, say, in therapeutics. It must be stressed that the aids to memory are aids to memorizing histories; that the new discoveries and the novel phenomena arise in the formation of natural histories; that the procedural rules derived from analogy arise from histories. There is not natural history and then some additional method of knowledge acquisition. Hypotheses and analogical reasoning find their domain of application in the compilation of natural histories.

---

[33] *A Defence of the Doctrine Touching the Spring and Weight of the Air* (LL 463), *Boyle Works*, Vol. 3, pp. 30 ff.
[34] *E* IV. xvi. 12, pp. 666–7.
[35] *E* IV. iii. 29, p. 560, IV. vi. 13, p. 588 and especially IV. viii. 9, p. 615.

Natural philosophy and the method of natural history

It is helpful to compare Locke here with Bacon, Boyle, and Hooke. According to Bacon, 'by far the noblest end of *Natural History* is to serve primarily for the founding of philosophy'. That is, 'to be the basic stuff and raw material of the true and legitimate induction [...] a proper preparative [*parasceve*] for the founding of philosophy' (ibid.).[36] By contrast, there is little indication in Locke that natural histories are preparatory for and the foundation of natural philosophy. Rather, given our current epistemic limits, Locke appears to consider the compilation of natural histories to be the primary task of natural philosophy.[37] Thus Locke never even discusses the next stage in the Baconian programme—that is, the inductive method. Of course Locke would also reject Bacon's ontology of form and essence and the prospects of demonstrative knowledge that derive from it. This is not because he rejects essences *simpliciter*, but rather because he denies that we can have any epistemic access to them. It is not that Bacon's demonstrative ideal is absent in Locke, but rather that Locke is far more sceptical about the range of resources available for human understanding to work on.

How, then, does Locke compare with Boyle and Hooke? In his most detailed treatment of natural histories, Boyle tells us that the preliminary to any history should include summary statements or 'a short survey' of the relevant hypotheses of philosophers such as the Cartesians, the Epicureans, and the Peripatetics. This is because the natural history might 'amplify & correct them'. Furthermore,

> the knowledg of differing Theorys, may admonish a man to observe divers such Circumstances in an Experiment as otherwise 'tis like he would not heed; and sometimes too may prompt him to stretch the Experiment farther then else he would (and so make it produce new *Phænomena*) & *partly* because these additional *Phænomena*, and accuratenes which these Theorys will ingage the Experimenter to imploy about some Circumstances, will conduce to make the History *both* more exact and compleat in it self, and more ready for use, and more acceptable to those that love to discourse upon *Hypotheses* [...][38]

Thus for Boyle there is a reciprocal relation between hypotheses and histories. Hypotheses might be corrected or extended by natural histories and, in turn, experiments used in compiling natural histories might be directed to produce new phenomena.[39] Locke could hardly have failed to be aware of this, not least because he reviewed Boyle's own 'Speculative discourse', which gave a corpuscular interpretation

---

[36] *Descriptio, Bacon Works*, Vol. 6, p. 104/105.
[37] So Romanell 1984, p. 198.
[38] Boyle to Oldenburg, 13 June 1666, *Boyle Correspondence*, Vol. 3, p. 171. See also Essay XIII of 'Texts and fragments of essays relating to *The Usefulness of Natural Philosophy, Part II, section 2*', *Boyle Works*, Vol. 13, pp. 350–4. It should be pointed out that Bacon allowed 'that received opinions, with all their varieties and sects, be succinctly reviewed as if in passing with no other object than to egg on the intellect', *Parasceve, Bacon Works*, Vol. 11, p. 470/471. For a similar prescription in Hooke's recommendations for writing a natural history see his *A General Scheme or Idea of the Present State of Natural Philosophy*, Hooke 1705, p. 19.
[39] For a detailed treatment of Boyle's 'Designe about Natural History', see Anstey and Hunter 2008.

of the operation of specific medicines.[40] (The content of Locke's review is discussed below.)

Hooke's view is even stronger than that of Boyle. For here is what Hooke claimed to be needed in order to discover the internal constitution of things 'together with the Method and Course of Nature's proceeding in them':

> These will require much deeper Researches and Ratiocinations, and very many Vicissitudes of Proceedings from Axiomes to Experiments, and from Experiments to Axiomes; and are indeed the Business of the Philosopher, and not of the Historian.[41]

The contrast with Locke here is very important. Boyle, in his experimental treatises, would explicitly state the various theories pertaining to the quality or phenomenon under investigation, in order both to test the hypotheses and to extend the range of the experiments. Hooke considered that the activity of testing axioms by experiments goes beyond the work of the natural historian, and he envisaged a kind of feedback loop whereby one proceeds 'from Axiomes to Experiments, and from Experiments to Axiomes'. Locke, by contrast, nowhere prescribes that the natural philosopher should review such theories; and, as we saw above, even his recommendations regarding them in *Some Thoughts concerning Education* are cautious.

> I do not hence conclude that none of them are to be read: It is necessary for a Gentleman in this learned Age to look into some of them, to fit himself for Conversation. But whether that of *Des Cartes* be put into his Hands, as that which is most in Fashion; or it be thought fit to give him a short view of that and several other also, I think the Systems of *Natural Philosophy*, that have obtained in this part of the World, are to be read, more to know the *Hypotheses*, and to understand the Terms and Ways of Talking of the several Sects, than with hopes to gain thereby a comprehensive, scientifical, and satisfactory Knowledge of the Works of Nature.[42]

For Boyle, then, the elaboration of hypotheses is an essential component in the compilation of a natural history, whereas Locke is all but silent on the interplay between a particular natural philosophical system (say, corpuscularianism) and the development of a natural history. For the Locke of the first edition of the *Essay*, natural history is not the handmaiden or nursing mother of natural philosophy, nor is it to be developed in relation to the best theories of the day. In this he was not alone; for, as Michael Hunter has noted, 'the aspiration to the accumulation of "complete" information and the postponement of hypotheses till this was achieved—however unrealistic it seems to us—was an aspiration of men at the core of the [Royal] Society'.[43]

There are, however, two passages after the publication of the *Essay* which reveal a position closer to the Boylean view on Locke's part, although neither passage concerns natural philosophy. In the second, 1694 edition of the *Essay*, Locke extended his

---

[40] Boyle says in the preface that 'the following Paper in its own nature, and in the direct and immediate design of it, is a Speculative discourse', and, again, that 'the ensuing discourse is for the main of a Speculative nature': *Specific Medicines, Boyle Works*, Vol. 10, pp. 353 and 354.
[41] *General Scheme*, Hooke 1705, p. 61.   [42] *SCTE*, §193, p. 247.   [43] Hunter 1995b, p. 175.

discussion at *E* II. i. 10 of the hypothesis that the mind always thinks by adding the following comment:

[H]e, that would not deceive himself, ought to build his Hypothesis on matter of fact, and make it out by sensible experience, and not presume on matter of fact, because of his Hypothesis, that is, because he supposes it to be so [...][44]

The important development here is Locke's claim, which can be generalized to natural philosophy, that hypotheses are to be *built* upon matters of fact. It is striking, however, that Locke did not adjust his discusson of hypotheses in natural philosophy in *E* IV. xii. 12–13 to make it reflect this change, in spite of all the minor adjustments that he made to these sections in subsequent editions.

The second passage dates from the mid-1690s and is a short discussion on how to evaluate the relative merits of competing speculative systems. This passage was probably intended for a revised edition of the *Essay*. His comments in this manuscript entry are important because, while they apply to speculative hypotheses in general and are not specifically related to natural philosophy,[45] it is reasonable to presume that the epistemic values they ascribe apply to speculative systems of natural philosophy. Locke first advises on how one should proceed in response to objections to a hypothesis or theory:

The way to finde truth as far as we are able to reach it in this our darke & short sighted state is to pursue the hypothesis that seems to us to carry with it the most light & consistency as far as we can without raising objections or sticking at those that come in our way.

Only after this pursuit is one to give consideration to objections. Locke then claims that competing hypotheses should be evaluated by considerations of comparative plausibility:

But to shew which side has the best pretence to truth & followers the Two whole systems must be set one by an other & considered entirely & then see which is most consistent in all its parts; which least clogd with incohærences or absurdities & which freest from begd principles & unintelligible notions This is the fairest way to search after Truth & the surest not to mistake on which side she is.[46]

Yet all of this is rather abstract. Let us turn to a concrete example from Locke's writings in which he employs the notions of hypothesis and analogy. This is the case of acids and alkalis, and its importance lies in the fact that it contains the only hypothesis about the

---

[44] E_{2-5} II. i. 10, p. 109.
[45] *Pace* Soles (2005, p. 18), who regards this fragment as 'displaying a subtle understanding of how working hypotheses are developed and evaluated, not to mention the role of probabilities in natural philosophy'.
[46] Quoting from Farr 1987, pp. 70 and 71, corrected. Farr cites the 'Method' entry as from Bodl. MS Locke c. 29, but it is actually found in Bodl. MS Locke c. 28, fol. 115.

sub-microscopic, other than the corpuscularian theory of matter, that Locke discusses in any depth.

Locke on the nature of acids and alkalis

Locke penned a review of Boyle's *Specific Medicines* in the *Bibliothèque universelle et historique* for his friend Jean Le Clerc. It was published in French in 1686; an (unauthorized) English translation appeared in 1692, and this will be our entry point into Locke's views on acids and alkalis.[47] Before discussing its contents, however, it is best to set it in context by introducing some of the issues that motivated Boyle's *Specific Medicines*.

It is well known that Boyle was interested in the nature of acids and alkalis. He was the first to publish the fact that indicator tests can be used to distinguish them. However, by the 1670s, a theory of matter had emerged which used as its primary explanatory resource the principles of acidity and alkalinity. This theory, first developed by Otto Tachenius, was not merely a new form of classification arising from the study of chemical reactions involving acids and alkalis, but a rival to the Aristotelian–Galenic four-element theory and the Paracelsian *tria prima*.[48]

The acid and alkali hypothesis stood in its own right, as a well-developed theory of matter, and arose as a competitor to the corpuscular theory of Robert Boyle, which denied that there were any such principles in nature. Boyle therefore attacked it in a short essay, entitled 'Reflections upon the Hypothesis of Alcali and Acidum' and published in 1675 in his *Mechanical Origine of Qualities*. One of Boyle's targets was no doubt François André, who in 1672 had published his version of the theory under the title *Entretiens sur l'acide et l'alcali*. André was quick to respond to Boyle's attacks, addressing them in a thoroughly revised second edition of his book (1677, LL 89ª). The dispute was over whether acids and alkalis acted by virtue of a principle or quality of acidity that was irreducible, or whether they acted through qualities that were ultimately reducible to the mechanical affections of bodies. In other words, do we need to posit a special quality of acidity, or is it just that acids share some common structural feature in the make-up of their corpuscles? Boyle held the latter view, André the former.

Now Locke had a copy of André's book and commented in his journal, on 19 September 1679: 'I feare his Doctrine wants proofs & that he does not always reason closely'.[49] Clearly Locke was unimpressed, although he conceded that the book contained some 'very good experiments'. Boyle returned to the issue of the nature

---

[47] The review appeared in French Le Clerc's *Bibliothèque universelle et historique* in 1686 (Locke 1686), and then in Dunton 1692, pp. 184–7.

[48] For background, see M. Boas [Hall] 1956. Locke owned copies of Tachenius' *Clavis* (1669), LL 2822ª and of his *Hippocrates chimicus* (1668), LL 2822ᵇ.

[49] Dewhurst 1963a, p. 174 (corrected).

of acidity and alkalinity in his *Specific Medicines*, published in 1685, though he did not mention André explicitly in that work. Let us turn, then, to Locke's review of the 1686 Latin edition of it.[50] Locke, mirroring Boyle, begins with a short historical sketch of the shift in explanations about the qualities of bodies. Occult qualities were once appealed to in order to explain certain qualities. In his day the situation was different:

> It was but in this latter Age, that People began to Discourse according to the Rules of Geometry, and to explain by Properties; by which we clearly conceive the different Effects of Bodies, the most universal Properties of Body and Extension, and Figure and Motion.[50a]

This is clearly a description of the corpuscular theory of qualities. Locke tells us that it is Boyle's intention to show that the corpuscular hypothesis is at least consistent with the common notion of specific medicines.[51] We are interested in the section relating to acids. Locke summarizes Boyle approvingly:

> [A]ll such *Menstruums* act by their Figure, Bigness or Solidity, or by some other such like Property, which is manifestly included in our Notion [l'idée] of a Body, and not by certain sensible Qualities as their Humidity and Acidity. An infinite number of Experiences persuade us that this is so; for whereas cold Water dissolves the White of an Egg, which the Spirit of Vinegar, of Salt, or the Oyl of Vitreal coagulates; the Spirit of Urine dissolves in a trice the filings of Brass, which the Spirit of Vinegar does but slowly; and on the contrary, the Spirit of Vinegar dissolves Crabs Eyes in a moment, upon which the Spirit of Piss had no Effect at all [...][52]

But then Locke departs from Boyle's text and draws the following conclusion:

> If there was nothing but Humidity and Acidity required for the dissolution of Bodies, *Aqua fortis* and *Aqua regalis* would be universal Dissolvers, whose force few Bodies could resist. They wou'd dissolve all such as are not extraordinary Solid. Whereas [we see that] quite contrary happens, because Dissolvers act by the figure of their Particles, it is not always proper to disunite the Particles of all sorts of Bodies.[53]

Locke here is glossing over Boyle's conclusion and giving it a more polemical twist than Boyle himself does. Indeed, Locke's comments are closer to those of Boyle in the 'Alcali and Acidum' treatise than to those made in the work under review. Locke's conclusion is clearly directed against the sort of view of acidity propounded by the likes of André. He is using experimental data to argue against the 'acid hypothesis'. Locke's claim is that the corpuscular explanation in which 'Dissolvers act by the figure of their

---

[50] Locke owned a copy of the English edition of *Specific Medicines* (LL 468). The book's full title, followed by Locke's usual description (including size, date and number of pages, '8° London 85. p225'), is found in Bodl. MS Locke d. 9, p. 146. He then quotes a reported remedy for heart palpitations from p. 128 of *Specific Medicines* on p. 288 of the same notebook.

[50a] Dunton 1692, p. 184.

[51] Locke, possibly under the influence of Boyle, acquiesced in specific medicines at least as early as 1678. See his Journal entry for 'Method of treatment', 22 July 1678 (quoted in note 31 above).

[52] Dunton 1692, p. 185 (corrected) = Locke 1686, pp. 268–9. See *Specific Medicines, Boyle Works*, Vol. 10, p. 371.

[53] Dunton 1692, p. 185 (corrected) = Locke 1686, p. 269.

Particles' is more consistent with the experimental data than the acid hypothesis is. What is relevant for our purposes is that Locke, tracking Boyle with some degree of deference, regards the results of chymical experiments as having implications for hypotheses about the unobservable qualities of bodies. In this case experiment and observation bear on the domain of the unobservable realm insofar as Locke is able to play off one hypothesis against another.

Locke retained strong views on the acidity hypothesis. This hypothesis appears again in section 40 of the *Conduct*, this time in connection with analogy:

§40. *Analogy*. Analogy is of great use to the mind in many cases, especially in natural philosophy; and that part of it chiefly which consists in happy and successful experiments. But here we must take care that we keep ourselves within that wherein the analogy consists. For example, the acid oil of vitriol is found to be good in such a case, therefore the spirit of nitre or vinegar may be used in the like case. If the good effect of it be owing wholly to the acidity of it, the trial may be justified; but if there be something else besides the acidity in the oil of vitriol which produces the good we desire in the case, we mistake for that analogy which is not, and suffer our understanding to be misguided by a wrong supposition of analogy where there is none.[54]

Locke is using a similar example to the one found in his review a decade earlier: just the fact that one acid has a particular effect implies neither that all acids will have that effect nor that the acid in question is acting by its property of acidity. Here he is giving us the example of an analogy overreaching itself, which will 'suffer our understanding to be misguided'. As in his other references to analogical reasoning, there is here a strong note of caution; and, like in his comments on the acidity hypothesis in the review, he is concerned with experimental observations arising from the behaviour of acids in chemical reactions. The focus is on the phenomenal level, and the caution pertains to the danger of making a false analogy with regard to the quality of acidity.

This example of analogy serves to augment the ones given in the *Essay*, which have been discussed above. It is a little more complex than the other three and will repay closer scrutiny. We could interpret this example as one using the analogical principle that same effect implies same cause. Alternatively, the example could be rationally reconstructed as an instance of Mill's method of agreement. Acid A has effect *e*, acid B has effect *e* and acid C has effect *e*, therefore acidity is the cause of *e*. Locke's point would then be explained in terms of the usual limitations of the method of agreement. Finally, one could rationally reconstruct Locke's example of analogy as an instance of the hypothetico-deductive method. Sulphuric acid, when applied to a particular substance, has effect *e*; the acid and alkali theory posits that all acids have similar effects; therefore we can test the hypothesis that nitric acid and ascetic acid, when applied to the same substance, will have effect *e*; and so on. The point is that we can reconstruct the example so as to suit our preferred form of scientific inference. Locke, however, used it as an example of analogical reasoning and nothing more. If hypotheses are in

---

[54] *Conduct*, p. 275.

view at all, it is only because of Locke's residual antagonism to the acid and alkali hypothesis.

Finally, the acid and alkali hypothesis appears again in Locke's correspondence. An important example is the letter to Thomas Molyneux of 20 January 1693, which, as we have seen, reinforces Locke's points about hypotheses and analogy, already made in the *Essay*. In extolling the virtues of Sydenham's method of compiling histories of diseases, Locke goes on to say:

> I fear the Galenists four humors, or the chymists sal, sulphur, and mercury, or the late prevailing invention of acid and alcali, or whatever hereafter shall be substituted to these with new applause, will upon examination be found to be but so many learned empty sounds, with no precise determinate signification.[55]

Locke's ongoing opposition to the acid and alkali hypothesis is striking. His remedy is to follow the method of natural history, which

> is a work of time, accurateness, attention, and judgment; and wherein if men, thro' prepossession or oscitancy mistake, they may be convinced of their error by unerring nature and matter of fact.[56]

The foregoing survey of Locke's discussions of the acid and alkali hypothesis serves very nicely to illustrate his comments on hypotheses and analogy in the *Essay*. The hypothesis of acid and alkali, like the *tria prima* or the four elements in the Arisotelian tradition, functions as a speculative explanation of the behaviour of observable bodies by positing the existence of unobservable qualities or principles. Locke argues against it by appeals to observation and experiment and by appeal to another hypothesis, which appears to be more consistent with the experimental data. This procedure is analogous to his use of the corpuscular hypothesis in elaborating on his primary and secondary quality distinction in the *Essay*, and it reveals that Locke is prepared to entertain hypotheses about the unobserved material realm—even if most of them, if not all, are 'castles in the air'.

The example of analogical reasoning about acids in the *Conduct* reveals that Locke is applying this reasoning at the phenomenal level in a way which might produce a novel effect and which (we can surmise) may have implications for a hypothesis like the acid and alkali theory. It is a very clear example of the sort of reasoning referred to at *E* IV. xvi. 12. The discussion also contains a warning about analogy overreaching itself. Indeed each of these discussions—apart from the review, which simply criticizes a particular hypothesis—contains warnings and cautions about the use of either hypotheses or analogy. The letter to Molyneux is clear about the natural historical context in which hypotheses and analogy should be situated. In short, all the features of the discussion of hypotheses and analogy in the *Essay* appear in this clutch of discussions of acids and alkalis. Together they confirm the overriding cautions that Locke applies to

---

[55] *Correspondence*, Vol. 4, p. 629.   [56] Ibid.

them and the natural historical context in which they are carried out. None of these discussions suggests that Locke was committed to a Laudanian method of hypothesis.

Locke and King Arthur

Before concluding this chapter, it should be said that there is one more, and very interesting, site for the examination of evidence concerning Locke's views on hypotheses and natural history. This is a series of letters between him and William Molyneux. In his letter of 27 May 1697, William Molyneux, after singing the praises of the physician and poet Sir Richard Blackmore and of his recently reissued poem *King Arthur*, mentions to Locke that he had asked Blackmore to compose a philosophical poem. He goes on to mention Blackmore's dislike of philosophical hypotheses and says:

> Were I acquainted with Sir R. Blackmore I could assure him [...] that I am as little an Admirer of Hypotheses as any Man, and never proposed that thought to him with a Designe that a Philosophick Poem should run on such a strain. A Natural History of the Great and Admirable Phænomena of the Universe is a subject, I think, may afford sublime Thoughts in a Poem.[57]

In his reply of 15 June 1697, Locke concurs with Molyneux:

> I have always thought, that laying down, and building upon hypotheses, has been one of the great hindrances of natural knowledge; and I see your notions agree with mine in it. And, though I have a great value for Sir R. Blackmore, on several accounts, yet there is nothing has given me a greater esteem of him, than what he says about hypotheses in medicine, in his preface to K. Arthur, which is an argument to me that he understands the right method of practising physick; and it gives me great hopes he will improve it, since he keeps in the only way it is capable to be improved in; and has so publickly declared against the more easie, fashionable, and pleasing way of an hypothesis, which, I think, has done more to hinder the true art of physick, which is the curing of diseases, than all other things put together.[58]

Needless to say, Locke gives as an example the hypothesis of 'acid and alcali'. So what, then, did Blackmore say in his (revised) preface?

> The raising of an Hypotheses in Philosophy obtains little more Credit with me, than the erecting a Scheme in Astrology; and the Judgments and Decisions that are given upon them seem to me alike Precarious and uncertain. [...] A clear and penetrating Understanding, Cultivated and

---

[57] *Correspondence*, Vol. 6, p. 134.
[58] Ibid., p. 144. It should be pointed out that Soles (2005), in his attempt to argue that Locke endorsed a kind of proto-hypothetico-deductivism, entirely ignores this evidence of Locke's attitude to hypotheses in the correspondence with Molyneux.

Matur'd by repeated, Diligent Observation, will in my Opinion, make a more able and accomplish'd Physitian, than any *Philosophical Scheme* that has yet obtain'd in the World.[59]

The correspondence continues with a reply from Molyneux, who says of Blackmore's views on hypotheses: 'I am wholy of his opinion [...] however the History and Phænomena of Nature we may venture at'.[60] Locke rounds off the correspondence (at least on this point) by reiterating:

there was nothing that I so much admired him for, as for what he says of hypotheses in his last [preface]. It seems to me so right, and is yet so much out of the way of the ordinary writers, and practitioners in that faculty [...][61]

Conclusion

If the argument of this chapter is correct, then a serious revision of current scholarship is required. For the interpretative trend, at least since the 1960s, has been to view Locke's pronouncements on hypotheses and analogy as placing him at the very beginning of the new 'way of hypothesis': a precursor to the hypothetico-deductive method to be sure, but on the right track none the less. But Locke was not developing a kind of 'proto-hypothetical method' of knowledge acquisition in natural philosophy. He was working rather with a Baconian conception of the knowledge of natural objects, but a mitigated Baconian conception at that. For he had no time for Baconian induction,[62] and little time for Boyle's robust reciprocal relation between hypothesis and experiment. He did see a role for hypotheses in aiding memory and discovery. But the burden of memory to be relieved in this way was the vast array of matters of fact, and the discoveries of hypotheses and analogy were to aid the overarching project of natural history. In this Locke's views on the nature and role of hypotheses were entirely consistent with those of an advocate of the experimental philosophy. The decrying of hypotheses and of speculative theories had been a defining feature of the experimental philosophy as promoted by members of the early Royal Society since the early 1660s. Locke's views were forged within that milieu.

---

[59] Blackmore 1697, Preface, pp. ix–x.   [60] *Correspondence*, Vol. 6, p. 164.
[61] Locke to William Molyneux, 11 September 1697, *Correspondence*, Vol. 6, p. 190.
[62] I am not claiming that Locke did not engage in what modern philosophers have come to call inductive inferences—that is, inferences from the observed to the unobserved. Rather I am claiming that Locke does not refer to Bacon's peculiar conception of induction, which is not equivalent to the modern conception.

5

Vortices, the deluge, and cohesion

> The Ingenious Mr. *Hook* did, some moneths since, intimate to a friend of his, that he had, with an excellent twelve foot Telescope, observed, some days before, he than spoke of it, (*videl*. on the ninth of *May*, 1664, about 9 of the clock at night) a small Spot in the biggest of the 3 obscurer *Belts* of *Jupiter*, and that, observing it from time to time, he found, that within 2 hours after, the said Spot had moved from East to West, about half the length of the Diameter of *Jupiter*.[1]

We have seen that Locke gives pride of place in natural philosophy to the construction of natural histories, and that hypotheses and analogical reasoning play a minor, subsidiary role in natural philosophy. This position is entirely in keeping with the experimental philosophy of Locke's day, which stressed the painstaking collection of matters of fact and decried the use of speculative hypotheses, and it can be further illustrated by Locke's more focused discussions of specific hypotheses. In this chapter we will examine in detail Locke's treatment of three hypotheses.

The first discussion of a hypothesis to be examined here is found in Locke's review of Newton's *Principia*, in the *Bibliothèque universelle et historique* in 1688.[2] There Locke paraphrases an argument which Newton brings against the Cartesian cosmological hypothesis to the effect that the planets in our solar system move in a large fluid vortex around the sun. This paraphrase furnishes us with a concrete example of the evaluation of a speculative hypothesis in natural philosophy, in which both observational and nomological considerations are brought to bear in the argument.

---

[1] Report of Robert Hooke's observations of what is now known to be a massive astrophysical vortex, the Great Red Spot in the atmosphere of Jupiter. The report appeared in the first issue of the *Philosophical Transactions*: 'A Spot in one of the Belts of Jupiter', *Philosophical Transactions*, 1, 1665, p. 3.

[2] Locke 1688b. J. R. Milton has recently pointed out that Le Clerc confirms Locke's authorship of the review in his own review of the second edition of the *Principia* in *Bibliothèque ancienne et moderne*, 1, 1714, p. 69. See Milton 2011. For a discussion of the context of writing and of content, see Axtell 1965.

Interestingly, Descartes' cosmology, tied as it was to a cosmogonical theory, was the stimulus for a new genre of cosmogonical writing both on the continent and in England. One such cosmogony, Thomas Burnet's *The Theory of the Earth*, was criticized by Locke in his correspondence. Locke's discussion of Burnet's hypothesis and his own alternative explanation of the deluge combine to provide a second interesting case study of Locke's treatment of hypotheses. But Locke's treatment of Burnet's cosmology and of the later cosmology of William Whiston nicely illustrate that his attitude to speculative hypotheses in natural philosophy was more subtle than *simpliciter* rejection.

A third example of a detailed treatment of a hypothesis is found in the *Essay*. Around the time when Locke was coming to terms with Newton's arguments against the vortex theory, he was also reflecting on a recent mechanical explanation of the cohesion of bodies, found in Jakob Bernoulli's *Dissertatio de Gravitate Aetheris*. His discussion of this hypothesis in the *Essay* provides us with another interesting example of Locke's specific deliberations on a speculative hypothesis in natural philosophy. Let us turn to Locke's treatment of these three hypotheses.

Locke, Newton, and the Cartesian vortex theory

The Cartesian vortex theory

Before turning to Locke's paraphrase of Newton's argument, it will be helpful to have before us a thumbnail sketch of the Cartesian vortex theory. Descartes claimed that all celestial bodies are moved mechanically in an extensive network of fluid vortices.[3] The system he developed was almost purely speculative and, while it was highly elaborate and accounts for almost all of the known celestial phenomena of his day,[4] it was not developed by using any quantitative arguments or experimental results, and it was bequeathed to his followers with a promissory note to the effect that further investigations will fill in the details.

A vortex is a whirlpool-like motion of fluid matter revolving about a central point or axis. Descartes' is not the first such theory, though he was the first to develop it in a sophisticated manner, so as to save the phenomena.[5] The theory is based on Descartes' account of fluid mechanics, a central premise of which is that fluids offer virtually no resistance. According to Descartes, bodies travelling in fluids can move with a circular inertial motion and a rotational inertial motion. Fluid systems contain a few simple forces. For example, there is a centrifugal force which acts on all the particles in the fluid and is a function of their size, density, and distance from the centre of the vortex. Further, the

---

[3] The theory is spelt out in Parts 3 and 4 of his *Principles of Philosophy*, Descartes 1991, pp. 84–311.
[4] Descartes to ?, 1648 or 1649: 'I have not described in my Principles all the motions of each planet, but I have supposed in general all those which observers have remarked upon'; Descartes 1996, Vol. 5, p. 259, cited in Aiton 1972, p. 43.
[5] For earlier discussions of the motion of objects in whirlpools, see Dear 2005.

vortex theory is set within a mechanical philosophy with no action at a distance, no occult powers and no qualities of matter other than shape, size, and motion.

Descartes claimed that, at the creation of the world, matter was an indefinitely large block of undifferentiated extended substance. Once God set this matter in motion, conserving the same quantity of motion in the universe at all times, matter gradually broke up to form objects of the same size. These had a rotational motion and were set in motion around certain centres, which remained the centres of vortices. Gradually the matter broke up into three differently sized elements: extremely small subtle matter, which fills all interstices and congregates at the centre of the vortex to form a star; spherical globules or *boules*, which fill the spaces between all celestial bodies; and a third kind of matter, out of which planets and everyday objects are made. All planets orbit their sun, which is at the centre of their vortex. The vortices are bunched together like an enormous cluster of balloons. However, they cannot touch each other at the poles, lest the matter of one enters the other, should they touch at opposite poles, or lest they hinder each other. Each planet remains in a state of equilibrium, at a fixed distance from the centre of its vortex, and the planets are carried along by the fluid matter and are at rest relative to it. The rotation of the sun causes the fluid matter to rotate in the same direction, and thus all the bodies in the vortex move in the same direction.[6] Furthermore, within our giant vortex are a number of smaller vortices: there is one around Jupiter carrying its moons, and one around the earth carrying its moon.

It is important to appreciate that the Ptolemaic/Aristotelian cosmology as an explanatory and predictive model had all but collapsed by the mid-seventeenth century. It had been undermined by new observational data—such as the appearance of new stars and the irregular surface of the moon—and by its main competitors, the Tychonian and Copernican hypotheses. The latter of these was consolidating its position in cosmology at the expense of its rival because of the simplicity of its account of planetary motions. Yet in the eyes of many the Copernican theory lacked a plausible account of the mechanism by which the celestial bodies moved; it lacked a mechanics.

The rotating celestial spheres of Aristotle had been done away with; but what was to replace them? Until Descartes there was no really satisfactory mechanical account of the motion of the celestial bodies. The vortex theory filled this explanatory gap and was widely adopted in Britain and on the continent. It soon became commonplace for natural philosophers casually to describe or refer to the solar system as 'our vortex'.[7] Locke, for example, in a Journal entry for 1 February 1679, writes: 'Mr Toinard shewd

---

[6] Descartes had a rather elaborate account of the variation of the speed of the planets relative to their distance from the sun. For a detailed discussion, see Schuster 2005.

[7] See Boyle's *A Free Enquiry Into the Vulgarly Receiv'd Notion of Nature; Made in an Essay, Address'd to a Friend*, 1686, *Boyle Works*, Vol. 10, p. 508, and Newton's letter to Thomas Burnet of January 1681 (Newton 1959–77, Vol. 2, p. 311). The theologian Richard Baxter also uses this expression in his *Reasons of the Christian Religion* (Baxter 1667, p. 563). Locke uses the term even as late as 2 July 1695, in a letter to William Molyneux, *Correspondence*, Vol. 5, p. 406.

me a new systeme of our Tourbillion [...]'.[8] Furthermore, given the intuitive and speculative nature of Descartes' theory and the ever-increasing public interest in cosmological phenomena and theories, the vortex theory was soon to capture the interest of the literate public. Various cosmogonies began to appear in mid-century. In England they were developed by Henry More, Thomas Burnet, and William Whiston.[9] At the same time, Descartes' thought was embroiled in theological controversies, and a number of neo-Cartesians saw fit to defend Descartes' theory of the formation of the cosmos as being consistent with the account of creation given in chapters 1–3 of Genesis. Their attempts include works such as Amerpoel's *Cartesius Mosaizans* (1669) in the Netherlands and Cordemoy's *Copie d'une lettre écrite à un sçavant religieux* (1668) in France. Surprisingly, even though the urgency and polemical intensity of these defences of Cartesianism gradually waned, interest and acceptance of the theory continued to increase.

But we should not regard all the enthusiasm for the vortex theory as issuing in a kind of proto-science fiction. For the theory was used by serious natural philosophers in their experimental work. Huygens for example used it to postulate that the earth is an oblate spheroid and to calculate the centrifugal acceleration on the surface of the earth.[10] He was a believer in the vortex theory even after the publication of Newton's critique of it in his *Principia*, in 1687. Indeed his posthumous *Cosmotheoros* (1698, LL 1537) develops a vortex theory and was read by Locke.[11]

Locke's review of the Principia

It is with all this as background that we need to approach Locke's review of the *Principia*. For it contains only one feature that is of any philosophical interest, the rest of the review being little more than a listing of the contents of the work, supplemented by the cosmographical detail that caught Locke's eye. The interesting feature is Locke's paraphrase of Newton's second argument against the vortex theory. In the final Scholium of Book II, section 9, Newton argues that the vortex theory is inconsistent with the Copernican hypothesis combined with the area law of planetary motion (Kepler's second law). Locke's paraphrase sticks quite closely to the text, although it omits one of the quantitative arguments altogether. Let us work through the arguments.

Locke's paraphrase begins thus: 'At the end of this section, the author proves that the planets are not carried by corporeal vortices'. He then gives a summary of the argument:

The reason of this being that, according to the Copernican hypothesis, they have their revolutions as ellipses of which the sun is the focus and they describe their areas proportionally to their times, by the radii which extend to the sun. However, the parts of a vortex cannot move in this manner as we see in the following figure.[12]

---

[8] British Library Add. MS 15642, pp. 8–9.   [9] More 1653; Burnet 1684; Whiston 1696.
[10] For details, see Aiton 1972, pp. 76–85.
[11] See *Elements of Natural Philosophy, Locke Works*, Vol. 3, p. 309.
[12] Locke 1688b, pp. 440–1; all translations of Locke are my own. See Newton 1999, p. 789–90 for Newton's arguments.

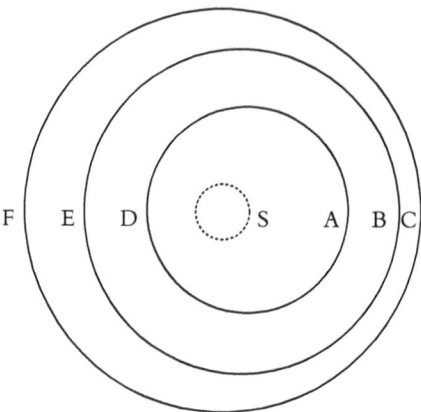

Figure 5.1. Vortex cross-section from Locke 1688b, p. 441

It should be noted that Locke is paraphrasing only the second argument that Newton brings against the vortex theory. The first argument, which immediately precedes the one discussed here, concerns the inability of the vortex theory to account for the 3/2 power rule of planetary motion—that is, for Kepler's third law. Locke reproduces almost exactly Newton's explanation of the diagram:

AD, BE, CF are three orbs described about the sun S: that the exterior CF is concentric to the sun and that the aphelia of the two interior planets are AB and their perihelia are DE. The body which makes its revolution in the orb CF, describing the areas proportionally to the time by the radius reaching to the sun will have a uniform motion.[13]

The aphelion is the point on an elliptical orbit that is furthest from the sun. The perihelion is the point on the orbit that is closest to the sun. The central argument is then introduced:

But the body which makes its tour in the orbit BE moves more slowly in the aphelion B and more quickly in the perihelion D [sic E], conforming to astronomical laws: whereas according to the laws of mechanics, the matter of the vortex which is in the narrower space AC must move more quickly than that which is in DF, where it can stretch more, so that it is necessary that the planet be carried by its vortex with more rapidity when it is more distant from the sun and that it go more slowly when it is closer to it.[14]

The reasoning here appears to be quite compressed when taken out of the context of the *Principia*; so let us work through it step by step. The area law claims that the radius drawn from the focus of the orbit to the planet will sweep out equal areas in equal times. When the planet is furthest from the sun, the radius is longer and therefore the motion of the planet will be slower. When the planet is closer to the sun, the radius is shorter and the planet moves more swiftly.

[13] Locke 1688b, p. 441.   [14] Locke 1688b, pp. 441–2.

VORTICES, THE DELUGE, AND COHESION 95

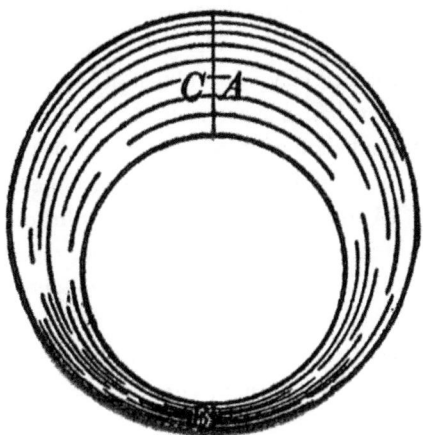

Figure 5.2. Vortex cross-section from Spinoza 1974, p. 77

However, according to the laws of mechanics, the opposite will happen in an elliptically shaped orbit. Newton (and Locke with him) is assuming the following principle of continuity for an incompressible fluid: density x velocity x cross-sectional area equals a constant.[15] Spinoza presents Descartes' theory with great clarity in his *Principles of Descartes' Philosophy*. He says:

If a circular canal, A, B, C, is filled with water or with some other fluid, and at A the canal is four times as broad as at B, when the water (or liquid) at A begins to move toward B, the water at B will move four times as fast as the water at A.

Demonstration
When the water at A moves toward B, the water at C, which is contiguous to A, takes its place (per Prop. 8); then from B an equal quantity must replace that at C. (per eandem). Therefore (per Ax. 14), it will move four times as fast. Q. E. D.[16]

Axiom 14 tells us that,

[i]f the tube A is of equal length with C, but C is twice as large as A, then if some liquid flows through A with double the velocity of that which passes through C, in the same time an equal amount will have passed through each. And if, in an equal time, an equal quantity has passed through each, the velocity through A will be double that of C.[17]

It is crucial here to note that in Fig. 5.2 the sun is in the centre of the outer circle, and therefore closer to CA than to B. Thus in the fluid vortex the perihelia are closer to the sun just because they are further away from the perimeter of the vortex.

---

[15] I thank George Smith for pointing this out to me and for alerting me to Spinoza's demonstration. Of course, Descartes' theory made no such assumption. He posited a constantly increasing force of motion gradient on the basis of changing sizes and speeds of *boules*. See for example Descartes' *Principles of Philosophy* III, §140, Descartes 1991, pp. 168–9 and Schuster 2005.
[16] Spinoza 1974, p. 77.   [17] Ibid., p. 61.

Locke then gives a slightly condensed version of the observational evidence that Newton cites against the vortex theory. The gist of the argument is as follows. The orbit of the earth is between that of Venus and that of Mars. Venus has an orbit that is nearly circular, whereas Mars has an appreciably eliptical orbit, such that the distance between their orbits at the aphelion of Mars compared to the distance between them at the perihelion of Mars is in a ratio of roughly 3:2. Now, at the time when Newton was writing, the aphelion of Mars was in Virgo and the perihelion of Mars was in Pisces (Locke omits this point). If the vortex theory were correct, the earth should speed up in the narrower region at Pisces and slow down in Virgo, and one would expect the apparent motion of the sun to be greater in Virgo than in Pisces. However, the observational evidence shows that the opposite is the case—namely that the apparent motion of the sun is greater in Pisces than in Virgo and therefore the earth moves faster in Virgo than in Pisces.

Locke sums it up by saying: 'The author concludes that the hypothesis of vortices does not serve to explicate the movements of the celestial bodies'.[18] But Newton's arguments here are hardly a knockdown case against the vortex theory, because he is using two incompatible analyses of the earth's motion. According to the first argument, relative to the sun and the outer vortex, the motion of the earth must slow down in its perihelion (contrary to the area law). According to the empirical argument, however, the motion of the earth is analysed relative to the orbits of Venus and Mars, such that the earth must slow down in the aphelion of Mars. But the perihelion of the earth does not coincide with the aphelion of Mars.[19] Furthermore, why should the Cartesian assume that the band of the solar vortex, which carries Mars, is of a similar shape to that of the orbit of Mars? It may be that Mars moves to the outer edge of this band when it is at its aphelion and the inner edge at its perihelion, and that the shape of the band of the vortex which carries Mars has no effect on the motion of the earth.

Now it should be pointed out that, historically, it was Newton's analysis of cometary motion that led to the rejection of the vortex theory—and not the arguments in Book II of the *Principia*. Locke, however, took Newton's word for it and appears to have been convinced that the vortex theory had been shown to be false. What is important here for our investigations into Locke's views on method in natural philosophy is that we have a concrete example of two widely held hypotheses being shown to be incompatible with each other. Crucial to the argument is the observational evidence of the motion of the planets, including the earth, and the role of the area law.

It is clear that Locke did not have the mathematical ability to follow the detail of the arguments of the *Principia*. However, the reasoning at the end of Book II, section 9 is easy enough for him to follow and seemed important enough for him to reproduce. It is a nice example of demonstrative reasoning in natural philosophy, containing as it

---

[18] Locke 1688b, pp. 442–3. For a discussion of the method underlying Newton's arguments against the vortex theory, see Ducheyne 2005, esp. pp. 125–6.

[19] For more criticisms of Newton's argument, see Neményi 1962, pp. 73–4.

does a principle which 'matters of fact justify', the area law, a principle of mechanics, the principle of continuity for fluids, and the obvious 'disagreement' of the Copernico-Kepler hypothesis with the vortex hypothesis. What is important to stress is that the vortex theory was, in Locke's day, a paradigm of speculative natural philosophy gone to seed. Newton's argument against it was therefore not simply a nice example of the sort of effects the correct method had in natural philosophy; it was of enormous worth in its own right—it seemed to have the power to knock out one of natural philosophy's most widespread new pests.

Locke was already somewhat sceptical of the vortex theory by the time he came to review the *Principia*. Note for example his comment to Nicolas Toinard in May 1680. When referring to the very large hailstones in London, he asks whether the French philosophers have any views on the weight at which objects can be suspended in the atmosphere. He then comments: 'I doubt whether the Cartesians can have any contrivances to help in this matter, and whether the Occult Qualities of the Peripatetics may not succumb to such a load'.[20] It is not surprising, therefore, that Newton's attack on the vortex theory is what Locke chooses to focus his interest on in his review of the *Principia*. There is no doubt that Locke was really taken with Newton's rebuttal of Descartes' hypothesis, for in his correspondence with Stillingfleet of the late 1690s, in a passage with a distinctively anti-speculative tone, Locke refers twice to Newton's demolition of the vortex theory, even citing the section from *Principia*, Book II, section 9:

When mathematical men will build systems upon fancy, and not upon demonstration, they are as liable to mistakes as others. And that Des Cartes was not led into his mistakes by mathematical demonstrations, but for want of them, I think has been demonstrated by some of those mathematicians who seem to be meant here [e.g., by] Mr. Newton Phil. Natur. Princip. Mathemat. L 2§9.

Mr. Newton has discarded Des Cartes's vortices, *i.e.* laid down principles from which he proves there is no such thing.[21]

Thomas Burnet's and William Whiston's theories of the deluge

Amongst the plethora of cosmogonies in Cartesian style that emerged in the latter decades of the seventeenth century, two English works proved to be hugely popular. The first was Thomas Burnet's *The Theory of the Earth* (1684, LL 534), which Locke discussed in a letter to James Tyrrell, and then again in *Some Thoughts concerning Education*. The second was William Whiston's *New Theory of the Earth* (1696,

---

[20] *Correspondence*, Vol. 2, p. 176, my translation.
[21] *Second Reply*, pp. 427 and 451. See also p. 390 for an ironical reference to Descartes' vortices.

LL 3142), which Locke briefly discussed in his correspondence with William Molyneux. We will deal with them in turn.

Burnet's cosmogony was first published in Latin, in 1681, under the title *Telluris Theoria Sacra*, and the first two books, which dealt with Noah's flood and the primeval paradisiac state of the world, were translated into English and published in 1684. His account of the formation of the earth is clearly inspired by that of Descartes; even the drawings in the work are reminiscent of those in Descartes' *Principles*.[22] Burnet's theory of the deluge is an account of the formation of the current state of the world which attempts to 'save all the phenomena' of the story of the flood in Genesis. It starts from the basic problem that there is not enough water in the oceans, rivers, and clouds of the present world to cover all the mountains. After dismissing various attempts to account for the Genesis flood—for instance by positing that God created sufficient water *ex nihilo* and subsequently destroyed it, or that the flood was a localized phenomenon—Burnet claims that before the deluge the surface of the earth was 'smooth, regular and uniform; without Mountains, and without a Sea'.[23] He also claims that the earth is egg-shaped (an oblate spheroid) consisting of a yoke-like fiery centre, a membrane around the yoke, a thick shell-like crust, and an abyss between the yoke–membrane and the shell.[24] At the deluge the outer crust collapsed into the abyss. The immediate short-term effect was that the entire crust which humankind inhabited was submerged. In the long term, however, various portions of the crust resurfaced and protruded from the abyss, such that the surface of the earth had something approximating its present form.[25]

This is how the outer crust caved in. First, the antediluvian earth did not wobble on its axis but rotated around a single axis. The effect of this movement was that the equatorial regions of the smooth crust heated up and dried out, while the subterranean waters of the abyss were agitated by the sun's heat. Eventually 'the whole fabrick brake, and the frame of the Earth was torn in pieces, as by an Earthquake; and those great portions or fragments, into which it was divided, fell down into the Abysse'.[26] At first the oceans were far larger than they are today, but they have gradually receded. Furthermore, the earth now wobbles on its axis of rotation, so that there are four seasons.[27] The account, according to Burnet, is consistent with that of Genesis and with all known natural phenomena. Burnet confidently asserts that 'the present form and structure of the earth [...] doth exactly answer to our Theory concerning the form and dissolution of the first Earth, and cannot be explain'd upon any other Hypothesis'.[28]

Locke was soon to disagree. He seems to have procured a copy of the English edition soon after it appeared, while he was in the Netherlands. He wrote to James Tyrrell expressing his appreciation of the style of the work, but also voicing serious reservations as to the plausibility and internal consistency of Burnet's theory. Here is the quotation, *in extenso*.

---

[22] For Burnet's criticisms of Descartes' theory, see Burnet 1681, pp. 181–8 (Book II, ch. 4).
[23] Burnet 1684, p. 51.   [24] Ibid., pp. 64 and 65.   [25] Ibid., pp. 103–4.
[26] Ibid., p. 72.   [27] Ibid., pp. 195–6.   [28] Ibid., p. 109.

The New Theory of the Earth I have read in English, and cannot but like the style and way of writing upon thoughts wholly a man's own; but since you desire my opinion, as to the treatise itself, though it be a good while since I read it, and that but cursorily; yet there sticks with me still some of those objections, which rose in my way as I perused it, and which offered themselves against the truth or probability of his hypothesis, which made me not able then to reconcile it either to philosophy, scripture, or itself. In the first part (as I remember) he makes the globe of the earth round, both by its schemes and hypothesis of its formation; and in the second part oval, without giving (as I remember) any reason for it.[29] He makes the circulation of the water to be drawn up by the sun as now, but all the clouds to go and empty themselves at the poles only. How he makes out the physical reason of this motion, I do not well remember, but this I am sure of, by this means there could be no rivers; for all the water that should fall in those parts he designs for it, must needs in that state he puts the world in (the sun being constantly in the equator,) must needs have fallen frozen, and so remained in mountains of snow. But granting water, though without a sea, where lived the whales[30] mentioned in the creation? But that, which seems to be the principle of his design, to make out [*viz.*] the history of the Flood, is that methinks, which he hath least succeeded in: for when this crust of earth broke, what hindered the broken pieces from sinking down into the abyss, and so being quite lost under water? And if the middle of the world, which lay under the sun, was that, which first failed, how comes it, that we find so much of the torrid zone above water? But if we may judge by the Andes (one of the highest and longest tracts of hills in the world) the crack (if there were any) seems to run the other way: but that which seems most incomprehensible of all is, how the water, that is now in the world, and was in his account no more then, could cover the tops of the highest hills, and remain above them so long a time as Moses mentions; for the flashing of it, upon the falling in of the earth, (which is the cause he assigns) will be found (if considered) impossible to raise them so high, much less to continue them there so long. I imagine, if I should trouble you with my fancies, I could give you an hypothesis would explain the deluge without half the difficulties, which seem to me to cumber this; but though I tell you, that I am not convinced of his doctrine, and have here sent you some of those doubts, which I had in reading of him, which is now almost two years ago; yet I must also assure you, that there are some chapters in him, that I cannot enough value, and the book is to be esteemed were it for those only.[31]

As it happens, Locke did proffer his own hypothesis in order to explain the deluge. It appears in section 192 of *Some Thoughts concerning Education*, and it is worth considering for the further light it sheds on Locke's view of hypotheses.

The context of Locke's deluge hypothesis is as follows. In *Some Thoughts concerning Education*, Locke recommends that the study of the Bible should precede the study of natural philosophy. This is because the very familiarity with material bodies might otherwise lead to the dismissal of spiritual beings, whereas in fact he believes that 'none of the great Phaenomena of Nature' can be fully explained by matter and motion alone:

---

[29] Within the space of a few pages, Burnet shifts from calling the earth spherical to calling it oval: ibid., cf. pp. 61–2 with p. 64. For Burnet's and Newton's discussion of the egg shape of the earth, see their exchange in January 1680/1 in Newton 1959–77, Vol. 2, pp. 327 and 329.
[30] Newton makes a similar objection in his extended discussion of Burnet's hypothesis. See Newton to Thomas Burnet, January 1680/1, in Newton 1959–77, Vol. 2, p. 332.
[31] Locke to James Tyrrell, 14/24 February 1687?, *Correspondence*, Vol. 3, pp. 139–40.

[I]t is evident, that by mere Matter and Motion, none of the great Phænomena of Nature can be resolved, to instance but in that common one of Gravity, which I think impossible to be explained by any natural Operation of Matter, or any other Law of Motion, but the positive Will of a Superiour Being, so ordering it. And therefore since the Deluge cannot be well explained without admitting something out of the ordinary course of Nature, I propose it to be considered whether God's altering the Center of gravity in the Earth for a time (a thing as intelligible as gravity it self, which, perhaps a little variation of Causes unknown to us would produce) will not more easily account for *Noah's* Flood, than any *Hypothesis* yet made use of to solve it. I hear the great Objection to this is, that it would produce but a partial Deluge. But the alteration of the Center of Gravity once allow'd, 'tis no hard matter to conceive that the Divine Power might make the Center of gravity placed at a due distance from the Center of the Earth, move round it in a convenient space of time, whereby the Floud would become Universal, and as I think, answer all the Phænomena of the Deluge as deliver'd by *Moses*, at an easier rate than those many hard Suppositions that are made use of to explain it.[32]

Locke is almost certainly alluding to Burnet's theory here. The reference to 'any other *Hypothesis* yet made use of to solve it' must include Burnet's theory and Locke's attempt to account for a universal rather than 'a partial Deluge' with a hypothesis consistent with the Mosaic account, is clearly sensitive to Burnet's own explanatory agenda. Furthermore, Burnet's own explanation of the cause of the inclination of the earth's axis is that it resulted from a change in the earth's centre of gravity at the time of the deluge.[33] Locke's alternative hypothesis of the cause of the deluge is therefore quite possibly inspired by Burnet's own explanation of the same phenomenon. It does appear to be an ill-considered speculation, thrown in to illustrate a serious point he was making about the appropriate structure of a curriculum for the education of a young man. Locke was stressing the need for biblical studies to precede the study of natural philosophy, not least because not all natural phenomena can be explained merely in terms of matter and motion. Gravity was a case in point; but his example of gravity quickly became a pretext for giving an explanation, not of a phenomenon that requires something over and above matter and motion, but of the deluge as recorded in Genesis.

Locke's hypothesis is also incorrect in so far as he seems to ignore that Newton had shown that the primary cause of the motion of the oceans was the gravitational pull of the moon, exerted as it orbits the earth. It follows that the relevant centre of gravity is determined by the location and density of the parts of the earth–moon system and not by the earth alone. Furthermore, the most natural way for an early modern corpuscularian to conceive of an alteration to the centre of gravity of the earth and of the moving around of the centre of gravity for a 'convenient space of time' is in terms of an increase in the density of matter in various parts of the core of the earth. This would be achieved through the motion of parts. But Locke is using the example of gravity in order to show that some phenomena cannot be explained solely in terms of matter and

[32] *SCTC*, §192, pp. 246–7. [33] Burnet 1684, p. 195.

motion. It may well be that the deluge required the special intervention of God, who had to manipulate the earth's centre of gravity; but the manner in which God achieved this operation could be explained in terms of matter and motion.

Locke concludes this section of *Some Thoughts concerning Education* with a hint that he might give further thought to the explication of the deluge in another place:

> But this is not a place for that Argument which is here only mentioned by the bye, to shew the necessity of having recourse to something beyond bare Matter and its Motion, in the explication of Nature; to which the Notions of Spirits and their Power, as deliver'd in the Bible, where so much is attributed to their Operation, may be a fit Preparative, reserving to a fitter Opportunity, a fuller Explication of this *Hypothesis*, and the Application of it to all the Parts of the Deluge, and any Difficulties can be supposed in the History of the Flood, as recorded in the Scripture.[33a]

And his friends Benjamin Furly and William Molyneux both picked up on this hint. Furly asked Locke '[w]hen shall we see your explication of the hypothesis by you mentiond concerning the Generall deluge',[34] and Molyneux also asked him for his view of William Whiston's *A New Theory of the Earth* (1696).[35] Whiston's *New Theory* is a speculative cosmogony like that of Burnet, though with some differences, the importance of which will become apparent below. Locke replied some five months later and, while he does not refer to his own hypothesis sketched in *Some Thoughts concerning Education*, he does give an opinion regarding the overall value of Whiston's theory:

> You desire to know, what the opinion of the ingenious is, concerning Mr. Whiston's book. I have not heard any one of my acquaintance speak of it, but with great commendation, as I think it deserves. And truly, I think he is more to be admired, that he has lay'd down an hypothesis, whereby he has explain'd so many wonderful, and, before, inexplicable things in the great changes of this globe, than that some of them should not go easily down with some men, when the whole was entirely new to all. He is one of those sort of writers, that I always fancy should be most esteem'd and encourag'd. I am always for the builders who bring some addition to our knowledge, or, at least, some new thing to our thoughts. The finders of faults, the confuters and pullers down, do but only erect a barren and useless triumph upon human ignorance, but advance us nothing in the acquisition of truth. Of all the motto's I ever met with, this, writ over a water-work at Cleve, best pleased me, *Natura omnes fecit judices paucos artifices*.[36]

Locke's comment is extremely interesting in the light of the interpretation of his views on hypotheses elaborated here, for it seems to imply an acceptance and even a commendation of speculative hypotheses. How could Locke, who is so critical of Burnet's hypothesis and so scathing of Descartes' cosmological speculations, wholeheartedly

---

[33a] STCE, p. 147.
[34] Furly to Locke, 21 December 1693, *Correspondence*, Vol. 4, p. 766.
[35] William Molyneux to Locke, 26 September 1696, *Correspondence*, Vol. 5, p. 702. As mentioned above, Locke also read John Woodward's *Natural History of the Earth* (1695).
[36] Locke to William Molyneux, 22 February 1697, *Correspondence*, Vol. 6, p. 6: 'Nature made all men critics but few craftsmen'.

embrace an alternative speculative hypothesis? Is Locke being inconsistent here, or is there more to Locke's comment to Molyneux than meets the eye?

The centrepiece of Whiston's new theory is the claim that a series of momentous events in the history of the earth are best explained by the interaction of the earth with comets: the earth was initially formed from a comet; the deluge was caused by the tail of a comet; and the final conflagration of the earth will result from the collision of a comet into the earth's surface. All of this might look like pure speculation. But on closer analysis it becomes clear that the garb in which Whiston's theory is wrapped is as remote as possible from being the product of speculation. For Whiston's *New Theory* is written in the style of Newton's *Principia*!

Like the *Principia*, it begins with two laws of motion and their corollaries and with a lemma concerning universal gravitation which applies to a corpuscular conception of matter. These three lemmata are followed, in Newtonian form, first by a scholium and then by more lemmata. Corollary 2 of Lemma IX is of direct relevance to Locke's point about gravity in §192 of *Some Thoughts concerning Education*; for there Whiston says:

Coroll. 2. *This universal force of Gravitation being so plainly above, besides, and contrary to the Nature of Matter; on the formention'd Accounts must be the Effect of a Divine Power and Efficacy which governs the whole World, and which is absolutely necessary to its Preservation.*[37]

Thus Whiston's *New Theory* parades as an application of Newtonian theory to the formation of the earth. And Whiston was not some crackpot interloper; he was to succeed Newton in the Lucasian Chair at Cambridge in 1702. Furthermore, his position on the correct method of natural philosophy is entirely consonant with that to which Locke was moving in the late 1690s, as he came to appreciate the power and importance of the Newtonian achievement. After approvingly referring to the *Essay* of 'the best of Metaphysicians, Mr Lock', Whiston goes on to claim:

[T]he knowledge of Causes is deduc'd from their Effects. Thus all Natural Philosophy, *i.e.* the knowledge of the Causes of the several visible *Phænomena* of the World, is solely deriv'd from those Effects, or *Phænomena* themselves, their accurate Correspondence to, and necessary dependance on certain supposed Causes, and their insolubility on any other *Hypotheses*, with the coincidence of the particular Calculations of the Quantities of Motion, Velocity, Periods, and Species of Figures to be every where accounted for. On the Universal Conspiration and Correspondence of which, with the impossibility of producing an instance to the contrary, depends what may be truly stil'd a *Physical Demonstration*.[38]

For his part, it is the natural philosopher who deploys hypotheses in this manner that Locke believes 'should be most esteemed and encouraged'. In fact, just as Whiston cites Newton's physical demonstration about universal gravitation as a prime exemplar of

---

[37] Whiston 1696, Bk 1, p. 6.   [38] Whiston 1696, Bk 2, pp. 128–9.

this natural philosophical method, so does Locke in *Of the Conduct of the Understanding*. Whiston claims:

This last method is that which our best of Philosophers has taken in his Demonstration of the Universal Affection or Property of Bodies, which he calls *Mutual Attraction* or *Gravitation*, and which accordingly he has establish'd beyond possibility of Contradiction.

And he adds a typical anti-speculative flourish:

this is the sole way of bringing natural Knowledge to perfection, and extricating it from the little *Hypotheses*, which in defect of true Science, the World has till lately been forc'd to be contented with.[39]

Compare this claim with Locke's following claim, from circa 1697:

There are fundamental truths that lie at the bottom, the basis upon which a great many others rest, and in which they have their consistency. These are teeming truths, rich in store, with which they furnish the mind, and, like the lights of heaven, are not only beautiful and entertaining in themselves, but give light and evidence to other things, that without them could not be seen or known. Such is that admirable discovery of Mr. Newton, that all bodies gravitate to one another, which may be counted as the basis of natural philosophy; which, of what use it is to the understanding of the great frame of our solar system, he has to the astonishment of the learned world shown; and how much farther it would guide us in other things, if rightly pursued, is not yet known.[40]

Thus, by endorsing Whiston's approach to the deployment of hypotheses, Locke is not being inconsistent with his commitment to the experimental philosophy. Rather he is revealing the extent to which his appreciation of Newton's achievement influenced his views on the nature of natural philosophical method.

Jakob Bernoulli's theory of cohesion[41]

Importantly for our purposes, the arguments against the vortex theory and the discussions of Burnet and Whiston are not isolated examples; for Locke also developed what appears to have been his own argument in mechanics against another theory which appeals to the powers of surrounding fluids. This was the view of Jakob Bernoulli (and others) that cohesion in material bodies could be accounted for by the pressure exerted by an ethereal fluid which envelops all things. But before we examine Locke's critique of Bernoulli's theory it is important that we first clarify Locke's view of the nature of matter.

---

[39] Ibid., p. 129. Whiston may even have in mind Burnet's theory of the earth here. He criticizes it in his *New Theory* (ibid., pp. 104–7). Interestingly, John Harris gave a copy of his *Remarks on Some Late Papers relating to the Universal Deluge* (Harris 1697) to Locke; see LL 1389.
[40] *Conduct*, p. 282.
[41] This section draws heavily on James Hill's excellent article on Locke on cohesion; see Hill 2004.

As we saw in Chapter 2, in Draft B Locke regarded the defining characteristics of matter to be extension and cohesion. It is not just that our *primary ideas* concerning the nature of matter are extension and cohesion, but that extension and cohesion underlie the other qualities of material things such as the sensible ones: 'Extension and Cohæsion of parts, all other qualitys we observe in, or Ideas we receive from body as destinguishd from spirit [...] are probably but the results & modifications of these'.[42] Extension and cohesion are, therefore, conceptually and ontologically prior to all the other qualities that matter might have.

With respect to the views of Locke's contemporaries and to his own views of a later period, the conception of matter in Draft B is significantly underdeveloped. By the time Locke had composed Draft C in 1685, his views had undergone substantial revision. In particular, he had come to see that the mechanical conception of cohesion is deeply problematic. In fact, as Roger Woolhouse has demonstrated, the manuscript of Draft C reveals that Locke's views on the plausibility of one of the standard mechanical theories of cohesion were changing even as the draft—written in the hand of his manservant Sylvester Brounower—was being checked by Locke.[43]

Another development in Draft C is the distinction between extension and expansion. Locke acknowledges in Draft C, at 2. 18. 1, that talk of extended space is potentially confusing, and therefore he determines to restrict the uses of the term 'extension' so as to mean by it 'distance only as to Solid parts of matter'.[44] He carried over this distinction into the *Essay*, even making changes to the fourth edition to reinforce the point.[45] But the decisive change came in the *Essay* itself, where Locke now defined extension in terms of cohesion.

At *E* II. iv. 5, in the chapter on the idea of solidity, Locke introduces his new conception of extension: 'The Extension of Body being nothing, but the cohesion or continuity of solid, separable, movable Parts'. This is a significant conceptual advance for Locke. It entails that there are no extended simples and, in terms of Locke's conception of intelligibility (see Chapter 8 below), it also entails that, if we cannot provide a coherent account of cohesion, there can be no coherent account of extension either. And Locke ends the chapter by warning the reader that he, Locke, will later show how difficult it is to give an explanation of either solidity or motion over and above the simple ideas we have of them. This is of course an allusion to the analysis of cohesion (and thereby extension) and motion in chapter 23, to which we now turn.

---

[42] Draft B, §94, p. 209.   [43] Woolhouse 2005, p. 149.   [44] See also Draft C 2. 18. 11.
[45] Draft C 2. 18. 1 is reworked at *E* II. xv. 1. The last sentence of *E* II. xiii. 26, p. 180, describing the distinction between expansion and extension, was added to the fourth edition. Locke also made a significant alteration to *E* II. xiii. 3 in the fourth edition. In the first three editions he had 'used the Word *Extension* for an Affection of Matter', but in the fourth edition he never called extension an affection of matter. See *E* II. xii. 3, p. 167.

At *E* II. xxiii, extension is again defined in terms of cohesion, and the primary ideas of body are now said to be '*the cohesion of solid, and consequently separable parts, and a power of communicating Motion by impulse*'.[46] It is not a demoting of extension,[47] but a redefinition of the notion in terms of cohesion of the parts. Having stated what the primary ideas of body are, Locke then spends sections 23–9 of chapter 23 demonstrating that these two ideas are inexplicable.

Like many features of material bodies, the phenomenon of cohesion posed serious problems for the mechanical philosophers. Given the very sparse ontology of the primary qualities or affections of matter, shape, size, motion, and texture, it was extremely difficult to account for the cohesion of different bodies, let alone the internal cohesion of the parts of the bodies themselves. The classical atomist solution was to appeal to the property of shape and to develop explanations in terms of hooks and eyes. But many were aware of the vicious regress that loomed when it came to explaining how hooks and eyes cohered with the other parts of minute bodies. One option was to declare that these shapes were irreducibly intensive qualities of the atoms, not subject to further analysis. But, for those who denied atomism and accepted infinite divisibility or for those who did not countenance hooked atoms, the problem remained. A mechanical solution to the problem was offered by Jakob Bernoulli. He argued that cohesion resulted from the pressure exerted by an ethereal fluid which surrounds all bodies. There were experimental precedents for this kind of hypothesis, for example von Guericke's hemispheres. And there was a well-publicized and much repeated experiment on cohesion, which consisted in pulling apart two flat smooth marble blocks.[48]

In the mid-1680s Locke, in keeping with his corpuscular pessimism, turned his mind to the problem of cohesion, and in particular to Bernoulli's theory. This theory is developed in Bernoulli's *Dissertatio de gravitate aetheris* of 1683 (LL 290). Locke discusses it in Draft C of the *Essay* and mentions Bernoulli and his theory in the *Abrégé* of 1688.[49] This material finds its way into chapter 23 of Book II of the *Essay*, though Bernoulli's name drops out. Let us turn to Locke's argument against the theory and examine its parallels with the sort of reasoning found in the argument against the vortex theory.

The theory is discussed at *E* II. xxiii. 23–7. Locke has three arguments against the ether theory of cohesion,[50] and their combined weight serves to reinforce his claim that we do not know the nature of matter, and in particular we do not have a coherent notion of what it is for matter to be extended.

---

[46] *E* II. xxiii. 17, p. 306.
[47] *Pace* Downing (2001, p. 530, n. 42), who says that Locke 'demotes extension, and makes *the cohesion of solid parts* one of the two primary ideas of body (the other being *impulse*)'. But, for Locke of the *Essay*, extension just is the cohesion of solid parts.
[48] Note the similar theory in Boyle's 'The History of Fluidity and Firmness' in his discussion of the polished marble experiment: *Boyle Works*, Vol. 2, pp. 158–61.
[49] Locke 1688a, p. 76.
[50] Locke's arguments are presented in reverse order in the *Abrégé*.

The regress argument

Running the familiar theme of our lack of knowledge of body, Locke claims that we do not know how bodies can be extended because we have no coherent explanation of the cohesion of parts of a body:

> For though the pressure of the Particles of Air, may account for the *cohesion of several parts of Matter*, that are grosser than the Particles of Air, and have Pores less than the Corpuscles of Air; yet the weight, or pressure of the Air, will not explain, nor can be a cause of the coherence of the Particles of Air themselves. And if the pressure of the Æther, or any subtiler Matter than the Air, may unite, and hold fast together the parts of a Particle of Air, as well as other Bodies; yet it cannot make Bonds for it self, and hold together the parts, that make up every the least corpuscle of that *materia subtilis*. So that that Hypothesis, how ingeniously soever explained, by shewing, that the parts of sensible Bodies are held together, by the pressure of other external insensible Bodies, reaches not the parts of the Æther it self; and by how much the more evident it proves, that the parts of other Bodies are held together, by the external pressure of the Æther, and can have no other conceivable cause of their cohesion and union, by so much the more it leaves us in the dark, concerning the cohesion of the parts of the Corpuscles of the Æther it self: which we can neither conceive without parts, they being Bodies, and divisible; nor yet how their parts cohere, they wanting that cause of cohesion, which is given of the cohesion of the parts of all other Bodies.[51]

Locke here points out the regress that will loom if one is to appeal to the pressure of ambient fluids to explain the cohesion of the parts of larger bodies. What is it that holds the particles of air together? If it is the ether, then what holds its particles together? And so on. This kind of regress argument against mechanical explanations of cohesion was common enough. Boyle discusses the regress of hooks and eyes and the regress of the parts of glue in 'Fluidity and Firmness'.[52] Locke uses the regress argument to bring home the point that this cuts to the heart of our conception of extended substance itself. The point is best posed as a dilemma. If extension is defined in terms of cohesion of the parts, then we must conceive of the constituents of the ether as being either composed of extended parts or composed of non-extended parts. But, if the constituents of the ether are extended, they must have cohering parts, which lands us back with the problem of explaining the cohesion of their parts. Whereas, if they are non-extended, then they are not material bodies, because material bodies are necessarily extended. Extended simples are ruled out *ex hypothesi*. Thus there is no need to follow Woolhouse in his claim that Locke's real concern here was with the 'self-coherence' of atomic corpuscles, or to follow Hill's claim that Locke's concern ultimately related to intra-particulate cohesion.[53] For the point applies to Lockean matter unqualifiedly.

---

[51] *E* II. xxiii. 23, p. 308.
[52] In *Certain Physiological Essays, Boyle Works*, Vol. 2, pp. 165 and 163.
[53] Woolhouse 2005, pp. 148–50 and Hill 2004, pp. 623–4. Hill claims that Locke's comment that we cannot account for the cohesion of the bonds, or cement, which binds corpuscles, 'or of the least Particle of Matter that exists' (*E* II. xxii. 26), is decisive evidence that he is concerned with intra-particulate cohesion

The lateral movement argument

Then in section 24 Locke addresses the Bernoullian hypothesis, and note that he calls it an hypothesis, as it applies to the experiment of the polished surfaces:

For, though such a pressure may hinder the avulsion of two polished Superficies, one from another in a Line perpendicular to them, as in the Experiment of two polished Marbles: Yet it can never, in the least, hinder the separation by a Motion, in a Line parallel to those Surfaces.[54]

The reason is that, if one piece of marble is moved laterally, it will encounter no more resistance than it would if it were completely surrounded by the ambient fluid. Indeed, ignoring friction (as Locke does) it is just as easy to move the two pieces of marble together in any direction as it is to move one of the adjoining pieces laterally. The consequence is only too clear:

[I]f there were no other cause of cohesion, all parts of Bodies must be easily separable by such a lateral sliding motion. For if the pressure of the Æther be the adequate cause of cohesion, wherever that cause operates not, there can be no cohesion. And since it cannot operate against such a lateral separation, (as has been shewed,) therefore in every imaginary plain, intersecting any mass of Matter, there could be no more cohesion than of two polished Surfaces, which will always, notwithstanding any imaginable pressure of a Fluid, easily slide one from another.[55]

The upshot is that, wherever there are two or more adjacent particles of matter, there is the possibility of lateral movement. Locke's conclusion is as follows:

[S]ince Body is no farther, nor otherwise extended, than by the union and cohesion of its solid parts, we shall very ill comprehend the *extension* of Body, without understanding wherein consists the union and cohesion of its parts; which seems to me as incomprehensible, as the manner of Thinking, and how it is performed.

It seems from this that Locke believes that extended bodies must have parts, that is, that there are no extended simples. As he puts it, extension is 'nothing but the cohesion of solid parts' (ll. 21–2). Locke concludes that the property of extension, which seems so obvious to us, is in fact as obscure as the nature of thinking substance:

[T]his primary and supposed obvious Quality of Body, will be found, when examined, to be as incomprehensible, as any thing belonging to our Minds, and *a solid extended Substance, as hard to be conceived, as a thinking immaterial one.*[56]

(p. 623). It is not clear from the context, however, that this phrase has to be read in this way. It could be that Locke is referring to the cohesion between the least parts of matter and other corpuscles. Likewise, Locke's comment in the *Abrégé*, cited by Hill (p. 624), that 'if there were no union between parts the body would be entirely destroyed and cease to exist' might refer to the destruction of the composite body rather than to the annihilation of the smallest parts of matter.

[54] *E* II. xxiii. 24, p. 309.   [55] Ibid.   [56] *E* II. xxiii. 26, p. 310.

The bounded universe argument

In section 27 Locke introduces his third argument against the Bernoullian hypothesis. He asks us to consider the pressure exerted by the ether, which is the *explanans* of the phenomenon of cohesion. If the matter of the universe is finite, claims Locke, then 'what conceivable Hoops, what Bond' can one 'imagine to hold this mass of Matter, in so close a pressure together'? A finite universe must have extremes, and there must be something that holds it together and in virtue of which pressure is able to be maintained within the ether. To be sure, one might 'throw himself into the Supposition and Abyss' that there is infinite matter in the universe and that this is infinite in extent; but Locke intimates that, whether or not one could explain cohesion on this supposition, the supposition itself is worse than the problem it is postulated to solve:

[L]et him consider, what light he thereby brings to the *cohesion* of Body; and whether he be ever the nearer making it intelligible, by resolving it into a Supposition, the most absurd and most incomprehensible of all other.[57]

And, of course, while Locke does not mention the point, the regress argument will reappear as soon as one tries to spell out just what sort of 'Wall of Adamant' is to be found at the extremities of the finite universe.[58] Locke draws the sobering conclusion that the simple ideas we receive through sensation and reflection

are the Boundaries of our Thoughts; beyond which, the Mind, whatever efforts it would make, is not able to advance one jot; nor can it make any discoveries, when it would prie into the Nature and hidden Causes of those *Ideas*.[59]

The example of extension shows that what we take to be a clear and distinct idea is, on further reflection, fraught with difficulties. For if extension is the cohesion of parts and we cannot have a clear idea of the nature of cohesion, it follows that we cannot have a clear conception of extension; and yet extension seems to be a necessary constituent of our general idea of material body. In fact, Locke argues elsewhere that solidity is essential to our idea of material body and that bodies cannot be solid without being extended.[60] Therefore solidity, cohesion, and extension stand or fall together. But Locke does not take the problem any further. In particular, he does not explicitly discuss the age-old complication of the possibility of extended simples in the *Essay*— and, it appears, with good reason; for it is fairly clear from his numerous discussions of the notion of the divisibility of matter that he, like Boyle, was uncommitted on the question of whether matter is infinitely divisible or not.[61]

---

[57] *E* II. xxiii. 27, p. 311.   [58] *E* II. xiii. 21, p. 176.   [59] *E* II. xxiii. 29, p. 312.
[60] *E* II. xiii. 11.
[61] See Hill 2005. For Locke's criticisms of John Sergeant's theory of cohesion, see Yolton 1951, pp. 539–41.

Conclusion

Where does this leave us with regard to the question of Locke's views on method in natural philosophy? It is well known that he did not have the mathematical ability to follow Newton's celestial dynamics in depth. He is, however, adept at following Newton's demonstrative reasoning regarding the vortex hypothesis. Indeed, for each hypothesis discussed, whether it be acid and alkali, the vortex theory, the cause of the deluge, or the ether as cause of cohesion, Locke shows how there are internal inconsistencies, inconsistencies with the phenomena, or better alternatives. Throughout his discussions of this range of hypotheses, his views are consistent with a cautious adherence to the experimental philosophy. But Locke's treatment of the problem of cohesion reveals that he was also acutely aware of the existence of deep problems in the conceptual foundations of corpuscular matter theory itself; and the consequence is that such problems, in Locke's view, force us back to the method of natural history.

6

Mathematics

> a natural Philosopher without Mathematicks is a very odd sort of person.
>
> John Arbuthnot[1]

I have argued above that for Locke, given our epistemic limitations, the construction of natural histories is the most appropriate way of acquiring knowledge in natural philosophy. That is, natural philosophy proceeds in the first instance through the accumulation of observations, even though at times it is guided by analogical reasoning and assisted by hypotheses. Natural philosophy as practised consists, then, of Locke's third type of knowledge—sensitive knowledge—combined with probable opinion. We have sensitive knowledge of those observations and experiments that we have made; we have well-confirmed testimony from others regarding their sensitive knowledge; and we have probable generalizations from phenomena. But, unfortunately, natural philosophy does not proceed through the sort of reasoning involved in the acquisition of demonstrative knowledge, the paradigm of which is mathematics. For this reason Locke bemoans the fact that natural philosophy might never be made a science, that is, a form of *scientia*.[2]

Now if this interpretation of Locke's views on method in natural philosophy is correct, it is not immediately clear how he can account for the successful application of mathematics to natural philosophy, and in particular for the success of Newton's *Principia*. It is well known that Locke was familiar with the contents of the *Principia*, even if he did not understand much of the mathematics in it. We have already examined the kernel of the review of the book which appeared in Jean Le Clerc's *Bibliothèque universelle et historique* in 1688 around the time when he was finishing the

---

[1] Arbuthnot 1701, p. 21. For this widely held sentiment, see also Flamsteed's Gresham lecture of 18 June 1684: '[n]or can any one be a good Philosopher (I affirme it positively) except he bee also well versed in Mathematicks & a good Geometrician': Flamsteed 1975, p. 436 and Molyneux 1685, Sig. a2.

[2] *E* IV. xii. 10 and *STCE*, §190, pp. 244–5.

Essay. The significance of the 'never enough to be admired book'[3] was probably dawning on Locke in the late 1680s, when the *Essay* was being prepared for publication, for he famously mentions Newton as one of the Master-Builders in the 'Epistle to the Reader'. But throughout the 1690s, as he prepared new editions of the *Essay* and befriended 'the incomparable Mr. Newton',[4] this awareness clearly intensified. The fact is reflected in subtle changes that Locke made to the second edition of 1694,[5] and it becomes glaringly obvious in the fourth edition of the *Essay*, where he refers to Newton by name twice in the body of the work.[6] Only a handful of other contemporary thinkers are mentioned by name in the body of the *Essay*: Descartes, Pascal, William Molyneux and Lord Herbert of Cherbury.[7] The problem is then to account for the success of the Newtonian achievement in the light of Locke's view that natural philosophy ought to proceed through the construction of Baconian natural histories and that it is not capable of being made a science.

Tackling this problem will take us to the heart of Locke's view of how we can acquire knowledge of nature. But Locke's thoughts on the matter were far from static, and it is most helpful to approach the problem by examining the stages through which his thoughts on the role of mathematics in the acquisition of knowledge of nature developed. Let us begin then with a summary and exposition of Locke's views in Draft A of the *Essay*.

Draft A

In Draft A Locke sets out to investigate the powers of the faculty of the understanding and the extent and certainty of human knowledge. As one might expect, he begins by stressing that knowledge is based on ideas and that all ideas have their origins in sensation or in reflection upon the operations of the mind. His general concern in Draft A is to examine the operations that the understanding performs on ideas in order for the subject to acquire knowledge. This leads him to analyse some of the basic epistemological categories of his day. To this end, he attempts to reveal the origins and epistemic status of *principles* or *maxims* and of *universal propositions* and to expound the nature of *demonstration*. On the question of principles or maxims, he claims that they are not innate; that they are not the basis of demonstrative reasoning in mathematics; and that they are learned through experience, in spite of being true by virtue of the meanings of the words.

---

[3] *E* IV. vii. 3 p. 599, 4th edn.
[4] *STCE*, §194, p. 248.
[5] For example, E_1 IV. xii. 7 speaks of how the mathematicians' 'Art of finding Proofs, and the *Ideas* that demonstratively shew the equality or inequality of unapplicable Quantities, is, I confess, of great help to them', whereas the second and subsequent editions have replaced 'I confess, of great help to them' with 'that which has carried them so far, and produced such wonderful and unexpected discoveries'.
[6] *E* IV. i. 9, p. 530 and IV. vii. 3, p. 599.
[7] References to Descartes are in *E* III. iv. 10, p. 424, and IV. vii. 12, 13, p. 604. For Pascal, see *E* II. x. 9, p. 154; for Molyneux, see *E* II. ix. 8, p. 145; and, for Lord Herbert of Cherbury, see *E* I. iii. 15, p. 77. Richard Hooker (d. 1600) is mentioned at *E* IV. xvii. 7, p. 680. Locke also refers more generally to Hobbists (*E* I. iii. 5, p. 68) and to Cartesians.

As for universal propositions, according to Locke in Draft A, these are of two kinds: there are verbal generalizations about the nature of things, and these are certain and uninstructive, and there are uncertain but instructive generalizations, which do inform us about the nature of things.[8] One of the examples he uses to illustrate this division is a comparison between the Cartesian definition of matter and a definition of matter as extension and impenetrability. He claims that it is easy to use demonstration and to show on the one hand, starting from the Cartesian definition, that a vacuum is impossible, and on the other hand, starting from the rival view, that a vacuum is possible. However,

> neither of these principles or ways of demonstrations prove to us or can prove that Body doth exist or what it is as it exists. but for that we are left only to our sense to discover to us as far as they can.[9]

This distinction between kinds of generalizations looks like what will come to be known later as the division between *a priori*/analytic on the one hand and *a posteriori*/synthetic on the other. Be that as it may; surprisingly, this distinction does not apply to mathematical demonstrations. For Locke claims that the operations which the understanding performs on ideas in mathematical demonstrations are reducible to comparing ideas in point of equality and inequality, and that this normally takes the form of measuring. Such measuring, which is applied either to extension or to number, is the basis of mathematical reasoning, and its certainty arises from the nature of the things themselves, not from true axioms or from the ideas involved in the demonstration. So, 'Mathematicall universall propositions are both true & instructive because as those Ideas are in our mindes soe are the things without us',[10] and therefore we could have certain demonstrative knowledge of the nature of things if we knew their inner natures. On the whole, however, because we lack this knowledge, the natural philosopher's certain knowledge of external objects consists of particular propositions, derived from the senses. This is 'the best ground of science he can have or expect'.[11]

Turning now to the text of Draft A (commencing at §11), we find that there Locke observes that we do not have accurate means of comparing simple ideas of whiteness, heat, and sweetness. The reason is that we do not have 'measures & standards whereby accurately to measure them'.[12] The implication is that, if we had such measures, then we would be able accurately to compare the ideas in question. Locke then claims that there are '2 grande & universal measures of all things extension & number'.[13] He discusses extension first: extension is the comparing of one extension with another by the use of lines or angles which we can measure with extensions that we do not know. The sense involved here is sight (though Locke is aware that we make similar judgments about sound)[14] and, importantly, the knowledge we have from comparing extensions is certain and demonstrative.

---

[8] Draft A, §27, p. 50 and §29, p. 55. [9] Draft A, §27, p. 46.
[10] Draft A, §30, p. 57 and §43, p. 75. [11] Draft A, §27, p. 43.
[12] Draft A, §11, p. 22. [13] Ibid.
[14] Draft A, §12, p. 23. See also Draft B, §45, pp. 153–4.

Locke then goes on to spell out the origins of this certainty. It comes from our constant observation that such-and-such quantities have such-and-such proportions— for example, 'that the 3 angles of a triangle are equall to two right ones', which being found in many triangles, 'passes into an universal acknowledgd truth, & is received as an undoubted axiom'.[15] Here in this early draft Locke seems to lack any conception of a geometrical proof. He clearly thinks that our knowledge of the certainty of geometrical propositions derives ultimately from observation; for he goes on to claim that even 'the more general axioms of geometry', such as the one stating that the whole is greater than its part, derive their certainty from observation: 'the whole of them & all where by they gain such an assent [...] is only by the testimony & assureance of our **senses**'.[16]

Next, Locke turns to the other means of comparing simple ideas, that of number. With numbers, our ideas are clearer, that is, more determinate and precise than ideas about extension, and a consequence of this state of things is that demonstrations about numbers are more evident. Locke illustrates this principle through a comparison between our certainty about different natural numbers and our inability to detect very slight differences of length in extended things.[17] He then claims, on the basis of the relative epistemic status of numerical and extensional demonstrations, that

the certainty of geometricall demonstration or knowledg is founded in & depends on arithmatique or the compareing of numbers & I thinke most of the axioms of geometry when well examind will amount to noe more but this that one & one compard togeather are equall.[18]

Locke then reiterates that both ideas of extension and ideas of number are derived from sense perception and that the certainty of demonstrations using such ideas is based on observation. He sums up his position as follows:

[H]aveing from our senses or sensation got the Ideas of Extension & number & by repeated observations about them atteind certeine knowledg of æquality or inequality of them compard to one another, which always retaine the same proportion when ever we compare them togeather, we collect from hence such propositions which haveing found to be true we call Maximes, & are indeed truths of eternall verity because where ever those numbers or extensions exist they must necessarily have all those propertys which we have demonstrated of them.[19]

It is important to stress here that Locke's overriding concern is to show that both the origins and the certainty of our ideas of number and extension and of our knowledge of geometrical axioms rest on the simple *comparing of numerical and metric proportions*. This thesis is, I believe, absolutely fundamental to Locke's later doctrine of the determination of the agreement or disagreement between ideas and therefore it is central to his

---

[15] Draft A, §11, p. 22. [16] Ibid., p. 23. [17] Draft A, §12, p. 24.
[18] Ibid. It is also important to point out that the relative status of geometry and arithmetic was a contested issue in Locke's day.
[19] Draft A, §12, p. 25. In his early *Essays on the Law of Nature*, written in the early 1660s, Locke had claimed that mathematical principles and axioms are derived from sense. See Locke 1954, pp. 148/149–150/151.

understanding of the nature of demonstration, the syllogistic, and the ideal natural philosophy. It is a thesis that Locke retained through to the end of his life, and it goes a long way to explaining some of the more difficult doctrines of the *Essay* and his long-term interest in metrology. We get some sense of this in Draft A, when Locke takes stock of the first half of the discussion and includes the following two points:

7. That two of these simple Ideas compard togeather have more lesse or equall proportion of that particular Idea in them one then other. which is mathematical demonstration
8. That two things compard togeather in one or more of these particular Ideas doe agree or disagree in them. which is that they are related.[20]

Here the notion of agreement or disagreement is tied to the comparison of proportions—and Locke clearly has metrical and numerical proportions in mind.

Furthermore, Locke claims that this sort of knowledge is not what the Schools define as knowledge of causes—that is, not the sort traditionally thought to be constitutive of natural philosophy.[21] And he goes on to contrast this certain knowledge with our ideas of substances, which are far less certain (§13)—a point he develops at length in Draft B.

Finally, Locke discusses the origin of the ideas of finitude and infinity. He is not concerned with the definition of 'infinity' or with its properties.[22] The origin of the idea of infinity presents a difficulty for Locke because it is not clear how such an idea could have any relation to things in the world. Some had apparently claimed that the idea of infinity is a *positive* one, and, since it is not derived from experience, it must be innate. Locke's strategy for dealing with this proposal in Draft A is to deny both that the idea of infinity is positive and that we have it innately. However, he does not define 'positive idea' until Draft B, to which we will turn in the next section.

For Locke in Draft A, the ideas of finite and infinite have only to do with quantity and nothing else (Draft A, §44). Since they relate to quantity, they are always considered under the notion of extension or number (Draft A, §44). The view of infinity that Locke considers is that of the negation of a limit or end, whether in extension or in duration. Locke doubts that the idea of infinity is as clear and distinct as one might suppose (Draft A, §45), and therefore he thinks it unlikely that it is a positive idea. If infinity derives from local extension, then, since God cannot have local extension, infinity must apply to body; but Locke cannot comprehend the notion of an infinite body.[23] If infinity derives from duration, does it include the notion of succession or not? Locke claims that he does not have a positive idea of infinity: 'such an Idea of Infinite I am sure I have, but this being but the negation of a positive thing [...] is not a positive Idea of Infinitie' (Draft A, §44, p. 81). However, he

---

[20] Draft A, §27, p. 43.   [21] Draft A, §12, p. 26.
[22] As rightly stressed by Dawson 1959.
[23] Draft A, §45, p. 80. The notion of infinitely extended matter remained incomprehensible to Locke. See *E* II. xxiii. 27, p. 311.

concedes that, if there were such a positive idea, it must be 'but a modus of Number or Extension, which Ideas of Number & Extension being taken from the grounds at first proposed viz sense or sensation' (ibid.), and therefore it cannot be an exception to his general claim that all our ideas are derived from sensation and reflection—in other words, it cannot be innate. As we shall see, Locke's views on the idea of infinity were to undergo significant changes in the *Essay* as a result of the doctrine of simple modes; but this is to get ahead of ourselves. Let us turn now to Locke's discussion of mathematical knowledge in Draft B.

Draft B

Locke's second draft of the *Essay* continues and develops the same themes outlined in Draft A. In §26, the faculty of comparing ideas is founded on the ideas of number. Locke regards this fact as the foundation of all mathematical demonstration and certainty, and declares that it pertains to all 'Ideas comprehended under relation'.[24] He tells us that he will discuss it after dealing with simple ideas in general. He then digresses to simple ideas in §§27–40 and returns to the faculty of comparing in §41.

In §41 he moves from knowledge acquired from simple ideas, derived from sensation and reflection, to mathematical knowledge, which he characterizes as the 'exactest knowledg' we have.[25] As he had earlier claimed in Draft A, here too, in Draft B, he asserts that this 'knowledg of mathematicall truths doth not (as I conceive) arise from the Generall axioms where on demonstrations are supposd to be founded'.[26] Locke is of the view that it arises instead from the ideas we acquire through the use of our senses, and that its universal certainty arises from the fact that, wherever those figures or angles really exist, they have the exact properties of our ideas of them:

But the certein knowledg we have of mathematicall veritys [...] depends on & rises from, the certeine destinct knowledg a man hath of the Ideas of his owne minde, & in this case of those Ideas which he hath at present of several extensions compared i e measured one with an other; which knowledg though it be but of those particular Ideas or diagrams which he then hath in his minde yet comes hence to be universall, that <u>when or where soever that line angle or figure &c doth realy exist</u> it must needs have all the propertys it hath in the minde when it is only there, in Idea.[27]

This knowledge, which derives from 'those particular Ideas or diagrams', 'comes hence to be universall' because those lines or geometrical figures that really exist must have all the properties that our ideas of them have in the mind, 'there being noe difference in the propertys of the same angle or figure whether it be drawn upon paper, carvd in marble, or only phansyd in my understanding'.[28]

---

[24] Draft B, §26, p. 137. [25] Draft B, §41, p. 149. [26] Draft B, §44, p. 151.
[27] Ibid., p. 152, underlining added. [28] Ibid.

Interestingly, Locke goes on in this section to elaborate on the claim about the nature of demonstration that he had made in Draft A. Concerning 'that great certainty which we call Demonstration' he says: 'We usualy appeale to our eyes & looke for noe greater certainty then what our eyes can afford us', and we come to know mathematical truths 'not by proofe but intuition', for proof really rests on observation and not the use of arguments.[29] As in Draft A, Locke seems here to lack a grasp of the nature and power of geometrical proofs, of the kind found in Euclidean geometry. Furthermore, he seems to take 'demonstration' in a sense closely related to etymology, which goes back to the Latin verb *monstrare* : 'to show' or 'point to' rather than 'to prove' (Draft A, §11, p. 22, §27, p. 50).

Furthermore, as in Draft A, Locke goes on to claim that it is likely that our geometrical reasoning is reducible to or founded upon numerical reasoning (Draft B, §48). The reason is that our ideas of number are clearer than those of extension, in other words our ideas of extension as derived from sense are less determinate: 'demonstrations about numbers are more evident & exact then in Extension because the Ideas of number are more determinate precise & destinguishable then in extension'.[30] This claim only serves to reinforce the suspicion that Locke is not working with an understanding of a geometrical proof, but rather sees the origin of arithmetic and geometry in ideas derived from sense perception.

Perhaps the most important development in the discussion of mathematics and geometry in Draft B is Locke's claim that, in spite of the importance of the comparison between numerical quantities and extensions, we have no standard by which to determine relative extensions. This is the subject of sections 41 and 42, where Locke elaborates on the following claim:

[A] man can never be sure that the foot rule he makes use of is exactly the same length with that of an other. & also because those things too, which are to be measurd by them are materiall also & soe cannot be brought punctualy to the standard, nor can our senses ever assure us that any two materiall things are perfectly of the same length.[31]

This was to become an overriding concern for Locke and he soon embarked on a long quest to develop his own metrical standards and to determine the relative metrical standards of other countries. In short, it is the wellspring of Locke's preoccupation with metrology. And this concern was not restricted to extension but also included duration. In fact, the question of the measure of time determines not only the logic of his chapter on duration in the *Essay*, but also his active interests in time-keeping and calendar reform.

Turning next to the idea of infinity, we find that Draft B has more to say on positive ideas than Draft A. The notion is introduced in §43, in the group of sections on mathematical reasoning and measuring (§§42–52). There Locke claims that the ideas we use for standards of measure are neither precise nor determinate, neither clear nor

---

[29] Draft B, §44, p. 153. [30] Draft B, §48, p. 155. [31] Draft B, §42, p. 150.

certain, and therefore they are not positive ideas. The notion of positive ideas is further elaborated upon in §58 (which, incidentally, is the basis of the discussion in *E* II. vii. 1–3) and in §97, and then resurfaces in the extended discussion of infinity, §§123–30. The discussion in §58 is important, for Locke there claims that simple ideas can be positive ideas even if the cause of the idea is a privation:

> Thus the Ideas of cold. heat light & darknesse, black & white, motion & rest are equaly cleare & positive Ideas in the minde, though perhaps some of the causes which produce these Ideas in our mindes are barely privations in those subjects.[32]

The point is that the existence of an objective positive cause does not determine whether an idea is positive, but rather whether it is clear and distinct. He had already denied (§43) that our ideas of 'inch' or 'yard' are clear or distinct, and he goes on to make the same claim about our idea of infinity.

The discussion of infinity (§§123–30) is set within a very long treatment of time and duration, which commences at §102. Our interest is in the developments which have occurred in Locke's view of the origin and nature of the idea of infinity. The significant development in Draft B is this: Locke now ignores the view that the idea of infinity is simply the negation of a limit or end and postulates that it derives from the active power of the mind to add the same idea together without ceasing. As in Draft A, the domains over which the notion of infinity applies are extension or duration, both of which can be reduced to number.[33] But, importantly, Locke now claims that, once we have a determinate measure of extension or duration, it is a simple function of the mind to add indefinitely equal quantities of that measure to itself and that this is how the idea of infinity arises.

> [I]n extension or duration haveing the Idea of any certain length litle or great the minde can repeate & multiply these Ideas as often as it pleases & adde them to any number before & this barely by the power it hath of recalling & bringing in view any of its owne Ideas as frequently as it will, & hence it comes to passe that we have the notions of endlesse space, duration and number.[34]

Locke does not believe that infinity is itself an actual number, and this counts against its being a positive idea: 'noe body I thinke haveing the Idea of an actuall infinite number, & soe the infinitie thereof can not be considerd by us as a thing whereof we have a positive Idea'.[35] Another consideration that counts against infinity being a positive idea is that it does not seem possible, according to Locke, to add infinities:

> if I could have an actuall positive Idea of an infinite length I could repeat it in my minde & adde these two infinities togeather nay I could adde as many of them togeather as I could of days or years, yards or miles, which are lengths of which I have actuall positive Ideas, & soe make one Infinite Infinitely biger then an other, which is an absurdity soe grosse that noebody can admit.[36]

---

[32] Draft B, §58, p. 161.
[33] Draft B, §126, p. 250.
[34] Draft B, §124, p. 248.
[35] Draft B, §123, p. 247.
[36] Draft B, §125, p. 249.

Cantor's paradise does indeed seem a long way off!

Locke has much more to say about the idea of infinity in Draft B. He discusses the idea of eternity, which is the number series extending infinitely from both ends; he discusses the limited range of ideas to which the idea of infinity is applicable; and he discusses the relation between the idea of infinity and the idea of God. But it is time to turn to his mature views on the nature of mathematical knowledge and to the idea of infinity as expressed in the *Essay*.

Essay

When we turn to the *Essay* we find that Locke's views on the nature of mathematical knowledge and on infinity have changed significantly from the early drafts. The material from the drafts on generalizations, mathematics, and infinity has been redistributed and new polemical agendas and doctrines are in play. Some of the material on these subjects from the early drafts has been taken over and reworked, but there is also a substantial body of new material. The key development in the *Essay* is the introduction of the doctrines of modes and essences.

It must be said at the outset that Locke's views on mathematical knowledge in the *Essay* have proven to be enormously difficult to interpret in a consistent way. In all honesty, I am not confident that a fully consistent interpretation of Locke's view is possible. Different scholars have located the problems for Locke's view in different places and we will have cause to discuss some of these as we proceed. In the remaining sections of this chapter I will reconstruct what I take to be a relatively consistent view of mathematical knowledge using the conceptual resources that Locke provides us with in the *Essay*. I will then raise several objections to this reconstruction on the basis of unambiguous passages from the *Essay* itself. These objections will provide grounds for suggesting diagnoses of several points at which I believe Locke's view of mathematical knowledge is not fully consistent. They will also, it is hoped, shed light on the points of emphasis that other interpreters have highlighted in their attempts to find just where the tension lies in Locke's account. Let us begin with the doctrine of modes.

Modes

Locke tells us that modes are a species of complex idea. It is easy to overlook this fact in the light of his distinction between simple and mixed modes. Indeed it is natural to correlate simple modes with simple ideas, but initially this must be resisted, for simple modes are a species of complex idea.[37] (We will have cause to qualify this statement below.) Locke defines modes as those complex ideas that 'contain not in them the supposition of subsisting by themselves, but are considered as Dependencies on, or

---

[37] This is rightly stressed in Carson 2005.

Affections of Substances' (*E* II. xii. 4, p. 165). His first examples of modes are not particularly helpful in bringing out the nature of these ideas. He lists triangle, gratitude, and murder (ibid.), and, when one combines them with Locke's notion that these ideas do not contain in themselves the 'supposition of subsisting by themselves', one is inclined to think of the ideas themselves as not supposing anything existing in the external world as their cause. However, it soon becomes clear that this does not capture the full semantic range of Locke's use of the term 'mode'.

The notion of modes or moods originates with Francisco Suárez (1548–1617). For Suárez, modes modify other entities. Both substances and accidents can be modified by modes. Thus modes do not subsist by themselves but are ontologically dependent on that which they modify. It is apparently this Suaresian doctrine, or some version of it, that Locke has in mind. The key clause in his definition of 'mode' is that modes are 'Dependencies on, or Affections of Substances'. This is the Suaresian view of modes. Boyle for example speaks of the primary modes of matter as being shape, size, and motion.[38] That Locke is partial to this Suaresian ontological category is evident as early as the period of redaction of Draft B, where he speaks of modes and substances as two categories and, in Cartesian style, alludes to modes of thinking.[39] This attitude is also clear early on in his discussion of modes in the *Essay*. When speaking of space, he tells us that '[e]ach different distance is a different modification of Space' (*E* II. xiii. 4, p. 167). Likewise, each different figure is a distinct mode of space, whether it is instantiated in space or not (*E* II. xiii. 6). Again, just as Descartes regards the modes of thinking substance to be understanding, imagination, memory, volition, and so on, so Locke considers the modes of thinking to be perception, recollection, and dreaming (*E* II. xix). We also find Locke speaking of the modes of motion, which itself is a paradigmatic mode in the Cartesian and Boylean ontology:

To *slide, roll, tumble, walk, creep, run, dance, leap, skip*, and abundance of others, that might be named, are Words, which are no sooner heard, but every one, who understands English, has presently in his Mind distinct *Ideas*, which are all but the different modifications of Motion. *Modes of motion* answer those of Extension.[40]

This implies that Locke was more comfortable with the Suaresian distinction between substantial and accidental modes than Descartes and Boyle were. But it is best not to put too fine a point on Locke's intellectual debts here. He seems to have found the category useful and to have plied it to his own purposes.[41]

This becomes clear when we consider that Locke's use of modal terminology is somewhat idiosyncratic. Indeed he confesses as much to the reader: 'if in this I use the

---

[38] Boyle, 'History of Particular Qualities', in *Tracts Written by the Honourable Robert Boyle About the Cosmicall Qualities of Things, Boyle Works*, Vol. 6, p. 267.
[39] Draft B, §§97 and 95, pp. 217 and 215 respectively.
[40] *E* II. xviii. 2, p. 224. See also *E* II. xxvii. 2, 3.
[41] The category of modes comes up in Locke's discussion with Stillingfleet on the nature of substance. See *Locke Works*, Vol. 4, pp. 8, 13, 445.

word *Mode*, in somewhat a different sence from its ordinary signification, I beg pardon' (*E* II. xii. 4, p. 165). Now it is helpful here to distinguish between the genealogy of Locke's term 'mode' and his deployment of the same term within his theory of ideas. In the first instance, when Locke speaks of modes he is referring to the way objects and properties in the external world are modified. Thus, when he occasionally speaks of the ideas of modes, he is referring to ideas of these modifications, that is, to ideas of the shapes of objects or of space and to modifications of motion such as swift or slow. For Locke, '[e]ach different distance is a different Modification of Space, and *each* Idea *of any different distance, or Space, is a simple Mode of this* Idea' (*E* II. xiii. 4, p. 167). In other words, we have the idea of space and we have the idea of the mode of space that is a determinate distance. So the idea is a modal idea insofar as it is an idea of a mode of space. It is not a modal idea in virtue of being a modification of an idea.

But Locke's deployment of the term in his theory of ideas tends to obscure the metaphysical context in which the term arose and from which it was borrowed. For when he speaks of simple modes he is referring to a kind of *idea*, and not to the modes of substances or attributes of bodies. Worse still, when he speaks of 'Modifications of the same Idea' he is speaking of modifying ideas in a way analogous to the manner in which modes modify substances or attributes. This is particularly common in his discussion of the modes of space and of the modes of number, where the relevant modes are the result of the operation of the understanding on a complex idea. The key point in each of these cases is that many of the modifications of the complex ideas of space and number (for example shapes, distances, and infinity) have no shape, distance, or aggregate corresponding to them in the actual world. Thus Locke's usage of modal terminology in the theory of ideas effectively swamps the metaphysical usage from which the term's meanings originated.

How is all this relevant to our quest to understand Locke's views on the nature of mathematical knowledge and on its role in natural philosophy? The answer is not hard to find. It is this compositional power of the mind, whereby it modifies ideas to create new simple modes, modes that go far beyond anything instantiated in the actual world, that is the salient doctrine for understanding Locke's views on the nature of mathematical knowledge. In order to see why this is so, we need to examine how the doctrine of modes intersects with the doctrines of essences, archetypes, real knowledge, and universal propositions. We start with the latter.

Universal propositions

All knowledge is either mental or verbal. Locke expresses a preference for what he calls mental propositions: the judging of ideas is the 'best and surest way to clear and distinct Knowledge' (*E* IV. vi. 1, p. 579), and he normally defines 'knowledge' in terms of agreement or disagreement between ideas. But he acknowledges that, as soon as propositions are formed from ideas, the verbal form takes over (*E* IV. v. 2–3). Once we begin to form verbal propositions, our knowledge can be expressed in either particular or general truths (*E* IV. vi. 2). General truths are much sought after and are 'very *seldom apprehended, but as conceived and expressed in Words*' (ibid., p. 579). Therefore it is important that we understand the truth and certainty of general truths, as expressed in universal propositions. We cannot be certain of the truth of any general proposition unless we know the real essence (to be discussed below) of the species terms in the proposition (*E* IV. vi. 4). In the case of general propositions that refer to substances, we cannot be certain that they are true. Locke devotes most of Book IV, chapter 6, to showing why this is so. We do not have epistemic access to the underlying real essence of substances, and therefore we cannot know whether our nominal essence of any particular substance is the same as the real essence of that substance.

So much, then, for general propositions concerning substances; what about mathematical propositions? In chapter 8 of Book IV Locke draws a distinction between certain and uninstructive propositions, what in the *Essay* he calls trifling propositions, and certain and instructive propositions. The example he gives of the latter is a mathematical one, namely that '*the external Angle of all Triangles, is bigger than either of the opposite internal Angles*' (*E* IV. viii. 8, p. 614). He concludes that 'this is a real truth, and conveys with it instructive *real Knowledge*' (ibid.). This conclusion, derived from a contrast between trifling and instructive propositions, is similar to what he had claimed two decades earlier in Draft A: 'Mathematicall universall propositions are both true & instructive'[42]—except that here in the *Essay* he also claims that mathematical general propositions convey '*real Knowledge*'. Real knowledge is an important species of knowledge for Locke, the nature of which he has spelt out four chapters earlier.

Real knowledge

In Book IV, Locke claims that knowledge is real 'only so far as there is a conformity between our *Ideas* and the reality of Things' (*E* IV. iv. 3, p. 563). To be sure, he admits that it is no easy matter to find a criterion for establishing which ideas conform to reality; however, he is certain that two types of ideas satisfy this requirement. The first type is that of simple ideas of sensation or reflection (*E* IV. iv. 4). The second is that of mathematical truths:

I doubt not but it will be easily granted, that the *Knowledge* we may have *of Mathematical Truths, is* not only certain, but *real Knowledge*.[43]

Hence mathematical knowledge is real knowledge. It is real knowledge because the mathematician 'is sure what he knows concerning those Figures, when they have barely *an Ideal Existence* in his Mind, will hold true of them also, when they have a real existence in Matter' (*E* IV. iv. 6, p. 565, underlining added). Thus, in the *Essay*, Locke appears to give the same reason for the certainty of the propositions of mathematics that

---

[42] Draft A, §30, p. 57. See also §43, p. 75. [43] *E* IV. iv. 6, p. 565.

he gave two decades earlier in Drafts A and B, where he claimed that mathematical propositions are true 'because as those Ideas are in our mindes soe are the things without us'.[44]

Real ideas and true ideas

If real knowledge is that wherein there is a conformity between the reality of things and our ideas of them, it is not surprising to find that real ideas are those that 'all agree to the reality of things' (*E* II. xxx. 2, p. 372). Locke devotes a chapter to real ideas in Book II. The doctrine of real knowledge, as developed in Book IV, is, then, an extension of this notion of real ideas. Of course, simple ideas are real because they always conform to the reality of things. However, Locke's notion of conformity is intentionally spelt out with some degree of imprecision. For he goes on to claim that those simple ideas are real that are constantly caused by the same thing in nature, whether they resemble their cause or are merely the 'constant Effects' of some externally existing cause (*E* II. xxx, 2, p. 373). This allows for the reality of simple ideas of secondary qualities, which Locke claims do not resemble anything in the body that causes them. By contrast, our ideas of substances are not real because they do not conform to the reality of things and in this respect they may even be the opposite of real, namely fantastical (*E* II. xxx. 5). Our complex ideas of substances are real only in so far as their constituent simple ideas conform to actually co-instantiated properties of substances. As for complex ideas, mixed modes (and one assumes simple modes) and relations are real in so far as 'there be a possibility of existing conformable to them' (*E* II. xxx. 4, p. 373).

Two chapters later, Locke introduces the notion of true ideas (*E* II. xxxii). Naturally, true ideas are opposed to false ideas. At first it is not easy to see just how true ideas differ from real ones, for true ideas end up being those ideas that have a conformity to a thing 'extraneous to them' (*E* II. xxxii. 4, p. 385). Simple ideas are true and our ideas of substances are false. The difference between real ideas and true ideas seems to lie in their opposites and in their relation to the ideas of other people. The opposite of a real idea is a fantastical idea, an idea composed by the imagination. The opposite of a true idea is a false idea, and falsehood can be relative to the ideas of others or to the nature of things in the external world. Descartes' idea of matter is different from Locke's, and therefore is false relative to Locke's idea. Fundamental to both types of idea, however, is the notion of conformity to real existents.

Real essences

The next important notion in Locke's theory is that of real essence. The essence of something is 'the very being of any thing, whereby it is, what it is' (*E* III. iii. 15, p. 417).

---

[44] Draft A, §30, p. 57.

For substances, the real essence is the inner corpuscular structure of the particular substance, be it gold or an oak tree. As Locke puts it at *E* II. xxxi. 6 (p. 379), the 'real Essence, or internal Constitution, on which these Qualities depend, can be nothing but the Figure, Size, and Connexion of its solid Parts'. Real essences are contrasted with nominal essences, which are general or abstract ideas—of, say, gold—that are formed by the mind. In the case of each simple idea, Locke tells us in a number of places that its real and nominal essences are (in a sense yet to be determined) the same. In the case of substances, however, the real and nominal essences are different. It may be that none of our abstract ideas of substances, in other words none of their nominal essences, is the same as the real essence of those substances, even though each of the constituent ideas of the nominal essence is a real idea and a true idea. This fundamental mismatch between our nominal essences of substances and their corresponding real essences is the reason why our ideas of substances, our nominal essences, are neither real nor true.

Archetypes

'Archetype' is another term which is common in Locke's discussion of modes and mathematics. While he uses the term forty-one times in the body of the *Essay*, Locke never defines it, and it is left to the reader to determine its precise signification.[45] Archetypes are of two kinds. There are '*Archetypes* made by Nature' in the world and there are archetypes made by the mind.[46] As for the former, Locke claims that there is a mismatch between our ideas of substances and these archetypes and therefore our knowledge of them is not real:

[t]here is another sort of *complex Ideas*, which being referred to *Archetypes* without us, may differ from them, and so our Knowledge about them, may come short of being real.[47]

But how do archetypes of nature differ from substances? While Locke is nowhere explicit about this, I suggest that he has in mind what, in the biological sciences, are called type-specimens. In Book III, chapter 3, Locke is adamantly of the view that there are no universals, and it is hard to see how archetypes could be identical to individual members of a species. It seems therefore that archetypes in nature are those token members of the species that are taken to be standards or patterns of the species in general.

Locke's primary concern in his doctrine of archetypes, however, is with archetypes in the mind, and most of his uses of the term refer to these rather than to archetypes in nature. Locke's main point about archetypes in the mind is that they are identical to mixed modes. At *E* II. xxx. 4 (p. 373) he tells us, concerning mixed modes, that '[t]hese *Ideas*, being themselves Archetypes, [unlike ideas of substances] cannot differ from their

---

[45] In fact, most of Locke's uses of the term are found in chapters 30 and 31 of Book II, on real, true and adequate ideas; in chapter 6 of Book III, where Locke is discussing species; and then in chapter 4 of Book IV.
[46] *E* III. vi. 51, p. 470 and II. xxxi. 3, p. 376.   [47] *E* IV. iv. 11, p. 568.

Archetypes'; and this is the ground upon which mixed modes are real ideas.[48] He reiterates the point in Book IV:

All our complex Ideas, *except those of Substances*, being *Archetypes* of the Mind's own making, not intended to be the Copies of any thing, nor referred to the existence of any thing, as to their Originals, *cannot want* [i.e. lack] *any conformity necessary to real Knowledge.*[49]

It is my view that Locke's archetypes in the mind are explanatorily redundant and that his theory of modal ideas could have been expressed more clearly without them. To be sure, they do provide some symmetry in the development of the theory: just as modes can be real essences which parallel real essences of substances in the world (as we shall see below), so Locke posits idea archetypes which are analogous to real world archetypes. However, in my own view, there is no role for archetypes of modal ideas beyond this feature of symmetry. I hope that the reasons for this conclusion will become clear in the following discussion.

The real essences of modes: An interpretation

We now come to the crucial issue in Locke's theory of ideas and in his account of mathematical knowledge. What is the status of those ideas which he calls mixed modes and simple modes, and, in particular, what are the real essences of mixed and simple modes? We have seen that ideas are real when they conform to the reality of things; that 'verbal' knowledge is real when our ideas (as referents of the constituents of propositions) conform to the reality of things; and that the real essences of substances are their inner corpuscular structure. In fact, Locke even invested the traditional scholastic term 'real quality' with a similar meaning, claiming that the primary qualities of things 'may be called *real Qualities*, because they really exist in those Bodies' (*E* II. viii. 17, pp. 137–8). We have also seen that in the early drafts Locke claimed that the certainty of mathematical knowledge arises from the way things are in the world. Might it not be that the real essences of modes are also things extraneous to the mind, to which our modal ideas conform? This would be consistent with the import of Locke's qualifier 'real' in 'real essence', in 'real idea', and in 'real knowledge'; and it would be consistent with the view of mathematical knowledge expressed in the early drafts.

There is textual support for this interpretation in the *Essay*. For example, at *E* IV. vi. 4 (p. 580), Locke says that in both simple ideas and modes

the real and nominal Essence being the same; or which is all one, the abstract *Idea*, which the general Term stands for, being the sole Essence and Boundary, that is or can be supposed, of the *Species*, there can be no doubt, how far the *Species* extends, or what Things are comprehended

---

[48] See also *E* II. xxxi. 14, pp. 383–4, which is discussed below.   [49] *E* IV. iv. 5, p. 564.

under each Term: which, 'tis evident, are all, that have an exact conformity with the *Idea* it stands for, and no other.

Locke's talk of things having 'an exact conformity with' ideas is unambiguously referring to the relation between things in the world and our abstract ideas of them. Therefore, when he claims that in the case of simple modes, such as figure and number, the nominal essence is the same as the real essence, he appears to be claiming that our complex idea of triangle is composed of exactly those properties which triangles in the world possess. The real essences of mathematical ideas are in space and exist independently of the mind. Thus it seems natural to take Locke to believe that, when we have the idea of a triangle and that triangle actually exists, the real and the nominal essence are the same. All of this is in the spirit of Locke's long-standing view, expressed in the early drafts of the *Essay*, that the certainty of mathematics derives from the way the world is.

If this is correct, then Locke's view developed from the early drafts, wherein the certainty of mathematical and moral knowledge derives from the conformity of our ideas with the way things are, to the mature view of the *Essay*, where the certainty of mathematics, and even of morality, is based on the congruity of the real and nominal essences of simple and mixed modes. Thus Locke can draw an analogy between the simple modes of mathematics and the mixed modes of morality, which are voluntarily constructed by the mind:

> Upon this ground it is, that I am bold to think, that *Morality is capable of Demonstration*, as well as Mathematicks: Since the precise real Essence of the Things moral Words stand for, may be perfectly known; and so the Congruity, or Incongruity of the Things themselves, be certainly discovered, in which consists perfect Knowledge.[50]

Here the 'Things moral Words stand for' are mixed modes. The real essence of mixed modes in the actual world can be perfectly known, and the congruity (or lack thereof) between 'the Things themselves' and the mixed modes can be discovered with certainty. And Locke goes on to stress that this is the case even when moral propositions include species terms that connote substances whose real essences are unknown. It is clear, then, on this interpretation that, while Locke has very little to say about the real essences of modes, they, like all other real essences, are in the world and not in the mind.[51]

The advantages of this interpretation are, first, that it is consistent with early drafts of the *Essay*; second, that it gives a neat explanation of the manner in which we can have certain and yet instructive knowledge in mathematics and morality; third, that it is consistent with Locke's claim about the knowledge of angels—their nominal essences

---

[50] *E* III. xi. 16, p. 516.
[51] Here I disagree with the interpretation of Cicovacki (1990, p. 522), who makes rather heavy weather of his claim that 'the real essence of mixed modes [and one assumes simple modes] is not ontologically different from their nominal essence'.

of substances are the same as real essences of substances and they can predict what properties substances have. In Book III he puts it this way:

> Spirits of a higher rank than those immersed in Flesh, may have as clear *Ideas* of the radical Constitution of Substances, as we have of a Triangle, and so perceive how all their Properties and Operations flow from thence.[52]

An exegetical excursus

There is, however, a serious exegetical problem facing this interpretation. Before we examine this problem, I would like to make a brief excursus using some of the fruits of philosophy that post-dates Locke. I would like to bring the notion of a truthmaker and the distinction between strict identity and equivalence to bear on Locke's theory of ideas and on his account of mathematical knowledge. These analytical tools can set us up to understand how we should best address the problematic feature of Locke's account of mathematical knowledge.

Let us begin by analysing the question of Locke's account of the certainty of mathematical knowledge in terms of the modern notion of a truthmaker. A truthmaker 'is just some existent, some portion of reality' in virtue of which a proposition is true.[53] The notion of a truthmaker is very old. It has been traced at least as far back as Aristotle. I suggest that it is found in Locke's Draft A, when he says that 'the measure & foundation of truth & error in these [our knowledge of things existing] is the real existing of the thing thus or thus'.[54] We have also seen how, for Locke, true ideas are true and real ideas are real in virtue of things in the world that make them true and real—though he is using 'true' in a peculiarly early modern sense when he makes these claims.[55]

Throughout the early drafts of the *Essay* Locke is committed to the view that the propositions of geometry and arithmetic are true in virtue of the way things are in the world. As he puts it in §12 of Draft A,

> [a]nd this is the knowledge we have of the truth or falshood of propositions wherein magnitudes or numbers are predicated one of another which can be noe otherwise but as biger or lesse or equall. & also of all other things that are measureable by number or extension, as motion, time weight &c, & of the certainty of this knowledge we are well enough assured. the ground whereof is the cleare knowledge of our owne Ideas, & the certainty that quantity & number existing have the same propertys & relations that their Ideas have one to another.[56]

It is clear from this claim that Locke believed that the truths of mathematics arise from properties of things in the world. Which properties does Locke have in mind? In the

---

[52] *E* III. xi. 23, p. 520. See also *E* III. vi. 3, IV. iii. 6 and IV. xvii. 14.
[53] Armstrong 2004, p. 5.
[54] Draft A, §25, p. 40.
[55] See for example Antoine Arnauld's *On True and False Ideas* (Arnauld 1990).
[56] Draft A, §12, p. 26.

Essay he claims that number is a primary quality of bodies (*E* II. viii. 23). This is the property of unity, and it is the most ubiquitous property there is: 'the most universal *Idea* we have' (*E* II. xvi. 1, p. 205). This primary quality is the truthmaker for the proposition <the number one exists>.

The mind can perform an additive function on the idea of unity, and so it can modify the idea by creating simple modes of the simple idea of one:

By repeating this *Idea* in our Minds, and adding the Repetitions together, we come by the *complex* Ideas *of the Modes of it.*[57]

Locke considers only the natural numbers (excluding zero), the rational numbers (*E* II. xvii. 12, 18), and infinity. Next, let us consider how Locke would give an account of the truthmakers of other existential truths concerning the natural numbers, truths such as <the number four exists>. If everything instantiates the property of unity or 'one', then mereological wholes will instantiate the natural numbers larger than one. Thus the real essence of the idea of unity (or 'one') is the primary quality *unity*, and the real essences of natural numbers larger than one are the combined primary qualities of unity in each part of the mereological whole.

What, then, of numbers that are not instantiated in the real world? Here Locke is silent, but from comments he makes concerning mixed modes it is likely that he would have approved of a possibilist account of uninstantiated natural numbers. Recall that, when stipulating the criterion for the reality of mixed modes, Locke claimed that they are real as long as 'there be a possibility of existing conformable to them' (*E* II. xxx. 4, p. 373). There is no problem about the mind conceiving of them, but there appears to be a problem when it comes to specifying the nature of their real essence.

What is the real essence of those simple modes of mathematics that are too large to be instantiated in the actual world? In particular, what is the real essence of our idea of infinity? Chapter 17 of Book II is entitled 'Of Infinity'. It contains two important developments of the account in Draft B from which it derives. First, as we would expect, Locke sets his treatment of the idea of infinity into his theory of modes:

Finite, and *Infinite*, seem to me to be looked upon by the Mind, as the *Modes of Quantity*, and to be attributed primarily in their first designation only to those things, which have parts, and are capable of increase or diminution.[58]

That is, this idea is a mode of duration, space, and number. The idea of infinity, then, is derived from the power of the mind to add, multiply, or divide without end the ideas of a determinate length or duration (*E* II. xvii. 3). Amongst the modes of quantity, number has a kind of epistemic priority because, in the cases of space and duration, the mind 'makes use of the *Ideas* and Repetitions of Numbers', such that it '*is nothing but the Infinity of Number applied to determinate parts*' (*E* II. xvii. 9 and 10, p. 215).

---

[57] *E* II. xvi. 2, p. 205. [58] *E* II. xvii. 1, p. 209.

The second important development in the *Essay*'s treatment is that Locke labels the idea of infinity as a *negative idea*. To be sure, he admits that the ideas that are modified to produce the idea of infinity are positive ideas, be they determinate ideas of extension, of duration or of unity (*E* II. xvii. 13–15); but the resultant idea of infinity itself is too indeterminate and unclear to be a positive idea. Recall that, in Draft B, §58 and then in the early sections of Book II chapter 8, Locke claims that positive ideas are those that are clear and distinct, even if they have privative causes. It seems that, by implication, negative ideas are those that are unclear and indistinct or indeterminate. Now the idea of infinity is the only idea that Locke labels as a negative one, and it seems to be unique among the mathematical ideas he discusses in the *Essay*. It may be that, because the idea of infinity is a negative one, Locke is wholly unable to consider its real essence and archetype. He is silent on these matters, but he is at pains to stress that those simple modes from which the idea of infinity is derived are themselves received from sensation and reflection (*E* II. xvii. 22). He is also firmly of the view, however, that the notion of an infinitely extended world is incomprehensible and that a consideration of the infinite divisibility of extension involves us in 'consequences impossible to be explicated, or made in our apprehensions consistent' (*E* II. xxiii. 31, p. 313).[59] All of this is consistent with the fact that in Locke's day the questions about infinity and the composition of the continuum were paradigm cases of things above reason.[60]

We are now in a position to bring into play our second modern notion, that of the distinction between identity and equivalence. When Bishop Butler introduced his loose and popular sense of 'identity' or 'sameness', he was referring to what is known in modern terminology as the distinction between strict identity and equivalence.[61] Both relations are transitive, symmetric, and reflexive; and in English the word 'same' can be used to refer to either of them. They are, however, different relations and, as all philosophers now know, the distinction between them is important. How, then, can this distinction between identity and equivalence be used to shed light on Locke's discussion of the nature of mathematical knowledge?

When Locke says that our nominal essence of gold is not real, is false and inadequate, this implies that our abstract idea of gold is not the same as its real essence. What would it be for it to be the same? In the case of spiritual beings without material bodies, Locke surmises that they may well know the real essences of substances such as gold. In this case the nominal essence of gold would be the same as the real essence of gold. That is, the nominal essence of gold would be *equivalent* to the real essence of gold in the sense that every constituent of the nominal essence of gold would correspond to some quality of the real essence of gold and that there would be no quality of gold that

---

[59] In a Journal entry of 16 July 1678, Locke claims that 'when we speake of infinite we speake of something at the same time we confesse we cannot comprehend and soe it seems to be conceptus negativus' (Locke 1936, pp. 111–12).
[60] See Boyle's *Things Above Reason*, *Boyle Works*, Vol. 9, pp. 367 and 369ff.
[61] Butler 1736, p. 303.

did not have a corresponding idea in the nominal essence. Clearly, here, the nominal and the real essences are not strictly identical: one is in the mind and the other in the world. Rather they are the same in a loose and popular sense—in other words they are equivalent.

If the interpretation of Locke on the question of the real essence of modes as sketched above is correct, it must be the case that, when Locke claims that the nominal essence of, say, a triangle is the same as the real essence, he means that the nominal essence of triangle is *equivalent* to the real essence of some triangle in the actual world. The same goes for our mixed modes of morality, such as justice or property. That is, on the interpretation I have presented, the relation between the nominal and the real essence of both simple and complex modes must be one of equivalence.

What, then, of those modes that do not have a corresponding real essence in the world? Well, as suggested in the case of very large natural numbers, Locke would subscribe to a possibilist account which would be cashed out in terms of counterfactuals. The following text reinforces Locke's possibilist account of the reality of modes:

These [complex ideas of modes and relations] being such Collections of simple *Ideas*, that the Mind it self puts together, and such Collections, that each of them contains in it precisely all that the Mind intends that it should, they are Archetypes and Essences of Modes that may exist; and so are designed only for, and belong only to such Modes as, when they do exist, have an exact conformity with those complex Ideas.[62]

Now clearly there would be a danger of anachronism if we took this line of interpretation too far. All we find in Locke is hints and suggestions that might entail what we would call a possibilist doctrine of uninstantiated real essences of modal ideas, and Locke shows no awareness of the formal differences between strict identity and equivalence. However, this suggestion that Locke regarded the nominal essences of modes to be merely equivalent to the real essences of things in the world faces a very serious problem. There are texts where Locke unambiguously claims that the nominal and real essences are *identical*.

The identity between nominal and real essences

In Book IV, chapter 12, Locke ceases to speak of the nominal and real essences of modes as being the same and uses the following locutions:

if other *Ideas* [than those of mathematics], that are the real, as well as nominal Essences of their Species, were pursued in the way familiar to Mathematicians, they would carry our Thoughts farther [...]

the *Ideas* that Ethicks are conversant about, being all real Essences [...]

[in mathematics and ethics] our abstract *Ideas* are real as well as nominal Essences.[63]

---

[62] *E* II. xxxi. 14, p. 384, underlining added. [63] *E* IV. xii. 7, 8, 9, pp. 643–4.

These passages claim very clearly that, in the case of modes, the real and the nominal essence are *identical*. This tends to pull us towards the interpretation of the 'ideality' of modes as recently developed by Emily Carson.

In a number of recent publications, Emily Carson has claimed that, for Locke, mathematics is certain because of the ideality of the objects of mathematical knowledge. She argues that, in Locke's view, 'the certainty of mathematics and ethics follows from the ideality of the objects of mathematical and ethical knowledge'.[64] For Carson ideas are ideational in so far as they 'do not purport to represent things or refer to things outside us: they are, in this sense, *ideal*'.[65] Her grounds for this claim are Locke's statements about the adequacy of modes. Her argument proceeds as follows. In his discussion of the adequacy of ideas, Locke claims that all modes are adequate. Now, to be adequate, an idea must represent its archetype perfectly. Simple ideas are adequate because they cannot but represent their causes in the external world or in the mind (*E* II. xxxi. 2). By contrast, the adequacy of modes resides in the fact that they are 'voluntary Collections of simple *Ideas*, which the Mind puts together, without reference to any real Archetypes, or standing Patterns, existing any where' (*E* II. xxxi. 3, p. 376). They cannot lack anything, 'they not being intended for Copies of Things really existing, but for Archetypes made by the Mind, to rank and denominate Things by' (ibid.).

But this only takes us halfway to Locke's conclusion. The second step comes by way of the doctrine of nominal and real essences. Locke claims that only in those cases where the nominal essence of a thing is *identical* to its real essence can we have demonstrative knowledge of that thing.[66] Further, in the case of modes, the nominal and the real essence '*are always the same*', that is, identical. This is because the real essence of, say, a triangle just is the complex idea of a triangle with all its properties. In this case, then, it appears that the real and the nominal essence coincide just because of the 'ideality' of the idea 'triangle'. Thus, given that the nominal and real essences do coincide in the case of mathematical ideas, we can reason demonstratively by using them and generate certain propositions.

Carson then finds a tension in Locke. She claims that, for Locke, mixed modes like courage or murder are *purely* ideational, but that simple modes such as geometrical shapes are constrained by the nature of Euclidean space itself. That is, the simple modes of geometry are not purely ideational. They function more like Locke's simple ideas. Thus on Carson's view there is an unresolved tension or inconsistency in Locke's account of the simple modes of geometry: on the one hand they are analogous to the purely ideational mixed modes of morality; on the other hand they are like simple ideas.

---

[64] Carson 2005, p. 28. See also Carson 2002, p. 364 and 2006, pp. 4–10.
[65] Carson 2005, p. 28.
[66] Ibid., pp. 29–30. Other interpreters who uncritically accept the identity of the nominal and real essences of modes include Jolley 1999, pp. 155–67; Atherton 2007, p. 275; and Bolton 2007, p. 97.

In my view, Carson has not correctly analysed Locke's theory of mixed modes and in consequence she has not correctly located the tension in Locke's account of the manner in which mathematical truths can be both certain and instructive. As Martha Bolton pointed out in 1976, at various points in the *Essay* Locke explicitly claims that mixed modes can, and sometimes do, have correlates in the world.[67] The key chapter here is *E* II. xxii, where Locke provides a number of illustrations to point out that, when it comes to mixed modes, 'I do not deny, but several of them might be taken from Observation' (*E* II. xxii. 2, pp. 288–9). Then, in section 9, Locke sums up his preceding discussion, claiming: 'There are therefore *three ways whereby we get the complex* Ideas *of mixed Modes*. 1. By Experience and *Observation* of things themselves . . .' (p. 291).

What he stresses, however, is that these real world correlates, be they actions or events, are transient. Even in the opening section of the chapter on mixed modes in Book II Locke tells us that these modes are 'not looked upon to be the characteristical Marks of any real Beings that <u>have a steady existence</u>' (*E* II. xxii. 1, p. 288, underlining added). Book III makes the point by contrasting the actions from which some mixed modes are derived from substances:

[T[he greatest part of mixed Modes, being Actions, which perish in their Birth, are not capable of a lasting Duration, as Substances, which are the Actors; and wherein the simple *Ideas* that make up the complex *Ideas* designed by Nature, have a lasting Union.[68]

It is not that mixed modes have no correlates in the world, but that, partly because of the transient nature of actions and events, in the formation of our mixed modes our minds have enormous freedom. This leads to a degree of arbitrariness and uncertainty in the signification of the names of mixed modes. In his extended treatment of the words used for mixed modes, Locke concludes that this signification is uncertain 'because there be no real Standards existing in Nature, to which those *Ideas* are referred, and by which they may be adjusted' (*E* III. ix 11, p. 481).[69] It is important not to take Locke's 'no real Standards existing in Nature' here as a categorical denial, for he later claims, echoing *E* II. xxxi. 3, that for mixed modes 'there are not always standing Patterns to be found existing' (*E* III. xi. 15, p. 516).

This feature of mixed modes, the fact that their correlates in the real world are transient, makes them analogous to the simple modes of mathematics insofar as their correlates may not be currently instantiated either. It seems then, *pace* Carson, that Locke's possibilist account of the reality of mathematical ideas also applies to the mixed

---

[67] See Bolton 1998, pp. 113–14. Interestingly, as late as 11 February 1759 philosophers in the Aberdeen Philosophical Society were still discussing 'Whether the Ideas of Mixed Modes are to be considered as the mere Creatures of the Mind, or formed after Patterns as well as the Ideas of the Substances whereof they are Modes'. See Question #22 in the list of questions for discussion in Ulman 1990, p. 191.

[68] *E* III. vi. 42, p. 465.

[69] See also *E* III. xi. 9, p. 513, 'This is very necessary in Names of Modes, and especially moral Words; which having no settled Objects in Nature, from whence their *Ideas* are taken, as from their Original, are apt to be very confused'.

modes of morality. If this is so, then neither mixed modes nor simple modes are purely 'ideational'. Moreover, if we follow the trajectory of Locke's comments, in the drafts of the *Essay*, that the certainty of mathematical truths arises from the nature of things in the world, it is natural to interpret him as believing that it is in virtue of the constraints of the nature of space on the formation of the simple modes of geometry that geometrical propositions are not only certain, but instructive. The same applies to the mixed modes: it is in virtue of the correspondence between our mixed modes of morality and real (or possible) actions and events in the world that moral propositions can be instructive.

Thus, when Locke appears to base the certainty of knowledge in morality and mathematics on the fact that mathematical and moral ideas are adequate and complete in themselves, it is important to point out that he goes on to ground the certainty of mathematics in the nature of geometrical figures themselves. His claim that

Certainty being but the Perception of the Agreement, or Disagreement of our *Ideas*; and Demonstration nothing but the Perception of such Agreement, by the Intervention of other *Ideas*, or Mediums, our *moral Ideas*, as well as mathematical, being *Archetypes* themselves, and so adequate, and complete *Ideas*, all the Agreement, or Disagreement, which we shall find in them, will produce real Knowledge, <u>as well as in mathematical Figures</u>[70]

at first sight might suggest that the self-contained nature of mathematical ideas is what grounds their certainty. However, the final clause gives the lie to this interpretation. Locke's view of the certainty of mathematics is never completely detached from the nature of figures in the real world. He is certainly aware of this danger and goes on immediately to address it:

Nor let it be wondred, that I place the Certainty of our Knowledge in the Consideration of our *Ideas*, with so little Care and Regard (as it may seem) to <u>the real Existence of Things</u>.[71]

Indeed,

If *moral Knowledge* be placed in the Contemplation of our own *moral Ideas*, and those, as other Modes [such as mathematics], be of our own making, What strange Notions will there be of *Justice* and *Temperance*? What confusion of Vertues and Vices, if every one may make what *Ideas* of them he pleases?[72]

Locke's answer is definitive:

No confusion nor disorder in the Things themselves, nor the Reasonings about them; no more than (in Mathematicks) there would be a Disturbance in the Demonstration, or a change in the Properties of Figures, and their Relations one to another.[73]

---

[70] *E* IV. iv. 7, p. 565, underlining added. See also the passage from *E* II. xxxii. 14 (quoted above), which caps off a long passage on the adequacy of modes.
[71] *E* IV. iv. 8, pp. 565–6, underlining added.
[72] *E* IV. iv. 9, p. 566.   [73] Ibid.

It is the nature of 'the real Existence of Things' that constrains real knowledge in mathematics and morality: 'as soon as the Figure is drawn, the Consequences and Demonstration are plain and clear' (*E* IV. iv. 9, p. 567).

What are we to make then of Locke's unambiguous and repeated claims that, in the case of modes, the nominal essence is identical to the real essence? There are two responses to this question. First, Locke may well have conflated the loose and popular sense of 'same' with strict identity; he may have slipped into strict identity talk about the relation between real and nominal essences when all he really meant to say was that they are equivalent. The example of angel knowledge suggests as much.[74] There is a sense in which it is true to say, of an angel whose nominal essence (that is, abstract idea) of gold corresponds exactly with the real essence of actual gold, that she knows the real essence. But surely the angel could know the real essence before gold is instantiated in the real world. In this case, it seems natural to say that the nominal and the real essence of gold are the very same abstract idea. Notice, however, that the referent of the term 'real essence' has shifted from something in the world to an abstract idea. In his elaboration of the doctrine of modes, Locke seems to have been untroubled by this shift in the denotation of the phrase 'real essence'.

A second response to Locke's claims about the identity between nominal and real essences is that he does not adequately develop the theory of essences in relation to modes and at some crucial points there is a mismatch between the theory of ideas and the theory of essences, such that no consistent or complete account of the nature of mathematical ideas and their truthmakers (so to speak) is given in the *Essay*. For example, according to Locke's theory of qualities, the idea of shape is a simple idea and, being a primary quality, it resembles the actual shape of the object that causes the idea (*E* II. viii. 9). However, according to his theory of ideas, shape is a simple mode of space; but all modes are complex ideas (*E* II. xiii. 5–6). So according to Locke shape is both a simple and a complex idea.[75]

This brings us back to the qualification of simple modes as complex ideas, which was mentioned above. As Carson rightly points out, Locke seems to treat simple modes as being closely analogous to simple ideas.[76] There is a sense, then, in which simple modes function for Locke like simple ideas. This comes out most clearly in his treatment of the names of simple ideas and of simple modes. He tells us at *E* III. iv. 17 (p. 428) that '[t]he Names of simple Modes, differ little from those of simple *Ideas*'. What does he have in mind here? He is referring to the sameness of the nominal and real essences of simple modes and simple ideas, for he had mentioned earlier in this chapter on the names of simple ideas, that the names of simple ideas and modes always signify both the real and nominal essence of their species.[77] But just what he means by this is not entirely clear.

---

[74] *E* IV. iii. 6, 23.
[75] Woolhouse 1970 discusses a similar problem for Locke's comments on the idea of extension. He rightly diagnoses that the problem lies in Locke's equivocation between ideas as images and ideas as concepts.
[76] Carson 2005, pp. 34–6.   [77] *E* III. iv. 3, p. 421.

There are two passages where he appears to fill out this blank with a thesis. The first occurs in chapter 6 of Book IV:

> Now, because *we cannot be certain of the Truth of any general Proposition, unless we know the precise bounds and extent of the Species its Terms stand for*, it is necessary we should know the Essence of each *Species*, which is that which constitutes and bounds it. This, <u>in all simple *Ideas* and *Modes*</u>, is not hard to do. For <u>in these, the real and nominal Essence being the same</u>; or which is all one, the abstract *Idea*, which the general Term stands for, being the sole Essence and Boundary, that is or can be supposed, of the *Species*, <u>there can be no doubt, how far the *Species* extends, or what Things are comprehended under each Term</u>: which, 'tis evident, are all, that have <u>an exact conformity with the *Idea* it stands for</u>, and no other.[78]

Here it seems that simple ideas and modes in general are analogous insofar as they allow us to determine which things in the world conform to them. But of course in the case of modes Locke is at pains to stress that our modal ideas are normally formed in the absence of anything that might be 'comprehended under' or might have 'an exact conformity with' our modal ideas. Perhaps it is at this point that simple ideas and modal ideas differ. Concerning the names of simple ideas, Locke claims that they '*intimate* also *some real Existence*, from which was derived their original pattern' (*E* III. iv. 2, p. 421), whereas, on the interpretation offered here, modal ideas intimate actual or *possible* existence.

Yet none of this goes very far in clarifying the sense in which the nominal essence and the real essence of a simple idea are the same thing. Throughout the *Essay* Locke stresses the deep connections between simple ideas and the world: simple ideas are real because they agree with the reality of things; simple ideas are adequate because they correspond—and, in the case of primary qualities, resemble—those powers of substances that cause them; simple ideas represent their archetypes in the world; the names of simple ideas intimate real existence. But how can this be the case, if the real essence of a simple idea is identical with its nominal essence? The most natural explanation, as suggested above, is that Locke is equivocating in his use of the word 'same' and that this is also the source of the tendency to assimilate simple ideas with modes, and in particular with simple modes. One final passage brings out this problem. It is found in Locke's discussion of essences in Book III, chapter 3:

> *Essences* being thus distinguished into *Nominal* and *Real*, we may farther observe, that *in the* Species of *simple* Ideas and Modes, they *are always the same*: But *in Substances, always quite different*. Thus a Figure including a Space between three Lines, is the real, as well as nominal *Essence* of a Triangle; it being not only the abstract *Idea* to which the general Name is annexed, but the very *Essentia*, or Being, of the thing it self, that Foundation from which all its Properties flow, and to which they are all inseparably annexed.[79]

---

[78] *E* IV. vi. 4, p. 580, underlining added. [79] *E* III. iii. 18, p. 418.

Does the phrase 'Figure including a Space between three Lines' refer to a real figure, or to an idea? Whatever the answer, Locke is assimilating here simple ideas and modes by using the example of a simple mode, triangle, which he has defined earlier, in a different context, as a simple idea.

It seems, then, that Locke is best interpreted as maintaining that mathematical propositions are certain and that mathematical ideas are real in virtue of the nature of things in the world (or in virtue of the way the world could be)—in particular, in virtue of the nature of Euclidean space. This is what accounts for the fact that mathematical propositions are not only certain but also instructive, and in consequence this also goes some way to showing how mathematics can play a role in natural philosophy. But this explanation does not enlighten us as to how mathematical propositions are generated. How is it that the mind can acquire mathematical knowledge, and what role does this knowledge play in advancing our knowledge of nature? The answer lies in Locke's doctrine of demonstration, which is the subject of the next chapter.

7

Demonstration

> Magnitude is the common Affection of all physical Things, it is interwoven in the Nature of Bodies, blended with all corporeal Accidents, and wellnigh bears the principal Part in the Production of every natural Effect [...] there is no Part of this [natural philosophy] which does not imply Quantity, or to which geometrical Theorems may not be applied, and consequently which is not some Way dependant on Geometry; I will not except even *Zoology* itself.
>
> Isaac Barrow[1]

Anyone perusing the logic texts of the eighteenth century will be struck by how often one encounters the claim that one of the functions of judgement, or reason, is the determination of the agreement or disagreement of ideas. Edward Bentham, in his *Reflections upon the Nature and Usefulness of Logick* (1740), introduces as follows the subject of the second part of his logic text:

In the second part [of this treatise on logic] is considered the Agreement and Disagreement of ideas, as signified by *Affirmation* and *Negation*.[2]

Similar references can be found in the logics of Isaac Watts and William Duncan.[3] The origins of this view can be traced back to Locke.

Today Locke is not known as a logician, or even as a friend of logic, but he had a profound influence on the development of a strand of logic in the century that followed the publication of the *Essay*.[4] In this chapter I will expound Locke's theory of demonstration. I will then trace its origins through the early drafts of the *Essay*,

---

[1] Isaac Barrow, *Lectiones mathematicae*, quoted from Barrow 1734, pp. 21–2.
[2] Bentham 1740, p. 18.
[3] See Watts 1725, pp. 222 and 274–5, Duncan 1748, pp. 6–11, and Reimarus 1766, §115, pp. 116–17 (Alberto Vanzo alerted me to this reference). For the permeation of the doctrine of agreement and disagreement into popular consciousness, see Fielding's *The True Patriot*, No. 8 from 1745, in Fielding 1987, pp. 161–2.
[4] See Buickerood 1985, Winkler 2003, and Schuurman 2004.

briefly survey some of the contemporary criticism of the theory; examine some of Locke's responses to these criticisms; and then examine his views on the application of the theory to natural philosophy. What emerges is a rather extraordinary approach to the acquisition of knowledge about nature—a theory that, so fas as I am aware, has never really been laid out in all its details, but which is extremely important for understanding the various facets of Locke's philosophical agenda in the *Essay* and, in particular, his views on the nature of natural philosophy.

Locke's theory of demonstration

According to Locke, knowledge consists in the perception of agreement or disagreement between ideas (*E* IV. i. 2). Some ideas are seen immediately to agree or to disagree with each other. The idea of black disagrees with the idea of white; the idea of three agrees with the sum of one and two. This immediate perception of the agreement or disagreement of ideas is called intuitive knowledge (*E* IV. ii. 1). However, in the case of many ideas, the mind cannot immediately perceive their agreement or disagreement. In these cases an additional idea is required to determine it. For example,

> the Mind being willing to know the Agreement or Disagreement in bigness, between the three Angles of a Triangle, and two right ones, cannot by an immediate view and comparing them, do it: Because the three Angles of a Triangle cannot be brought at once, and be compared with any other one, or two Angles; and so of this the Mind has no immediate, no intuitive Knowledge. In this Case the Mind is fain to find out some other Angles, to which the three Angles of a Triangle have an Equality; and finding those equal to two right ones, comes to know their Equality to two right ones.[5]

When this happens, the intervening ideas enable the identification of agreement or disagreement between ideas. In the case at hand, the intermediate ideas are additional angles which sum to 180 degrees. The knowledge acquired through the use of intermediate ideas is called demonstrative knowledge. The intermediate ideas are called proofs.

> Those intervening *Ideas*, which serve to shew the Agreement of any two others, are called *Proofs*; and where the Agreement and Disagreement is by this means plainly and clearly perceived, it is called *Demonstration*, it being shewn to the Understanding, and the Mind made to see that it is so. A quickness in the Mind to find out these intermediate *Ideas*, (that shall discover the Agreement or Disagreement of any other,) and to apply them right, is, I suppose, that which is called *Sagacity*.[6]

Locke uses the word 'proof' over 150 times in the *Essay* with various senses, but when it comes to the nature of demonstration and the process by which demonstrative knowledge is acquired, 'proof' refers to an intermediate idea.

It should be clear by now that Locke's conception of demonstrative knowledge bears little resemblance to the traditional Aristotelian notion of demonstration. In Aristotelian logic, a demonstration is a syllogism which conforms to one of the fourteen

---

[5] *E* IV. ii. 2, p. 532. [6] *E* IV. ii. 3, p. 532.

valid forms, which has necessarily true premises, and which yields 'scientific' knowledge.[7] A syllogism is a valid argument with two premises and a conclusion, each one of which is a syllogistic proposition—that is, each of which has the form A*x*B, where *x* is one of the four syllogistic relations.[8] According to Locke, demonstrative knowledge does *not* involve inferences from propositions. Therefore it does not involve the notion of validity at all.[9] Rather it involves *perceptions* of the relations between ideas. Locke denies that demonstrations are syllogisms. He denies that a science is a finite set of connected syllogisms based upon axioms.

Let us fill out this claim a little more by examining Locke's description of what happens when reason carries out a mathematical demonstration. In section 3 of the infamous chapter on reason (*E* IV. xvii), Locke describes the different functions of the faculty of reason and then illustrates them with an analysis of what happens when we perform a mathematical demonstration. (I should add that this section immediately precedes the critique of the syllogistic.) Here is what Locke claims:

> [W]e may in *Reason* consider these *four Degrees*; the first and highest, is the discovering, and finding out of Proofs; the second, the regular and methodical Disposition of them, and laying them in a clear and fit Order, to make their Connexion and Force be plainly and easily perceived; the third is the perceiving their Connexion; and the fourth, the making a right conclusion. These several degrees may be observed in any mathematical Demonstration: it being one thing to perceive the connexion of each part, as the Demonstration is made by another; another to perceive the dependence of the conclusion on all the parts; a third, to make out a Demonstration clearly and neatly ones self, and something different from all these, to have first found out those intermediate *Ideas* or Proofs by which it is made.[10]

So reason has four degrees. They are:

A. the discovery or finding out of proofs [sagacity, intermediate ideas] = 4
B. their regular and methodical disposition, and laying them [all the ideas] in a clear and fit order, to make their connexion and force be plainly and easily perceived [ordering the proofs and ideas correctly] = 3
C. the perception of their connexion [perceiving the connection between the proofs and the ideas in order to determine the agreement or disagreement] = 1
D. drawing a right conclusion [making a correct determination of agreement or disagreement] = 2

These degrees are evident in the way reason carries out a mathematical demonstration whereby we:

---

[7] For the more nuanced view of Aristotle himself, see Barnes 1975.
[8] See Barnes 1994, p. xvi.
[9] The notion of formal validity is almost entirely absent from the *Essay*. David Owen rightly comments that '[i]t is highly misleading to talk of premises and conclusions when thinking of Locke's demonstrations': Owen 1999, p. 38.
[10] *E* IV. xvii. 3, pp. 669–70. This analysis is consistent with two other discussions of mathematical demonstration, in *E* IV. xii. 7 and 15.

1. perceive the connection of each part as made by someone else [= C]
2. perceive the dependence of the conclusion on all the parts [= D]
3. make out a demonstration neatly for oneself [= B]
4. have first found out those intermediate proofs by which it is made [=A]

Now Jonathan Barnes calls this description of mathematical demonstration 'less than limpid',[11] but this is because he mistakenly takes Locke to be glossing on an Aristotelian demonstration in terms of his own theory of ideas. For example, Barnes takes Locke's phrase 'to perceive the dependence of the conclusion on all the parts' to mean that 'at the end of the proof, you may grasp that its conclusion depends on its premisses'.[12] But the whole thrust of Locke's discussion here is to the effect that mathematical demonstration does *not* involve inferences from premises to a conclusion. Rather it involves the use of intermediate ideas to enable the understanding to *perceive* the agreement or disagreement of ideas. Mathematical demonstration is fundamentally an act of perception of the relations among ideas, and not the derivation of new propositional knowledge on the basis of true premises. Locke's theory of demonstration does not include deductive arguments. This also puts paid to Barnes' very ingenious suggestion that Locke's theory of demonstration might be a theory of what early modern logicians called material inference.[13] This refers to valid inferences which are not in syllogistic form, such as:

1. Caius runs
2. Therefore, Caius moves.

It is tempting to think, given Locke's objections to syllogisms, that it is these material inferences that he has in mind, for it is pretty clear that Locke's theory of demonstration has no truck with the notion of *formal* validity. However, as I have stressed already, the notions of inferring from one proposition to another and of validity are not constituents of Locke's account of demonstration, so material inference is ruled out as well.

In fact, the case of material inference can be used further to illustrate Locke's view. For it may be objected that material inferences are really enthymemes and that in our example the suppressed premise is 'Everything that runs, moves', which allows the construction of a Barbara syllogism (with a singular term). But Locke's rejoinder would be that this just highlights the manner in which the syllogism is a *post hoc* propositional construction based upon the pre-propositional perception of the agreement of the idea of running with the idea of moving.[14]

---

[11] Barnes 2006, p. 308.
[12] Ibid. Barnes is not the only scholar who interprets Locke's view of demonstration as applying to the relations between propositions. See also Aaron 1971, pp. 224–5, Wolterstorff 1996, pp. 57–9, Soles 2005, pp. 7–8.
[13] Barnes 2006, pp. 320ff.
[14] For further discussion of the treatment of material inferences as enthymemes, see Read 1994. It is of some relevance here to note that in some recent epistemology there has been renewed interest in non-propositional understanding. See for example Roberts and Wood 2007, pp. 42ff and Gabbay and Woods 2003. Rod Girle alerted me to the latter reference.

So Locke's account of the generation of knowledge is a foundational, pre-propositional, even pre-linguistic theory. In the first three short sections of chapter 6 of Book IV, he concedes that, in fact, the pure pre-propositional perception of the relations between ideas 'is very seldom practised' and that this makes '*the consideration of Words and Propositions, so necessary a part of the Treatise of Knowledge*' (*E* IV. vi. 1, p. 579).[15] On this basis he distinguishes between '*Certainty of Knowledge*' and '*Certainty of Truth*'. One might wonder, therefore, just what role this pre-propositional form of perception plays in the acquisition of knowledge. Perhaps it is, after all, only a very minor role. However, Locke's subsequent discussion makes it clear that our lack of epistemic access to the real essences of substances significantly undermines the prospects of certainty for any general propositions involving species terms. And by the end of the chapter Locke is reaffirming after all that the grounds of the certainty of general propositions are, in fact, the agreement or disagreement of the ideas to which the terms used in the propositions refer. He says:

General Propositions, of what kind soever, are then only capable of *Certainty*, when the Terms used in them, stand for such *Ideas*, whose agreement or disagreement, as there expressed, is capable to be discovered by us. And we are then certain of their Truth or Falsehood, when we perceive the *Ideas* the Terms stand for, to agree or not agree, according as they are affirmed or denied one of another.[16]

Origins of Locke's theory

Now the origins of Locke's theory of demonstration can be traced all the way back to the early drafts of the *Essay* of 1671. They reveal that, from early on, Locke was highly critical of traditional logic and that he adumbrated the theory in his early reflections on the nature of ideas and on knowledge acquisition.[17] It is testimony to Locke's independence of mind that his terms of reference for working out the theory were not constrained by the standard approach to demonstration that he encountered at Oxford. The fine detail of his early view will be discussed below, when we come to examine the application of the theory. For now it will suffice to give a taster by quoting some of Locke's early references to mathematical certainty and demonstration.

In Draft A, §11 Locke says:

Now the certainty of mathematical knowledg arises thus 1° That by constant observation of our senses espetialy our eys we come to finde that such & such quantitys have such & such proportions compard with other v.g. that the 3 angles of a triangle are equall to two right ones, or that one side of a triangle being produced the exterior angle is equal to the two interior opposite angles. which being tried in several tryangles & by noe body found in any one triangle

---

[15] See also *E* IV. v. 4. [16] *E* IV. vi. 16, pp. 590–1.
[17] For Locke's early criticisms of traditional logic, see Draft B, §88, pp. 194–7.

otherwise, passes into an universal acknowledgd truth, & is received as an undoubted axiom, & is as it were a standard to measure other proportions by.[18]

Locke's emphasis in these very early and rather undigested thoughts is on sensory observation. It is not that he is ignorant of the fact that geometrical theorems are ultimately based upon axioms. After all, he does go on, immediately after this excerpt, to speak of the 'more general axioms of geometry' and he lists some of them. But what has struck Locke about the way in which geometrical reasoning proceeds is that it relies on drawing and on visual comparisons. This is reinforced in the description of mathematical demonstration in Draft B, which was also written in 1671. There Locke makes the following claim:

the certein knowledg we have of mathematicall veritys [...] depends on & rises from, the certeine destinct knowledg a man hath of the Ideas of his owne minde [...] For haveing in my minde framd the Idea of an equilaterall triangle, (the Idea of figure being one of those I have receivd by my senses & is noething but the modification or termination of Extension) & there by measureing the angles found them equall to 2 right ones, & soe have a cleare infallible knowledg of it. I cannot but be sure that wherever that figure exists it will always have all the same propertys it had when I contemplated it in my owne understanding there being noe difference in the propertys of the same angle or figure whether it be drawn upon paper, carvd in marble, or only phansyd in my understanding for being once truly & clearly measured there I could never more doubt of the truth of this proposition in generall that the 3 angles of an equilaterall triangle are equall to two right ones where ever such a triangle did exist.[19]

Here again Locke claims that the certainty of the proposition that the internal angles of a triangle sum to 180° rests on observation. The description of geometrical reasoning is a fairly accurate account of the way in which a seventeenth-century mathematician would approach the derivation of what we now call a theorem. There is no evidence that Locke regarded the derivation of new mathematical knowledge in mathematical demonstration as analogous to the formation and articulation of arguments with propositions as premises and conclusions, or that the syllogistic is playing any role in his conception of demonstration. This is confirmed by the immediately following passage, where Locke discusses the nature of demonstration. There he says:

I thinke I may adde that when we would arive at that great certainty which we call **Demonstration**. we usualy appeale to our eyes & looke for noe greater certainty then what our eyes can afford us, the whole evidence of this assureance being noe more then what the word **Demonstration** doth naturaly import; which is to shew any thing as it is & make it be perceived soe that in truth what we come to know this way is not by proofe but intuition, all the proofe that is used in this way of knowledg being noe thing else but shewing men how they shall see right & observe the equality or proportion of parts without useing arguments to perswade them that they are soe.[20]

---

[18] Draft A, §11, p. 22.   [19] Draft B, §44, p. 152.   [20] Ibid., p. 153.

Once again, the emphasis is on immediate epistemic access through the senses. Demonstration is not understood in Aristotelian terms, but rather is related to intuition through perception. (Perhaps there is a hint of awareness of the nature of geometrical proof in the final clause, which alludes to 'arguments to perswade'.)[21] It is clear, then, that Locke's theory of demonstration, as developed in the *Essay*, is continuous with these comments on mathematical certainty and on demonstration, but contains much more besides.

Criticism of Locke's theory of demonstration

Not surprisingly, Locke's theory of demonstration was subject to some very harsh criticism. The most stinging attacks came at the end of the 1690s, in the writings of John Sergeant and Edward Stillingfleet. (Locke was later to be criticized on the same points by Henry Lee and Leibniz.)[22] As a result, Locke made substantial revisions to his chapters on reason (which contains the critique of the syllogistic: *E* IV. xvii), on the improvement of our knowledge (*E* IV. xii), and on maxims (*E* IV. vii). He also wrote an extensive reply to Stillingfleet's charges, and we have his annotations to his copy of Sergeant's *Solid Philosophy Asserted* (1697), which pertain to his theory of demonstration. I will ignore the comments on Sergeant here, which add little to our understanding of Locke's view,[23] and deal with the reply to Stillingfleet.

In his reply to Locke's second letter, written in 1698, Stillingfleet sets Locke's 'way of ideas' against the traditional 'way of reason'. Stillingfleet's way of reason generates knowledge by deducing one thing from another, whereas Locke's way of ideas determines the agreement or disagreement of ideas. Stillingfleet brings three charges against Locke's way of ideas. First, he criticizes Locke's notion of reason.[24] Second, he repeatedly claims that the certainty of the perception of agreement or disagreement between ideas is undermined by the fact that many of our most important ideas are not clear and distinct.[25] Third, he claims that Locke denies the very principles of reason upon which the certainty of deductions is based.

On the question of the nature of reason, Stillingfleet argued, with some justice, that 'your Idea of Reason is as obscure as that of Substance'.[26] By the end of the seventeenth century it was standard practice in logic texts to present a tripartite division of the functions of the understanding, namely perception, judgement, and reason. Perception deals with the apprehension of ideas or notions; judgement deals with the formation of

---

[21] In Draft A Locke has a long discussion of the role of proofs in assent to probable propositions, but here the notion is one of 'sensible proof', where 'seeing is believing' is the notion under scrutiny. See Draft A, §§38–42, pp. 65–74.
[22] See Lee 1702, pp. 311–18 and Leibniz 1996, pp. 475–95. For a discussion of Leibniz's criticisms of Locke, see M. D. Wilson 1999.
[23] See Yolton 1951 for a discussion of Locke's comments on Sergeant's criticisms.
[24] Stillingfleet 1698, p. 104.
[25] Ibid., pp. 110–14, 120–2, 125–7, 134ff.
[26] Ibid., p. 104.

propositions of perceived ideas, and reason deals with the relations between propositions. Locke's own lecture notes from the logic he was taught at Oxford contain this very tripartite division.[27] It is also to be found in the *Port Royal Logic* and in Aldrich's logic of 1691.[28] Locke, however, completely reconfigures these functions. In effect, he collapses reason and perception, such that reason just is the perception of the agreement or disagreement of ideas, and he makes judgement to be the faculty of determining the degree or probability of agreement or disagreement of ideas when certainty is not to be had: '*Judgment* [...] is the putting *Ideas* together, or separating them from one another in the Mind, when their certain Agreement or Disagreement is not perceived, but *presumed* to be so' (*E* IV. xiv. 4, p. 653). By contrast, Stillingfleet conceives of reason in the standard manner, as the faculty of making inferences from propositions according to certain self-evident principles of reason.

With respect to these principles of reason, Stillingfleet claims that 'our true Grounds of Certainty depend upon some *general Principle of Reason*'.[29] He provides a survey of the principles of reason that were offered by the ancient philosophers as the grounds of the certainty of deductions:

I now come to the *Certainty of Reason in making Deductions*. And here I shall briefly lay down the *Grounds* of *Certainty*, which the Ancient Philosophers went upon, and then compare your way of *Ideas* with them.[30]

After this survey, he concludes:

But your Way of *Certainty by Ideas* is so wholly New, that here we have no *general Principles*; no *Criterion*, no *Antecedents and Consequents*; no *Syllogistical Methods* of *Demonstration*; and yet we are told of a better Way of Certainty to be attained, meerly by the help of *Ideas*.[31]

In his reply, Locke fastens on one particular principle of reason that Stillingfleet mentions:

Now of the certainty in making deductions, I see none of the ancients produced by your lordship, who say any thing to show, wherein it consists, but Aristotle; who, as you say, 'in his method of inferring one thing from another, went upon this common principle of reason, that what things agree in a third, agree among themselves'. And it so falls out, that so far as he goes towards the showing wherein the certainty of deductions consists, he and I agree, as is evident by what I say in my Essay.[32]

So Locke claims that he agrees with the principle that 'what things agree in a third, agree among themselves'. Moreover, he claims that Aristotle would definitely have concurred with him, on the grounds of the certainty of this principle:

---

[27] See Bodl. Library MS Locke f. 33, fol. 185v. See also Buickerood 1985, p. 160.
[28] See Arnauld and Nicole 1996 and Aldrich 1691, pp. 1–2.
[29] Stillingfleet 1698, p. 109.   [30] Ibid., p. 114.
[31] Ibid., p. 120.   [32] *Second Reply*, p. 383.

if Aristotle had gone any farther to show, how we are certain, that those two things agree with a third, he would have placed that certainty in the perception of that agreement, as I have done, and then he and I should have perfectly agreed. I presume to say, if Aristotle had gone farther in this matter, he would have placed our knowledge or certainty of the agreement of any two things in the perception of their agreement.[33]

Locke's claim is that the certainty of the principle of reason, on which the certainty of deductions is grounded, rests on the perception of agreement between the ideas:

For who can doubt that the knowledge, or being certain, that any two things agree, consists in the perception of their agreement? What else can it possibly consist in? It is so obvious, that it would be a little extraordinary to think, that he that went so far could miss it. And I should wonder, if any one should allow the certainty of deduction to consist in the agreement of two things in a third, and yet should deny that the knowledge or certainty of that agreement consisted in the perception of it.[34]

And in fact this is exactly what Locke has already argued in the *Essay*. For at *E* IV. xii. 6 (pp. 642–3) he claims:

But since the Knowledge of the Certainty of Principles, as well as of all other Truths, depends only upon the perception, we have, of the Agreement, or Disagreement of our *Ideas, the way to improve our Knowledge*, is not, I am sure, blindly, and with an implicit Faith, to receive and swallow Principles; but is, I think, *to get and fix in our Minds clear, distinct, and complete* Ideas, as far as they are to be had, *and annex to them proper and constant Names*. And thus, perhaps, without any other Principles, but barely considering those *Ideas*, and by *comparing them one with another*, finding their Agreement, and Disagreement, and their several Relations and Habitudes; we shall get more true and clear Knowledge, by the conduct of this one Rule than by taking up Principles, and thereby putting our Minds into the disposal of others.

Where Stillingfleet claims that Locke rejects the 'way of reason', that is, the syllogistic, because he rejects the principle of reason, Locke claims that he can accept the syllogism because the certainty of the principle of reason on which it is founded (at least in Aristotle's version) is based on the perception of the agreement of ideas. Not only has he already argued for this in the *Essay*, but a careful reading of the drafts of that work reveals that the kernel of Locke's view was already in existence in 1671.

Locke's application of the theory of demonstration: A corpuscular metric

How, then, did Locke believe his theory of demonstration should be applied? One of his concerns is that this method should be properly applied in the domain of natural philosophy. Here is Locke's prescription for that science:

---

[33] *Second Reply*, pp. 383–4.   [34] Ibid., p. 384.

But whether natural Philosophy be capable of Certainty, or no, the *ways to enlarge our Knowledge*, as far as we are capable, seem to me, in short, to be these two:

First, The *First* is *to get and settle in our Minds* determined *Ideas* of those Things, whereof we have general or specific Names; at least of so many of them as we would consider and improve our knowledge in, or reason about. And if they be *specific* Ideas of *Substances*, we should endeavour also to make them as complete as we can, whereby I mean, that we should put together as many simple Ideas, as being constantly observed to co-exist, may perfectly determine the *Species*: And each of those simple Ideas, which are the ingredients of our Complex one, should be clear and distinct in our Minds. For it being evident, that our knowledge cannot exceed our *Ideas*; as far as they are either imperfect, confused, or obscure, we cannot expect to have certain, perfect, or clear Knowledge.

Secondly, The other is the Art of *finding out* those *Intermediate Ideas*, which may shew us the Agreement, or Repugnancy of other *Ideas*, which cannot be immediately compared.[35]

But all of this is rather vague. It is one thing to be told that the perception of the agreement or disagreement of ideas is the way to advance knowledge in natural philosophy; however, what is needed is some idea of how the understanding engages in this process. Fortunately Locke has a theory about this too, and it goes to the core of how he believes the science of natural philosophy would proceed, should we gain epistemic access to the inner natures or real essences of things.

That theory was inspired by mathematics. Locke believed that geometry and arithmetic present us with paradigm examples of the sort of demonstrative reasoning that would be involved in a science of nature, that is, a demonstrative natural philosophy. But he understood this kind of reasoning in a peculiar way. The kernel of Locke's conception of demonstrative reasoning in mathematics is the procedure of extensional and numerical measuring. On his view, these are very precise forms of determination of agreement or disagreement between ideas, which are potentially available to those who studied natural philosophy. The origins of Locke's view can be traced to Draft A. He tells us there that of the means for determining the affirmation or negation of simple ideas 'all the measures that have been or are to be found depending upon & resolveing into those 2 grande & universal measures of all things extension & number' (Draft A, §11), and that the first of these 'is noething but the compareing one extension with an other that is by lines or angles which we doe know [...] to measure those that we doe not know' (Draft A, §11, p. 22). This method of comparison is certain because it is founded on the sense of sight, and it is therefore aptly called demonstration (Draft A, § 11). The second method of affirming or negating ideas is by comparisons of number 'whereof the Ideas are clearer then that of extension [...] & the demonstrations about numbers are more evident then in extension because, the Idea of number is more determinat & precise then in extension' (Draft A, §12, p. 23). This analysis of demonstration is carried over into Draft B and then into the *Essay* itself, where Locke reaffirms (at *E* IV. ii. 10, p. 535):

---

[35] *E* IV. xii. 14, p. 648.

> [T]he Modes of Numbers have every the least difference very clear and perceivable: and though in Extension, every the least Excess is not so perceptible; yet the Mind has found out ways, to examine and discover demonstratively the just equality of two Angles, or Extensions, or Figures, and both these, *i.e.* Numbers and Figures, can be set down, by visible and lasting marks, wherein the *Ideas* under consideration are perfectly determined, which for the most part they are not, where they are marked only by Names and Words.

Thus, from the early drafts to the *Essay* itself, Locke stressed that numerical measuring is superior to geometrical or extensional measuring, but that both are superior to what the mind can do with its simple ideas of the sensible qualities. For Locke, then, extensional and numerical measuring would be the fundamental means of generating demonstrative natural philosophical knowledge if we could gain epistemic access to the primary qualities of the inner corpuscular structure of things. The aim for natural philosophy is to acquire a quantitative analysis of qualitative difference, but because we lack knowledge of the internal constitution of things this knowledge is not available to us. In section 41 of Draft B Locke expresses this using the example of degrees of whiteness:

> There is yet another knowledg which we have by these simple Ideas. which is by compareing the degrees & proportions of those of the same kinde to know their æquality or excesse one to an other. as when the degree of whitenesse heat or sweetnesse are compard one with an other [...] But because the accurate knowledg of these is not of that universall use nor hath the world had measures & standards whereby exactly to measure them. we have noe measures of the graduall & least excesses of extension.[36]

In the *Essay* Locke recycles the example of whiteness giving an extended treatment to the comparison of degrees of whiteness in corpuscular terms (*E* IV. ii. 10–13). He concludes that, given our ignorance of the inner structures that cause ideas of whiteness, 'we cannot demonstrate the certain Equality of any two degrees of *Whiteness*, because we have no certain Standard to measure them by, nor Means to distinguish every the least real difference' (*E* IV. ii. 13, p. 536). The same applies to all the secondary qualities. Locke's vision for a demonstrative natural philosophy is in terms of a metric of corpuscles, though he is at pains to stress that he is not committed to any speculative corpuscular accounts of colour or other secondary qualities (*E* IV. ii. 11 and 12). Scholars of Berkeley's philosophy will note the parallel here with Berkeley's *minimum visibile*, which is the idealist's analogue to Locke's standard of measure for corpuscles.[37]

An important consequence of Locke's ideal of a corpuscular metric is his ongoing concern with metrology. Again and again, he states that we lack 'measures & standards' and possess only relative measures, and his concern is not only with measures of

---

[36] Draft B, §41, p. 149.
[37] See Berkeley's *A New Theory of Vision*, §§79–87, in Berkeley 1965, pp. 317–20.

extension but also with measures of duration and weight. Not content with this situation, Locke set out to gather data on comparative measures and to establish a standard measurement of length. To this end he developed a decimal measure, which he called the gry; he sought out information on time-keeping; and he even developed his own proposal for calendar reform.[38] It is not surprising, therefore, that the longest sustained discussion in Draft B and his main concern in the chapter on duration in *E* II. xiv are of, and with, the metrics of time.[39]

Locke's ideal of a corpuscular metric was certainly the driver of his interest in metrology, but he was well aware that, even if such a metric were available, it would still not deliver a complete natural philosophy. That is, even if a standard of measure could be established and we had epistemic access to the inner natures of material substances, there would still remain much about which we were consigned to ignorance. The reason for this belief is to be found in Locke's views on the limits of reason's ability to determine the agreement or disagreement between ideas.

In the opening chapter of Book IV of the *Essay*, Locke explains that there are four sorts of agreement or disagreement. These are: 1. Identity or diversity; 2. Relation; 3. Coexistence or necessary connection; 4. Real existence. A corpuscular metric would go a long way towards determining the agreement or disagreement of ideas in terms of identity or diversity (1) and in terms of relation (2), but it would provide little assistance when it comes to determining agreement or disagreement in terms of co-existence or necessary connection (3). We may one day be able to give a quantitative explanation of the perceived difference between ideas of two different shades of white, but we would still be ignorant of the '*Co-existence*, or *Inco-existence*' of the qualities of things (*E* IV. iii. 12). Locke takes up this problem in *E* IV. iii. 9–17 and concludes that we are only able to have 'experimental *Knowledge*' of the co-existence and necessary connections between the qualities of things and their 'original *Rules* and *Communication of Motion*' and that 'we are not capable of a philosophical *Knowledge* of the Bodies that are about us'. The upshot is that 'we cannot but ascribe them to the arbitrary Will and good Pleasure of the Wise Architect' (*E* IV. iii. 29, p. 560). A corpuscular metric, then, will offer a kind of demonstrative natural philosophy, but it will be, at best, a truncated science: the determination of the agreement or disagreement between many ideas of qualities in terms of coexistence and necessary connection will remain beyond our reach.

---

[38] Locke seems to have devised the gry in August 1677 while he was in Paris; see Lough 1953, pp. 161 and 185. He may even have hoped that others would take it up as a standard of measure, for he mentions it in the *Essay*, claiming: 'I think, it would be of general convenience, that this should be the common measure in the Commonwealth of Letters' (*E* IV. x. 10, p. 624). He also uses it in his report on the horny excrescencies that he saw on a young Frenchman's nails, which was published in the *Philosophical Transactions* in 1697. For Locke and the calendar reform, see Milton 2006.

[39] Draft B, §§102–30, pp. 225–53.

Principles and bottoming

Now it is all very well for Locke to speculate about natural philosophy in the ideal state in which we have epistemic access to the corpuscles themselves, but what about Newton's achievements in Locke's day? How could Locke account for the fact that mathematics had enabled much progress to be made in our understanding of large objects such as planets and comets? How can Locke's theory of demonstration and his ideal of a corpuscular metric help him to explain the role of mathematics in natural philosophy in general? The answer to these questions (which have been raised at the end of Chapter 6 above) lies in Locke's late adoption of the Newtonian notion of principles of natural philosophy.

We have seen that, from the early drafts of the *Essay*, Locke was highly critical of innate or speculative principles and maxims.[40] This was entirely in keeping with his broad commitment to the experimental philosophy, and it provided one of the motivations for the development of his critique of innate principles in general. This negative appraisal of principles was carried over into the first edition of the *Essay* itself, and from chapter 6 of Book IV of the *Essay* Locke is at pains to stress the futility of basing our knowledge or our opinions upon general principles and maxims. In particular, he has in mind metaphysical maxims such as 'Whatever is, is'—the very principles about which he has argued in Book I that they are not innate:

> But yet, I think, I may say, that neither that received Maxim, nor any other identical Proposition teaches us any thing: And though in such kind of Propositions, this great and magnified Maxim, boasted to be the foundation of Demonstration, may be, and often is made use of to confirm them, yet all it proves, amounts to no more than this, That the same Word may with great certainty be affirmed of it self, without any doubt of the Truth of any such Proposition; and let me add also, without any real Knowledge.[41]

We have also seen (in Chapter 4) that the futility of this approach to knowledge, of this starting from first principles, is what lies behind his comments on the use of hypotheses at *Essay* IV. xii. 13. But this railing against principles and maxims, which in a sense is the polemical impetus of the middle third of Book IV, begins to be somewhat compromised by another line of thought which develops in the book. For Locke acknowledges that, in demonstrative moral reasoning as well as in mathematics, we do start with principles and build up demonstrations from them. As he put it in the first edition, we might develop a demonstrative morality 'from Principles, as incontestable as those of the Mathematicks, by necessary Consequences' (E_1 IV. iii. 18, p. 549). No doubt these principles are not innate, and they are formulated through an examination of our ideas; but they remain the foundation of demonstrations. Indeed Stillingfleet took Locke to task on this very point and, to my mind, it is one of the few places where the good bishop had Locke on the back foot.[42] Once we leave the first edition of the *Essay*,

---

[40] See Draft A, pp. 44–50. [41] *E* IV. viii. 2, p. 609.
[42] See *Second Reply*, pp. 407–8.

however, and we survey the writings of the 1690s, this admission ceases to apply only to mathematics and morality and is extended to natural philosophy as well. How did this dramatic change come about?

In March 1690, just months after the publication of the *Essay*, Newton gave Locke 'A Demonstration That the Planets by their gravity towards the sun may move in Ellipses'.[43] The text begins with a geometrical proof of Kepler's area law of planetary motion—the very law that Locke knew, from his review of Newton's *Principia*, to be incompatible with the Cartesian analysis of planetary motions. If Locke lacked a clear conception of geometrical proof when composing the early drafts of the *Essay*, if he lacked such a conception even at the time of the publication of the first edition of that work, the situation was soon to change. For by early 1690 he had in his possession an excellent example of a proof of a law that he had already carefully considered and mentioned in print. Interestingly, too, the proof begins with three hypotheses. After establishing the area law by reasoning from the three hypotheses, the 'Demonstration' then goes on to prove a second proposition, namely that,

[i]f a body be attracted towards either focus of any Ellipsis & by that attraction be made to revolve in the perimeter of the Ellipsis, the attraction shall be reciprocally as the Square of the distance of the body from that focus of the Ellipsis.[44]

Perhaps Locke's contemplation of this document was one of the catalysts that caused him to change his views. The first inkling that Locke was altering his views with regard to the role of principles in natural philosophy came in 1693, in a new section written for *Some Thoughts concerning Education*, a section that does not derive from the earlier correspondence with Edward Clarke, which formed the backbone of the book. Locke tells us that

the incomparable Mr. *Newton*, has shewn, how far Mathematicks, applied to some Parts of Nature, may, upon <u>Principles that Matter of Fact justifie</u>, carry us in the knowledge of some, as I may so call them, particular Provinces of the Incomprehensible Universe.[45]

It is the 'Principles that Matter of Fact justifie' that are the basis of Newton's success. What might these principles be? Well, in the *Conduct*, begun around 1697, we get another insight; for there Locke tell us that

[t]here are fundamental truths that lie at the bottom, the basis upon which a great many others rest, and in which they have their consistency. These are teeming truths, rich in store, with which they furnish the mind, and, like the lights of heaven, are not only beautiful and entertaining in themselves, but give light and evidence to other things, that without them could not be seen or known. <u>Such is that admirable discovery of Mr. Newton, that all bodies gravitate to one another,</u>

---

[43] Bodl. MS Locke c. 31, fols 101–4 transcribed in King 1858, pp. 210–16 and collated with a similar document from among Newton's papers in Herivel 1965, pp. 248–56. For a facsimile of the version among Newton's papers, see Newton 1989, pp. 239–46; for analysis of these manuscripts, see Brackenridge 1993.
[44] Bodl. MS Locke c. 31, fol. 102 = Herivel 1965, p. 251.
[45] *STCE*, §194, p. 248 (=§ 182 in the first edition), underlining added.

which may be counted as the basis of natural philosophy; which, of what use it is to the understanding of the great frame of our solar system, he has to the astonishment of the learned world shown; and how much farther it would guide us in other things, if rightly pursued, is not yet known.[46]

One cannot help but regard the fundamental truth that 'all bodies gravitate to one another' as one of the principles which 'matter of fact justify'. This is confirmed by Locke's *Elements of Natural Philosophy*, also composed at this time. There Locke claims:

> Two bodys, at a distance; will put one another into motion by the force of attraction: which is unexplicable by us, tho' made evident to us by experience, and so to be taken as a Principle in Natural Philosophy.[47]

This notion of principles of natural philosophy is in fact central to Newton's understanding of the method of his *Principia*, and it is no doubt one of the reasons for the title of that book.[48] In the Introduction to Book III, Newton claims:

> In the preceding books I have presented principles of [natural] philosophy that are not, however, philosophical but strictly mathematical—that is, those on which the study of [natural] philosophy can be based. [...] It still remains for us to exhibit the system of the world from these same principles.[49]

And this is the very task that Newton undertook in Book III. In the first edition of the *Principia*, however, he does not elaborate further on the nature of the derivation and role of these principles; but he takes up these issues in the draft preface to the *Opticks* composed in 1703. In that document Newton posits four natural philosophical principles, including the principle of gravitational attraction, and, after dismissing the speculative approach to natural philosophy, he claims of the principles:

> There is no other way of doing any thing with certainty than by drawing conclusions from experiments & phaenomena untill you come at general Principles & then from those Principles giving an account of Nature. Whatever is certain in [natural] Philosophy is owing to this method & nothing can be done without it.[50]

Then, in a related fragment, he claims:

> Thus in the Mathematical Principles of Philosophy I first shewed that all bodies endeavoured by certain force proportional to their matter to approach one another, that this force in receding from the body grows less & less in reciprocal proportion to the square of the distance from it & that it is equal to gravity & therefore is one & the same force with gravity. Then using this force as

---

[46] *Conduct*, p. 282, underlining added.
[47] Locke 1720, p. 183 = *Locke Works*, 3, pp. 305, underlining added.
[48] It is surprising, therefore, that I. Bernard Cohen fails to mention Newton's actual principles of philosophy in his discussion of Newton's choice of a title for the book in his splendid 'Guide to Newton's *Principia*'; see Cohen 1999, pp. 43–9.
[49] Newton 1999, p. 793.
[50] Quoted from McGuire 1970, p. 183.

a Principle of Philosophy I derived from it all the motions of the heavenly bodies and the flux & reflux of the sea [...][51]

These reflections fill out the brief introductory comments that preface Book III of the *Principia* (quoted above). But, more importantly for our purposes, they nicely parallel Locke's sentiments on Newton's principles as expressed in the *Conduct*.

It is evident, then, that by the late 1690s Locke had come to the view that principles are, after all, legitimate bases for reasoning in natural philosophy, as long as they are principles that matter of fact justify and not speculative hypotheses.[52] In accordance with this view, toward the conclusion of the *Conduct* he develops the conception of 'bottoming' as an alternative to the scholastic general maxims and principles.[53] Locke recommends that 'the examination of our principles', along with an 'indifferency for all truth', is one of the key means of achieving 'that freedom of the understanding which is necessary to a rational creature, and without which it is not truly an understanding'.[54] The foundational maxims of mathematics in the *Conduct* become the paradigm of the method of bottoming in general: 'in all sorts of reasoning, every single argument should be managed as a mathematical demonstration; the connection and dependence of ideas should be followed, till the mind is brought to the source on which it bottoms, and observes the coherence all along'.[55] It is hardly surprising, then, that in the fourth edition of the *Essay* Locke added an extended discussion of the purposes served by maxims, which includes new material on Newton. According to Locke, Newton did not proceed from general maxims to find 'so many new Truths', but, once he had found his principles, he proceeded to reason demonstratively from them, according to the Lockean theory of demonstration:

Mr. *Newton*, in his never enough to be admired Book, has demonstrated several Propositions, which are so many new Truths, before unknown to the World, and are further Advances in Mathematical Knowledge: But, for the Discovery of these, it was not the general *Maxims, What is, is*; or, *The whole is bigger than a part*, or the like, that help'd him. These were not the Clues that lead him into the Discovery of the Truth and Certainty of those Propositions. Nor was it by them that he got the Knowledge of those Demonstrations; but by finding out intermediate *Ideas*

---

[51] Quoted ibid., pp. 185–6.
[52] *Pace* Soles, who claims that, for Locke, '[e]xplanations in natural philosophy are grounded in hypotheses, and Locke repeatedly provides examples. He, for example, appeals to Newton's hypothesis about gravitational attraction' (Soles 2005, p. 15; see also p. 10). Newton, in his letter to Roger Cotes of 28 March 1713, stresses that his principles of natural philosophy are not hypotheses: 'in experimental Philosophy [the term 'hypothesis'] is not to be taken in so large a sense as to include the first Principles or Axiomes which I call the laws of motion' (here Newton has the inverse square law in mind), Newton 1959–77, Vol. 5, p. 397.
[53] *Conduct*, §§43–4, pp. 281–3. See also the reference in 'Method', in Farr 1987, p. 71. Talk of bottoming on principles was fairly common in early modern British philosophy. See for example Samuel Parker's discussion of the problem of 'bottoming' hypotheses (Parker 1666, pp. 44–6). Locke uses the term in Draft B, §130 to refer to the senses as the foundation of our idea of space: 'the foundation of it bottoms there' (p. 253).
[54] *Conduct*, §12, p. 231.
[55] *Conduct*, §7, p. 222.

that shew'd the Agreement or Disagreement of the *Ideas*, as expressed in the Propositions he demonstrated. This is the greatest Exercise and Improvement of Humane Understanding in the enlarging of Knowledge, and advancing the Sciences; wherein they are far enough from receiving any Help from the Contemplation of these, or the like magnified *Maxims*.[56]

It is beyond doubt, therefore, that the Newtonian achievement forced Locke seriously to reconsider the source and foundational role of principles in natural philosophy in the 1690s.[57] Newton himself may well have had a hand in this. Apart from Newton's 'Demonstration', received by Locke in early 1690, we know that Newton had some involvement in Locke's revisions of his discussion of the creation of matter for the second edition of the *Essay* (E_2 IV. x. 18),[58] and this may have coincided with his preparation of *Some Thoughts concerning Education* for the press—a work in which he mentions natural philosophical principles for the first time.

I argued in Chapter 3 that, when he composed the *Essay*, Locke believed that the method of natural history is the most appropriate and efficacious one for pursuing knowledge of the natural world. At this point Locke was generally negatively disposed to admitting any role for principles or maxims in natural philosophy and emphasized the massive task of fact gathering for the enterprise of constructing natural histories. However, as Newton's achievement slowly dawned on him, he became aware of the efficacy of reasoning demonstratively by using principles; that is, he became aware that mathematical reasoning from principles derived from experience could generate knowledge of nature. Thus there was a certain amount of backtracking in Locke's mind on the question of the role of principles in natural philosophy. After a peroration against them in early Book IV of the first edition of the *Essay*, Locke came to see that there are foundational principles derived from phenomena and experiment which have a central place in natural philosophy.

It is tempting to infer, then, that Locke identified such 'Principles in Natural Philosophy' with laws of nature, and that in Locke's mature natural philosophy laws of nature 'made evident to us by experience' came to play the role that principles and maxims played in the traditional natural philosophy. However, I argue in the following chapter that Locke seems to have had little use for nomological explanation. Let us turn, then, to Locke's account of explanation in natural philosophy.

---

[56] *E* IV. vii. 11, p. 599.

[57] Here I am in broad agreement with Axtell 1968, pp. 72–4, and I differ from the views of G. A. J. Rogers. Rogers (1978, p. 230) claims that '[t]he *Principia* was for Locke the vindication of a general methodological approach to which he had subscribed for perhaps twenty years'. For a recent discussion, complementary to my own, see Winkler 2008.

[58] For discussion, see Stein 2002, pp. 272–3.

8
Explanation

> It is usuall in things we doe not comprehend as a cover of our ignorance for the explaining what we doe not understand to substitute something as unintelligible & hard to be explaind with this pretence that without such a supposition it can not be explained. whereby we are made much vainer in an opinion of our Knowledg though not one jot the more Knowing.
>
> John Locke[1]

In the previous two chapters we examined Locke's vision of a corpuscular metric of the unobservable entities that make up everyday material bodies, and we saw just how Locke accommodated demonstrative reasoning in his method for natural philosophy. No doubt Locke came to believe that the corpuscular metric would ideally produce a kind of analogue to what Newton had achieved in celestial physics. It would include reasoning according 'Lockean demonstration' from natural philosophical principles derived from observation. In this chapter we turn to Locke's views on the nature of the explanation of the phenomena we experience in the external world. The issue is important, because an analysis of his views on empirical explanation is the final piece in the exposition of Locke's views on the nature and prospects of the science of natural philosophy. We will proceed by examining some principles of explanation to which Locke is committed and some constraints on the application of those principles which seem to be implied in his discussions of natural philosophical reasoning. The principles and their constraints, when taken together, enable us to construct a coherent picture of Locke's view of natural philosophy.

Lockean principles of empirical explanation

Locke does not have a *theory* of empirical explanation. Rather, what we find in the *Essay* and elsewhere is a wide range of claims about the nature of properties, matter,

---

[1] Extract from 'Ignorantia', by Locke, Bodl. MS Locke c. 33, fol. 27v.

and the phenomena of nature, all of which reveal that Locke is committed, implicitly at least, to two principles of explanation. The first and most explicit explanatory principle is the Contact Criterion:

Contact Criterion—all change in the material world, so far as we can conceive of it, occurs by contact of bodies in motion (apart from gravitational attraction).

Locke states this explicitly in the *Essay*. In the first three editions (E_{1-3} II. viii. 11), Locke says:

The next thing to be consider'd, is, how *Bodies operate* one upon another, and that is manifestly *by impulse*, and nothing else. It being impossible to conceive, that Body should operate on what it does not touch, (which is all one as to imagine it can operate where it is not) or when it does touch, operate any other way than by Motion.[2]

In his subsequent correspondence with Stillingfleet, Locke acknowledged that Newton's claims about gravity in the *Principia* had prompted him to change his view:

It is true, I say, 'that bodies operate by impulse, and nothing else'. And so I thought when I writ it, and can yet conceive no other way of their operation. But I am since convinced by the judicious Mr. Newton's incomparable book, that it is too bold a presumption to limit God's power, in this point, by my narrow conceptions. The gravitation of matter towards matter, by ways inconceivable to me, is not only a demonstration that God can, if he pleases, put into bodies powers and ways of operation above what can be derived from our idea of body, or can be explained by what we know of matter, but also an unquestionable and every where visible instance, that he has done so. And therefore in the next edition of my book I shall take care to have that passage rectified.[3]

He did rectify the passage by removing the clause 'and nothing else' and by changing it from a claim about body–body interaction to a claim about how bodies produce ideas in us.[4] But he left other statements of the contact criterion untouched, as we see for example just six sections later, where he claims that the pain and sickness caused by manna

are confessedly nothing, but the effects of its operations on the Stomach and Guts, by the size, motion, and figure of its insensible parts; (for by nothing else can a Body operate, as has been proved:).[5]

In fact, Locke even made a countervailing change to his concession to Stillingfleet in the fourth edition, at *E* IV. x. 19. There he changed '[w]e cannot conceive how Thought (or any thing but motion in Body) can move Body' to 'we cannot conceive how anything but impulse of Body can move Body' (taken also in the fifth edition).[6] Thus it is not entirely clear just how far Locke really modified his views in the light of Newton's discoveries about gravity.

---

[2] For minor textual variations between editions, see the critical apparatus of the *Essay*, p. 135.
[3] *Second Reply*, pp. 467–8.
[4] For further discussion, see Downing 1997.
[5] *E* II. viii. 18, p. 138.   [6] See the critical apparatus in Locke 1975, p. 629.

What is clear is that he was committed to the Contact Criterion in a fairly strong form. This criterion is a central tenet of the mechanical philosophy, as espoused by the likes of Descartes and Boyle.[7] It is, in effect, a criterion of causal explanation which privileges efficient causation over other forms of causation, though Locke does not present it as such.

A second principle of explanation to which Locke is committed can be stated as follows:

The Reduction Principle—all observable natural phenomena can, in principle, be explained by the small number of qualities possessed by the imperceptible parts of matter.[8]

Locke nowhere in the *Essay* explicitly states that this is an explanatory principle, but there is ample evidence that this principle is implicit in his articulation both of the primary/secondary quality distinction and of the nominal/real essence distinction. In Book II, chapter 8 (and elsewhere), Locke speaks of secondary qualities as powers which 'depend on', 'flow from', 'spring from', and are 'produced' by the primary qualities of the imperceptible parts of matter that make up the relevant object.[9] Yet the clearest statement of this Reductive Principle is found in the last sentence of Locke's *Elements of Natural Philosophy*, composed in the late 1690s:

By the figure, bulk, texture, and motion, of these small and insensible corpuscles, all the Phenomena of bodies may be explained.[10]

The principle is reductive in so far as a large range of qualities and phenomena are claimed to have their ontological ground in a small set of underlying qualities, and this ontological reduction is explanatory.

It is well known that these two principles are central tenets of the mechanical philosophy of Descartes and Boyle. However, it is unlikely that they are sufficient to mark a commitment to the mechanical philosophy. An additional explanatory principle is required; and that is the claim that all explanations of natural phenomena are to be made by analogy with the functioning of machines. With respect to the machine analogy, Locke does use some common mechanical tropes, in the *Essay* and elsewhere;[11] but, unlike Boyle, he does not seem to employ the machine analogy as an explanatory device.

Nevertheless, it is clear that he was well disposed to the corpuscular hypothesis (as distinct from the mechanical philosophy). Here the work of Lisa Downing has,

---

[7] See for example Boyle's 'About the Excellency and Grounds of the Mechanical Hypothesis', *Boyle Works*, Vol. 8, p. 105.
[8] Gaukroger 2008 downplays the significance of reductive explanations in Locke and emphasizes the autonomy and explanatory adequacy of phenomenal explanations vis-à-vis mirco-corpuscular explanations.
[9] Locke's secondary qualities are said at *E* II. viii. 14, 23, 26, II. xxiii. 9, IV. iii. 12, etc. to depend on primaries; at *E* II. xxxi. 13, to flow from primary qualities; at *E* IV. iii. 11, to spring from primary qualities; at *E* IV. iii. 13, to be produced by primary qualities.
[10] *Elements of Natural Philosophy*, *Locke Works*, Vol. 3, p. 330.
[11] See for example *E* IV. vi. 11. For other uses of 'machine' to refer to the world, see also *STCE*, §194, p. 248 (quoted below), and Locke's Journal entry for 8 February 1677, in Locke 1936, pp. 86 and 89. Locke denies the Cartesian doctrine of the *bête machine* at a number of places in the *Essay*: *E* II. xi. 11 (section entitled 'Brutes abstract not'), *E* II. xxvii. 5.

I believe, gone a long way to establishing that, while Locke was not an unequivocal adherent of the corpuscular matter theory, he did regard it as the most intelligible hypothesis in terms of the clarity of its primary concepts and of its explanatory potential.[12] Wherein does its explanatory potential lie? Why does Locke give the example of 'the corpuscularian Hypothesis, as that which is thought to go furthest in an intelligible Explication of the Qualities of Bodies'?[13] As Downing has pointed out,[14] the answer lies in Locke's theory of material qualities.

The centrepiece of Locke's theory of qualities, the primary and secondary quality distinction, maps nicely onto a similar distinction, adumbrated by Boyle, between the mechanical affections and the non-mechanical or secondary qualities of bodies. Now Boyle's theory of material qualities was central to his corpuscularian hypothesis and, in particular, it was tied to his account of the explanatory superiority of that hypothesis. For Boyle as for Descartes, the new theory of qualities required an inversion of the explanatory direction of the traditional theory of qualities. Instead of the *primae qualitates* of bodies (hot, cold, wet, and dry), which were used to explain the elemental make-up of bodies and their peculiar accidents, the new mechanical affections of shape, size, motion, and texture became the *explanans*. Thus, for the corpuscularians, the properties of hot, cold, wet, and dry were to be explained in terms of the mechanical affections of shape, size, and motion.[15] So by adopting, and even by developing, the corpuscularian theory of properties in the drafts and then in the *Essay*, Locke implicitly committed himself to a new approach to explanation.

There is, however, another point that needs to be made with regard to the Reduction Principle, and this has to do with one particular property of the microstructure of the unobservable parts of bodies. Numerous comments that Locke makes throughout the *Essay* and elsewhere imply that he is committed to a particular form of the Reduction Principle, a form that has been dubbed by Ernan McMullin 'structural explanation'.[16] Locke's talk of the possibility of God superadding thought to matter 'fitly disposed' is perhaps the most notorious of the many passages in which he reveals a commitment to the view that the powers of material bodies derive from the structural arrangement of their constituent parts.[17] The technical term for this property is 'texture', and Locke does include texture in a number of his lists of primary qualities.[18] Moreover, structural explanations were championed by the mechanical philosophers and were a natural mode of explanation for those who emphasized the efficacy and comprehensiveness of explaining natural phenomena by analogy with the functioning of machines. We have seen that Locke does not fully appropriate the machine metaphor as an explanatory principle; yet his commitment to structural explanation

---

[12] Downing 1998. [13] *E* IV. iii. 16, p. 547, underlining added.
[14] Downing 1998, pp. 356–63. [15] For further discussion, see Anstey 2000, pp. 24–8.
[16] McMullin 1978. [17] *E* IV. iii. 6. See also *E* II. viii. 19.
[18] 'Texture' appears in lists of primary qualities at *E* II. viii. 10, 14, 18, 23 and 24, *E* II. xxi. 3, 73, *E* II. xxiii. 8.

was such that he used the underlying structure of functional systems as a criterion of the preservation of identity in living things over time.[19]

Lockean explanatory constraints

In addition to the Contact Criterion and to the Reduction Principle, Locke appears to be committed to two very important explanatory constraints on empirical explanation. The first is what I have elsewhere dubbed the Familiarity Condition:[20]

Familiarity Condition—all explanations of the unobserved must be made in terms of properties and causes with which we are familiar.

Before we examine the textual warrant for the claim that Locke implicitly adhered to this condition, it is worth drawing attention to just how important this thesis was to some of Locke's closest natural philosophical mentors. When Robert Boyle discusses the nature of natural philosophical explanation in *The Origine of Forms and Qualities, (According to the Corpuscular Philosophy)* (hereafter *Forms and Qualities*) he speaks in the following terms:

to explicate a *Phænomenon*, being to deduce it from something else in Nature more known to Us, then the thing to be explain'd by It.[21]

Again, in his *Defence of the Doctrine Touching the Spring of the Air*, he claims: 'to *explain* a thing is to deduce it from something or other in Nature more known'.[22] Boyle's younger contemporary Isaac Newton agreed. His third rule of philosophizing, given in the second edition of the *Principia*, says,

Those qualities of bodies that cannot be intended and remitted and that belong to all bodies on which experiments can be made, should be taken as qualities of all bodies universally.[23]

Amongst the claims which Newton is making here and in his extensive elaboration of this rule is the claim that the properties of the unobservable parts of matter are to be inferred by analogy with those of the observable parts of matter. A manuscript comment on this rule is revealing: 'This seems to be the foundation of all Philosophy. For otherwise one could not derive the qualities of imperceptible bodies from the qualities of perceptible (bodies)'.[24]

What is more interesting still is that in Locke's copy of the *Principia*, which was given to him by Newton, there is an annotation on p. 402 'correcting' Hypothesis III. This is an ancestor of what was to become Rule III in the second edition of 1713. It says:

---

[19] *E* II. xxvii. 4–5. [20] Anstey 2000, pp. 54–8.
[21] *Boyle Works*, Vol. 5, pp. 351–2. [22] *Boyle Works*, Vol. 3, p. 42.
[23] Newton 1999, p. 795. 'Intended and remitted' means roughly increase or decrease in magnitude.
[24] Quoted from Cohen 1966, p. 176.

Hypoth. III. The qualities of bodies that cannot be intended and remitted, and that belong to all bodies in which one can set up experiments, are the qualities of bodies universally.[25]

Unlike Rule III, this is a strongly metaphysical claim. Instead of the injunction that universal qualities of observable bodies 'should be taken as' qualities of those bodies that we cannot observe, Newton asserts that they *are* the universal qualities of bodies. This, as far as we know, is the only version of Rule III that Locke ever saw and, while it postdates the publication of the first edition of the *Essay*, it certainly reflects the confidence with which the Familiarity Condition was held by those within Locke's ambit.

It is clear, then, that Boyle and Newton are both committed to the Familiarity Condition.[26] Part of the motivation for adopting this condition on natural philosophical explanation derives from the polemic against the speculative excesses of scholastic natural philosophy, which was more than ready to postulate the existence of a host of occult or inexplicable qualities in order to explain various natural phenomena. One need only allude to the hackneyed example of the dormitive virtue of opium to make the point.[27]

Turning to Locke's discussion of analogical reasoning in *E* IV. xvi. 12, we have already encountered the following claim about reasoning from the observed to the unobserved micro-structure of material objects:

Analogy in these matters is the only help we have, and 'tis from that alone we draw all our grounds of probability.

Locke gives the example of rubbing two sticks together, producing heat, and inferring from this that 'what we call Heat and Fire, consists in a violent agitation of the imperceptible minute parts of the burning matter'.[28] He clearly regards analogical reasoning from the observed to the unobserved micro-structure of material objects to be our only legitimate method of reasoning about the unobserved parts of bodies. The implication of the words 'only' and 'alone' is that Locke was committed to the Familiarity Condition of two of his Master-Builders.[29] A crucial instance of this, as we have seen, is the manner in which Locke accepted Newton's inductive generalization that all bodies have the power of gravitational attraction; and this is a direct application of analogical reasoning.

As stated, the Familiarity Condition is an epistemic constraint on natural philosophical explanation; we cannot infer the existence of any new properties or laws at the sub-microscopic level. However, the condition rides closely alongside the stronger metaphysical thesis that Newton toyed with, namely that there are in fact no properties

---

[25] Quoting Cohen's translation in Cohen 1971, p. 24. For a facsimile of this annotation, see ibid., p. 48.
[26] For Descartes and the Familiarity Condition, see his *Principles*, Part 4, §201 (Descartes 1985, p. 287), and his *The World*, ch. 6 (ibid., p. 91). For Cordemoy, see Cordemoy 1679, p. 73 (Mihnea Dobre alerted me to this passage).
[27] See Hutchison 1982. For Locke's references to the properties of opium, see *E* II. xxiii. 8 and IV. iii. 25.
[28] *E* IV. xvi. 12, pp. 665–6.
[29] See the related discussion in R. A. Wilson 2002, pp. 207–8.

at the unobservable level that are not also at the observable level. It is important that we do not saddle Locke with this thesis, for he did conceive that spiritual beings might have additional senses to our own, and he implies that they might be able to perceive qualities of bodies to which humans do not have epistemic access.[30] We must therefore stress that Locke is committed only to the epistemic cousin of this stronger metaphysical thesis.

The Familiarity Condition also needs to be considered alongside a common vice in the conduct of the understanding: taking words for things that really exist in the world. Locke regards this as a particularly pernicious error in human reasoning, and one that he himself attempts to guard against: 'I endeavour, as much as I can, to deliver my self from those Fallacies, which we are apt to put upon our selves, by taking Words for Things' (*E* II. xiii. 18, p. 174). He has a sustained discussion of this error in *E* III. x. 14–16, and returns to it in the section on words in the *Conduct* (§29). Locke gives numerous examples of this kind of error, from various speculative systems of philosophy, and even from the new philosophy. The causes of the vice are various, ranging from uncritical acceptance of authority to prepossession by a speculative system or to lack of clarity and distinctness among ideas. Furthermore, while Locke does not make the connection, the problem is compounded by the tendency to take certain qualities, such as cold, to be positive when they are merely privative (Draft B, §58, *E* II. viii. 1–6). At *E* III. xi Locke prescribes a raft of techniques in the use of language, all designed to combat this and other abuses of words. And these techniques can be seen to complement the Familiarity Condition in so far as they will militate against the postulation of the existence of theoretical entities that are mere posits of theory and not real existents.

Now, while the advantage of a commitment to the Familiarity Condition is the proscribing of appeals to bizarre and *ad hoc* properties, there is also a severe cost to it. The history of science since Locke has revealed that nature is replete with qualities at the sub-microscopic level (as measured in Locke's day) that bear no resemblance to properties with which Locke and his contemporaries were familiar.[31]

A second condition for natural philosophical explanation to which Locke is committed has to do with the way of ideas. Let us call it the Simple Ideas Condition.

Simple Ideas Condition—if an idea is in the mind, then it arrived there as a simple idea (or simple ideas) via sensation or reflection.

The Simple Ideas Condition is a further epistemic constraint on empirical explanation for Locke. It lies at the heart of his theory of knowledge and ideas, and it has the

---

[30] *E* II. xxiii. 13, p. 304: 'though we cannot but allow, that the infinite Power and Wisdom of God, may frame Creatures with a thousand other Faculties, and ways of perceiving things without them, than what we have: Yet our Thoughts can go no farther than our own, so impossible it is for us to enlarge our very Guesses, beyond the *Ideas* received from our own Sensation and Reflection'. In Draft A, §2, p. 11, Locke suggests that spiritual beings might be distinguished by qualities 'whereof we have noe notion'. See also Draft B, §20, pp. 131–2.

[31] See Friedman 1974.

important consequence that we cannot conceive of new properties for which we lack simple ideas. Locke uses the example of the man born blind, who lacks ideas of colour and who, barring a miracle, has no prospect of receiving such ideas.[32] (Of course, Locke denies that the mind is equipped with any innate principles or ideas.) This constraint is closely allied to the Familiarity Condition insofar as it limits the range of possible inferences humans can make about the unobserved. Were we even to believe that there are unfamiliar properties at the sub-microscopic level, we could have no conception of what they might be like. Therefore the route to such properties is doubly blocked: *ex hypothesi* we cannot perceive them, and we cannot reason to them analogically because they are unfamiliar.

Furthermore, the Simple Ideas Condition and the Familiarity Condition, together with the primary and secondary quality distinction, appear to entail the Contact Criterion. Thus, while the Contact Criterion and the Reduction Principle might seem at first sight to be important and independent explanatory principles from which one might develop a theory of empirical explanation, it is really Locke's theory of ideas and the Familiarity Condition that are at the heart of Locke's views on how we can explain the phenomena of the material world.

The argument from intelligibility

But on what grounds could Locke claim that this new theory of qualities was explanatorily superior to its rivals? 'Intelligibility' was a buzz word amongst the mechanical philosophers. Conversely, 'unintelligible' was a term of abuse frequently levelled against Aristotelian natural philosophical categories, against the Galenic theory of disease, and often against the principles of the chymists. Boyle uses the term and its cognates scores of times, with reference to the new theory of qualities and to the corpuscularian hypothesis in general. Such uses are easy to spot in other mechanical philosophers as well. The term and its cognates occur eighteen times in the *Essay* alone.

Now there was a generic intelligibility argument, propounded by the adherents of the mechanical philosophy, which was normally stated in a fairly imprecise manner. For example, Descartes famously claims at *Principles* IV, §198:

Now we understand very well how the different size, shape and motion of the particles of one body can produce various local motions in another body. But there is no way of understanding how these same attributes (size, shape and motion) can produce something else whose nature is quite different from their own—like the substantial forms and real qualities which many {philosophers} suppose to inhere in things; and we cannot understand how these qualities or forms could have the power subsequently to produce local motions in other bodies. Not only is all this unintelligible, but we know that the nature of our soul is such that different local motions are quite sufficient to produce all the sensations in the soul. What is more, we actually experience

---

[32] *E* II. ii. 2, III. xxii. 11, III iv. 11–13, IV. iii. 23, IV. xvii. 9. See also Draft A, §43, Draft B, §20, pp. 75 and 131.

the various sensations as they are produced in the soul, and we do not find that anything reaches the brain from the external sense organs except for motions of this kind. In view of all this we have every reason to conclude that the properties in external objects to which we apply the terms light, colour, smell, taste, sound, heat and cold—as well as the other tactile qualities and even what are called 'substantial forms'—are, so far as we can see, simply various dispositions in those objects which make them able to set up various kinds of motions in our nerves {which are required to produce all the various sensations in our soul}.³³

Boyle produces an analogous argument in *Forms and Qualities*:

I do not remember, that either *Aristotle* himself, (who perhaps scarce ever attempted it,) or any of his Followers, has given a solid and intelligible solution of any one *Phænomenon* of Nature by the help of substantial Forms; which you need not think it strange I should say, since the greatest Patrons of Forms acknowledg their Nature to be unknown to Us, to explain any Effect by a substantial Form, must be to declare (as they speak) *ignotum per ignotius*, or at least *per æquè ignotum*. And indeed to explicate a *Phænomenon*, being to deduce it from something else in Nature more known to Us, then the thing to be explain'd by It, how can the imploying of Incomprehensible (or at least Uncomprehended) substantial Forms help Us to explain intelligibly This or That particular *Phænomenon*? For to say, that such an Effect proceeds not from this or that Quality of the Agent, but from its substantial Form, is to take an easie way to resolve all difficulties in general, without rightly resolving any one in particular; and would make a rare Philosophy, if it were not far more easie then satisfactory.³⁴

Analyses of the various versions of these arguments suggest that the notion of intelligibility was closely tied with conceivability, with familiarity, with parsimony, and with observation. Normally the first step of the implicit argument is of the form:

1. If x is conceivable (or familiar or parsimonious) then x is intelligible
2. x is conceivable (or familiar or parsimonious)
3. Therefore, x is intelligible.

This is followed by an argument by elimination or by an argument from comparative plausibility. The argument from comparative plausibility suffers from the threat of circularity, for it is tempting to cash out plausibility in terms of intelligibility.

Locke gives a rather vague eliminative version of the intelligibility argument in Draft B, appealing to conceivability and to the Simple Ideas Condition. He claims that material effects in nature are 'noething else but modifications of motion'. He continues:

I thinke we cannot conceive [material effects] to be any other [...] for what ever sort of action besides [this] produces any effect I confesse my self to have noe notion nor Idea of & soe are as far from my thoughts apprehension & knowledge & as much in the darke to me as the Ideas of colours to a blinde man.³⁵

---

[33] Descartes 1985, p. 285.   [34] *Boyle Works*, Vol. 5, pp. 351–2, underlining added.
[35] Draft B, §150, p. 262. For the use of the term 'unintelligible' against the School philosophers, see Draft B, §§72 and 88, pp. 176–7 and 195.

We should not make too much of this intelligibility argument as an argument for the Contact Criterion, for Locke's concern here in Draft B is to elucidate the notion of power, and the passage is recycled in the chapter on mixed modes in the *Essay* (II. xxii. 11), where the focus is on the idea of causation. Moreover, Locke uses a similar argument form and the very same terminology at *E* II. xxiii. 28 (p. 311), when arguing against the intelligibility of the transfer of motion from one body to another by impulse: 'the passing of Motion out of one Body into another; [...] I think, is as obscure and unconceivable, as how our Minds move or stop our Bodies by Thought'. However, of interest here is the argument form, together with Locke's early appeal to the Simple Ideas Condition.

Locke's claim, at *E* IV. iii. 16, p. 547, about 'the corpuscularian Hypothesis, as that which is thought to go farthest in an intelligible Explication of the Qualities of Bodies' suggests a comparative plausibility form of the intelligibility argument. But it must be said that Locke nowhere goes to any pains to spell out an intelligibility argument for the corpuscularian philosophy. Rather, informal intelligibility arguments are deployed by him on the one hand for the new theory of qualities, and on the other hand against the intelligibility of the fundamental notions of corpuscular theory. In Locke's discussions of the new philosophy, intelligibility arguments cut both ways.

Nomological explanation

Rather surprising, however, is the fact that Locke has so little to say about nomological explanation. As we have seen, he is certainly aware of the recent discovery of determinable laws of nature in optics and mechanics; and there are at least fifteen specific references to laws of nature in his writings.[36] However, unlike Boyle, who infers by transdiction that 'the Laws of Motion take place [...] in the smallest Fragments of Matter',[37] Locke never offers nomological explanations of natural phenomena, and he makes almost no mention of laws of nature in the *Essay*. There are only two places in his published writings where he mentions their explanatory power. The first occurs in the opening paragraph of his review of Newton's *Principia* in 1688. There he says:

[T]he philosophers and principally the moderns imagine that God has prescribed the same laws for the formation and the conservation of his works and they have tried to explicate by

---

[36] For references to laws of nature in Locke's writings, see his *Essays on Law of Nature* (= Locke 1954), p. 109; his review of Newton's *Principia* in Locke 1688, pp. 436–7; *STCE*, §192, p. 246; *Examination of Malebranche*, *Locke Works*, Vol. 9, p. 217 (motion of animal spirits, rules of refraction and dioptrics); *Second Reply*, p. 427; *Elements of Natural Philosophy*, *Locke Works*, Vol. 3, p. 304; *Discourse of Miracles*, ibid., Vol. 9, pp. 256 and 264; and *Conduct*, p. 282. There is a note made by Locke in 1690 upon reading Cudworth's *True Intellectual System of the Universe* (LL 896), which refers to phenomena that cross 'the laws of Mechanisme': see Bodl. MS Locke c. 33, fol. 28r. This note was copied in 1700 into Bodl. MS Locke d. 11, fol. 51v.

[37] 'About the Excellency of the Mechanical Hypothesis', *Boyle Works*, Vol. 8, p. 107.

them divers effects of nature. Mr Newton sets himself the same aim and takes the same way in this treatise.[38]

This is merely a paraphrase of Newton's description of the project of the *Principia* in his 'Preface to the Reader'.[39] The second reference to the explanatory role of laws is found in Locke's *Second Reply* to Stillingfleet, and there Locke's comments are laced with irony:

> Your second argument against accommodating mathematics to the nature of material things is, 'that mathematicians cannot be certain of the manner and degrees of force given to bodies so far distant as the fixed stars; nor of the laws of motion in other systems'. A very good argument why they should not proceed demonstratively in this our system upon laws of motion, observed to be established here: a reason that may persuade us to put out our eyes, for fear they should mislead us in what we do see, because there be things out of our sight.[40]

The implication of Locke's ironic reply to Stillingfleet is that we *should* proceed demonstratively from the laws of motion (just as Newton has done). But there is no hint of this in the *Essay*, where laws of nature are only mentioned three times, and then only in passing.[41]

I claimed in the previous chapter that in the 1690s Locke came to acquiesce in Newton's notion of principles of natural philosophy and that, while this notion does not appear in the *Essay*, changes that Locke made to his discussion of principles and maxims in Book IV indicate the impact of Newton's demonstrative reasoning from principles. It is natural to ask, therefore, whether Locke believed that these principles are laws of nature.

It is beyond doubt that Newton regarded the principles of the *Principia* as laws. He says as much in the Introduction to Book III: '[t]hese principles are the laws and conditions of motions and of forces, which especially relate to [natural] philosophy'.[42] Later, after Locke's death, Newton reiterated the point when writing to Roger Cotes about 'the first Principles or Axiomes [of experimental philosophy] which I call the laws of motion' and by claiming that the principles 'are deduced from Phænomena & made general by Induction' and are therefore as certain as we can expect in natural philosophy.[43] But in the draft preface to the *Opticks*, written in 1703, Newton is working with a broader conception of principles of natural philosophy, one which encompasses impenetrability, the particulate nature of matter, and the existence of an infinite, eternal spirit.[44] These latter three principles are hardly laws of nature.

---

[38] Locke 1688b, pp. 436–7. [39] Newton 1999, p. 382.
[40] *Second Reply*, p. 427.
[41] *E* IV. iii. 13 and 29, twice. Locke mentions the 'Rules of Geometry' in the context of corpuscular explanations in his review of Boyle's *Specific Medicines* (Dunton 1692, p. 184), and again in his review of Newton's *Principia*, Locke 1688b, p. 437.
[42] Newton 1999, p. 793.
[43] Newton to Cotes, 28 March 1713, in Newton 1959–77, Vol. 5, p. 397. He is even more explicit in a draft of this letter that was never sent: ibid., p. 399.
[44] McGuire 1970, pp. 183–4. See also p. 181 for the claim that Newton's principles are 'broader in scope' than laws are.

I contend that this broader conception has primacy in Locke's own use of the notion of principles of natural philosophy. For Locke nowhere makes an explicit connection between principles and laws. He does intimate the identity between principles and laws, at least in relation to gravity, in the *Elements of Natural Philosophy*. I quote *in extenso*:

It appears, as far as human observation reaches, to <u>be a settled Law of Nature</u>, that *all Bodies have a Tendency, Attraction, or Gravitation towards one another.*

The same force applied to two different bodies, produces always the same quantity of Motion in each of them. For instance, let a Boat, which with its loading is one tun, be tied at a distance, to another Vessel, which with its lading [cargo] is twenty six tuns: if the rope that ties them together be pulled, either in the less or bigger of these Vessels; the less of the two, in their approach one to another, will move twenty six foot, while the other moves but one foot.

Wherefore the quantity of matter in the Earth being twenty six times more, than in the Moon; the motion in the Moon towards the Earth, by the common force of attraction by which they are impell'd towards one another, will be twenty six times as fast as in the Earth; that is, the Moon will move twenty six miles towards the Earth, for every mile the Earth moves towards the Moon.

Hence it is, that in this natural tendency of Bodys towards one another, that in the lesser is consider'd as *Gravitation*; and that in the bigger as *Attraction*: because the motion of the lesser body (by reason of its much greater swiftness) is alone taken notice of.

This Attraction is the strongest, the nearer the attracting bodies are to each other: and in different distances of the same bodys, is reciprocally in the duplicate proportion of those distances. For instance, if two bodys, at a given distance, attract each other with a certain force, at half the distance, they will attract each other with four times that force; at one third of the distance, with nine times that force: and so on.

Two bodies, at a distance; will put one another into motion by the force of attraction: which is unexplicable by us, tho' made evident to us by experience, <u>and so to be taken as a Principle in Natural Philosophy</u>.[45]

But he nowhere seems to make the general claim that laws are identical to, or a subset of, the principles of natural philosophy. Evidence of this is found in a telling passage of the *Essay* that hardly changed from the first to the fourth editions. At *E* IV. iii. 29 (p. 560), Locke speaks thus:

The Things that, as far as our Observation reaches, we constantly find to proceed regularly, we may conclude, do act by a Law set them; but yet by a Law, that we know not: whereby, though Causes work steadily, and Effects constantly flow from them, yet their *Connexions* and *Dependancies* being not discoverable in our *Ideas*, we can but have an experimental Knowledge of them.

Had he clearly identified some of his natural philosophical principles with laws, he might have modified this passage, for he would have seen that we can, and we do, have experimental knowledge of some laws of nature, and that these laws in some sense explain the necessary connections or constant regularities in nature. Such a change to

---

[45] Locke 1720, pp. 181–3 = *Locke Works*, 3, pp. 304–5, underlining added. For another comment that hints that the principle of gravity is a law, see also *STCE*, §192, p. 246.

the *Essay*, however, would have ramified through Locke's theory of knowledge and would have required additional changes elsewhere in the text. For, according to Locke's theory, sensitive knowledge—that is, experimental knowledge—is only of particulars (*E* IV. iii. 5), and all general propositions concerning substances—for instance 'All bodies gravitate towards one another'—while keenly sought after, are not knowledge at all (*E* IV. v. 10; IV. vi. 16). Yet his principles of natural philosophy are general propositions that are 'teeming truths', 'fundamental truths' from which new truths can be generated. Little wonder, then, that the principles that matters of fact justify do not appear in the later editions of the *Essay*. There remains, therefore, a discontinuity between Locke's mature thoughts on the method of natural philosophy and what he presented in the *Essay*, even in its final form of the fourth edition.[46]

The Newtonian doctrine of natural philosophical principles also bears on another issue in Locke's account of natural philosophy given in the *Essay* and in the correspondence with Stillingfleet: the evident tension between Locke's ideal of a demonstrative natural philosophy and the passages in which he posits that God might superadd certain qualities to matter. The various attempts to resolve this tension have polarized Locke's interpreters. Some, like Michael Ayers, claim that Locke maintained that a demonstrative science of nature is possible, though 'out of our reach' (*E* IV. iii. 26, p. 556).[47] Others, such as Matthew Stuart, claim that the superaddition passages reveal that a demonstrative science of nature is ruled out in principle and that Locke ultimately succumbs to natural philosophical scepticism.[48]

In my view, the most honest assessment,—and here I am in agreement with Margaret Wilson[49]—is that Locke has two ostensibly inconsistent lines of reasoning on the nature of our knowledge of material substances. On the one hand, he had long held to the ideal of a demonstrative natural philosophy which is based upon a corpuscular metric once we gain epistemic access to the determinate qualities of corpuscles. On the other hand, he could genuinely see no way in which, say, the quality of gravity would derive from what we know about matter.[50] The principles of natural philosophy, however, provide a means of resolving this tension. For example, the principle of gravitational attraction, the prime example of a superadded quality, just is a principle which matters of fact justify: the general proposition 'All bodies gravitate to one another' is a teeming truth, the foundation of all natural philosophy, and therefore a principle upon which a demonstrative natural philosophy can be based. The key move here is to see that the superadded quality, gravity, is *identical* to the quality that features in the foundational principle.

---

[46] On this point I am in broad agreement with John Yolton, who claims that Locke 'was unwilling or unable to adjust his theory of knowledge and his account of the science of nature to take account of this new understanding [the method of Newton's *Principia*]': Yolton 1970, p. 89.

[47] Ayers 1981a and 1991, Vol. 2, pp. 142–53.

[48] See Stuart 1996.

[49] See M. D. Wilson 1979.

[50] See *Second Reply*, pp. 467–8. Gravity is not mentioned in the *Essay*.

Now the unresolved tension in Locke's view of gravity arises from the fact that we cannot demonstrate that gravity derives or flows from the nature of matter. But, if the principle of gravity is the foundation of natural philosophy, then there is no need to derive it from anything more fundamental. It should be stressed that the contingency of the laws of nature is not relevant here—and not because, as we have seen, Locke had little time for nomological explanation. The fact that God might be able to impose laws (or qualities) on bodies independently of their inner natures (and of the natures of bodies with which they causally interact) does not entail that we cannot, in principle, have a demonstrative science of nature. Should God change the laws, we would have a different science of nature, but a science of nature nonetheless. Thus, had Locke identified principles with laws, such 'nomological principles' would have formed the foundation from which a demonstrative science of nature would have developed. It is even in keeping with Locke's views that there may be different sciences of nature at different times, or in different worlds. In my view, then, Locke did have the resources at hand to resolve the tension between his ideal of a demonstrative natural philosophy and the doctrine of superaddition. Locke was not a natural philosophical sceptic. Unfortunately, however, the doctrine of the principles of natural philosophy never found its way into the *Essay*.

Conclusion

Where does this leave Locke? What sort of natural philosophy can one reasonably construct, given these theses about empirical explanation? Given the current limits of observation in Locke's day, which enabled microscopic magnification up to x500 (though this was extremely rare) and telescopic magnification up to x100 and above (though the field of view was very limited), the prospects of actually getting epistemic access to the corpuscular realm were extremely remote.

First, let us consider the knowledge of celestial bodies. Here the situation is markedly more encouraging. In the case of forces, we have a highly developed celestial dynamics with (determinable) laws of motion and gravitational attraction; we have epistemic access to determinate properties of celestial bodies; we have causal explanations of macro-terrestrial and celestial phenomena (movement of the tides, planetary and cometary motions, and the like); we have predictive power. This represents a significant advance, and in *Some Thoughts concerning Education* Locke rightly praises the Newtonian achievement, seeing it as a model for approaching other parts of natural philosophy:

Though the Systems of *Physicks*, that I have met with, afford little encouragement to look for Certainty or Science in any Treatise, which shall pretend to give us a body of *Natural Philosophy* from the first Principles of Bodies in general; yet the incomparable Mr. *Newton,* has shewn, how far Mathematicks, applied to some Parts of Nature, may, upon Principles that Matter of Fact justifie, carry us in the knowledge of some, as I may so call them, particular Provinces of the

Incomprehensible Universe. And if others could give us so good and clear an account of other parts of *Nature*, as he has of this our Planetary World, and the most considerable *Phænomena* observable in it, in his admirable Book *Philosophiæ naturalis principia Mathematica*, we might in time hope to be furnished with more true and certain Knowledge in several parts of this stupendious Machin, than hitherto we could have expected.[51]

However, when Locke turns to *transdictive* inferences, that is, inferences from the observed to the sub-microscopic, the situation is very different. In the case of forces, we cannot posit, say, repulsive forces between corpuscles by the Contact Criterion; nor can we posit, by the Contact Criterion, any attractive forces apart from gravity; and we cannot give an explanation of cohesion, in spite of the Reduction Principle. In the case of qualities of sub-microscopic bodies, we cannot posit any new qualities by the Familiarity Condition and by the Simple Ideas Condition; we can infer the existence of familiar properties through analogy, by the Familiarity Condition, but we cannot give any determinate corpuscular explanations, in spite of the Reduction Principle.

Not surprisingly, therefore, Locke is far less sanguine about the prospects of this aspect of *experimental* natural philosophy than he is about the progress that has been made in celestial mechanics:

I deny not, but a Man accustomed to rational and regular Experiments shall be able to see farther into the Nature of Bodies, and guess righter at their yet unknown Properties, than one, that is a Stranger to them: But yet, as I have said, this is but Judgment and Opinion, not Knowledge and Certainty. This *way* of getting, and *improving our Knowledge in Substances only by Experience* and History, which is all that the weakness of our Faculties in this state of *Mediocrity* which we are in in this World, can attain to, makes me suspect, that natural Philosophy is not capable of being made a Science.[52]

As for *speculative* natural philosophy, as we have already seen, Locke sees here little hope of any advance. We have already encountered his comment, in *Some Thoughts concerning Education*, that 'Natural Philosophy, as a speculative Science, I imagin we have none, and perhaps, I may think I have reason to say, we never shall be able to make a Science of it'.[53] One important consequence is that Locke does not regard the corpuscular hypothesis or the mechanical philosophy as having any special heuristic value.[54] He does not view them as setting *desiderata* for an experimental programme, but rather as the outcome of speculative reflection on the collection of observations and experiments performed by chymists and others on material bodies. On this point

---

[51] STCE, §194, pp. 248–9.
[52] E IV. xii. 10, p. 645. See also E IV. iii. 26, pp. 556–7: 'And therefore I am apt to doubt that, how far soever humane Industry may advance useful and *experimental* Philosophy *in physical Things, scientifical* will still be out of our reach: because we want perfect and adequate ideas of those very bodies which are nearest to us, and most under our command'.
[53] STCE, §190, pp. 244–5.
[54] For Boyle's view of the heuristic value of his speculative corpuscular philosophy, see Anstey 2002d.

then, Locke had a more realistic grasp of the yawning gap between theory and the current science than Boyle did.

A second point to note is the extent to which Locke's approach to empirical explanation is still wedded to the Aristotelian ideal of a demonstrative natural philosophy. To be sure, he has his own objections to the syllogistic, and the process of demonstrative reasoning is cashed out by using the Lockean theory of ideas. But there is nothing in his approach to explanation that resembles the hypothetico-deductive method, and this is what makes it so different from a modern conception of empirical explanation.

Finally, it is now clear, with hindsight, that Locke was unduly pessimistic about the prospects of natural philosophy and that, within one hundred years of the publication of his *Essay*, significant advances were to be made in chemistry that would deliver quantitative results. Therefore Locke should not be regarded as a modern when it comes to empirical explanation: he should not be regarded as pioneering, providing, or even adumbrating a promising new approach to the acquisition of natural philosophical knowledge.

9

Iatrochemistry

> I have forborn to say any thing against multiplication in general because you seem perswaded of it.
>
> Newton to Locke.*

The foregoing analysis of Locke's views on the correct method for pursuing natural philosophy, the use of hypotheses and analogy, the role of mathematics, the nature of demonstrative reason, and natural philosophical explanations might incline us to the view that Locke evaded natural philosophical speculation altogether. To be sure, he conceded that the corpuscular hypothesis was the most intelligible of the systems available, but, given his reservations about some of its fundamental notions such as cohesion and the transfer of motion, it would be understandable on his part to have left speculation to others. Indeed the numerous passages in the *Essay* itself where Locke refrains from indulging in 'physical inquiries' tend to reinforce the view that Locke was not inclined to speculation. However, a close analysis of Locke's manuscripts and correspondence, and even of the *Essay* itself, reveals that, although he was cautious, Locke did not evade speculative theory altogether. In fact it is possible to reconstruct with a fair degree of precision the speculative theory of matter to which Locke adhered and to identify his sources of influence. Locke's theory of matter is found in his medical and chymical writings.

Chymistry

Mention of the remains of Locke's medical and chymical writings brings us to the important background question of the relation between physic and chymistry in Locke's day. By the early seventeenth century, the preparation of medical remedies was one of the primary applications of chymistry. In fact the Wittenberg chymist Daniel Sennert claimed:

---

* 2 August 1692, *Correspondence*, Vol. 4, p. 490.

Chymistry is not a peculiar Art, but belongs to Physick, and is the perfection of it, for it is the part only of the Physitian to use and apply Chymical medicines for cure, and [he] may be called then a Chymical Physitian, and the Medicines Chymical, which are the perfection of Physick.[1]

The theory of disease, its diagnosis and treatment, as well as many facets of animal physiology, such as respiration and digestion, were founded upon chymical theories of one sort or another. Almost every leading chymist in England in the 1660s practised physic.[2] The diversity amongst them can be accounted for, in part, by differences in the respective chymical theories and techniques that they deployed.

Locke's involvement in chymistry, and therefore in chymical medicine, probably began in 1659 and continued well into the 1690s. There were two important strands to Locke's chymistry. First, it is clear that he was deeply influenced by the mercurialist school and practised chymistry in conformity with its teachings. This school believed that the Philosophical Mercury, an essential ingredient in preparing the Philosopher's Stone, could be obtained from common mercury. But there is a second, Helmontian strain in Locke's chymistry, which is evident in his chymical notebooks, his correspondence, and his medical receipts and which is easily accounted for in terms of important sources of influence such as Boyle and his good friend, the Helmontian physician David Thomas. To be sure, it is slightly artificial to separate out these two strands of Locke's chymical thought and practice, and yet it is true to say that the mercurialist strand is the most fascinating one when it comes to Locke's chymical practice, while the Helmontian elements are most important for understanding his approach to medicine or physic. I will deal with each of these strands of Locke's chymistry in turn. The evidence presented is illustrative rather than exhaustive.

Locke and mercurialist chymistry

The derivation of the Philosophical or 'Sophic' Mercury involved two processes: first, the removal of 'external' impurities, which was done by using well-established purification techniques such as washing, grinding, and distillation; second, the removal of internal impurities. This process was believed to be essential for the animation of the Sophic Mercury. Once purified, Sophic Mercury was then able to liberate and nourish the seeds of gold and so enable transmutation.[3] The actual process that Boyle used in order to develop the Sophic Mercury involved combining mercury with an alloy of pure metallic antimony and silver. William Newman has shown that Boyle learnt this technique from George Starkey, who in turn had derived it from Alexander von Suchten. Where does Locke fit into all of this?

---

[1] Debus 1990, p. 174. Further discussion on the relation between chymistry and medicine ibid.

[2] The one notable exception is Boyle. For a discussion of the relation between his chymistry and medicine, see Principe 1998, pp. 186–8, 305, 307. For Boyle on the Galenists, see Hunter 2000b. For Starkey, see Newman 2003, pp. 176–7, and Starkey's notebook entry entitled 'A Book on Paper of George Starkey', published in Starkey 2004, pp. 319–27.

[3] Summarizing Principe 1998, pp. 153–5.

On 20 May 1660 Dr Ayliffe Ivye wrote to Locke at Oxford, hoping for his assistance:

> I hope Sir, you will lett slippe noe occasion whereby you may better your selfe, and soe me, by your aquaintance with Mr. Boyle, I longe to have an accounte of my Quæries; I made Panacæa[4] Last weeke and have sent you two dragmes, tis the First preparation calcined via humida, liquore alkahestico then, washed and dryed you may go higher and with spirite of wine acuated etc. drawe off his perfect tincture; but truelye this worketh admirable well and noethinge standeth in his way, and tis most safe to administer it secundum Glauberi modum [...][5]

Ivye's request suggests that he had sent some chymical queries to Boyle and hoped that Locke would follow them up for him. It is clear from this letter that Ivye believed Locke to be interested in his chymical preparations, not least because he had sent Locke two drachms of his Panacea and some details of his method of preparation of the expectorant: he refers to the *via humida* (the use of liquid solvents), alludes to van Helmont's alkahest, and mentions the method of the German chymist Glauber. Moreover, this is the earliest known connection between Locke and Boyle and it suggests that they were already discussing chymistry together by May 1660.

Three months later, we find Locke writing to a certain J. O. that he had failed to find in the study of Mr B (that is Robert Boyle) the second part of a work by Alexander von Suchten, which he had promised him; he was sending instead a newly arrived work by Glauber.[6] In fact, Locke had probably promised J. O. a manuscript translation of the second treatise of von Suchten's 1604 work on the secrets of antimony, *Tractatus secundus de antimonio vulgari*.[7] Two copies of a Latin translation of von Suchten's *Concordantia chymica* (1606) survive amongst the Boyle Papers.[8] It is therefore of great interest to note that Locke seems to have believed that Boyle also had a copy of a translation of von Suchten's tract on antimony. It is important not to be misled by Locke's comment in this letter that 'Mr B prefers Glauber to Sutchen' because, as mentioned above, von Suchten's method of preparing his Sophic Mercury, as spelt out in the second treatise to which Locke refers, was absolutely crucial to George Starkey's preparation of Philosophical Mercury—a preparation that Starkey transmitted to Boyle.[9] And, of course, we now know that Boyle was preoccupied with the preparation of the Sophic Mercury for over four decades because this process was thought to be a necessary preliminary to the preparation of the Philosopher's Stone.[10]

---

[4] Glauber's Panacea is probably Antimony pentasulphide, an expectorant. See Bodl. MS Locke f. 25, p. 279 and Bodl. MS Locke d. 9, p. 288 for entries on panacea.

[5] Ivye to Locke, 20 May 1660, *Correspondence*, Vol. 1, pp. 146–7. For notes from Ivye, see Bodl. MS Locke d. 9, p. 6; Bodl. MS Locke f. 27, pp. 33–4, 38; Bodl. MS Locke f. 25, pp. 117, 185, 262, 271, 290/303–5, 317a.

[6] Locke to J. O., August 1660, *Correspondence*, Vol. 1, p. 151. Esmond de Beer suggests that J. O. might be John Oliver, whom Locke mentions in a previous letter: ibid., p. 150.

[7] Printed in Suchten 1604; the first treatise was Suchten 1575.

[8] BP 34, fols 1–152, and BP 14, fols 47–74.

[9] Newman 2003, pp. 135–41; Newman and Principe 2002, pp. 50–6.

[10] See Principe 1998. Interestingly, in a diary entry of 1681, during a period of renewed chymical activity between Locke and Boyle, Locke records the following comment by Boyle: 'Suckten a very good chymist' (Dewhurst 1963a, p. 207).

Was the young Locke cognizant of all of this? The remains from his chymical works reveal that he was. For in Bodl. MS Locke f. 18, which he used from 1659–60—that is, at the time of his correspondence with Ivye and J. O.—Locke records an opinion of a substance called Hews Powder, described by his chymical friend and physician Dr William Currer (d. 1668). Currer, it should be noted, was a chymical physician and had had an acrimonious dispute with Starkey in 1657–8.[11] Locke records Currer's view of Hews Powder as follows:

> My opinion is Hews his powder is noething but mercury of antimony fixed with gold which worketh as this doth witnesse Suchtenius.[12]

Interestingly, a near identical entry in John Ward's diary, deriving from Currer, can be dated to 1661.[12a] In c. 1659–61, in Bodl. MS Locke d. 11, Locke made a bibliographic entry for von Suchten's *De secretis antimonii* (1575).[13] Clearly he was fully aware of the importance given to von Suchten's 'mercury of antimony' in the early 1660s. But was he, under the influence of Boyle, to become a covert chrysopoeian (that is, a gold-maker) seeking the recipe for the Sophic Mercury? Was he a mercurialist when it came to developing techniques for generating the Stone? Did he also seek the alkahest, the universal solvent, through the purification of salts after the manner of van Helmont, Starkey, and Boyle? Was Locke a philosopher by fire? And, most importantly, what light does this shed on his views on the nature of matter?

Around 1660, there was clearly a need in Oxford for some sort of instruction in chymistry for the clutch of young talented physicians who were associated with those practising the new philosophy there. To this end, Boyle arranged for the German chymist Peter Stahl to teach a course in chymistry, and Locke attended such a course from 23 April to late May 1663.[14] Detailed notes from this course survive in Bodl. MS Locke f. 25, and we can glean from it—as well as from similar notes recorded by others—a fairly clear picture of what Locke was taught. Stahl was a physician; he taught basic laboratory techniques for preparing chymical remedies, many of which, according to John Ward, derived from Oswald Croll, a student of the German chymist Hartmann.[15] If there is any truth to Anthony Wood's charge that during the course Locke was 'prating and troublesome', this might have happened because Locke had already been inducted into the chymical arts and had well-developed chymical views of his own.[16]

But Locke's chymical notebook (Bodl. MS Locke f. 25) contains far more than simply notes from the course with Stahl. Interestingly, it includes extensive entries

---

[11] For Currer's dispute with Starkey, see Newman 2003, p. 190.
[12] Bodl. MS Locke f. 18, p. 52. The entry begins on p. 43 and continues on p. 52. It was later copied to Bodl. MS Locke f. 25, pp. 317a–b.
[12a] See the transcription in Wellcome MS 6175, p. 11.
[13] Bodl. MS Locke d. 11, fol. 81v. Locke noted, correctly, that the work has forty-nine pages.
[14] See Walmsley and Milton 1999.
[15] 'Stall hath most of his praeparations out of Crollius and others notwithstanding what hee pretends of their being left him by his father', John Ward's Diary, Folger MS V.a.291, fol. 90r. (Michael Hunter provided me with this reference.)
[16] Wood 1891–1900, Vol. 1, p. 472.

relating to antimony and mercury, and in particular mercury of antimony, the alkahest, and even the Philosophical Mercury.[17] Their presence is strong evidence that an important seam in Locke's own chymical outlook was mercurialist and that the various preparations relating to antimony were conceived within the theoretical framework deriving from the lineage of von Suchten→Starkey→Boyle.[18] On the whole, Locke's preoccupation was with chymical preparations that had some application in physic, and the entries in Bodl. MS Locke f. 25 coincide with the period in which Locke was equipping himself as a physician. So, for example, the fact that the chymist John Read, who was associated with the plans, in 1665, for a Society of Chymical Physicians, could write to Locke in 1666 asking him '[w]hat it is in mettells & Minnerall that is Medicinal',[19] indicates that Locke was associated with the medicinal applications of chymistry. Moreover, as we have seen, it is but a small step from the medical applications of the mercurialist theoretical framework to a full engagement in the teleological structure of this approach to chymistry, which the quest for the Stone represented. Yet soon after this period Read and his friend Thomas Williams (who was later to become Chymical Physician to Charles II) were to run into trouble over a chymical substance through which Locke feared 'all nature might be discovered'. Is it surprising, then, that Locke supplied Boyle in secret, *sub sigillo*, with his own recipe for a mercury of antimony which still survives in the Boyle Papers?[20]

Locke's chymical notebook also contains records of recipes derived from various chymists and chymical physicians within his ambit, including William Currer and Thomas Williams (with whom Locke had had an altercation).[21] The most important of these people is Boyle himself, and in fact Boyle remains the single most important source of chymical advice and opinion in all of Locke's notebooks; many of Locke's chymical connections triangulate in various degrees with Boyle. One important example is Johann Schard, whom Locke met on his visit to Cleves during the winter of 1665–6. Locke had complained to Boyle of Cleves that 'their physicians go the old road, I am told, and also easily guess by their apothecary's shops, which are unacquainted with chemical remedies. This, I suppose, makes this town so ill furnished with books of that kind, there being few here curious enough to enquire after chemistry or

---

[17] The same is true of the chymical entries in Bodl. MS Locke f. 27. See for example the entry on *Aurum* at pp. 43–4: 'to purify gold, melt the gold & put to it 2 or 3 times its weight of antimony that takes away the impuritys of the gold, & to carry away the Antimony put to it a quarter of its weight of sublimate. to know whether the sublimate be good put it upon the tongue & it will stick to it'.

[18] See for example Locke's entry on mercury of antimony from Boyle on p. 76: 'Mercury of antimony: Take as much vitriol as you like and distill it in the usual manner. Pour the chaos over very finely powdered antimony and distill in a retort to dryness. Take what remains in the retory and sublime. Grind the sublimate upon a marble with oil of tartar and let the mercurial globules combine together into larger ones. Mr. Boyle' (Translation from Latin by L. M. Principe).

[19] John Read to Locke, *Boyle Correspondence*, Vol. 3, p. 14.

[20] BP 26, fol. 102.

[21] For William Currer, see Bodl. MS Locke f. 25, pp. 23, 63, 277, 317b, Bodl. MS Locke f. 27, pp. 47, 51 *bis*. For Thomas Williams, see Bodl. MS Locke f. 25, fols 39, 60, 249, 316, 359, 361, Bodl. MS Locke f. 19, p. 207, Bodl. MS Locke c. 44, pp. 60–1 (notes derived from Boyle's papers). Locke even received some receipts from Prince Rupert, such as a recipe for *Auri tinctura* 'communicated by his own mouth', Bodl. MS Locke d. 9, p. 16. For Locke and Prince Rupert, see Dewhurst 1963b.

experimental learning'.²² By 'the old road' Locke was referring to the traditional Galenic approach to physic, but in Schard he found an up-to-date chymical physician. The many chymical recipes from Schard in Bodl. MS Locke f. 25 derive from the notebook Bodl. MS Locke f. 27, which Locke took with him to Cleves and Bodl. MS Locke f. 27 reveals that Locke almost certainly spent time in Schard's chymical laboratory and that in addition to the preparation of various chymical remedies, they worked on mercury of antimony.²³

After his return from Cleves in February 1666 Locke engaged in another period of chymical experimentation for which notes also survive in Bodl. MS Locke f. 25. 1666 was also an important year in Locke's development as a physician and we will have cause to examine his medical writings from this period below. Locke seems to have been practising chymistry with his friend David Thomas throughout the period from his return from Cleves on 18 February 1666 to the time of his departure for the household of Anthony Ashley Cooper in early April 1667. On 18 November Thomas wrote to Locke, who was visiting Lord Ashley in London, saying: 'If you bring with you mercury [...] we will make mercury sublimate our selves which wilbe much cheaper then to buy it'.²⁴ Once established in Ashley's household, he wrote to Boyle that his fingers still itched to practise chymistry again.²⁵ In fact there was a chymical laboratory at Exeter House, but there is little evidence of his engaging in chymical experimentation. He did, however, practise physic, and the period from September 1667 to September 1670 proved to be the most intense years of medical practice that Locke was ever to experience.²⁶ During these years Locke was able to start to apply some of the vast knowledge of chymical remedies he had begun to accumulate in the late 1650s.

Locke's chymical interests never waned. There are chymical preparations, notes, and observations in his journal that testify to his ongoing interest in chymistry during his travels in France. Of particular interest is his discussion of Samuel Cottereau Duclos' potable gold, one of the most prized medicines in the armoury of chymical medicine. Locke's entry for 22 June 1678 contains the recipe for Duclos' potable gold, which had apparently 'cured quartans and dropsy', though Locke records that 'Mr. Briot told me Duclos was a great liar'.²⁷ He goes on to enter a query which he intended for Thomas Williams:

Q. of Sr T. Williams concerning the processe of this aurum potabile of Dr. F. Anthony found amongst the papers of the Bishop of Winchester.²⁸

---

²² *Correspondence*, Vol. 1, p. 228.

²³ Bodl. MS Locke f. 27, pp.75–6 copied into Bodl. MS Locke f. 25, pp. 201/309. Locke's drawings of glassware and descriptions of apparatus (pp. 72, 80–1, 90) render it very likely that his notes were made in Schard's laboratory.

²⁴ David Thomas to Locke, 18 November 1666, *Correspondence*, Vol. 1, p. 296. For Thomas' process for mercury of antimony, see Bodl. MS Locke f. 25, p. 31.

²⁵ Locke to Boyle, 12 November 1667, *Correspondence*, Vol. 1, p. 315.

²⁶ See British Library Add. MS 5714, which contains Locke's medical case notes from this period.

²⁷ Dewhurst 1963a, p. 128.

²⁸ Quoted in ibid. A copy of this entry is in Bodl. MS Locke f. 28, p. 184. Francis Anthony (1550–1623) had a run in with the College of Physicians over his potable gold. See Debus 2002, pp. 184–5 for a summary discussion and references.

Later, near the end of Locke's exile in the Netherlands, Thomas wrote again to him, this time about the potable gold:

I receaved the chymicall processes and have read Philalethes[29] more then once and doubt whether water in the receavor in the purification of the mercury may prejudice it That being in other processes prescribed. I desire you to read Jodocus Greverus in Theatr Chym vol. 3: p. 699 to the same purpose. I entend and am now preparing materialls for the potible gold which Mr Boyle assures though formerly of a contrary opinion is of very greate use and efficacy in physicke.[30]

Boyle had indeed been sceptical of the potable gold in his *Usefulness of Natural Philosophy*, published in 1663.[31] However, his view changed, perhaps due to his involvement with Georges Pierre, the mysterious ambassador of the asterism, who sent him a recipe for the potent medicine. In fact Boyle finally published his own recipe for the potable gold in his *Observationes physicae* in 1691.[32]

After Locke's return from France, David Thomas wrote to him on 11 January 1682 hoping to see him, because 'this wilbe a convenient time for chemestry', and expressing to Locke that he believed he could make a 'principall remedy' approaching the alkahest.[33] The next notable episode in Locke's chymical engagements involved Francis Mercurius van Helmont, the son of the great Flemish chymist, whom Locke met in the Netherlands in late 1686, while he was in exile. Francis Mercurius van Helmont had edited his father's literary remains, which were published as *Ortus medicinae* in 1648. Locke was reading them carefully as early as 1657/8.[34] Francis Mercurius van Helmont was a peripatetic chymist and theologian whose most distinctive views concerned the transmigration of souls. In December 1690, after Locke had returned to England, Francis Mercurius, Locke's 'Chymicall freind',[35] provided him with a new furnace.[36] This signals on Locke's part a return to chymical trials that is almost certainly tied to his involvement with Boyle.[37]

---

[29] Thomas refers to Eirenaeus Philalethes' *Introitus*, first edition Amsterdam, 1667 (LL 1554). Unbeknownst to Thomas and Locke, this was written by George Starkey.
[30] David Thomas to Locke, 20 October 1688, *Correspondence*, Vol. 3, p. 511.
[31] *Usefulness of Natural Philosophy*, II, i, *Boyle Works*, Vol. 3, pp. 381–2. For Starkey's attempts to make von Suchten's potable gold, see Newman and Principe 2002, pp. 107–14.
[32] *Observationes physicae*, *Boyle Works*, Vol. 11, p. 419. For Georges Pierre and the potable gold, see Pierre to Boyle, 3/13 May 1678, *Boyle Correspondence*, Vol. 5, pp. 77–8. For further discussion, see Principe 1998, p. 145, Malcolm 2004, and Principe 2004a.
[33] David Thomas to Locke, *Correspondence*, Vol. 2, p. 474.
[34] See Bodl. MS Locke e. 4, pp. 43–4 and 123–5.
[35] David Thomas to Locke, 7 July 1688, *Correspondence*, Vol. 3, p. 481. For chymical notes from F. M. van Helmont, see Bodl. MS Locke d. 9, p. 156 (Rugæ), p. 205 (Ferrum).
[36] *Correspondence*, Vol. 4, p. 177.
[37] Locke carried out a chymical experiment from 28 April to 6 July 1691; see Bodl. MS Locke d. 9, p. 223.

We now know that, some months before Boyle's death, Locke received from him a part of the recipe for the Sophic Mercury. It is recorded in shorthand and code in Locke's Journal entry for 25 September 1691.[38] A month later, in a letter to Boyle, he declares: 'I have water, and I have vessels, I only want soap to be at work'.[39] Lawrence Principe has shown that the 'soap' is the cleansing alloy for the internal process of purification of common mercury. After Boyle's death on 31 December 1691, Locke corresponded with Newton about the various constituents, or periods, of the recipe for the Sophic Mercury.[40] On 10 May 1692 he visited Newton in Cambridge with the express purpose of discussing Boyle's chymistry. Newton immediately gave him Boyle's recipe for a solvent prepared from butter of antimony, which he had intended to ask Locke to publish.[41] On the next day Locke recorded in his Journal the second and third periods for the recipe for the Sophic Mercury, using the fairly transparent cypher 'per Van Notwen', that is, Newton's name spelt backwards. He quickly copied into another notebook, in Latin and in shorthand, both the periods and the recipe for the solvent.[42]

Soon, however, Locke was to have access to Boyle's very own recipes for the three periods, for in mid-July he became aware that he had been named as one of the executors of Boyle's chymical papers. He informed Newton of this development in a letter of 26 July, in which he recorded the first period for the recipe. Newton's reply to Locke's letter claims that it was for this recipe that Boyle 'procured the repeal of the Act of Parl. Against Multipliers'. But the letter also sheds light on Locke's own attitude to transmutation at this later stage in his life: 'I have forborn to say any thing against multiplication in general because you seem perswaded of it'.[43] Newton's claim is reinforced by the fact that, amongst the roughly two-hundred pages of chymical notes that Locke had copied from Boyle's papers, we find not only the crucial letter of early 1651, from Starkey to Boyle, outlining the method of von Suchten for preparing the Sophic Mercury, but also the second and third periods.[44] There is no

---

[38] Bodl. MS Locke f. 10, p. 105; expanded in Principe 1998, p. 174.

[39] Locke to Boyle, 21 October 1691, *Correspondence*, Vol. 4, p. 321.

[40] Locke to Newton, 26 July 1692, *Correspondence*, Vol. 4, pp. 485–6. See Principe 1998, pp. 175–7. See also Principe 2004b.

[41] The recipe is recorded in Locke's Journal on 10 May 1692, Bodl. MS Locke f. 10, p. 138. Newton's draft letter containing this recipe (#X.398.1, Newton 1959–77, 7, pp. 393–4) was rewritten and sent to Locke after his visit in early May. See Newton to Locke, 2 August 1692, *Correspondence*, Vol. 4, pp. 488–90. In fact Newton asked Locke to publish two of Boyle's recipes, the second of which is probably the one, found in the CHF Newton manuscript, for making an acid capable of dissolving gold by subliming sal ammoniac and quicklime, extracting the caput mortuum, and putting the extracted salt into aqua fortis. This manuscript also contains the recipe for the solvent derived from butter of antimony. I am grateful to Lawrence Principe for this information.

[42] The second and third periods in shorthand are in Bodl. MS Locke c. 42 first part, p. 69. Newton had apparently given them to Locke 'per memoriam'. The recipe for the solvent is on p. 88.

[43] Newton to Locke, 2 August 1692, *Correspondence*, Vol. 4, pp. 488 and 490. For further discussion of the repeal of the act against multipliers, see Hunter 2000c, pp. 111–13.

[44] Newman and Principe 2004, pp. 12–31. Locke's copies of Boyle's chymical notes are in Bodl. MS Locke c. 44, pp. 24–212. The Starkey letter is on pp. 142–53. The second and third periods are on p. 70 (combined under the head 'The 3rd Period'), and a recipe for mercury of antimony appears on p. 39. For

doubt, then, that in the early 1690s Locke was still keenly interested in Boyle's chrysopoeian ambitions and that he took measures to record them and to try them out experimentally.

Finally, in October 1694, in a letter to Locke, James Tyrrell says: 'I have no more but to assure you that as for the Manuscript you mention of the Course of Chymistry I doe not remember I ever so much as saw it'.[45] This suggests that Locke remained interested in chymical matters even as late as 1694. It also seems likely that the manuscript containing the 'Course of Chymistry' is Bodl. MS Locke f. 25, which we have discussed above. All of this evidence shows that Locke maintained a keen interest in chymistry, and specifically in mercurialist transmutational chymistry, over four decades.

Locke and Helmontian chymistry

Van Helmont died in 1644 and his substantial manuscript remains were published by his son Francis Mercurius van Helmont in 1648. His writings exerted a significant impact on the Hartlib circle, including George Starkey and the young Robert Boyle. By 1660, when Locke was beginning in chymistry, Helmontian iatrochemisty was embedded in reformist English medicine and had become one of its mainstays.[46]

The story of the transmission and assimilation of Helmontian ideas in England from the 1650s is multifaceted. However, as in the case of the mercurialist approach to chrysopoeia, Locke's main instructor in the application of Helmontian ideas was Robert Boyle. But Locke also read widely amongst the works of van Helmont and counted a number of Helmontian physicians amongst his friends—including, as we have seen, David Thomas, whom Locke seems to have befriended in the mid-1660s and who remained one of his closest friends.

Van Helmont's chymistry is predicated upon the view that the fundamental elements are water and air and that water is the primal principle to which all substances can be reduced. Van Helmont claimed that there is a universal solvent, the alkahest, which can reduce vegetables and minerals to their constituents and then to primal water. He identified Paracelsus' *sal circulatum* with his own alkahest. The alkahest operates by stripping substances of their forms, which are produced by the seminal principles that reside in the substance. Once the reduction has taken place, the alkahest can be separated off and reused, because it is not affected by that upon which it works. Of particular importance for medicine was the fact that the alkahest could work on the essence of a substance and isolate the active ingredient within it from its inert and noxious matrix. This in turn enabled the development of more powerful specific medicines which, stripped of their

---

early laboratory notes by Starkey that Locke almost certainly acquired from Boyle, see Bodl. MS Locke c. 29, fols 115r–18v, transcribed and translated in Newman and Principe 2004, pp. 3–11.

[45] James Tyrrell to Locke, 16 October 1694, *Correspondence*, Vol. 5, p. 163.
[46] See Clericuzio 1993. Newman and Principe (2002, p. 296) claim that 'Van Helmont's writings constituted what was probably the most wide-ranging and influential chymical theory of the second half of the seventeenth century'.

noxious matrix, were able to work in harmony with the *archeus* of each person, to be absorbed by the intestines, and thence to ameliorate the diseased condition of the patient. By contrast, Galenic remedies were rejected by the *archeus*, which purged the body of their gummous poisons.

According to van Helmont, other substances over and above the alkahest had medicinal value. Of particular importance was the volatile salt of tartar, which worked, not on the essence or 'crasis' of the substance to be ingested, but on its noxious impurities. This process converted natural substances into perfected sulphurs, which were thus prepared for ingestion by the patient. The volatile salt of tartar was, therefore, an important succedaneum to the aklahest in Helmontian medicine. Other Paracelsian medicines promoted by van Helmont include the tincture of Lili and *Mercurius diaphoreticus*.[47]

It was mentioned above that van Helmont identified his alkahest with Paracelsus' *sal circulatum* and thus regarded it as a special species of salt. In fact, van Helmont had a well-developed classification of salts and a theory concerning their manner of interacting with other chymical substances. Van Helmont's tripartite distinction between acid, alkaline, and urinous salts was taken up and adapted by Boyle, who also derived a further tripartite division of spirits from Starkey. Boyle also adopted the Helmontian theory of exantlation, by which it was supposed that acids lost their corrosive power when acting upon other substances, which Boyle explained in terms of the mechanical affections of the subtle bodies involved rather than through the more vitalistic explanatory categories of van Helmont.[48]

Now, in the service of his iatrochemistry, van Helmont deployed two features derived from Renaissance chymistry. First, he developed and applied quantitative techniques of gravimetrics for his chymical analyses of substances. Second, he used corpuscular explanations of the sub-microscopic material changes that gave rise to the chymical phenomena he observed. He also developed the Paracelsian ontological conception of diseases as pathogenic *semina*, each one with its own *archeus*, which comes into conflict with the *archeus* of the patient. This conception of disease was naturally tied to the chymical theory which went with the therapeutic applications of the alkahest and of the volatile salt of tartar, and it had radical implications for the traditional Galenic *methodus medendi*. No longer was disease to be considered a form of humoural imbalance and treatment determined by the idea of addressing excesses and privations of the primary qualities (hot, cold, wet, and dry). In fact van Helmont decried the use of venesection and of other traditional therapeutic techniques and advocated the development of chymical remedies based upon his conception of the operation of the *archei* and of the transformative power of his solvent and salts.[49]

---

[47] See Porto 2002, p. 16. For Mercurius diaphoreticus dulcis in Locke, see Bodl. MS Locke f. 25, pp. 124, 126. For Helmont's mercury diaphoreticus, see Bodl. MS Locke f. 27, p. 46.
[48] Newman and Principe 2002, pp. 289–96.
[49] For a thorough treatment of van Helmont's theory of disease, see Pagel 1982, pp. 141–61.

Van Helmont's was not the only existing conception of the alkahest, nor is it clear that the term 'alkahest' referred to one determinate substance in his *oeuvre*.[50] Others such as the German chymist Glauber developed and applied their own alkahests.[51] There was also a plethora of seminal theories of disease deriving from Paracelsus. In this regard, the views of the Dane Severinus provide a nice counterpoint to the Helmontian seminal theory of disease.[52] However, Helmont's ideas and laboratory techniques were undoubtedly the most influential in mid-seventeenth-century English medicine, and the most important locus of their development and deployment was in the work of Starkey and Boyle.

As it happens, all of these Helmontian substances and notions (of the alkahest and of the volatile salt of tartar in medicine; the theory of salts; the seminal theory of disease; a concern with quantitative chymical experimentation; and even the *archeus*) are to be found in Locke's chymical and medical notebooks and correspondence.[53] Locke also sought out specific receipts deriving from van Helmont. Let us first examine the trail of Helmontian ideas in Locke's chymical notebooks and in his correspondence before turning to his more focused treatments of the nature of disease and animal physiology. We turn first to the alkahest. In late 1666 Locke wrote:

Sal Circulatus Paracelsi est Alkahest Cellarius p. 26 <u>61</u>.[54]

Clearly he was aware of the relation between van Helmont's solvent and Paracelsus' circulatory salt. In the same year he recorded a long note on Schard's recipe for alkahest in Bodl. MS Locke f. 25, pp. 194/301. Another entry from around the same time records Boyle's view of the medicinal value of the alkahest or of a similar substance:

Alkahest   Or a menstruum like it dissolvd crud antimony, & when drawn of⟨f⟩ left christall of very great efficacy in physick, pourd upon salt of tartar & drawn of⟨f⟩ & the remainder dissolvd in water afforded strange chrystalls Mr Boyle

Just before leaving for London to join Ashley's household, Locke wrote to Boyle concerning one of van Helmont's recipes for the use of warts cut from horses. There he wonders

[w]hether they are to be taken from live horses, since (if I forget not) Helmont some where says, that if in histerical fits, (for in that disease he commends them) you use those that are taken from an horse, *æstuante venere*, they have different effects from others.[55]

---

[50] Porto 2002.   [51] For Glauber's alkahest, see Roos 2007, pp. 33–46.
[52] For Severinus, see Shackleford 2004, and, for a survey of theories of *semina* from the Renaissance to the period up to Boyle, see Hirai 2005.
[53] For Locke's extensive notes on Salt of Tartar, see Bodl. MS Locke f. 25, pp. 106–17/320/339.
[54] Bodl. MS Locke f. 25, p. 33. The work by Andreas Cellarius is *Harmonia macrocosmica*, Amsterdam, 1661 (not listed in Locke's library). In Bodl. MS Locke d. 9, p. 132, Locke has notes on Paracelsus' 'Hilech', 'Paracelsus vocat Hilech magnum et sal circulatis minor', and 'Alkahest Paracelsi videtur esse mercurius philosophorumet et non circulatum minus quod est Alkahest Helmontii'.
[55] Locke to Boyle, 24 March 1667, *Correspondence*, Vol. 1, p. 309.

Locke also seeks from Boyle's advice on the correct dosage of *sal ammoniac*.[56] Years later Thomas tells him

> I thinke a principall remedy may be made by Armoniacke salts satiated with acid salts and volatilized which I beleeve may be by a short way effected and farther advanced to allmost the Alkahest.[57]

Of course the alkahest was not the only Helmontian substance in which Locke took an ongoing interest. He also seems to have adopted, probably via Boyle, Helmont's theory of salts. For example, in Bodl. MS Locke d. 9, we find a signed entry implying a belief in the Helmontian tripartite division:

> Whether volatil or urinous salts, acid & alkali may by any art of chymistry be changed one into another & what difference is to be found amongst the particulars of each of these 3 species JL[58]

Locke is clearly aware of the Helmontian origins of this theory. The very next entry concerns the derivation of volatile salts from herbs, and makes a reference to van Helmont's *Ortus*:

> How the oyls of hearbs may be turned into volatil salts v. Helmont de Feb. c. 15 §7 52.[59]

Moreover, as will become apparent below, the Helmontian view of salts and spirits plays an important role in Locke's views on the use of respiration in animals and humans.

It may be objected that much of what Locke appropriated from van Helmont was undergirded by a speculative theory that included abstruse ontological categories such as *gas*, *blas*, and ferments, and that this is inconsistent with the experimental philosophy's opposition to speculation and hypotheses. However, this is to miss three crucial features of the Helmontian legacy in Locke's thought.

First, almost all of Locke's chymical notes concern practical chymistry, and there is no sustained discussion of underlying ontological categories. Locke's Helmontianism was practically and therapeutically oriented. Where Helmontian notions do appear, such as in his theory of seminal disease (to be discussed below), there is no detailed explanation of what these categories actually are.

Second, on the rare occasions when Locke actually does report explanations of what is happening in chymical reactions at the sub-microscopic level, he is either reporting Boyle's corpuscular explanations or offering corpuscular musings of his own. For example, a marginal comment in Bodl. MS Locke f. 25, p. 309 to an entry on 'Mercury of Antimony made by ascending at an intense heat by distilling in a retort' says: 'This calx fixes the oyly parts, & ~~fastens~~ imbibes them to its self Mr Boyle'.[60] The important

---

[56] Ibid., p. 310.

[57] David Thomas to Locke, 11 January 1682, *Correspondence*, Vol. 2, p. 474.

[58] Bodl. MS Locke d. 9, p. 30. See ibid., p. 222 for a reference to Daniel Coxe's article on alkali and fixed salts in the *Philosophical Transactions*, 9, 1674, pp. 150–8.

[59] Bodl. MS Locke d. 9, p. 30. For the process of converting oils into salts in the work of Starkey, Starkey's 'grand design for medicine', see Newman and Principe 2002, pp. 136–46.

[60] Entries on mercury of antimony from Schard and Petrus de Nicol begin at Bodl. MS Locke f. 25, p. 201 and continue on pp. 309/310/313.

point here is that, as Newman and Principe have shown,[61] Boyle tended to give mechanical explanations of Helmontian processes; and it is this 'de-vitalized' Helmontianism that he transmitted to Locke.

Nosology and therapeutics

Turning now to Locke's views on the nature of disease, we find that they are typical of those held by the chymical physicians of the 1660s and that the salient doctrines were widely held amongst Locke's peers. The *locus classicus* of Locke's view of disease is his 'Morbus' entry in British Library Add. MS 32554, about which much has been written. This text espouses a seminal theory of some diseases as a *via media* between the views of the Paracelsians and the Galenists. Locke's treatment of disease in this long entry from c. 1666 is strongly Helmontian and illustrates the manner in which Helmontian medical ideas were seen to oppose Paracelsian notions.

Of particular interest in 'Morbus' is the strong corpuscularism that underlies the theory. Locke delimits generation to two kinds: generation by seed and generation by the mixtion of parts:

some things are producd by seminall principles, & some other by bare mistion of the parts, to which might be added the circumstantiall assistances of heat & cold &c, by seminall principles or ferments I meane some small & subtile parcelles of matter which are apt to transmute far greater portions of matter into a new nature & new qualitys, which change could not be brought about by any other knowne means, soe that this change seems wholy to depend upon the operation or activity of this seminall principle, & not on the difference of the matter its self that is changd.[62]

Note, too, the reference to the Helmontian notion of ferments, which on this conception were endowed with the formative power of seeds. Locke also speaks of the *archeus* of the disease:

How these small & insensible ferments, this potent Archeus works I confess I cannot satisfactorily comprehend, though the effects are evident but yet I believe 'twould be worth considering, to finde what deseases spring from these ferments, such as I beleive are contagions.[63]

This is strongly Helmontian in tone and typical of the theories of disease which Locke was reading in the mid-1660s.[64] The seminal ferments are regarded, following van Helmont, as invasive pathogenic agents which have their own *archeus*. Interestingly, Locke's discussion contains a residue of Galenism in his references to temperaments:

it may be observd that in many deseases of this nature, the particular constitution of the body doth not make the deseases though some tempers be better fitted to be wrought on by this & some by that ferment, though if the seminall virtue be strong enough it will lay hold on any soe most seeds will grow almost in any soyle, though in some they thrive much better & others starve & dwindle.

---

[61] Newman and Principe 2002, pp. 289–96.
[62] British Library Add. MS 32554, p. 232 (= Walmsley 2000, pp. 390–1).
[63] British Library Add. MS 32554, p. 237 (= Walmsley 2000, p. 391).
[64] See Thomson 1666, LL 2891^a.

182   JOHN LOCKE AND NATURAL PHILOSOPHY

Soe sanguine complexions are observd most easily to admit the seminall principles of the plague easily melancholy tempers more difficultly.[65]

The seminal theory of disease combined naturally with the miasmatic theory, which was propounded by Fracastoro and others and promoted by Boyle, by Hooke, and later by Sydenham.[66] Locke's own later foray into 'environmental' medicine with Charles Goodall, which was discussed in the chapter on natural history, was predicated upon this miasma theory and is evidence for his continued belief in the seminal theory itself. And in fact we find in his Journal entry for 22 July of 1678 that he claims: 'certain body types may carry seeds of certain diseases, or are more predisposed to contract them'.[67]

As many scholars have pointed out, this ontological conception of disease lends itself to the view that there are different species of pathogenic agents. Interestingly, Thomas Sydenham's nosology lacked any clear conception of pathogens, but even in his earliest book, the *Methodus curandi febres* (1666), he emphasized the need to classify the different 'species' of fever which he took to be 'substantial forms' engendered from bodily humours in particular seasons and atmospheric conditions (constitutions).[68] And, while Locke maintained a radically different conception of disease, he may have been attracted to Sydenham's particular classification of fevers and may have realized its susceptibility to the method of natural history. (This would be consistent with the likelihood that the assembling of natural histories of disease became the hallmark of Sydenham's medical methodology through Locke's own influence.[69]) It is important to stress, however, that Locke concedes that not all diseases are caused by seminal agents:

Other deseases I suppose may probably be conceivd to be producd by a bare mistion of two unfitt ingredients, as when acid & volatile salts are mixd, there presently is producd an ebullition, & then the two differing salts coagulate into a 3^d substance far enough different from either of the ingredients. Which I suppose not to be donne by any seminall principle.[70]

One cannot help but note the implicit commitment to an Helmontian theory of salts, which seems to have played an important role in Locke's understanding of his own medical receipts as he went on and practised physic in later years. The depth of this commitment to this common theory of salts at this early stage in Locke's development as a physician is perhaps best illustrated in his short disputation on the use of respiration; and we turn now to Locke's physiology.

---

[65] British Library Add. MS 32554, p. 237 (= Walmsley 2000, pp. 391–2).
[66] See Nutton 1990 and Keele 1974.
[67] Romanell 1984, p. 139 and Dewhurst 1963a, p. 136.
[68] See Sydenham 1987, pp. 52/3–54/5, and 1848, Vol. 1, pp. 19–20. For Sydenham's view of constitutions, see Meynell 1988, pp. 48–9.
[69] For further discussion, see Anstey and Burrows 2009.
[70] British Library Add. MS 32554, p. 248 (= Walmsley 2000, p. 392).

Physiology

In 1666 Locke drafted in Latin a medical disputation on the use of respiration, entitled 'Respirationis usus'. It now survives in the Shaftesbury Papers in the National Archives in Kew.[71] Before we examine some of its contents, a note of caution is in order. Locke despised the disputations of the Schools, which he regarded as vacuous performances designed to titillate rather than to instruct. It seems most likely that he composed this disputation in order to cover himself, or at least his conscience, in his bid to have the degree of Doctor of Medicine conferred on him without fulfilling the requirements of the degree. With this in mind, we can surmise that there was in Locke's heart a degree of reluctance as he composed this draft and that its contents were designed more for the occasion than to record his own precise theoretical reflections on a very vexed problem in animal physiology. In other words, we should not take too seriously all of what Locke says in the 'Respirationis usus'—at least not as a definitive statement of his views. It was not composed as a record of research findings but as an academic exercise, a necessary evil in order to secure a Medical Studentship at Christ Church.

With these preliminaries in hand, let us turn to the text. The first thing to notice is the dramatic disputational form it takes. While this is most evident to the reader of Latin, there is enough in translation to capture the theatricality of the prose. It opens thus:

Nature never hides and flees from us more than when she seems to come forth openly and to show herself to anyone as obvious and easy. The vital breath of air that we draw in and expel with continuous labor from the first moment of life to its final extent seems merely to jeer at us. It pours itself into our inner breast only to slip away, and it cheats the embraces into which it rushed at first, and with the same subtlety it escapes the sharpness of both mind and eyes.[72]

And it is not long before the Helmontian themes start to leap off the page. After speaking of the 'vestal fire of life', which nourishes us, we are told that it is not the function of respiration to cool this fire, but rather

there are so many kitchens [*culinae*] of digestion and coction in the body, hence there are such various ferments of the internal parts all of which appear to work together so that there is finally something that can be inflamed and so that the vital flame may have tinder; to this purpose above all else, respiration seems to be devoted.[73]

The kitchen metaphor is classic van Helmont and the reference to the 'various ferments of the internal parts' speaks of the Helmontian theory of digestion. Locke then moves on to the role of fermentation in the generation of animal spirits, which he describes in terms redolent of Helmontianism:

---

[71] TNA PRO 30/24/47/2, fols 71r–74v. All translations and transcriptions of extracts from 'Respirationis usus' are by Lawrence Principe. Walmsley and Meyer 2009 provides a full translation.
[72] TNA PRO 30/24/47/2, fol. 73r.
[73] Ibid., fol. 73v.

It is now generally acknowledged by everyone that the life of animals consists in the continuous generation and flow of subtle spirits. It is evident that these spirits of the heart are generated either by heat or fermentation by means of a previous digestion of ingested substances in the stomach, the intestines, the mesentery, and other workshops [*officinis*].[74]

The next stage of the process brings us to the Helmontian theory of salts:

Animal life turns upon this hinge, that a continuous and constant supply of animal spirit be produced, that is, that the parts of the blood be exalted into a subtle and volatile material.[75]

This 'subtle and volatile material' is diffused throughout the body; and, when it has 'played its role',

these mature effluvia of the blood finally transpire and fly off into the breeze, thus furnishing a place for the spirits following behind them. In this way, by repeated circuits through the heart and lungs the mass of blood furnishes material to the vital flame, and finally the whole mass of blood, having been made volatile (leaving no residue behind) and transmuted into the nature of spirits, is breathed out and vanishes through sweat; this could never be done without the air's fellowship.[76]

What is the solvent in the air that enables it to 'agitate, subtilize, volatilize, and finally kindle' the body? Following Robert Hooke, Locke speculates that

[i]t would seem to be a certain highly volatile nitrous spirit, ⟨for⟩ some have not unaptly observed that saltpeter is the proper menstruum for sulphureous and inflammable bodies. Especially since it is well known that the volatile salts of animals (for example, of blood and of urine) produce niter when cofermented with earth exposed to solar rays.[77]

This is, in fact, the widely held Helmontian account of the role of the volatilization of venous blood in respiration. Locke even deploys the corpuscular terminology so characteristic of Van Helmont:

---

[74] 'Vita animalium in continua spirituum subtilium generatione et fluxu consistere apud omnes jam in confesso est. Istos spiritus cordis sive calore sive fermentatione generari praevia ingestorum in stomacho intestinis mesenterio aliisque officinis digestione constat', ibid. For *culinae* in van Helmont, see for example Van Helmont 1648: *Ortus medicinae*, 'Sextuplex digestio alimenti humani', numbers 67–8, pp. 222–3.

[75] 'cum enim eo in cardine versatur vita animalis, ut continuus constansque fiat proventus spirituum animalium, hoc est ut sanguinis partes in materiam subtilem et volatilem exaltentur', TNA PRO 30/24/47/2, fol. 73v.

[76] 'haec sanguinis effluvia exoleta tandem transpirent et in auras evolent, succedentibus spiritibus locum praebentia. et ita sanguinis massa repetitis per cor et pulmones circuitionibus flammae vitali materiam praebeat et tota tandem volatilis facta nulla relicta faece in spirituum naturam transmutata per διαπνοη difflatur et evanescat, quod nunquam fieri possit sine aeris commercio', ibid., fols 73v–72r. For van Helmont's view that the purpose of respiration is the volatilization of the blood, see van Helmont 1648: *Ortus medicinae*, 'Blas humanum', pp. 178–92, especially numbers 22, 31, 34–37 and 46.

[77] 'esse spiritum quendam nitrosum summe volatilem, qui non inepte nonnulli observarunt salem petrae corporum sulphureorum et inflammabilium esse menstruum appropriatum. praesertim cum constet sales animalium volatiles sanguinis puta et urinae terrae radiis solaribus expositae confermentata nitrum progignere', TNA PRO 30/24/47/2, fol. 72r. For the connection with Hooke, see Bodl. MS Locke f. 19, p. 158. The notion of an aerial nitre was widely discussed amongst the Oxford physiologists; see Frank 1980. For the origins of the notion, see Debus 1964.

it is probable that it is air which consumes bodies and makes them burn, not fire, which seems to be nothing other than the greatest agitation of the minute parts, while the air loosens their texture and shatters them.[78]

The point here is not that Locke was a thorough-going Helmontian, but that these were the tropes, the turns of phrase, the theoretical framework that Locke had at hand to work with. To be sure, in his *obiter dicta* concerning respiration and air he is more circumspect and less flowery, but even there the stamp of Helmontian chymistry and physiological theory are everywhere apparent.[79]

Conclusion

Locke was a chymical physician,[80] a mercurialist, and a Helmontian. He was almost certainly inducted into the chymical arcana by Robert Boyle, at least by early 1660, when he had access to his chymical papers and laboratory. It is little wonder, then, that Locke was one of the three physicians to whom Boyle entrusted his chymical papers on his death-bed and that one of the keys to unlocking Boyle's own quest for the Sophic Mercury was discovered through this inheritance. It is somehow appropriate that Locke should be a key to the chymical Boyle because so much of Locke's own development as a chymical physician was inspired by Boyle.

Four things are worth noting in conclusion. First, while Locke was a mercurialist and was tantalized by the prospect of securing the Sophic Mercury, there is, to my knowledge, no evidence of Locke as a crypto-chrysopoeian. Unlike Boyle, who secretly pursued transmutation and was even duped by unscrupulous pretenders such as Georges Pierre, Locke remained, first and foremost, one who sought to apply mercurialist and Helmontian chymistry in physic. Locke was not attempting to be an adept of chrysopoeia.

Second, Locke was not uncritical of his sources, his teachers, and the authors he read. He would have had no truck with the likes of Starkey, or even van Helmont himself, when it came to their pretensions to revelation. This, for Locke, would smack of enthusiasm, although to my knowledge there is no record of his response to the revelatory claims of the chymists.

Third, it should be noted, however, that there is a natural fit between Locke and van Helmont. Van Helmont was a serious experimenter, who contributed significantly to experimental method in chymistry. In this he was a significant source for the experi-

---

[78] TNA PRO 30/24/47/2, fol. 72r. For Locke's notes on nitre, see Bodl. MS Locke f. 25, pp. 147–51.
[79] See, for example, British Library Add. MS 32554, pp. 91/93; Bodl. MS Locke f. 19, p. 158 (adapted from Bodl. MS Locke f. 27, pp. 3–4 (rear)).
[80] One should not conclude, from the fact that Locke was aligned with the chymical physicians in the 1660s, that he was strongly opposed to the College of Physicians. In his final years he gave much valued advice to Dr Robert Pitt on problems within the College. See the letters from Pitt to Locke, of 22 November 1701 and of 27 December 1701, in *Correspondence*, Vol. 7, pp. 507–9 and 522–3.

mental philosophy: his gravimetric techniques were deployed by Boyle, who also performed some of his experiments, most famously the willow-tree experiment.[81] We have seen above that, from the early drafts of the *Essay* composed in 1671, Locke was deeply concerned with standards of measure, and his ideal natural philosophy was to be based upon a corpuscular metric. The corpuscular matter theory of Boyle was conducive to Locke's ideal for a fully quantified natural philosophy and at the same time was part and parcel of the Boylean application of Helmontian ideas.

Locke's appropriation of Helmontian medicine also dovetails nicely with his other natural philosophical interests and methodological views. A life-long interest in botany fed into Locke's training and practice as a physician, as did his involvement in Boyle's researches into the air. As we saw in Chapter 3, all of this was subsumed under the Baconian rubric of the need to assemble the natural histories, the classification of plants, the classification of diseases, the meteorological readings, and even the forays into environmental medicine form parts of an integrated whole, which preoccupied Locke for four decades.

And this brings us, fourth and finally, to the historiography which underlies so much Lockean interpretation. How are we to square Locke's commitment to seminal principles and the teleological sub-structure of a mercurialist theory of matter with a commitment to the sparse ontology of a corpuscular theory of matter and to the primary/secondary quality distinction? There are three considerations that need to be brought to bear on this question. First, as is typical of Locke in many areas of natural philosophy, he declares his nescience concerning the manner of operation of the seeds: '[h]ow these small & insensible ferments, this potent Archeus works I confess I cannot satisfactorily comprehend' (for further discussion see Chapter 10).[82] This reflects Boyle's own claims of ignorance about the mode of operation of seminal principles and is consistent both with Locke's reflections in the 'Anatomia' of 1668 and with the corpuscular pessimism of the drafts and of the *Essay* itself. A second important consideration is that Locke's commitment to transmutational mercurialist chymistry is predicated upon a homogeneous matter, which underlies the corpuscular concretions—that is, the stable materials with which the chymists worked. It is this homogeneous, solid matter that Locke describes in the *Essay* as being 'every where the same, every where uniform'[83] and that, when modified by determinate shape, size, and motion, gives rise to the conceptual problems for the corpuscular philosophy that were discussed above (Chapter 5).

However—and this is the third consideration—not only did Locke bring corpuscular analyses to bear upon matters of chymical analysis and interpretation wherever he could, but he clearly thought that such analyses would eventually be constituents of a demonstrative natural philosophy. Here is how he puts it in the chapter on universal propositions in Book IV:

---

[81] See Webster 1965. [82] See also Clericuzio 1990 and Anstey 2002c.
[83] *E* III. x. 15, p. 498.

[c]ould we begin at the other end, and discover what it was, wherein that Colour consisted, what made a Body lighter or heavier, what texture of Parts made it malleable, fusible, and fixed, and fit to be dissolved in this sort of Liquor, and not in another; if (I say) we had such an *Idea* as this of Bodies, and could perceive wherein all sensible Qualities originally consist, and how they are produced; we might frame such abstract *Ideas* of them, as would furnish us with matter of more general Knowledge, and enable us to make universal Propositions, that should carry *general Truth* and *Certainty* with them.[84]

Such universal propositions would not be merely general and certain truths, but, like the truths of mathematics and like the principles of natural philosophy discovered by Newton, they would be *instructive*.

Locke left no lasting legacy in chymistry or in medicine, and it is possible, when reading the *Essay*, to be blissfully ignorant of his involvement in the experimental chymistry of his day. However, apprized as we now are of his mercurialist commitments, shall we wonder that the most common illustrations in Book III, in which Locke discusses the nature of species, are chymical ones—gold, antimony, and vitriol? Is it any wonder that Locke claims:

[t]hat we find many of the Individuals that are ranked into one Sort, called by one common Name, and so received as being of one *Species*, have yet Qualities depending on their real Constitutions, as far different one from another, as from others, from which they are accounted to differ *specifically*. This, as it is easy to be observed by all, who have to do with natural Bodies; so Chymists especially are often, by sad Experience, convinced of it, when they, sometimes in vain, seek for the same Qualities in one parcel of Sulphur, Antimony, or Vitriol, which they have found in others.[85]

[84] *E* IV. vi. 10, p. 584.   [85] *E* III. vi. 8, p. 443.

10

Generation

> All stones, metals, and minerals, are real vegetables; that is, grow organically from proper seeds, as well as plants.
>
> John Locke*

Locke's own speculative natural philosophy was not confined merely to the matter theory that underlies his commitment to mercurialist transmutational chymistry, or to the kind of 'armchair' cosmogonical speculations he offers us in *Some Thoughts concerning Education* when discussing Burnet's theory. We have also seen that he uses the notion of seminal principles in his early speculations on the nature of some diseases and, as it happens, this notion of *semina* was applied by Locke more generally in his wide-ranging discussions of generation. In the present chapter we will examine Locke's views on the nature of generation. Our discussion will be an important preliminary for the discussion of Locke's view of species in the final chapter.

Few if any of the philosophical discussions of Locke on species or on natural kinds make even a cursory use of the manuscript notes and comments in his correspondence and journals on generation and seminal principles.[1] Yet it is clear that, if Locke accepts the existence and efficacy of seminal principles, this will have implications for his account of the replication of substances in nature and therefore it will impinge on any analysis of his views on species and kinds in general.

In this chapter I want to examine Locke's numerous notes and comments on seminal principles and generation in order to situate his views in their wider natural philosophical and theological context. I aim also to tease out the implications of these views for the interpretation of his more widely known comments on species in Book III of the *Essay*, a subject that will be taken up in the following chapter. Furthermore, I plan to use the contemporaneous views of Richard Burthogge not so much as a foil to Locke,

---

* *Elements of Natural Philosophy, Locke Works*, Vol. 3, p. 319.
[1] For a recent discussion of Locke's interest in generation, see P. Walmsley 2003, ch. 2.

because their views are similar, but to fill out the picture. Burthogge was one of Locke's enthusiastic readers and correspondents who was writing on generation and seminal principles and corresponding with Locke in the late 1690s.

The chapter proceeds as follows. First, I sketch the natural philosophical background to Locke's comments on generation and seeds. Second, I summarize the relevant sources of Locke's discussions and comments from which his views can be reconstructed. Third, I attempt to reconstruct these views by examining what Locke claims about the scope of the operation of seminal principles, their mode of operation, and the variation of their operation. Then the chapter turns to Locke's discussion of re-generation or resurrection in his *Second Reply* to Stillingfleet, and to Burthogge's endorsement of Locke's views. Finally, we will be in a position to assess the implications of Locke's views for the interpretation of his comments on species in the *Essay* and elsewhere.

However, before proceeding, I should like to make three 'topographical' clarifications. First, it is clear that in contemporary philosophy the problem of natural kinds is *not* co-extensive with the problem of the species. In view of recent developments in debates in the philosophy of biology, the problem of species should be regarded as intersecting with the problem of natural kinds. Thus, some philosophers have claimed that biological species are not natural kinds at all, but are individuals.[2] It would be nice if, in general, we could restrict the criteria for classifying stars or atoms, regarding them as part of the problem of natural kinds, and maintain that this problem does not pertain to that of species. That is, we could claim that the species problem is confined to biological species only. But, for Locke, the waters are a little muddy on this point, because he believed that some inanimate things reproduce by seminal principles; and of course he speaks of species in a broad sense, as sorts, following the Aristotelian tradition. Thus he frequently mixes examples of animate, inanimate, and artefactual kinds in the same discussion (*E* III. vi. 39–41). A second point that should be stressed is that there is no necessary connection between the denial of universals and species nominalism. The notion of exact resemblance, or even the loose and popular sense of 'same', suffices to enable us to carve nature up into equivalence classes even if there are no universals. It is entirely consistent to be a realist about species and to deny the existence of universals.

Third, there are two motivations for conventionalism about species, or about natural kinds in general. First, there is species nominalism, which entails conventionalism about species. That is, if one denies that there exist objective determinate kinds or species, then the referents of species terms will be determined purely by convention. However, one can be a conventionalist about species and accept that there are objectively existing species. In other words, one can deny species nominalism and yet be a conventionalist about species by claiming, for instance, that we do not have

[2] Hull 1978.

epistemic access to actual kinds and therefore our terms for kinds refer by convention. I believe that this is roughly Locke's position, and I will argue here that his theory of generation is a strong argument in favour of attributing him the belief in the existence of species and of some natural kinds. But more of this anon. Let us turn to the intellectual background to Locke's discussions of generation and seeds.

Background

Almost every major natural philosopher from the early modern period believed that seminal principles were the primary agents in the generation of bodies and the guarantors of the replication of form. Descartes, Gassendi, Digby, Charleton, Willis, Sennert, and Boyle all espoused theories of seminal principles, accepting them as the primary explanatory category in the theory of generation. For example, Robert Boyle discusses or refers to seminal principles in twenty-eight extant works, in addition to the two lost works entitled 'Of Seminal Principles' and 'About the Concealments and Disguises of Seminal Principles'.[3]

Now it is helpful, if somewhat artificial, to conceive of the plethora of views on seeds in Locke's day as being influenced by two quite different notions of seeds. The first was the corpuscular notion, which derived from Epicureanism: there seeds were conceived as invisible clusters of atoms or corpuscles, which somehow operated upon their surrounding matter in order to structure it so as to make it resemble closely other members of the relevant kind. The second was the more vitalistic notion deriving from the *logoi spermatikoi* of the Stoics, which was deployed by the neo-Platonists and reworked in the natural philosophies of Paracelsus and Joan Baptista van Helmont. For example, on the Helmontian view, seeds are the most complex in a whole series of psycho-physical entities responsible for the maintenance and generation of material substances. Seeds accompany such entities as odours, ferments, *gas*, and the *archeus*, and each one has its own special role in generation.

Locke's discussions of seeds and generation

Having briefly sketched the background to Locke's numerous comments on generation and seminal principles, we now turn to a selective survey of Locke's discussions of these topics. Not surprisingly, the nature of generation is one of Locke's earliest interests in his extensive medical notebooks. Some of Locke's earliest entries on generation are reading notes from William Harvey's *Exercitationes de generatione animalium* (1651, LL 1398), which appear in Bodl. MS Locke f. 20 and were probably made around 1659–60, at the time when Locke was turning in a serious way to medical reading. For instance, Locke records Harvey's distinction between epigenesis and

---

[3] For Boyle's notion of seminal principles, see Anstey 2002c. For pre-Boylean theories, see Hirai 2005.

metamorphosis, and he carefully summarizes Harvey's discussion of the efficient cause of generation in point form.[4] The manner in which these notes were made indicates that Locke had made a serious effort to understand Harvey's account of the cause of generation. However, it seems that no distinctively Harvean elements found their way into Locke's later views on generation. Further evidence of Locke's interest in the subject during this period is found in Bodl. MS Locke f. 18, where Locke took notes from 'Hypomnemata physica' in Volume 1 of Daniel Sennert's *Opera omnia* (1656, LL 2617) and which contains an extensive discussion of generation. Entries under the heads 'Generatio' (pp. 28–9, 33, 35), 'Plantæ' (p. 36), 'Spontenea' (p. 35), and 'Semen' (p. 82) show an interest in Sennert's view of generation. In particular, Locke notes Sennert's reference to a 'principium seminale' as a cause of spontaneous generation (p. 35). Some of these notes were later copied into Bodl. MS Locke d. 11, which also contains an extensive topical index for Velthusius' tract 'De generatione' and a note dating from the 1660s, which is typical of Locke's interest in Boyle's opinion on the best authorities.[5] Locke quotes Boyle:

Generatio. Amongst the accuratist of our moderne writers I suppose you will readily allow me to reckon Dr Harvey & Dr Highmore, who in their excellent treatises of Generation Boyle: Phys[iological] Ess[ays] p. 87.[6]

The next important source relating to generation is found in Locke's entry 'Morbus', where, as we have seen, Locke discusses a theory of diseases as seminal principles or seeds, which are responsible for the replication and growth of some diseases. He describes these seminal principles as follows:

by seminall principles or ferments I meane some small & subtile parcelles of matter which are apt to transmute far greater portions of matter into a new nature & new qualitys, which change could not be brought about by any other knowne means, soe that this change seems wholy to depend upon the operation or activity of this seminall principle [...][7]

Here the seminal principles are the agents of generation for a given disease, and they function analogously to the seeds of plants. Locke develops the analogy between seminal disease and plants and the formation of the chick in the egg. As we have

---

[4] Bodl. MS Locke f. 20, pp. 4–5. This entry was copied to Bodl. MS Locke f. 14, p. 1. Locke also made a note from George Ent's *Apologia pro circulatione sanguinis* (1641, LL 1054) on generation in Bodl. MS Locke f. 20, p. 227.

[5] 'Generatio' is copied to Bodl. MS Locke d. 11, p. 3v as 'Anima', and Bodl. MS Locke f. 18, p. 33 entry under 'Licetus' is copied to Bodl. MS Locke d. 11, p. 32v as 'Generatio'. The topical index for Velthusius' *De generatione* (the second tract of *Tractatus duo medico-physici*, LL 3063^8) was copied from Bodl. MS Locke c. 29, fols 9v–10r to (the rear of) Bodl. MS Locke d. 11, fols 271v–72r. In fact most of the notes in the six folded pages that form the booklet Bodl. MS Locke c. 29, fols 9–18, were copied into the rear of Bodl. MS Locke d. 11 not earlier than 1662.

[6] Bodl. MS Locke d. 11, fol. 32v. Boyle refers to Nathaniel Highmore's *Disquisitio anatomica* (1651, LL 1451^a).

[7] British Library Add. MS 32554, p. 232 (= Walmsely 2000, p. 391).

seen, such theories were common and are to be found in a range of works that Locke read in the mid-1660s.[8]

Then, in Draft A and Draft B of the *Essay*, which were written in 1671, we find the following comments on generation. Draft A, §16 tells us that, in addition to creation, there is another form of beginning, to the following effect:

> When a thing is made up of particles which did all of them before exist, but that very thing soe constituted of præexisting particles which considerd altogeather constitute or make up soe many particular simple Ideas had not any existence before, as an eg a rose a cherry. And this when referd to substance producd in the ordinary course of nature by <u>an internal principle</u> but set a work by & received from some externall agent or cause workeing by insensible ways which we comprehend not we cal **Generation**.[9]

Note here the particulate view of matter and the reference to 'an internal principle', most likely a reference to the power of seminal principles. The passage reappears in Draft B, §134[10] in almost identical form, and then in Draft C (II. xxx. 3). It is reproduced in the *Essay* at II. xxvi. 2, in the chapter entitled 'Of Cause and Effect, and other Relations', but with the interesting modification of 'insensible ways which we comprehend not' to 'insensible ways, which we <u>perceive</u> not'.[11] All of this is continuous with the 'Morbus' entry, but is less explicit as to the nature of the 'internal principle'. Then, in the extended discussion of species in Draft B, we find the following comment:

> Not that I doubt but that nature workeing regularly & uniformly for the most part doth produce great numbers of Individuals agreeing in qualitys one with an other & that are constantly soe [...][12]

Here the uniformity of generation is attributed to nature. This passage is reworked in the *Essay* and appears at III. vi. 37 thus:

> I do not deny, but Nature, in the constant production of particular Beings, makes them not always new and various, but very much alike and of kin one to another [...]

The continuity between the Drafts and the *Essay* itself is mirrored in parallels between the early 'Morbus' entry and Locke's comments on generation in his Journal. In an entry from 19 September 1676 entitled 'Species', Locke writes:

> [N]ature in things that have life keepes them in the distinct classes by the order of generation wherein those of the same species produce their like but the inhærent qualitys or essentiall differences whereby we pretend to destinguish them into species are unknowne.

---

[8] Locke's examples of mint and marjoram are almost certainly taken from Boyle's *The Sceptical Chymist: or Chymico-Physical Doubts & Paradoxes* (1661, LL 444), *Boyle Works*, Vol. 2, p. 256. For further discussion, see Walmsley 2000, Anstey 2002b, and Walmsley 2002.
[9] Draft A, §16, pp. 31–2, underlining added.   [10] Draft B, §134, p. 255.
[11] As pointed out by Mattern 1981, p. 845.   [12] Draft B, §77, p. 184.

Here Locke is claiming that classes within nature, biological kinds in our terminology, are propagated and maintained through generation. He goes on to contrast generated species with inanimate beings, which

> without any organical constitutions or parts adapted to nutrition or generation may be capable of infinite variety of mixtures where we are able to make noe destinction whereas the principall difference of animate beings seems to depend on that internall principle that organizes the parts and contributes to and is the principall cause of generateing the like.[13]

Locke's 'internall principle', a phrase which we have just encountered in the Drafts and in the *Essay* (*E* II. xxvi. 2), almost certainly refers to the seminal power, or to what he had earlier called (with Helmontian echoes) the *archeus* which resides in the seed. The contrast between species which are, and species which are not propagated through seeds also recurs in the *Essay*, where Locke is more specific about their differences:

> Of sensible Substances there are two sorts; one of organiz'd Bodies, which are propagated by Seed; and in these, the Shape is that, which to us is the leading Quality, and most characteristical Part, that determines the *Species*: And therefore in Vegetables and Animals, an extended solid Substance of such a certain Figure usually serves the turn.[14]

And the point about indefinite mutability also recurs in the *Essay*.[15] There are other references to seeds and generation in Locke's Journal and medical notebooks which we will discuss below, but enough has been cited to establish the prevalence of the notions of seeds and generation in Locke's thought and its continuity up to the publication of the *Essay* in 1690. What, then, about Locke's discussions of these issues after the first edition of the *Essay*?

The first interesting site is a discussion of spontaneous generation in 1694, in Locke's correspondence with Hans Sloane. Even more fascinating is a note on the theological implications of the discovery of spermatozoa in Locke's interleaved Bentley Bible, which is datable to the period after 1691. There is an extended discussion of the role of 'seminal parts' in the resurrection, in the Stillingfleet correspondence. This treatment of the resurrection is taken up in a letter from Richard Burthogge to Locke in 1699, which will repay careful study. Meanwhile, Locke also referred to seminal principles in his *Elements of Natural Philosophy*, which he began after 1697. Each of these references will be discussed below, but it is important to note here another interest of Locke's which bears on the problem of species and generation. I have in mind Locke's long-term interest in botanical classification. It has long been known that Locke kept a herbarium in the mid-1660s and that he corresponded with botanists and continued to collect plant specimens and botanical works. However, it is now clear that Locke made a modest, but none the less important, contribution to early modern botany. He did this through the distribution of seeds and plant parts which were cultivated in his day

---

[13] Locke 1936, p. 83.   [14] *E* III. vi. 29, p. 456.
[15] See for example *E* III. iii. 19, p. 419.

and entered the major contemporaneous herbaria: Jacob Bobart's Hortus siccus; the Morisonian Herbarium; and above all the Sloane Herbarium, which was used by Carl Linnaeus. So, when Locke discusses seeds and generation, when he explores the philosophical problem of species, or when he considers the nature of original sin and of bodily resurrection, his views need to be seen against a backdrop of extensive interest and involvement in botanical taxonomy.[16]

Locke's view of seeds: The scope of their operation

Locke believes that seeds or seminal principles are responsible for the generation of animals, plants, insects, some diseases, and some minerals. That seeds are responsible for the generation of plants is entirely uncontroversial. Indeed vegetable seeds are the fundamental natural analogy upon which the conception of seminal principles is based. This is not to say, however, that Locke never speculated about the roles of seeds in vegetable generation. For example, at one point in notes taken in 1686 on articles in the *Acta Eruditorum*, Locke enters the following note and query:

Del Chiaccio, e della coagulatione del P. Dan: Bartoli Soc. Jes: 4° Rom 81 In which he treats of vegetation & says the seed is made of the most active subtil parts of the plant combined with an oyly substance & derived from the pith of the plant & hence he says tis that a citron inoculated on an orange will beare the fruit citron with seeds of Orange in it 350. Q whether hence may not be taken a rule in grafting. Viz. that plants will graft one on another which have seeds alike JL.[17]

That animals are generated by seeds is also uncontroversial: this is the standard early modern view. It should, however, be noted that there is, to my knowledge, no evidence in Locke of the kind of 'Harvean ovism' that flourished after the discovery of ovaries in female animals in the late 1660s.[18] While Swammerdam championed Harvey's *ex ovo omnia* and Boyle in the late 1660s could call eggs 'seeds', Locke was always content simply to call seeds 'seeds' or 'seminal principles'. Thus plants and animals are the two most natural genera to be generated by seeds; and these are the very examples that Locke uses at *E* III. vi. 29, when he claims that sensible substances divide into two classes—those that are generated by seed and those that are not.

We have already encountered Locke's early view that some forms of disease are caused by seminal principles. He is still speaking of seminal diseases in 1678; in the Journal entry for 22 July he claims that 'certain body types may carry seeds of certain diseases, or are more predisposed to contract them'.[19] Furthermore, it is unlikely that Locke's views on disease changed. This is because his belief in diseases as invasive seminal pathogenic agents seems to have been the motivation behind the primitive epidemiological research he undertook with Dr Charles Goodall in the 1690s, when

---

[16] See Anstey and Harris 2006; Harris and Anstey 2009.
[17] Bodl. MS Locke f. 9, pp. 91–2. See Bartoli 1681.
[18] See Swammerdam 1681.   [19] Romanell 1984, p. 139, and Dewhurst 1963a, p. 136.

they distributed questionnaires on bills of mortality as well as on seasonal weather patterns and on the incidence of disease to various British and continental physicians.

So Locke believes that seeds are responsible for the generation of plants, animals, and some diseases. The situation with minerals, however, is not so clear. In a notebook entry in Bodl. MS Locke d. 11, fol. 52v, placed under the head 'Metalla' and datable to the 1660s, Locke quotes Boyle saying:

> That metalline bodys have a power to propagate their nature you may finde many notable testimonies in the physico-chymicall questions of Jo: Conradus Gerardus, & most of them recitd with some of his owne by the learned Sennertus Boyle useful: p. 1. p. 80 63.[20]

This is one in a number of references to metalline seeds in Locke's notebooks and in interleaved books in his library.[21] Then, in the *Elements of Natural Philosophy* begun in the late 1690s, Locke claims:

> All stones, metals, and minerals, are real vegetables; that is, grow organically from proper seeds, as well as plants.[22]

Thus it would appear that he unequivocally accepted the view that all minerals are propagated by seminal principles. However, in the *Essay*, at III. vi. 29 (p. 456), when discussing the salient properties of his two natural classes, Locke implies that the metal gold is not propagated by seed. He says:

> As in Vegetables and Animals 'tis the Shape, so in most other Bodies, not propagated by Seed, 'tis the Colour we most fix on, and are most led by. Thus where we find the Colour of Gold, we are apt to imagine all the other Qualities, comprehended in our complex *Idea*, to be there also.

The clear implication is that gold is not generated by seed. I do not want to digress so as to attempt to explain this apparent inconsistency here. It may be that Locke regards gold as somewhat different from other metalline bodies in the light of his chymical views and interest in transmutation. It may be that the real contrast here is between 'organiz'd Bodies' and masses of stuff. However, enough evidence has been presented in this section to show that seminal principles played a central role in Locke's account of generation. The more controversial question now arises: What is their mode of operation?

---

[20] See *Boyle Works*, Vol. 3, p. 254. It is worth noting that at Bodl. MS Locke d. 11, p. 32v Locke also records Boyle's comment, made in *Certain Physiological Essays*, p. 87, on Harvey and Highmore, whom he ranks 'among the accuratist of our moderne writers' on generation. This note was probably made in the mid-1660s. See also Bodl. MS Locke f. 14, p. 24 for a similar record from Boyle's *Usefulness of Natural Philosophy*.

[21] For example, see Locke's interleaved copy of Johnson's *Lexicon chymicum* (1660, LL 1577), page facing p. 217, for 'Sperma seu sulphur metallorum Becher Oedip p. 138. 64'. As was his habit, Locke has underlined the 'S' of 'Sperma' in his edition of Becher's *Oedipus chimicus* (LL 248) for easy reference. Another entry relating to seeds is on page facing p. 223, where Locke writes 'Sperma mundi [...]' and cross-references to Matthias Untzer's *Opus chymico-medicum* (1660, LL 3023), p. 611.

[22] *Locke Works*, Vol. 3, p. 319.

Locke's view of seeds: The mode of their operation

As we have seen, Locke speaks of an 'internal principle' which guides generation in plants and animals. At *E* II. xxvi. 2, when contrasting creation with generation, he says:

> when referred to a Substance, produced in the ordinary course of Nature, by an <u>internal Principle</u>, but set work on by, and received from some external Agent, or Cause, and working by insensible ways, which we perceive not, we call *Generation*.[23]

It is hard to resist the conclusion that these internal principles are not the seeds themselves, but the power or powers by which these seeds work. When Locke tells us, in the 'Morbus' entry,

> [h]ow these small & insensible ferments, this potent Archeus works I confess I cannot satisfactorily comprehend,[24]

he is expressing a similar claim of nescience to that found later in the *Essay*. We just do not know how these things work. To be sure, the *archeus* is a Helmontian notion, but Locke seems to use it as a general term for an unspecified generative power and nowhere explores the ontological implications of this notion. Thus, while the seeds themselves are corpuscular—'some small & subtile parcelles of matter which are apt to transmute far greater portions of matter into a new nature & new qualitys'—Locke seems never to have taken the issue of the mode of their operation any further. Nonetheless, he seems to be quite clear that, whatever it is, this mode is responsible for the generation of species. In the Journal entry of 19 September 1676, as we have seen, he says:

> [N]ature in things that have life <u>keepes them in the distinct classes by the order of generation wherein those of the same species produce their like</u> [...] the principall difference of animate beings seems to depend on that internall principle that organizes the parts and contributes to and is the principall cause of generateing the like.[25]

But are seminal principles solely responsible for the generation of species? This brings us to the question of spontaneous generation.

In the early modern period, the phrase 'spontaneous generation' could be used in a strict sense, to refer to generation *by chance* in the absence of seeds, and in a loose and popular sense (derived from Aristotle), to refer to phenomena of generation which appear not to involve eggs or parents. Thus some natural philosophers accepted spontaneous generation (in the loose sense) because they explained the absence of eggs or parents by recourse to a notion of matter which is naturally impregnated with seeds. Now, a vigorous and ongoing debate over the influential Aristotelian notion of

---

[23] *E* II. xxvi. 2, p. 325, underlining added.
[24] British Library Add. MS 32554, p. 237 (= Walmsley 2000, p. 391).
[25] Locke 1936, p. 83, underlining in original.

spontaneous generation was undertaken by the members of the Royal Society in the 1660s. Committees were formed and experiments undertaken, including the famous experiments on may-dew,[26] but no decisive results emerged. Then Francesco Redi's *Esperienze intorno alla generazione degl'insetti* (LL 2454ª, 1671 edn) was published in 1668, and immediately the nature of the debate changed. In a series of simple experiments which involved covering rotting meat, Redi showed decisively that insects do not generate spontaneously from putrefying matter. Yet Redi himself was not convinced that the phenomenon could be ruled out entirely. He conceded that plants may contain in themselves the power to generate worms. The publication of Redi's book was the catalyst for a fascinating correspondence between Henry Oldenburg, John Ray, and Martin Lister. Ray's comment to Oldenburg is relevant here:

Whether there be any spontaneous or anomalous generation of animals, [...] I think there is good reason to question. It seems to me at present most probable that there is no such thing. [...] F. Redi hath gone a good way in proving this, having cleared the point concerning generation *ex materia putrida*. But still there remain the two great difficulties. The first is to give an account of the production of insects bred in the by-fruits & excrescensies of Vegetables, which Redi doubts not to ascribe to the Vegetative soul of the plant which yields those excrescencies [...] the second to give an account of the generation of insects bred in the bodies of other animals.[27]

This letter was written on 3 July 1671. Let us now turn to Locke's letter to Hans Sloane of 14 September 1694. There Locke says:

The notion of equivocal generation I should quite lay aside as a groundlesse phansy if you could resolve me some instances that puzel me in that affair. One is the strange and new creatures that have been often found in the bodys of men and other animals, which could not be reduced to any species of animals that in that country or else where from which they might derive their original. Another is the production of lice in any one who changes not though in a place and circumstances where there cannot be supposed to be any propogation by seed from other animals of that species. These and others that might be mentiond I think can hardly be accounted for by univocal generation according to the ordinary philosophie.[28]

The parallels are striking: both Ray and Locke give two examples which prevent them from dismissing spontaneous generation outright, and one of these examples is the same. Locke had read Redi and no doubt was aware of some of the literature on the issue; he may well have read Ray's letter, which was published in the *Philosophical Transactions* of 14 August 1671.[29] What is surprising is that Locke's views are almost identical with those of Ray, expressed some twenty-three years earlier. It may have been around that time, that is, in the early 1670s, that Locke came to a settled view on the matter. Whatever the case with regard to the formation of Locke's views, it is

---

[26] On the early research on may-dew, see Taylor 1994.
[27] *Oldenburg Correspondence*, Vol. 8, pp. 132–3.
[28] *Correspondence*, Vol. 5, p. 128.   [29] *Philosophical Transactions*, 74, 1671, pp. 2219–20.

interesting to turn now to the writings of Richard Burthogge, who discusses at length this issue of spontaneous generation in his *Of the Soul of the World* (1699)—a treatise written for Locke. In this work Burthogge is arguing for an *anima mundi* (a world soul), and he mobilizes spontaneous generation as a natural phenomenon which, he argues, can only be explained through such a vitalistic principle.

I acknowledg it almost a Scandal but to name *equivocal* Productions at this time, they are now so generally disbelieved and exploded; but for my part, I am not ashamed to confess that as yet I have not observed so much said by the excellent *Redi*, or by any other Author against the Reality of them, as to oblige me to depart from a Sentiment that hath been the common Belief of most Inquirers into Nature, in all Ages before this last. And the *Hypothesis* of a mundane Soul will make Productions of that kind conceivable [...][30]

Where Locke would dismiss the phenomena as a 'phansie' but for a few anomalous instances, Burthogge fully endorses it. Of course, Locke would have no truck with a world soul. In a guardbook entry on 'Ignorantia' prompted by Ralph Cudworth's belief in a world soul, Locke wrote:

Thus because we cannot comprehend how a blinde jumble of Atoms can frame the curious bodys of animals, nor yet thinke it fit to engage the immediate hand of god in the production of every mite and insect an anima mundi without knowledg & consciousnesse is substituted as the conducter of physical generations and productions. But yet how this material unthinkeing soule, (for if it be immaterial it will be yet harder to be understood) should be a better guide & artificer than unthinkeing matter or how it differs from it will be always equally hard to be explaind and soe in effect amounts to noe more but a new name of noething more intelligible than what we would explain by it. JL[31]

While he remained highly sceptical of the residual phenomena of spontaneous generation, he could not dismiss spontaneous generation outright. It is interesting, therefore, to speculate as to just how Locke would have explained the anomalous instances. But speculation it must remain; for he does not discuss the issue further.

Locke's view of seeds: Generative variation

One issue that Locke does discuss on a number of occasions is generative variation. This is a particularly interesting feature of his theory of generation and, to my knowledge, it is the first application of this phenomenon in the philosophical treatment of the problem of species. In the 'Morbus' entry, Locke claims that the operation of seminal principles is the sole determinant of the generative process, and he illustrates this idea with the following observation:

---

[30] Burthogge 1699, pp. 31–2.
[31] Bodl. MS Locke c. 33, fol. 27v.

[T]his change seems wholy to depend upon the operation or activity of this seminall principle, & not on the difference of the matter its self that is changd, soe severall seeds set in the same plot of earth, change the moisture of the earth which is the common nourishment of them all into far different plants which, differ both in their qualitys & effects, which I thinke is not donne by bare streineing the nourishment through their pores which in different plants are of different shapes & sizes.[32]

Locke seems to be claiming that the very same seeds, in the same soil, can produce different plants.[33] Stephen Harris alerted me to the fact that in Locke's Herbarium there are instances of mutant forms and double flowers. For example, in Volume 1 (1664), f. 1381 there are two specimens labelled 'Cichorium sativum fl:(alb) White Garden sucory June' and 'Cichorium sativum fl:(caer.) Blew Garden sucory July', both of which appear to be Cichorium endivia (endive), yet one has white flowers and the other blue. Interestingly, both are mounted on the same page, and double-mounting is not common in Volume 1 of the Herbarium. Does this indicate that Locke believed that they were of the same species? It is difficult to decide from the Herbarium, or to determine the extent of Locke's understanding of phenotypic variation; but, once we have examined the herbarium, the comments on variation in the 'Morbus' entry come as no surprise. Furthermore, we know from Robert Sharrock's *History of the Propagation and Improvement of Vegetables* (1660) that the Bobarts, Locke's main botanical contacts at this time, were speculating about genuine species transmutation, though Sharrock himself was somewhat sceptical.[34] The picture becomes clearer in the following Journal entry, from 19 November 1677, written during Locke's time in Paris:

Species   The species of things are distinguishd & made by chance in order to nameing & names imposd on those things which either the conveniencys of life or common observation brings into discourse. The greatest part of the rest sine nomine turba, lie neglected neither differencd by names nor destinguishd into species. E.g. how many flies & wormes are there & which though they are about as in great plenty we have not yet named nor ranked into species but come under the generall of flies or wormes which yet are as destinct as an horse & a sheepe though none have had noe grat occasion to take notice of them. Soe that our Ideas of species are almost voluntary or at least different from the Idea of nature by which she formes & destinguishes them. Which in animals she seems to me to keepe to with more constancy & exactnesse than in other bodys & species of things which being various engines doe perhaps require a greater accuratenesse for their

---

[32] British Library Add. MS 32554, fols 118v–119r (= Walmsley 2000, p. 390).
[33] This was pointed out to me by J. C. Walmsley.
[34] See Sharrock 1660, pp. 29–30: 'It is indeed growen to be a great question, whether the transmutation of a species be possible either in the vegetable, Animal, or Minerall kingdome. For the possibility of it in the vegetable: I have heard Mr *Bobart* and his *Son* often report it, and proffer to make oath that the Crocus and Gladiolus, as likewise the Leucoium, and Hyacinths by a long standing without replanting have in his garden changed from one kind to the other'. Sharrock discussed this with Boyle and in his presence sought to find examples, though without success. Sharrock's book is dedicated to Boyle. Of changes in colour, Sharrock claims: 'this transmutation ends not at all in another divers kind; but in severall small diversities of the same kind', i.e. not new species (p. 29). Locke notes that Sharrock's book was commended by John Evelyn: Bodl. MS Locke f. 14, p. 188.

propagation & continuation of their race. For in vegetables we finde that severall sorts come from the seeds of one & the same individuall as much different species as those that are allowed to be soe by philosophers. This is very familiar in apples & perhaps other sorts of fruits, whereof some have destinct names & other only the generall. Though they begin every day to have more & more given them as they come into use soe that species in respect of us are but things ranked into orders because of their agreement in same ædios which we have made essentiall in order to our nameing them. Though what it is to be essentially belong to any species in reference to nature be hard to determin. For if a woman should bring forth a creature perfectly of the shape of a man, that never shewd any more appearance of reason then an horse nor had noe articulate language. And another woman should produce an other with noe thing of the shape but the language & reason of a man I ask which of these you would call by the name man? Or both or neither?[35]

The phenomenon Locke is discussing is variation between parent and progeny and between siblings in the plant and animal kingdoms, and this variation is more pronounced in the plant kingdom than in the animal kingdom. Locke's example of apples is entirely natural, given that he was collecting copious amounts of information on the cultivation of fruit trees in France by interviewing farmers and botanists during this period.[36] He would have been familiar with the problems of keeping cultivars true to type. But Locke claims that this variation is sometimes so pronounced that the differences between progeny are greater than, say, the differences between one of the progeny and an entirely different species. This is what he means when he says 'severall sorts come from the seeds of one & the same individuall as much different species as those that are allowed to be soe by philosophers'. The implication is that this phenomenon is enough to show that phenotypic characteristics are neither necessary nor sufficient to guarantee species membership. This is an important claim, and it constitutes significant background evidence for the discussion of species in the *Essay*—a discussion that was already well developed in Draft B of 1671.[37] It is to be distinguished from the argument from monstrous births, which Locke includes for good measure at the end of the entry.

Re-generation

As Locke's observations on spontaneous generation and generative variation show, he was quick to see the implications of advances in natural philosophical knowledge. And it was not only in philosophy, but also in theology that Locke could deploy his knowledge of natural philosophy. In a comment on Romans 5:12 in his interleaved Bentley Bible, Locke mentions the discovery of spermatozoa and its implications for original sin.

And thus it is noe harder a figure to say in him all have sinned than it is to say In Adam all die 1 Cor. XV. 22. Which I think have just the same meaning with the words here. Viz. That al men

---

[35] Bodl. MS Locke f. 2, pp. 356–8 (= Locke 1936, pp. 98–9, corrected).
[36] See Harris and Anstey 2009. [37] Draft B, pp. 163–92.

in Adam did soe far partake in eating of the forbidden fruit as there by to be made mortal. How far the modern philosophie, & the late discoveries of live animals in the masculin seed may favour this in a literal sense I need not mention. JL[38]

But his most notorious discussion of seeds occurs in the correspondence with Stillingfleet over the nature of the resurrection body. In his *Second Letter*, Stillingfleet argues that the resurrection body is the same as the mortal body, in other words the body that is in the grave. And he claims, further, that Locke is committed to denying the identity of the resurrection body with the mortal body in spite of this being a Christian doctrine. The argument hinges around a point of biblical interpretation of the passage in I Corinthians 15: 36–8 where Paul draws an analogy between seed and the resurrection. Locke's reply is very long and, in my view, involves some sophistries;[39] but that need not detain us here. What is important is Locke's comment on the role of seminal agents and of God in the production of species. On the question of the expression *to idion soma* (one's own body), Locke says that,

in the production of wheat and other grain from seed, God continued every species distinct; so that from grains of wheat sown, root, stalk, blade, ear, and grains, of wheat, were produced, and not those of barley; and so of the rest: which I took to be the meaning of 'to every seed his own body'.[40]

He repeats this point further on, when he claims:

For I do not know of any seminal body in little, contained in the dead carcass of any man or woman; which, as your lordship says, in seeds, having its proper organical parts, shall afterwards be enlarged, and at the resurrection grow up into the same man. For I never thought of any seed or seminal parts, either of plant or animal, 'so wonderfully improved by the providence of God', whereby the same plant or animal should beget itself; nor ever heard, that it was by divine Providence designed to produce the same individual, but for the producing of future and distinct individuals, for the continuation of the same species.[41]

---

[38] Bodl. Locke 16. 25, p. 787. Victor Nuovo has alerted me to this entry and has informed me that it was made some time after 1691. Compare Locke's paraphrase and comments in *A Paraphrase and Notes on the Epistles of St Paul*, Locke 1987, 1, p. 252 and 2, p. 524. Locke observed spermatozoa on 22 June 1686; see his Journal, Bodl. MS Locke f. 9, p. 15 where he says: 'Some of the small animals which he [Leeuwenhoek] said were taken out of the womb of a dog post coitum I saw sticking to a small plate of glasse they were a very great number in a very small area they being taken by only applying the glasse to an equall area of the womb. they seemed to me like very small beads & twas with much difficulty I could perceive the tailes he describes of them if at least I did perceive any at all. for these being long since taken were dead & dried on to the plate of glasse'. Locke also comments that 'the best of all his glasses & those by which he describes his spermatique animals we saw not, nor (as I heare) does he shew them to any one' (ibid., p. 17). See Dewhurst 1963a, p. 273.

[39] Locke appears to switch from strict to loose and popular identity and to charge Stillingfleet with a commitment to mereological essentialism, which it is clear that Stillingfleet denies. Stillingfleet's claim that the mortal body is the same as the resurrection body could easily be interpreted by Locke as a claim that the human individual involved is the same; thus Locke's threefold distinction between the body, the human, and the person would be preserved.

[40] *Secord Reply*, p. 317.   [41] Ibid., p. 319.

Note here the claim that the seminal parts of plants and animals are not 'by divine Providence designed to produce the same individual, but for the producing of future and distinct individuals, for the continuation of the same species'. We have already encountered this claim, that seeds are responsible for the propagation of species, in Locke's Journal. We should also note here *en passant* that Locke denies the doctrine of 'vicarious' or pre-existing seeds; that is, the view that matter is impregnated with seminal principles which can operate independently of sexual union and which, under the right conditions, generate animate beings.[42] Locke says: 'I do not know of any seminal body in little, contained in the dead carcass of any man or woman; which, as your lordship says, in seeds, having its proper organical parts, shall afterwards be enlarged, and at the resurrection grow up into the same man'.

But the most salient point from Locke's discussion of the resurrection or re-generation is his denial that seminal principles are responsible for the generation of the resurrection body. This is not only because St Paul did not have observational evidence for this belief and hence could not have been alluding to it in speaking to the Corinthians, although Locke does drive home this point:

It does not appear, by any thing I can find in the text, that St. Paul here compared the body produced with the seminal and organical parts contained in the grain it sprang from, but with the whole sensible grain that was sown. Microscopes had not then discovered the little embryo plant in the seed.[43]

The real reason why seeds are not responsible for the resurrection body is that seeds replicate species members and not the individuals from which the seed originates. Interestingly, Richard Burthogge heartily concurs. In his letter to Locke of 19 September 1699 he says:

I am much of the same opinion that you are concerning the Resurrection [...] so much seems plain that it consists not in this That the Body which is SOWN contains not (sic) in it a Seminal Body of that which SHALL BE. For if the discovery be certain that grain tho' it be not divided into Lobes as other seeds are yet upon seperating the membranes these seminal parts are discerned in them which afterwards grow up to that body with we call corn; yet that discovery being Microscopical (as you judiciously observe) it was not made at the time when the Apostle wrote [...][44]

---

[42] For Boyle on vicarious seeds, see *Boyle Works*, Vol. 13, pp. 287–8; for discussion, see Anstey 2002c, pp. 612–13.

[43] *Second Reply*, p. 319. Locke continues: 'and supposing it should have been revealed to St. Paul (though in the Scripture we find little revelation of natural philosophy) yet an argument taken from a thing perfectly unknown to the Corinthians, whom he write to, could be of no manner of use to them, nor serve at all either to instruct or convince them. But granting that those St. Paul writ to knew as well as Mr. Lewenhocke; yet your lordship thereby proves not the raising of the same body', ibid., pp. 319–20.

[44] *Correspondence*, Vol. 6, pp. 685–6.

He adds that, if seminal principles are at work here, then the resurrection body must be 'an Earthly Carnal and Corruptible Body'—which is certainly not the point that St Paul is making.

What is interesting about the views of Locke and Burthogge on seeds and the resurrection is not so much the exegetical point about *to idion soma*, as the fact that the notion of seminal principles is so natural in their view of generation, that it is deployed quite unselfconsciously in the analysis of the nature of bodily resurrection. It is clear, then, that Locke's speculative natural philosophy went well beyond mere matter theory and was even applied in his theological reflections. Yet the point at which his views on generation are of the greatest interest is their relation to his difficult discussion, in Book III of the *Essay*, on the nature of species. This is the subject of the next and final chapter.

11

Species

> I hope I have no where said, *there is no such sort of creatures in nature as birds*; if I have, it is both contrary to truth and to my opinion.
>
> Locke to William Molyneux*

The analysis of the extensive references in Locke's writings on generation, which I have undertaken in the previous chapter, reveals that Locke believes that seminal principles are responsible for the generation of plants, animals, some diseases, and some (if not all) minerals. As such, these principles are the primary determinant of the propagation of species, even if Locke is unclear as to their precise mode of operation. What, then, are the implications of this account of seminal principles for his views on species and kinds?

If, in order to account for the generation of species, Locke consistently posits the existence of entities, many of which have never been observed, yet which have powers that are difficult to explain, it would be bold indeed for someone to claim that Locke denied the existence of species in nature. Surprisingly, however, the majority of Locke's interpreters on the subject of species and natural kinds argue that he believed none of these to exist in nature. Here is a sampling of recent claims. Paul Guyer says:

On Locke's account, we cannot simply intend that our system of classification rigidly designate differences of microscopic real essence, not merely because we are—or were—largely ignorant of such differences, but because there are none.[1]

Susanna Goodin, echoing Guyer, claims:

Locke was denying naturally existing specific essences, that is, essences out in the world that determine a thing to be a sort of thing independently of human input.[2]

In his book *The Species Problem*, David Stamos has recently claimed that 'Locke was a species nominalist' for whom

---

* Locke to William Molyneux, 20 January 1693, *Correspondence*, Vol. 4, p. 626.
[1] Guyer 1994, p. 140.   [2] Goodin 1999, p. 166.

biological species are nothing else but abstract ideas existing in the mind. No minds, no species.[3]

It might be thought that we can rest easy on this point, because Locke was very explicit about it to his friend William Molyneux. Molyneux wrote to Locke:

What you say concerning Genera and Species is Unquestionably true, and yet it seems hard to assert, that there is no such sort of Creatures in Nature as Birds; for tho we may be Ignorant of the Particular Essence that makes a Bird to be a Bird, or that Determines and Distinguishes a Bird from a Beast, of the just Limits and boundarys between each; Yet we can no More doubt of a Sparrows being a Bird, and an Horses being a Beast, than we can of this Colour being Black and tother White, tho by Shades they may be made so Gradually to Vanish into each other, that we cannot tell where either Determines.[4]

Locke replied soon, saying:

I hope I have no where said, *there is no such sort of creatures in nature as birds*; if I have, it is both contrary to truth and to my opinion. This I do say, that there are real constitutions in things from whence these simple ideas flow, which we observ'd combined in them. And this I farther say, that there are real distinctions and differences in those real constitutions one from another; whereby they are distinguished one from another, whether we think of them or name them or no.[5]

This comment must have been reassuring for Molyneux: it is a clear denial of species nominalism. But can we take it as settled that nominalism is neither the motivation for, nor the implication of, Locke's conventionalism about species as expressed in the *Essay*? It is the aim of the present chapter to settle this issue.

Locke's conventionalism

First, it is important to state from the outset that, in spite of Locke's apparent belief in objectively existing species,[6] he was a conventionalist about the classification of species. Locke famously tells us that 'the sorting of Things, is the Workmanship of the Understanding'; and there is no doubt that this expresses Locke's conventionalism. Not surprisingly, this claim has come to be known as 'the workmanship of the understanding' thesis. But it is important to take the claim in context—or, better still, not to take it out of context. In Book III, chapter 2, Locke is at pains to stress that

Words in their primary or immediate Signification, stand for nothing, but the Ideas *in the Mind of him that uses them.*[7]

---

[3] Stamos 2003, pp. 45 and 41.
[4] 22 December 1692, *Correspondence*, Vol. 4, p. 601.
[5] Locke to William Molyneux, 20 January 1693, *Correspondence*, Vol. 4, p. 626.
[6] The extended discussion of species in Draft B (§§72–84, pp. 176–92) is more explicit about the objective existence of kinds in nature than is the *Essay* itself.
[7] E III. ii. 2, p. 405.

General terms signify general (or abstract) ideas, which are formed by abstraction from particulars. And it is crucial to note the extent to which this process of abstraction presupposes the perception of equivalence classes in nature. At *E* III. iii. 6, in explaining the origins of our general ideas, Locke says:

> By this way of abstraction they [that is general ideas] are made capable of representing more Individuals than one; each of which, having in it a <u>conformity</u> to that abstract *Idea*, is (as we call it) of that sort.[8]

So individuals in nature have a conformity to the general idea and are members of that sort. This is not enough to get us species in nature, but it is a claim about objective resemblances. But one can confidently presume that Locke has species in mind; for in the immediately following section Locke tells us how children form the general idea of human. He speaks of how the infant encounters its nurse and its mother, and then,

> [w]hen time and a larger Acquaintance has made them observe, that there are a great many other Things in the World, that in some common agreements of Shape, and several other Qualities, resemble their Father and Mother, [...] they frame an *Idea*, which they find those many Particulars do partake in.[9]

What are we to make, then, of the subsequent claim, in section 9, that the whole of the '*mystery* of *Genera* and *Species*' in the Schools 'is nothing else but abstract *Ideas*' (*E* III. iii. 9, p. 412)? Well, it is important not to be misled here. At first blush, Locke appears to be saying that species are simply ideas. But let's go back a step.

Locke is emphasizing in sections 9–12 that general ideas are formed by abstraction from particulars or tokens and that there is no actual type to which they refer: there is no universal man to which the term 'man' refers, only particular men. Just as there is no real 'average Australian' or 'typical politician'. So, when he says, in §12, that '*Species* of Things, are nothing else but these abstract Ideas', he is not saying that there are no species in nature, but that there are no types that exist, though of course there are individual tokens.[10] Locke's statement, then, makes more sense to us if we substitute the word 'type' for 'Species', because we are so familiar with the token/type distinction. Thus 'Types of Things, are nothing else but these abstract Ideas' makes perfect sense. The point is reinforced when we consider that Locke is arguing here against the scholastic view that there really are substantial forms, which give a substance its specificity as a particular kind of thing.

This brings us to the first 'workmanship of the understanding' passage. Having stressed that general terms signify abstract ideas and not really existing types or universals, Locke goes on to say that 'the sorting of Things, is the Workmanship of the Understanding' (*E* III. iii. 12, p. 415). Again, taken on its own, this clause seems to say that the way we carve up the world is entirely up to us. But Locke qualifies the

---

[8] *E* III. iii. 6, p. 411, underlining added.   [9] *E* III. iii. 7, p. 411.
[10] See also *First Reply to Stillingfleet*, *Locke Works*, Vol. 4, pp. 24–7.

clause by saying, immediately, 'since it is the Understanding that abstracts and makes those general *Ideas*'. So sorting is cashed out in terms of the formation of general ideas.

As if he anticipates a misunderstanding on this point, he immediately adds: 'I would not here be thought to forget, much less to deny, that Nature in the Production of Things, makes several of them alike' (*E* III. iii. 13, p. 415).[11] He then goes on to use the workmanship image again, and to clarify it further: 'But yet, I think, we may say, the *sorting* of them under Names, *is the Workmanship of the Understanding, taking occasion from the similitude* it observes amongst them [...]'. This is nothing more than the claim that the observation of equivalence classes in nature and the naming of such classes is the work of the human mind. It is not the claim that the mind constructs or determines which classes there are in nature.[12]

Up to this point in Book III, it appears that what is doing the classificatory work is the similitudes in nature and that convention is only choosing the names. But from §15 of chapter 3 Locke clarifies the notion of essence and introduces his distinction between real and nominal essence;[13] and from this point the true breadth of his conventionalism becomes apparent. Real essences are the 'unknown constitution of Things, whereon their discoverable Qualities depend' (*E* III. iii. 15, p. 417). It is 'a real, but unknown Constitution of their insensible Parts, from which flow those sensible Qualities' (*E* III. iii. 17, p. 418).[14]

By contrast, the nominal essence of a substance is that cluster (or complex idea) made up of ideas which are caused by the sensible qualities of members of particular species. Locke develops this doctrine further in chapter 6. Thus 'the *nominal Essence* of *Gold*, is that complex *Idea* the word *Gold* stands for, let it be, for instance, a Body yellow, of a certain weight, malleable, fusible, and fixed. But the *real Essence* is the constitution of the insensible parts of that Body, on which those Qualities, and all other Properties of *Gold* depend' (*E* III. vi. 2, p. 439). And Locke accepts the inference that, if substances have the same observable qualities, then they have the same internal structure. He puts this most clearly in his later discussion of species in the Stillingfleet correspondence:

where we find all the same properties, we have reason to conclude there is the same real, internal constitution, from which those properties flow.[15]

In fact, this is a guiding assumption behind the form of mercurialist transmutational chymistry to which Locke was committed. So far, the assumption appears to be a form of corpuscular essentialism. But there is a problem. Because we lack epistemic access to the real essences of things, we must form our notions of the essences of things through

---

[11] Cf. Draft B, §77, p. 184. [12] See also *E* III. vi, §§30, 36, 37.
[13] The doctrine of real and nominal essences is not present in either Draft A or Draft B of the *Essay*.
[14] This is the same terminology that he uses in the letter to Molyneux quoted above, in which he claims that he believes in species in nature. There Locke says 'that there are real constitutions in things from whence these simple ideas flow'.
[15] *First Reply to Stillingfleet, Locke Works*, Vol. 4, p. 91.

our complex ideas of them, that is, through their nominal essences. Locke goes on to explain this process at *E* III. vi. 7 (p. 443):

> The next thing to be considered is, by which of those Essences it is, that *Substances are determined into* Sorts, or *Species*; and that 'tis evident, is *by the nominal Essence*.

The first reason he gives is the confusion we suffer when we encounter variation within species, and the resemblances between species is a clear sign that we do not sort them by their real essences. And then in section 9 the core of the problem is spelt out:

> Nor indeed *can we* rank, and *sort Things*, and consequently [...] denominate them *by their real Essences*, because we know them not. Our Faculties carry us no farther towards the knowledge and distinction of Substances, than a Collection of those sensible *Ideas*, which we observe in them [...][16]

This is where Locke's conventionalism is established. He is now ready to bring out a whole swag of problems relating to variability and arbitrariness in our complex ideas of substances, such that the very notion of species appears to be problematic. There is variability in the nominal essence of a species from one person to another (*E* III. vi. 26, p. 453); if there is a great chain of being, then our species boundaries seem indeterminate, or even arbitrary (*E* III. vi. 12, pp. 446–7);[17] there are anomalous instances such as monstrous births (*E* III. vi. 16–17, pp. 448–9);[18] reproductive isolation fails in many cases (*E* III. vi. 23, pp. 451–2); any particular substance has potentially infinite relational properties (*E* III. vi. 47, p. 469, III. ix. 13, p. 482); and, as we saw in the previous chapter, there is variation such that members of the same species can differ from each other as much as they differ from another species (*E* III. vi. 8, p. 443 and III. x. 20, p. 502). The moral is that these problems arise because we rely on nominal essences to determine species, and nominal essences are human constructs. Locke develops these sceptical arguments against an essentialist account of species with such sustained intensity that the reader can form the impression that Locke was dismissive of the very notion of species essentialism and was a species nominalist. When he says:

---

[16] *E* III. vi. 9, p. 444.

[17] Cf. *E* III. vi. 30. The point about indeterminate boundaries is first expressed in Draft B, §75, where Locke says: 'though there be a foundation in nature for the divideing of things into sorts & tribes, yet because we seldom know the precise bounds where one ends & the other begins & where the destinction is made between them, [...] we devide them into species in respect of our selves' (Draft B, §75, p. 183). Locke uses the notion of a great chain of being elsewhere in the *Essay* (*E* IV. xvi. 12). His belief in distinct species of angels and spiritual beings is evident from Draft B, §81 (p. 188) to his *First Reply to Stillingfleet*, *Locke Works*, Vol. 4, p. 18, where he says: 'it cannot be doubted but there are distinct species of separate spirits, of which we have no distinct ideas at all'.

[18] See also *E* III. iii. 17, p. 418, III. vi. 12, p. 447, III. vi. 23, p. 451, III. vi. 26–7, p. 453–5, III. x. 21, p. 502, III. xi. 20, p. 519 and IV. iv. 13–16. It is worth noting here that Boyle's first three publications in the *Philosophical Transactions* concerned monstrous births, and the first two of these, concerning a monstrous calf, were communicated to him by Locke's Oxford medical colleague David Thomas. See *Boyle Works*, Vol. 5, pp. 495–9. Locke's interest in mutant plant varieties is discussed in Anstey and Harris 2006.

if Things were distinguished into *Species*, according to their real Essences, it would be as impossible to find different Properties in any two individual Substances of the same *Species*, as it is to find different Properties in two Circles, or two equilateral Triangles,[19]

this presumption is hard to resist and few commentators have resisted it. However, I argue that it should be resisted. And this, not only on grounds extrinsic to the text of the *Essay*—such as Locke's views on generation and his comments to Molyneux—but in the light of further theses, spelt out in the *Essay* itself.[20]

A constrained conventionalism

Locke's conventionalism about species is *constrained*. Let me explain. Locke posits that there are 'real constitutions' and differences amongst them. This is an objective fact about the world. In the *Essay* he calls these real constitutions 'real essences', and it is clear that he regards them in terms of corpuscular structure. The problem is that we do not have epistemic access to determinate real constitutions. We do, however, have epistemic access to clusters of properties which flow from real essences. These properties cause simple ideas in us. These clusters are not arbitrarily assembled, because there are constraints on the range of possible properties which can give rise to ideas in us. Indeed, Locke frequently points out that groups of these ideas, ideas that constitute the nominal essences of species, always occur together (see below for references).

I think that we should regard these groups of ideas as an epistemological analogue to Richard Boyd's homeostatic property clusters—HPCs—and that we can use Boyd's HPC view of natural kinds, or a version of it, as an interpretative tool for understanding Locke's own position.[21]

A homeostatic property cluster view of kinds is defined by Rob Wilson as follows:

[N]atural kind terms are often defined by a cluster of properties, no one or particular n-tuple of which must be possessed by any individual to which the term applies, but some such n-tuple must be possessed by all such individuals. The properties mentioned in the [homeostatic property cluster] definitions are *homeostatic* in that there are mechanisms that cause their systematic coinstantiation or clustering.[22]

The homeostatic nature of the clusters is determined by underlying causal mechanisms, which put constraints upon which properties can be co-instantiated in any individual. As Boyd put it in an early discussion of this notion, 'there are a number of scientifically

---

[19] *E* III. vi. 8, p. 443.
[20] This conventionalism is present in Draft B, though it is more muted there and not developed with the corpuscular pessimism and doctrine of essences which we find in the published work.
[21] The homeostatic property cluster view of species has been mentioned in connection with Locke on species in Kornblith 1993, ch. 2 and in Stuart 1999, pp. 278–80. The interpretation of this chapter is in broad agreement with Stuart's article. For a discussion of non-essentialist accounts of species before Darwin, see Winsor 2003. Ironically, Boyd himself appears to regard Locke as a nominalist about species. See his 1999, pp. 142 and 146.
[22] R. A. Wilson 1999a, p. 197.

important kinds (properties, relations, etc.) whose natural definitions are very much like the property-cluster definitions postulated by ordinary-language philosophers except that the unity of the properties in the defining cluster is mainly causal rather than conceptual'.[23]

The idea of a homeostatic property cluster is clear enough; how can it be used to illuminate Locke's account of species? Well, if we think in terms of clusters of ideas caused by properties rather than in terms of the properties themselves, we can see the utility of the HPC view. The clusters of ideas that make up the nominal essence of a species may not always correspond exactly to those properties that a member of the species instantiates, and no idea is itself essential; but the clusters are relatively stable collections of ideas. Variation can come from differences in experience, as Locke points out, or from different determinate members of the species, but the clusters easily and naturally allow us to form equivalence classes that enable naming, reidentification, and communication about species.

Locke's nominal essences are analogous to homeostatic idea clusters—HICs: they are *constrained* both by the range of actual properties that can flow from the real essence (or constitution) and by the epistemic limits of the percipients. This rules out arbitrary or *ad hoc* clusters of ideas. Locke says:

> But though these *nominal Essences of Substances* are made by the Mind, they are *not yet made so arbitrarily, as those of mixed Modes* [...] the Mind, in making its complex Ideas of Substances, only follows Nature; and puts none together, which are not supposed to have an <u>union in Nature</u>. No body joins the Voice of a Sheep, with the Shape of a Horse; nor the Colour of Lead, with the Weight and Fixedness of Gold.[24]

It is this 'union in nature' that puts constraints on the formation of the HIC that gives rise to the complex idea of gold. The real constitution or essence gives rise to a certain range of properties, which in turn cause ideas in us that constitute the nominal essence of the species. Locke explains: 'By this *real Essence*, I mean, that real constitution of any Thing, which is the foundation of all those Properties, that are combined in, and are <u>constantly found to co-exist</u> with the *nominal Essence*' (*E* III. vi. 6, p. 442, underlining added). This fact, that the properties 'are constantly found to co-exist', is grounded in the nature of the real essence, which is the 'foundation of all those Properties'. The idea expressed here is not simply that the nominal essence 'depends' upon or 'flows from' the real essence, something which Locke says again and again.[25] Rather, the key notion is that the co-occurrence of the properties within the cluster has its ontological ground in the nature of the real essence. This is why Locke can say:

---

[23] Boyd 1991, p. 141.
[24] *E* III. vi. 28, pp. 455, underlining added. See also *E* III. iii. 11, p. 435 and III. ix. 13, p. 483 ('the Union in Nature of these Qualities, being the true Ground of their Union in one complex *Idea* [...]') and *First Reply to Stillingfleet, Locke Works*, Vol. 4, p. 87.
[25] See *E* III. iii. 15 *bis*, III. vi. 2.

Supposing the nominal Essence of *Gold*, to be Body of such a peculiar Colour and Weight, with Malleability and Fusability, the real Essence is that Constitution of the parts of Matter, on which these Qualities, <u>and their Union</u>, depend.[26]

It is this claim made by Locke, that the *union* of the ideas that make up the nominal essence has its ground in a union of properties in the real essence, that renders his view epistemologically analogous to the modern HPC view of species. It is analogous, namely, to the way in which, in some contemporary accounts of species, clusters of, say, phenotypic characteristics of a species are related to an underlying genetic structure.[27]

Furthermore, it is the grounding of the co-occurring ideas in the nominal essence in those properties which have a union in nature that marks an important difference between species of *substances* and species of *mixed modes*. Thus, from *E* III. v. 10 on, Locke is at pains to stress that, for species of mixed modes, 'the connexion between the loose parts of those complex *Ideas*, being made by the Mind, <u>this union</u>, which has no particular foundation in Nature, would cease again, were there not something that did, as it were, hold it together' (p. 434, underlining added). We saw in Chapter 6 that Locke does not categorically deny that mixed modes can have 'truthmakers' in the world, but this does not undermine the distinction between our ideas of mixed modes and our ideas of substances. The implication is that, for the nominal essences of substances, it is the union of qualities in nature that 'holds together' the constituents of the abstract ideas of each sort of substance. As Locke puts it:

when we speak of a *Horse*, or *Iron*, whose specifick *Ideas* we consider not, as barely in the Mind, but as in Things themselves, which afford the original Patterns of those *Ideas*. But in mixed Modes, at least the most considerable parts of them, which are moral Beings, we consider the original Patterns, as being in the Mind.[28]

The point is repeated a number of times throughout the remainder of Book III; it marks the critical difference between ideas of mixed modes and ideas of substances. And Locke uses it to introduce a number of other notions, which both reinforce the idea of properties having a union in nature and presuppose the objective existence of sorts, or species. Locke uses both the notion of a *standard* of nature[29] and nature's *archetypes*.[30]

Now, not only does the HIC account for the co-instantiation of properties, it also accounts for the fact that members of the same species may not instantiate any particular property or n-tuple of properties in the HPC. Thus Locke observes that 'we find many

---

[26] *E* III. vi. 6, p. 442, underlining added.
[27] Of course, I am not claiming that Locke believed in, or even anticipated, the notion of a homeostatic property cluster. Rather, I am simply using this modern notion to shed light on his view.
[28] *E* III. v. 12, p. 436. Therefore, according to Locke, ideas of substances are far more constrained than those of mixed modes. See *E* III. vi. 27–8 and III. x. 33.
[29] See III. vi. 46, p. 468 and III. ix. 11, p. 481.
[30] See *E* III. vi. 46 and 51, III. xi. 15 and 17. The precursor of this discussion is in Draft B, §79, pp. 185–7.

of the Individuals that are ranked into one Sort, called by one common Name, and so received as being of one *Species*, have yet Qualities depending on their real Constitutions, as far different one from another, as from others, from which they are accounted to differ *specifically* [i.e. as species]' (*E* III. vi. 8, p. 443=Draft B, §83). The HIC quite naturally allows this variability. Locke also observes that no particular property of any substance can be said to be essential in the sense that the substance in question cannot exist without it. This point is stressed at *E* III. vi. 4–6.[31] Having said this, however, Locke emphasizes in a number of places that most substances have a group of 'leading Qualities' by which they are commonly identified and which one would normally expect to find in any member of a sort. In substances that reproduce by seed, this is normally their shape, and for inanimate natural substances it is their colour (*E* III. vi. 29, p. 456).[32]

Moreover, this view also allows us to account for the discovery of new properties, properties not previously known to flow from the real essence, such as the ductility of gold (*E* III. vi. 47, p. 469). And it allows for the natural differences in the nominal essences of the same species that arise from casual acquaintance with individuals of the species, or from self-interest or expertise. As Locke says:

the number [...] [of ideas the mind] combines [to form the nominal essence], *depends upon the various Care, Industry, or Fancy of him that makes it*. Men generally content themselves with some few sensible obvious Qualities; and often, if not always, leave out others as material, and as firmly united, as those that they take.[33]

This allows for an element of conventionalism in the use of general terms, but it is a conventionalism constrained by the fact that there is an ontological ground which guarantees the co-occurrence of ideas that make up the nominal essence.

A convergent conventionalism

If the nominal essence is constrained by the underlying real essence, it is also convergent. The homeostatic idea cluster is *convergent* in so far as discoveries about new properties—for instance solubility in *aqua regis*, relative weights—enable more fine-grained nominal essences to be assembled, and ultimately (though Locke was supremely pessimistic on this point) a knowledge of real constitution. And this convergence comes in grades. There are and always will be cases of speakers whose use of general terms signifies impoverished nominal essences:

because by familiar use from our Cradles, we come to learn certain articulate Sounds very perfectly, and have them readily on our Tongues, and always at hand in our Memories; but yet

---

[31] *E* III. vi. 6, p. 442: 'there is no individual parcel of Matter, to which any of these Qualities are so annexed, as to be *essential* to it, or inseparable from it'.
[32] See also *E* III. ix. 15. p. 484 and III. xi. 19, p. 518.
[33] *E* III. vi. 29, p. 456.

are not always careful to examine, or settle their Significations perfectly, it *often* happens that *Men*, even when they would apply themselves to an attentive Consideration, do *set their Thoughts more on Words than Things*. [...] Therefore some, not only Children, but Men, speak several Words, no otherwise than Parrots do.[34]

But one of the great benefits of the new science, according to Locke, is that we are constantly learning about new properties that individuals of particular kinds possess, and we are able to make finer distinctions between kinds. So in his list of remedies for the imperfection and abuse of words Locke recommends that experts should construct a dictionary which would specify the nominal essences, or the HICs, of all general terms:

It were therefore to be wished, That Men, versed in physical Enquiries, and acquainted with the several sorts of natural Bodies, would set down those simple *Ideas*, wherein they observe the Individuals of each sort constantly to agree. This would remedy a great deal of that confusion, which comes from several Persons, applying the same Name to a Collection of a smaller, or greater number of sensible Qualities, proportionably as they have been more or less acquainted with, or accurate in examining the Qualities of any sort of Things, which come under one denomination. But a Dictionary of this sort, containing, as it were, a Natural History, requires too many hands, as well as too much time, cost, pains, and sagacity, ever to be hoped for...[35]

Locke is less sanguine here about the prospects of such a dictionary than he is in Draft B of 1671 when this suggestion was first mooted.[36] But in this section of the *Essay* he does go on to express a hope that at least a dictionary containing 'little Draughts and Prints' could be produced which would aid the non-expert. He gives examples of plant and animal species and of artefacts as well.[37] Of course, Locke's library contained many such taxonomical works. In fact, it now appears likely that he even supplied seeds for specimens which appeared in the herbarium which formed the basis for at least one work of this kind: Robert Morison's *Plantarum historiae universalis Oxoniensis pars tertia* (1699).[38] So, while there is an element of variability and convention in the formation of nominal essences, it is hoped that they will gradually converge to map more accurately their underlying real essences.

Let us then summarize Locke's constrained and convergent conventionalism about kinds. There are naturally occurring clusters of properties, which have their foundation in the real essences or corpuscular structures of objectively existing kinds. These clusters of properties cause clusters of ideas in us. Clusters of ideas are nominal essences; they are

---

[34] *E* III. ii. 7, pp. 407–8.   [35] *E* III. xi. 25, pp. 521–2.
[36] Draft B, §84, pp. 191–2. See also §72, p. 176.
[37] *E* III. xi. 25, p. 523. Locke had been particularly impressed by examples of such works that he saw in the KING'S library in Paris, of which he wrote in his journal that the drawings were 'soe exactly well donne that who ever knew any of the plants or birds before, would there know them at first sight, the figure, proportions, & colours being all soe lively & naturall', Lough 1953, p. 160.
[38] The work was assembled by Locke's associate Jacob Bobart the younger. For a discussion of Locke's distributing seeds to botanists, see Harris and Anstey 2009.

quickly formed by the understanding into one complex idea and given a general name. The clusters of ideas are not arbitrarily formed, but correspond to the naturally co-instantiated properties which flow from their underlying causes. They are constrained insofar as they should only include ideas of properties which are constituents of this underlying union. And, while the nominal essence of a general term may vary from person to person in accordance with age, experience, and so on and over time, depending upon the current state of our knowledge of bodies, we are gradually forming more and more accurate nominal essences of kinds. To be sure, in some cases the boundaries between kinds are blurry; there are anomalous cases; and there is enormous generative variation. And in these cases, at least in the short term, the understanding, and not nature, demarcates between species and must judge whether an individual qualifies as a member of a species. But, if our knowledge and our accuracy in the use of words improve, this should happen less and less.[39]

The relativized real essence

On the view presented here, it is the nominal essence that is caused by, and has its ontological ground in, the real essence or the corpuscular constitution of a member of a kind. But perhaps the most widely held view about Locke's theory of kinds maintains the exact opposite. Following Michael Ayers, David Owen and others have argued that, for Locke, the real essence is relativized to the nominal essence.[40] That is, of all the many properties an individual has in virtue of its corpuscular structure, it is only those that correspond to ideas in the nominal essence that form part of the real essence. The internal corpuscular constitution may have many properties and relations which are not part of the nominal essence, and these are therefore not constituents of the real essence. As the nominal essence of a general term changes, so too does the underlying real essence. This interpretation effectively turns the view I have presented on its head. Instead of the nominal essence being constrained by the natural union of properties in the real essence, the real essence is relativized to the nominal essence. This is a far stronger form of conventionalism than I credit to Locke. What are we to make of it?

Well, if we start from the premise that Locke was a species nominalist, it is an appealing view. It enables us to make sense not just of his talk of real essences, but also of the manner in which the properties which cause the ideas that make up our nominal essences 'flow from' or 'depend upon' real essences. There is no reason to break the causal nexus between real and nominal essences; it is just that real essences are to be demarcated by our epistemic proclivities and not by anything in nature.

---

[39] Locke sketches a simple taxonomy of animals, vegetables and minerals in his *Elements of Natural Philosophy*, chs VIII to X. See *Locke Works*, Vol. 3, pp. 317–23. This work was composed for the education of the young Francis Cudworth Masham.

[40] Owen 1991. See also Goodin 1998. A variant of this view is found in Conn 2003.

The strongest textual evidence for this interpretation is found at *E* III. vi. 6 (p. 442, underlining added) where Locke says:

But *Essence*, even in this sense [real essence], <u>relates to</u> *a sort*, and <u>supposes</u> a *Species*: For being that real Constitution, on which the Properties depend, it necessarily <u>supposes</u> a sort of Things, Properties belonging only to *Species*, and not to Individuals; *v.g.* Supposing the nominal Essence of *Gold*, to be Body of such a peculiar Colour and Weight, with Malleability and fusibility, the real Essence is that Constitution of the parts of Matter, on which these Qualities, and their Union depend; and is also the foundation of its Solubility in *Aqua Regia*, and other Properties accompanying that complex *Idea*. Here are *Essences* and *Properties*, but all upon supposition of a Sort, or general abstract *Idea*, which is considered as immutable: but <u>there is no individual parcel of Matter, to which any of these Qualities are so annexed, as to be *essential* to it</u>, or inseparable from it. [...] as to the *real Essences* of Substances, we only suppose their Being, without precisely knowing what they are: But that which annexes them still to the *Species*, is the nominal Essence, of which they are the supposed foundation and cause.

Locke's talk of real essences *relating* to a sort, of *supposing* a species, and of being *annexed* to a species *may* suggest that the boundaries of the cluster of properties that makes up the real essence are determined by the constituents of the nominal essence. That is, the real essence just is the ontological ground of those properties, and only of those, which cause in us the ideas that constitute the nominal essence. On this view, then, the property of being soluble in *aqua regia* only becomes part of the real essence of gold when it is discovered: real essences are demarcated by an epistemological criterion. As Michael Ayers says,

real essences could not determine species ontologically because real essences are relative to nominal essences.[41]

I have five arguments against this view.

First, the passage quoted above neither explicitly claims nor implies that the real essence is to be relativized to the nominal essence. It is important to point out that the immediate context of the passage is a discussion of the manner in which properties can only be said to be essential in so far as they relate to the nominal essence. No individual property of the real essence is essential, because each one is separable without the substance losing its identity. By contrast, if one simple idea of the nominal essence is removed, we have in effect a new nominal essence (*E* III. vi. 4–5).[42] We might say that, for Locke, mereological essentialism applies to nominal but not to real essences; and that it does not make sense to talk of malleability being an essential property of gold, but it makes sense to say that the idea of malleability is an essential part of the nominal essence of gold.[43] But a further qualification is required here; for different users of the term, 'gold' will have different nominal essences of gold, and the idea of malleability

---

[41] Ayers 1991, Vol. 2, p. 74. See also Ayers 1981b.
[42] See also *First Reply to Stillingfleet*, *Locke Works*, Vol. 4, p. 90.
[43] For Locke's original discussion of this point, see Draft B, §73, p. 179. See also §78, p. 185.

may be an essential part of one person's nominal essence of gold, but not of another's. Thus essence *qua* essential property relates to/supposes a nominal essence, but essence *qua* inner nature relates to/supposes inner corpuscular structure.

Second, elsewhere in this very chapter Locke explicitly says that the real essence is that on which *all* the properties of a body depend:

> But the *real Essence* is the constitution of the insensible parts of that Body, on which those Qualities [causing the nominal essence], and all the other Properties of *Gold* depend.[44]

Locke also speaks of our *ignorance* of properties of the real essence. That there are properties of the real essence that we do not know entails that the real essence is not demarcated by the nominal essence. Locke says:

> We can never know what are the precise number of Properties depending on the real Essence of *Gold*, any one of which failing, the real Essence of Gold, and consequently Gold, would not be there, unless we knew the real Essence of Gold it self.[45]

On the relativized real essence view, Locke's talk of our being ignorant of the real essences of things and therefore ignorant of all the properties which flow from it, would make no sense. For the relativized real essence, there just are no properties of the real essence that we are ignorant of, because this sort of essence is defined by those properties which cause the ideas that make up our nominal essences.

Third and most importantly, there is the argument from correspondence. Locke sometimes speaks in evaluative terms of the relation between nominal and real essences. These evaluations only make sense if the nominal essence is relativized to the real essence. For example, he claims that '*artificial* Things are distinguished, with less Doubt, Obscurity, and Equivocation' than 'Things natural' (*E* III. vi. 40, p. 465, underlining added). At *E* III. vi. 37 (p. 462), Locke speaks of man-made nominal essences being 'seldom adequate to the internal Nature of the Things they are taken from'. Again, at *E* III. vi. 19, p. 449, he speaks of 'having framed perfect complex ideas of the *Properties* of things, flowing from their different real Essences'. And at *E* III. xi. 24 (pp. 520–1) he says:

> [I]n Substances, we are not always to rest in the ordinary complex *Idea*, commonly received as the signification of that Word, but must go a little farther, and enquire into the Nature and Properties of the Things themselves, and thereby perfect, as much as we can, our *Ideas* of their distinct Species.[46]

What, I ask, would make the nominal essence *adequate*, except for the fact that it is derived from the real essence? And does not the notion of a *perfect* complex idea or

---

[44] *E* III. vi. 2, p. 439.
[45] *E* III. vi. 19, p. 449.
[46] Underlining added. See also: *E* III. vi. 30, p. 457, where Locke speaks of nominal essences as imperfectly copied from nature; III. vi. 31, p. 458, where Locke speaks of complex ideas (i.e. nominal essences) being formed 'some more, and others less accurately'; *E* III. xi. 6, p. 511, where 'imperfect *Ideas*' of birds and bats are made more complete by examination of actual birds and bats.

nominal essence imply a standard over and above the nominal essence itself, a standard that is most naturally found in the properties grounded in the real essence?

Fourth, the relativized real essence view seems to run counter Locke's broader philosophical methodology as we find it in the *Essay*. For on the whole Locke sets his metaphysics first, and then addresses epistemological issues. Thus, in his theory of ideas, it is taken as a given that external objects exist and that they are the cause of our ideas, which are acquired by sensation. There is no hint that the existence of external objects is something that is to be established on the basis of the theory of ideas. And so too with the account of the relation between real and nominal essences. This is why we constantly encounter in Book III the following locutions: uses of general names are to 'conform their *Ideas* to the Things they would speak of' (vi. 28, p. 456); clusters of qualities are observed in nature (ibid.) or to be found in nature (vi. 36, p. 462); the mind has thus 'borrowed [...] from Nature' (vi. 29, p. 456) or 'copied from Nature' (vi. 30, p. 457); nominal essences are to follow nature (vi. 32, p. 459, ix. 11, p. 481), and they 'must agree with the Truth of Things' (xi. 24, p. 520; underlining added *passim*).

Fifth, adopting the relativized real essence interpretation is but a short step from attributing to Locke the view that we cannot, in principle, have knowledge of the real essence of substances because we are confined to our nominal essences. This would be to saddle Locke with what the late David Stove called 'The Worst Argument in the World', namely, that we cannot have knowledge of the way things are because all of our knowledge is relativized to our own conceptual scheme. Different intellectual beings would carve up the world in different ways, and there is no correct division.[47]

Furthermore, even if we grant relativized real essences, we still have to account for Locke's claims about the co-instantiation of the properties that cause the nominal essences to have a 'union in nature' and to co-exist regularly: we still have to account for 'the real distinctions and differences' whereby species 'are distinguished one from another'. On the relativized real essence view, this union is explained by conventions in language use and by the interests and preoccupations of the classifier, whereas on the view I am urging here it has its ground in the nature of the real essence itself. And this difference in interpretation brings to the fore the utility of the HPC view of kinds for understanding Locke's position. For, if Locke believes in objectively existing natural kinds, this union of their defining properties will be cashed out in terms of something like homeostasis rather than human convention.

Conclusion

To my mind, then, the weight of background evidence and of textual evidence inclines heavily in favour of the interpretation of Locke on species that I have presented above. In spite of the limitations of Locke's views concerning the nature of language and in

---

[47] See Franklin 2002. For a recent attribution of Stove's Gem to Locke, see Kim 2008.

spite of his pessimistic outlook in natural philosophy, he came up with a reasonable account of terms of natural kinds and their referents. He also wrote a very nuanced, if somewhat undirected, critique of the essentialist theory of species. His is the first sustained philosophical critique of essentialism about kinds in the modern period. If Locke's protracted discussion of kinds in the *Essay* causes some trouble for his contemporary interpreters, it is comforting to know that it gave Locke himself much trouble as well. He told Molyneux that

[s]ome parts of that third book concerning words, though the thoughts were easy and clear enough, yet cost me more pains to express than all the rest of my Essay.[48]

[48] *Correspondence*, Vol. 4, p. 626.

Conclusion

> I both honour his Person, and admire his Book [the *Essay*], which [...] I think to be one of the most Exquisite Pieces of Speculation that is Extant.
>
> John Norris[1]

In concluding this study of Locke and natural philosophy, let us return to the famous under-labourer passage of 'The Epistle to the Reader' in Locke's *Essay*. Locke's four Master-Builders might be construed as covering the whole domain of natural philosophy in England and abroad: Boyle the chymist; Sydenham the physician; Huygens the continental master of mechanics; and Newton the master of celestial physics.[2] Of the four, Locke knew personally three when he penned this passage, and Newton was very soon to become his friend.[3] The passage might also be construed as a list of those for whom Locke had the greatest admiration and whose work 'in advancing the Sciences' he believed would most likely be 'lasting Monuments to the Admiration of Posterity'.

In the case of Boyle, we have seen that he was the formative influence on Locke's views on the importance of the role of the method of natural history and on his chymistry. In the case of Newton, the late-comer in the English triumvirate, we have seen the manner in which his achievements in the *Principia* led Locke to revise his views on the role of principles in natural philosophy and on the explanatory reach of the mechanical philosophy. Moreover, for Locke, Newton's reasoning in the *Principia* became a paradigm of demonstrative reasoning. Locke was later to recommend the reading of Boyle's works and of Newton's *Principia*, works which were seminal contributions to the development of modern science.

The case of Sydenham is somewhat more difficult to assess. There is no lasting monument to posterity from his works, and his professional career was marked by

---

[1] Norris 1692, p. 64.   [2] This point was put to me by Antonio Clericuzio.
[3] Sadly for Locke, Sydenham died within weeks of the publication of the *Essay*, and Boyle two years later.

opposition and controversy. Only in the late 1680s did he come in from the cold and find acceptance by the College of Physicians. Indeed, it could be argued that two of the key factors in establishing his posthumous reputation as 'the English Hippocrates' were the occurrence of his name in the under-labourer passage in the *Essay* and Locke's subsequent promotion of him amongst British and continental physicians. What Locke promoted and what scholars abroad picked up on was Sydenham's decrying of hypotheses and speculation and his promotion of natural histories of disease; both these approaches were hallmarks of the experimental philosophy. Ironically, however, the text in which Sydenham is most explicit about this medical methodology was most likely written with the assistance of John Locke.[4] Moreover, there appears to be little definitive evidence that Locke's philosophical views were influenced by Sydenham, although Locke clearly learnt much from his therapeutics.[5] With hindsight, then, Sydenham's status as Master-Builder is far more ambiguous than that of Newton and Boyle, but his status as a proponent of the experimental philosophy is beyond dispute.

The case of Christiaan Huygens is also worthy of comment. Not much is known of Locke's direct relations with him, but all the evidence we have confirms that they held each other in very high regard. As for Huygens' status as an advocate of the experimental philosophy, two crucial pieces of evidence are worth citing here. First, it is most likely that his recommendation that the Parisian Académie develop a programme of Baconian natural history was adopted by Colbert in 1666.[6] Indeed, it seems highly probable that he came to acquiesce in such a conception of method in natural philosophy through his contacts with Henry Oldenburg and Sir Robert Moray, and as a result of his close engagement with Boyle's publications. Be that as it may, Huygens was the most eminent experimentalist amongst the natural philosophers of the Parisian Académie and, in spite of his preference for a Cartesian speculative philosophy, he was only too ready to declare that Newton had 'destroyed' Descartes' vortices and was scathing of Descartes' speculative 'chimeres'.[7]

What unifies the four masters in Locke's eyes, then, is their adherence to and practice of the experimental philosophy. This study has shown just how embedded Locke's thought was amongst that of the experimental philosophers of his day. It now seems remarkable, therefore, that François Duchesneau could claim that 'the point of view of Sydenham and that of Locke seem opposed to the experimentalist doctrine of

---

[4] See Meynell 2006.

[5] The evidence is assessed in Anstey and Burrows 2009; Burrows and Anstey forthcoming; and Anstey 2011b. Like many other students of Locke's thought, I took the 'Sydenham influence' thesis on trust, and I wrongly claimed in my 2005, p. 228 that Sydenham's influence on Locke's view of hypotheses and histories of disease 'is well documented'.

[6] See Stroup 1990, p. 70. For Huygens' recommendations, see Huygens 1888–1950, Vol. 6, pp. 95–6 and Vol. 19, pp. 268–71.

[7] Huygens 1888–1950, Vol. 21, p. 437 and Vol. 10, p. 405.

Bacon and revived by Boyle'.[8] Duchesneau's careful study, important in its time, built on the work of David E. Wolfe, who himself had concluded that

> [t]he ideas of Sydenham and Locke on observation, classification, and explanation differ from those of Bacon and Boyle and entail a general rejection of experimental biological inquiry, especially of anatomization with instruments.[9]

But Wolfe and Duchesneau entirely overlooked the wider medical context within which Locke's comments on anatomy were written and, in particular, the widespread opposition of the chymical physicians to Galenist claims for the efficacy of gross anatomy in physic. In fact, Wolfe erroneously regards Locke's views on anatomy as entailing not simply a 'rejection of microscopy', but the rejection of 'an entire method, the way of anatomization and experimentation'![10]

I believe that the weight of evidence assembled in this study argues for exactly the opposite conclusion: that, far from being anti-experimental, Locke was a proponent of the experimental philosophy; far from breaking with the natural philosophical methodology of Bacon and Boyle, Locke derived his neo-Baconian method of natural philosophy from Boyle and from the many virtuosi and chymical physicians with whom he interacted in the 1660s. One key shift in our thinking about the evidence on Locke's views on natural philosophy and medicine consists in breaking away from the 'Sydenham influence' historiography, which has so dominated our understanding of Locke's early philosophical development—as is rightly suggested by Romanell in his *John Locke and Medicine* of 1984. Yet we should not go all the way with Romanell, who claims that Locke's historical plain method was derived from the empirical medicine of his day, and ultimately from ancient medicine.[11] For Romanell was unaware of the interplay between the methodological views of natural philosophers and of chymical physicians in the 1660s; and he ignored the overt attempts of the latter to adopt the kind of methodology that was found in the new philosophy. It is more accurate to treat the medicine of that period as continuous with natural philosophy— as it appears to be in Boyle, especially insofar as medicine included physiological research and iatrochemistry. In the case of Locke, then, to privilege one of these disciplines, say, medicine, over the other is to misunderstand the milieu in which his intellectual formation took place and to ignore the major influence on Locke in these years, Robert Boyle.

Looking beyond the formative 1660s, other scholars have had much to say about the general cast of Locke's conception of natural philosophy vis-à-vis his Cartesian heritage and his realization of the importance of Newton's achievements. For example, in the early 1990s G. A. J. Rogers claimed that, because Locke realized that the prospects for a science of nature were almost nil, he resisted and all but rejected the idea:

---

[8] Duchesneau 1973, p. 85.
[9] D. E. Wolfe 1961, p. 203. This view has recently been reasserted in C. T. Wolfe 2010.
[10] D. E. Wolfe 1961, pp. 194, 195.   [11] Romanell 1984, p. 9.

This rejection of the certainty of natural science was also a rejection of the a priori route to knowledge of nature, which Locke had detected in Descartes and some of his followers and which he (with Newton) wholeheartedly wished to resist.[12]

Now, as we have seen, there is some truth in this claim insofar as Locke was supremely pessimistic about the prospects of a science of nature and he opposed speculative systems based upon general maxims. However, I have argued here that, from the early drafts to the *Essay* itself, he envisaged a kind of corpuscular metric that would enable us to develop a demonstrative science of material bodies, a science of nature founded on a quantitative analysis of their constituent parts. This ideal of a science of nature is carried over into the *Essay*, where a theory of demonstration is developed which articulates, in terms of the theory of ideas, the actual mechanism by which the mind could determine the relations between qualities—should we get epistemic access to real essences. Locke never gave up on, or rejected, this kind of science of nature, and therefore we should not infer from his pessimism that such an ideal natural philosophy is not desirable, or that the method of natural history is, in principle, a better way to knowledge of material things.

For that reason, it is important correctly to delimit the place of the construction of natural histories in Locke's prescriptions for natural philosophy. In an earlier article I claimed that, for Locke, the construction of natural histories is 'constitutive of natural philosophy'.[13] In fact Locke's position is more nuanced than this earlier analysis suggested. Locke's view is that the way of natural history is constitutive of *experimental* natural philosophy. But the construction of such histories is not an end in itself. It has its own heuristic structure: it is aimed at assembling and ordering observational evidence and, perhaps in time, at converging on the real essences of those substances to which we can apply a genuine corpuscular metric. From this we will eventually be able to determine the agreement or disagreement of ideas, so that we will have demonstrative rather than mere sensitive knowledge of phenomena such as the difference between two shades of white. Thus Locke's position is not an outright rejection of natural philosophy as a form of *scientia*. It is, rather, that such a natural philosophy, such a science of nature, will have to wait until we gain epistemic access to the real essences of terrestrial bodies.

What Locke did reject was speculative natural philosophical systems that were not founded on observation and experiment but on metaphysical principles, maxims, and

---

[12] Rogers 1994a, p. 18. See also Rogers 1979, p. 23 (= Rogers 1998, pp. 109–10); 'he [Locke] is not at all attracted to the Cartesian ideal of a completely deductive physics [...] Neither Locke nor Newton shared this aspiration'.

[13] Anstey 2003a, p. 33. Soles 2005 is rightly critical of this overstatement of Locke's view, though I do not accept his counterclaim that the 'conclusions or axioms derived from the natural histories by a wary induction of particulars are hypotheses and are central to Locke's conception of natural philosophy' (pp. 14–15). It should be pointed out that the passage which Soles cites (*Conduct*, pp. 233–4) as the basis of this claim is concerned with the correct conduct of the understanding in the *reading* of histories, whether civil or natural, and not in the practice of natural philosophy.

hypotheses. But, again, it is important not to miss the subtlety of Locke's position here. As we have seen, it is not that he was opposed to speculation *tout court*. He did acquiesce in speculative theories himself—theories that were propounded and developed by other experimental philosophers—but his overarching concern was that one should never lose sight of the hypothetical nature of these theories and that they should be subjected to the evidence accumulated in natural history. For Locke, then, natural history is to be given precedence over speculation; it is to be the arbiter of theory. Thus Locke's solution to the problem of corpuscular pessimism is not to allow speculative natural philosophy in through the back door, so to speak, but to bring it before the court of natural history. Moreover, Locke's ideal of a corpuscular metric from which a science of nature could derive was reinforced by his gradual realization, in the 1690s, that his ideal is analogous to what Newton had achieved by applying a mathematical method to heavenly bodies. In the 1690s Locke came to accept the Newtonian notion of principles of natural philosophy which, while derived from experiment and observation, are themselves an adequate foundation for a demonstrative natural philosophy. Unfortunately, however, Locke was either unwilling or unable to make the requisite changes to his theory of universal propositions in the *Essay* to reflect this development. Had he done so, he may also have diffused the evident tension between his vision of a demonsrative natural philosophy and his view that some qualities can only be explained by appeal to divine superaddition.

I take it, then, that the foregoing study has established the four theses stated in the Introduction. There is no doubting that Locke emphasized the utility of experimental natural philosophy and remained sceptical as to the epistemic status of speculative natural philosophical systems (Thesis 1). There is overwhelming evidence that Locke believed that the development of Baconian natural histories was the most efficacious method of natural philosophy (Thesis 2). In spite of this, however, Locke, like Boyle and Hooke, did engage in speculative natural philosophy and, like Boyle, he favoured the corpuscularian hypothesis, mercurialist transmutational chymistry, and various Helmontian conceptions (Thesis 3). Yet Locke's views did not remain static, for, by the end of his life, he had come to appreciate the efficacy of the mathematical experimental method of Newton. This is reflected in changes to his views in the 1690s, not least his admission that natural philosophy could be founded upon principles that matters of fact justify (Thesis 4).

It remains, in conclusion, to determine the extent to which the *Essay* itself is a work of experimental philosophy, or even a work of natural history. To what extent is Locke's project of explicating the nature of the understanding, the scope and limits of human knowledge, and the demarcation between knowledge and opinion an exercise in experimental philosophy?

Some recent discussions of Locke suggest that the answer to these questions is: 'Not much!'. Take, for example, Ian Hacking's portrayal of Locke's approach to philosophy. In his book *Historical Ontology*, in a chapter entitled 'Two kinds of "New Historicism" for Philosophers', Hacking turns to Locke's *Essay* in the context of a discussion of the need for philosophers to 'take a look'. Hacking urges that philosophers need to take a look at the genesis and history of the problems they address and to situate and contextualize their problems rather than continuing with the presumption that they are dealing with abstract and timeless problems. Here is what he says about Locke:

> Locke's *Essay Concerning Human Understanding* is as nonhistorical a work as we could imagine

and

> Locke is the model empiricist: our ideas and our knowledge originate in experience. But his methodology is rationalist. His book is one great thought experiment. Aside from anecdotes, he almost never takes a look.[14]

Hacking commends Locke for his pursuit of an account of the origins of our ideas, but he implicitly castigates him for not 'taking a look'. He argues that philosophers need to be more historically informed; otherwise they end up doing the sort of philosophy of which Locke was guilty. These are methodological prescriptions for how philosophy should be done now. Yet, Locke's understanding of experimental natural philosophy, as discussed in this book, constitutes part of the background evidence for what is actually a very strong case for the claim that the *Essay* is a genuine attempt at a natural history of the understanding; a natural history both of the genealogy of our ideas in general (Hacking's main concern) and of our ideas about the particular sorts of substances that are to be found in nature. Indeed, a detailed analysis of Locke's published works, of his manuscripts, and of his correspondence reveals the broad scope, the pains, and the care with which Locke examined the history of reflection as well as the current state of knowledge in those particular disciplines—and their associated problems, with which he was concerned in the *Essay*. It is therefore simply wrong to charge him with not having 'taken a look', or to claim, as Hacking does in an earlier work, that Locke was 'fashioning a parable when he pretended to practice the natural history of the mind'.[15]

There is no doubt that Locke's speculations extend beyond the theory of matter and the theory of generation, to the way of ideas itself. This is why, in 1692, John Norris could rightly call the *Essay* 'one of the most Exquisite Pieces of Speculation that is Extant'. But Locke's claims to have written the work according the 'Historical, plain Method' are not empty rhetoric or wishful thinking. On numerous occasions he asks his reader to 'experiment in himself'[16] and to find in their understanding phenomena which are the evidential basis of his 'system'.[17] Moreover, Locke's *Essay* was quickly understood and emulated as an 'application of experimental philosophy to moral

---

[14] Hacking 2002, p. 63.
[15] Hacking 1983, p. 131. Greg Radick alerted me to this reference.
[16] See, for example, Draft A, §27, p.44, Draft B, §93, p. 200 and §94, p. 208, *E* II. xxi. 47; II. xxiii. 6, 32, 33, 36; IV. vii. 4.
[17] Locke to William Molyneux, 20 September 1692, *Correspondence*, Vol. 4, p. 523.

subjects'.[18] In fact, it is not too much to say that Locke's *Essay* inaugurated a new genre of writing experimental histories of the understanding, which was to flourish well into the eighteenth century.[19] The *Essay* is not just the work of an under-labourer for the experimental philosophy; it is a work of experimental philosophy in its own right. Little wonder that Voltaire could say of Locke:

Such a Multitude of Reasoners having written the Romance of the Soul, a Sage at last arose, who gave, with an Air of the greatest Modesty, the History of it. Mr. *Locke* has display'd the human Soul, in the same Manner as an excellent Anatomist the Springs of the human Body.[20]

[18] See for example Hume 2007, Vol. 1, p. 4.
[19] See Anstey 2009.
[20] 'On Mr. Locke' in *Letters concerning the English Nation*', Voltaire 1994, p. 56.

List of Manuscripts

Bodleian Library, Oxford

Lovelace Collection

MS Locke b. 7: Herbarium, vol. 2.
MS Locke c. 28: Philosophical papers.
MS Locke c. 29: Medical papers.
MS Locke c. 31: Miscellaneous papers.
MS Locke c. 33: Notes on books read by Locke.
MS Locke c. 42A: Medical commonplace book.
MS Locke c. 44: Chymical and medical notes copied from Boyle's papers.
MS Locke d. 9: 'Adversaria 5', medical commonplace book, from c. 1665.
MS Locke d. 11: 'Lemmata Physica', Medical commonplace book, c. 1660–c. 1675, 1693–1701.
MS Locke e. 4: Medical notebook, 1650s.
MS Locke f. 10: Journal, 1689–1704.
MS Locke f. 14: Commonplace book, c. 1659–c. 1666.
MS Locke f. 18: Medical notebook, c. 1659–c. 1660.
MS Locke f. 19: 'Adversaria 3', medical commonplace book, c. 1662–c. 1669.
MS Locke f. 20: Medical notebook, c. 1659–c. 1660.
MS Locke f. 21: Medical notebook, c. 1669–c. 1672, 1679–81.
MS Locke f. 22: Medical notebook, c. 1665–c. 1666.
MS Locke f. 25: 'Adversaria 4 Pharmacopaea', chemical notebook, 1663–1667.
MS Locke f. 27: Pocket memorandum book, 1664–1666.
MS Locke f. 28: Pocket memorandum book, 1678–1685.
MS Locke f. 29: Pocket memorandum book, 1683–1702.
MS Locke f. 33: Student notebook.

Microfilm

MS Film 77: 'Adversaria 1661', notebook.

British Library, London

Additional MS 5714: Medical case notes from September 1667 to September 1670.
Additional MS 15642: Locke's Journal, 1679.
Additional MS 32554: Commonplace book, 1659–c. 1667.
Sloane MS 2502: 'Topics for the History of Diseases', fols 1v–2.

Royal Society Library, London

Boyle Papers

Vol. 9: Philosophy[1]
Vol. 10: Philosophy
Vol. 14: Theology
Vol. 18: Physiology
Vol. 26: Science
Vol. 34: Science

Boyle notebooks

MS 186: Boyle notebook, c. 1690.

Wellcome Library, London

MS 6175: Transcription by Sir D'Arcy Power of some notebooks of John Ward.

Royal College of Physicians Library, London

MS 572: Thomas Sydenham's 'Medical Observations'.

The National Archives, Kew

Shaftesbury Papers: 'Locke's letters and papers'
NA PRO 30/24/47/2: Medical papers, c. 1666–c. 1674.
NA PRO/30/24/47/30: Miscellaneous papers.

Folger Shakespeare Library, Washington, DC

Folger MS V.a.291: Notebook of John Ward.

Chemical Heritage Foundation, Philadelphia

Roy G. Neville Historical Chemical Library
Alchemical manuscript by Isaac Newton, fol.1 (Sotheby Lot 18[c]).

---

[1] Volume titles of the Boyle Papers derive from nineteenth-century contents leafs.

Bibliography

Aaron, R. I. (1971) *John Locke*, 3rd edn, Oxford: Clarendon Press.
Aarsleff, H. (1964) 'Locke on Leibniz on language', *American Philosophical Quarterly*, 1, pp. 165–88. [Reprinted in Aarsleff 1982.]
—— (1982) *From Locke to Saussure: Essays on the Study of Language and Intellectual History*, London: Athlone.
Acosta, J. de (1604) *The Natural & Moral History of the Indies*, London.
Aiton, E. (1972) *The Vortex Theory of Planetary Motions*, London: Macdonald.
Aldrich, H. (1691) *Artis Logicae Compendium*, Oxford.
Alexander, P. (1985) *Ideas, Qualities and Corpuscles: Locke and Boyle on the External World*, Cambridge: Cambridge University Press.
Amerpoel, J. (1669) *Cartesius Mosaizans*, Leeuwarden.
André, F. (1672) *Entretiens sur l'acide et l'alcali*, Paris [2nd edn 1677].
Anstey, P. R. (2000) *The Philosophy of Robert Boyle*, London: Routledge.
—— (2002a) 'Locke, Bacon and natural history', *Early Science and Medicine*, 7, pp. 65–92.
—— (2002b) 'Robert Boyle and Locke's "Morbus" entry: A Reply to J. C. Walmsley', *Early Science and Medicine*, 7, pp. 358–77.
—— (2002c) 'Boyle on seminal principles', *Studies in History of Biological and Biomedical Sciences*, 33, pp. 597–630.
—— (2002d) 'Robert Boyle and the heuristic value of Mechanism', *Studies in History and Philosophy of Science*, 33, pp. 161–74.
—— (2003a) 'Locke on method in natural philosophy', in Anstey, ed., 2003b, pp. 26–42.
—— (2005) 'Experimental versus speculative natural philosophy', in Anstey and Schuster, eds, pp. 215–42.
—— (2009) 'The experimental history of the understanding from Locke to Sterne', *Eighteenth Century Thought*, 4, pp. 143–69.
—— (2011a) 'The matter of medicine: New medical matter theories in mid-seventeenth-century England', in Jalobeanu and Anstey, eds, pp. 61–79.
—— (2011b) 'The creation of the English Hippocrates', *Medical History*, 55, pp. 457–78.
—— ed. (2003b) *The Philosophy of John Locke: New Perspectives*, London: Routledge.
—— ed. (2006) *John Locke: Critical Assessments*, 4 vols, Abingdon: Routledge.
Anstey, P. R. and Burrows, J. (2009) 'John Locke, Thomas Sydenham, and the authorship of two medical essays' *electronic British Library Journal*. Accessible at http://www.bl.uk/eblj/2009articles/articles.html.
Anstey, P. R. and Harris, S. (2006) 'Locke and botany', *Studies in History and Philosophy of Biological and Biomedical Sciences*, 37, pp. 151–71.
Anstey, P. R. and M. Hunter (2008) 'Robert Boyle's "Designe about Natural History"', *Early Science and Medicine*, 13, pp. 83–126.
Anstey, P. R. and J. A. Schuster, eds (2005) *The Science of Nature in the Seventeenth Century: Patterns of Change in Early Modern Natural Philosophy*, Dordrecht: Springer.

Arbuthnot, J. (1701) *An Essay on the Usefulness of Mathematical Learning*, Oxford.
Aristotle (1984) *The Complete Works of Aristotle*, 2 vols, ed. J. Barnes, Princeton: Princeton University Press.
—— (1994) *Posterior Analytics*, 2nd edn, ed. and transl. J. Barnes, Oxford: Clarendon Press.
Armstrong, D. M. (2004) *Truth and Truthmakers*, Cambridge: Cambridge University Press.
Arnauld, A. (1990) *On True and False Ideas* [1683], ed. S. Gaukroger, Manchester: Manchester University Press.
Arnauld, A. and Nicole, P. (1996) *Logic or the Art of Thinking* [1662; 4th edn 1683], ed. J. V. Buroker, Cambridge: Cambridge University Press.
Ashcraft, R. (1990) 'John Locke's Library: Portrait of an Intellectual', in J. S. Yolton, ed., pp. 226–45. [First published in *Transactions of the Cambridge Bibliographical Society*, 5, 1969, pp. 47–60.]
Atherton, M. (1991) 'Corpuscles, mechanism, and essentialism in Berkeley and Locke', *Journal of the History of Philosophy*, 29, pp. 47–67.
—— (2007) 'Locke on essences and classification', in Newman, ed., pp. 258–85.
Axtell, J. L. (1965) 'Locke's Review of the *Principia*', *Notes and Records of the Royal Society*, 20, pp. 152–61.
—— ed. (1968) *The Educational Writings of John Locke*, Cambridge: Cambridge University Press.
Ayers, M. (1981a) 'Mechanism, superaddition, and the proof of God's existence in Locke's *Essay*', *Philosophical Review*, 90, pp. 210–51.
—— (1981b) 'Locke versus Aristotle on natural kinds', *Journal of Philosophy*, 78, pp. 247–72.
—— (1991) *Locke: Epistemology and Ontology*, 2 vols, London: Routledge.
Bacon, F. (1622) *Historia naturalis et experimentalis ad condendam philosophiam*, London.
—— (1653) *Scripta in naturali et universali philosophia*, ed. Issac Gruter, Amsterdam.
—— (1733) *The Philosophical Works of Francis Bacon*, 3 vols, ed. P. Shaw, London.
—— (1859) *The Works of Francis Bacon*, 7 vols, ed. J. Spedding, R. L. Ellis, and D. D. Heath, London: Longman & Co.
—— (1996–) *The Oxford Francis Bacon*, 15 vols, ed. Graham Rees et al., Oxford: Clarendon Press.
Barnes, J. (1975) 'Aristotle's theory of demonstration', in Barnes, Schofield, and Sorabji, eds, pp. 65–87.
—— (1994) 'Introduction', in Aristotle, pp. xi–xxii.
—— (2006) 'Locke and the syllogism', in Anstey, ed., Vol. 2, pp. 297–326. [First published in Sharples 2001, pp. 105–32.]
Barnes, J., M. Schofield, and R. Sorabji, eds (1975) *Articles on Aristotle: 1 Science*, London: Duckworth.
Barrow, I. (1734) *The Usefulness of Mathematical Learning Explained and Demonstrated*, London.
Bartoli, D. (1681) *Del Ghiaccio e della coagulatione*, Rome.
Baxter, R. (1667) *The Reasons of the Christian Religion*, London.
Becher, J. (1664) *Oedipus chimicus*, Amsterdam.
Bédoyère, G. de la, ed. (2005) *Particular Friends: The Correspondence of Samuel Pepys and John Evelyn*, new edn, Woodbridge: Boydell Press.
Belon, P. (1589) *Plurimarum singularium & memorabilium rerum in Graecia, Asia, Aegypto, Iudaea, Arabia*, Antwerp.

Bentham, E. (1740) *Reflections upon the Nature and Usefulness of Logick as it has been Commonly Taught in the Schools*, Oxford.
Berkeley, G. (1965) *Berkeley's Philosophical Writings*, ed. D. M. Armstrong, London: Macmillan.
Bernoulli, J. (1683) *Dissertatio de gravitate aetheris*, Amsterdam.
Blackmore, Sir R. (1697) *King Arthur. An Heroick Poem in Twelve Books*, London.
Blount, Sir T. P. (1690) *Censura celebriorum authorum*, London.
Boas [Hall], M. (1956) 'Acid and alkali in seventeenth-century chemistry', *Archives Internationales d'Histoire des Sciences*, 34, pp. 13–28.
Bolton, M. B. (1998) 'Substances, substrata, and names of substances in Locke's *Essay*', in Chappell, ed., pp. 106–28. [First published in *Philosophical Review*, 85, 1976, pp. 488–513.]
—— (2007) 'The taxonomy of ideas in Locke's *Essay*', in Newman, ed., pp. 67–100.
Boyd, R. (1991) 'Realism, anti-foundationalism and the enthusiasm for natural kinds', *Philosophical Studies*, 61, 1991, pp. 127–48.
—— (1999) 'Homeostatis, species, and higher taxa', in Wilson, ed., 1999b, pp. 141–85.
Boyle, R. (1660) *New Experiments Physico-Mechanical, Touching the Spring of the Air and its Effects*, Oxford.
—— (1661) *Certain Physiological Essays*, London.
—— (1664) *Experiments and Considerations Touching Colours*, London.
—— (1665) *New Experiments and Observations Touching Cold*, London.
—— (1684) *Memoirs for the Natural History of the Humane Blood*, London.
—— (1685) *Of the Reconcileableness of Specific Medicines to the Corpuscular Philosophy*, London.
—— (1686) *De specificiorum remediorum cum corpusculari philosophia concordia*, London.
—— (1692) *The General History of the Air*, London.
—— (1999–2000) *The Works of Robert Boyle*, 14 vols, eds. M. Hunter and E. B. Davis, London: Pickering and Chatto.
—— (2001) *The Correspondence of Robert Boyle*, 6 vols, eds. M. Hunter, A. Clericuzio, and L. M. Principe, London: Pickering and Chatto.
—— (2005a) *Robert Boyle's 'Heads' and 'Inquiries'*, eds. M. Hunter, Robert Boyle Project Occasional Papers No. 1, ISBN 978-0-9551608-0-6.
—— (2005b) *Unpublished Material Relating to Robert Boyle's* Memoirs for the Natural History of Human Blood, eds. M. Hunter and H. Knight, Robert Boyle Project Occasional Papers No. 2, ISBN 978-0-9551608-1-3.
—— (2008) *The Text of Robert Boyle's 'Designe about Natural History'*, eds. M. Hunter and P. R. Anstey, The Robert Boyle Project, Occasional Papers No. 3, ISBN 978-0-9551608-2-0.
Brackenridge, J. B. (1993) 'The Locke/Newton manuscripts revisited: Conjugates, curvatures, & conjectures', *Archives internationales d'histoire des sciences*, 43, pp. 280–92.
Brown, S. C., ed. (1979) *Philosophers of the Enlightenment*, New Jersey: Harvester Press.
Buchdahl, G. (1969) *Metaphysics and the Philosophy of Science*, Oxford: Blackwell.
Buickerood, J. G. (1985) 'The natural history of the understanding: Locke and the rise of facultative logic in the eighteenth century', *History and Philosophy of Logic*, 6, pp. 157–90.
Burnet, T. (1681) *Telluris Theoria Sacra*, London.
——(1684) *The Theory of the Earth*, London.
Burrows, J. and P. R. Anstey (forthcoming) 'John Locke, Thomas Sydenham, and the "Smallpox Manuscripts"', *English Manuscript Studies*.
Burthogge, R. (1699) *Of the Soul of the World*, London.

Butler, J. (1736) *The Analogy of Religion, Natural and Revealed, to the Constitution and Course of Nature*, London.
Carey, D. (1996) 'Locke, travel literature and the natural history of man', *The Seventeenth Century*, 11, pp. 259–80.
—— (1997) 'Compiling nature's history: Travellers and travel narratives in the early Royal Society', *Annals of Science*, 54, pp. 269–92.
—— (2006) 'Travel, geography, and the problem of belief: Locke as a reader of travel literature', in Rudolph, ed., pp. 97–136.
Carson, E. (2002) 'Locke's account of certain and instructive knowledge', *British Journal for the History of Philosophy*, 10, pp. 359–78.
—— (2005) 'Locke on simple and mixed modes', *Locke Studies*, 5, pp. 19–38.
—— (2006) 'Locke and Kant on mathematical knowledge' in Carson and Huber, eds, pp. 3–19.
Carson, E. and R. Huber, eds (2006) *Intuition and the Axiomatic Method*, Dordrecht: Springer.
Cellarius, A. (1661) *Harmonia macrocosmica*, Amsterdam.
Chappell, V., ed. (1994) *The Cambridge Companion to Locke*, Cambridge: Cambridge University Press.
—— ed. (1998) *Locke*, Oxford: Oxford University Press.
Cicovacki, P. (1990) 'Locke on mathematical knowledge', *Journal of the History of Philosophy*, 28, pp. 511–24. [Reprinted in Anstey, ed., 2006, Vol. 2, pp. 327–40.]
Clericuzio, A. (1990) 'A redefinition of Boyle's chemistry and corpuscular philosophy', *Annals of Science*, 47, pp. 561–89.
—— (1993) 'From van Helmont to Boyle: A study of the transmission of Helmontian chemical and medical theories in seventeenth-century England', *British Journal for the History of Science*, 26, pp. 303–34.
Cohen, I. B. (1966) 'Hypotheses in Newton's philosophy', *Physis*, 8, pp. 163–84.
—— (1971) *Introduction to Newton's* Principia, Cambridge: Cambridge University Press.
—— (1999) 'A Guide to Newton's *Principia*', in Newton, pp. 1–370.
Cohen, I. B. and G. E. Smith, eds (2002) *The Cambridge Companion to Newton*, Cambridge: Cambridge University Press.
Colton, J. (1976) 'Merlin's Cave and Queen Caroline: Garden art as political propaganda', *Eighteenth-Century Studies*, 10, pp 1–20.
Conn, C. H. (2003) *Locke on Essence and Identity*, Dordrecht: Kluwer.
Cook, H. J. (1990) 'The new philosophy and medicine in seventeenth-century England', in Lindberg and Westman, eds, pp. 397–436.
Cordemoy, G. de (1668) *Copie d'une lettre écrite à un sçavant religieux*, Paris.
—— (1679) *Le discernement du corps et de l'âme, en six discours*, 2nd edn, Paris.
Corneanu, S. (2011) *Regimens of the Mind: Boyle, Locke, and the Early Modern Cultura animi Tradition*, Chicago: University of Chicago Press.
Coxe, D. (1674) 'A discourse denying the prae-existence of alcalizate or fixed salt in any subject, before it were exposed to the action of the fire', *Philosophical Transactions*, vol. 9, #107, pp. 150–8.
Cudworth, R. (1678) *The True Intellectual System of the Universe*, London.
Davidson, A. I. and N. Hornstein (1984) 'The primary/secondary quality distinction: Berkeley, Locke, and the foundations of corpuscularian science', *Dialogue*, 23, pp. 281–303.
Dawson, E. E. (1959) 'Locke on number and infinity', *Philosophical Quarterly*, 37, pp. 302–8.

Dear, P. (2005) 'Circular argument: Descartes' vortices and their crafting as explanations of gravity', in Anstey and Schuster, eds, pp. 81–97.

Deason, G. B. (1986) 'Reformation theology and the mechanistic conception of nature', in Lindberg and Numbers, eds, pp. 167–91.

Debus, A. G. (1964) 'The Paracelsian aerial nitre', *Isis*, 55, pp. 43–61.

—— (1990) 'Chemistry and the universities in the seventeenth century', *Estudos Avançados*, 4, pp. 173–96.

—— (1991) *The French Paracelsians: The Chemical Challenge to Medical and Scientific Tradition in Early Modern France*, Cambridge: Cambridge University Press.

—— (2001) *Chemistry and Medical Debate: Van Helmont to Boerhaave*, Canton, MA: Science History Publications.

—— (2002) *The Chemical Philosophy, Paracelsian Science and Medicine in the Sixteenth and Seventeenth Centuries* [1977], Mineola, NY: Dover.

Descartes, R. (1985) *The Philosophical Writings of Descartes*, Vol. 1, ed. J. Cottingham, R. Stoothoff, and D. Murdoch, Cambridge: Cambridge University Press.

—— (1991) *Principles of Philosophy* [1644, Lat. edn], Dordrecht: Kluwer.

—— (1996) *Œuvres de Descartes*, rev. edn, 11 vols, ed. C. Adam and P. Tannery, Paris: Vrin.

Dewhurst, K. (1956) 'The genesis of state medicine in Ireland', *Irish Journal of Medical Science*, 363, pp. 365–84.

—— (1960) 'Locke's Essay on Respiration', *Bulletin for the History of Medicine*, 34, pp. 257–73.

—— (1962) 'Locke's contribution to Boyle's researches on the air and on human blood', *Notes and Records of the Royal Society*, 17, pp. 198–206.

—— (1963a) *John Locke (1632–1704): Physician and Philosopher*, London: Wellcome Historical Medical Library.

—— (1963b) 'Prince Rupert as a scientist', *British Journal for the History of Science*, 1, pp. 365–73.

—— (1966) *Dr. Thomas Sydenham (1624–1689): His Life and Original Writings*, London: Wellcome Historical Medical Library.

—— ed. (1980) *Thomas Willis's Oxford Lectures*, Oxford: Sandford Publications.

Downing, L. (1992) 'Are corpuscles unobservable in principle for Locke?', *Journal of the History of Philosophy*, 30, pp. 33–52.

—— (1997) 'Locke's Newtonianism and Lockean Newtonianism', *Perspectives on Science*, 5, 1997, pp. 285–310.

—— (1998) 'The status of mechanism in Locke's *Essay*', *Philosophical Review*, 107, pp. 381–414.

—— (2001) 'The uses of mechanism: Corpuscularianism in Drafts A and B of Locke's *Essay*', in Lüthy et al., eds, 2001, pp. 515–34.

Duchesneau, F. (1973) *L'Empirisme de Locke*, The Hague: Martinus Nijhoff.

Ducheyne, S. (2005) 'Bacon's idea and Newton's practice of induction', *Philosophica*, 76, pp. 115–28.

Duncan, W. (1748) *The Elements of Logick. In Four Books*, London.

Dunton, J. (1692) *The Young-Students-Library*, London.

Ent, G. (1641) *Apologia pro circulatione sanguinis*, London.

Farr, J. (1987) 'The way of hypotheses: Locke on method', *Journal of the History of Ideas*, 48, pp. 51–72.

Fielding, H. (1987) *The True Patriot and Other Writings*, ed. W. B. Coley, Oxford: Clarendon Press.

Flamsteed, J. (1975) *The Gresham Lectures of John Flamsteed*, ed. E. G. Forbes, London: Mansell.

Frank, R. G., Jr (1979) 'The physician as virtuoso in seventeenth-century England', in Shapiro and Frank, Jr, pp. 57–114.
—— (1980) *Harvey and the Oxford Physiologists: Scientific Ideas and Social Interaction*, Berkeley: University of California Press.
Franklin, J. (2002) 'Stove's discovery of the worst argument in the world', *Philosophy*, 77, pp. 615–24.
Friedman, M. (1974) 'Explanation and scientific understanding', *Journal of Philosophy*, 71, pp. 5–19.
Gabbay, D. M. and J. Woods (2003) *A Practical Logic of Cognitive Systems: Agenda Relevance: A Study in Formal Pragmatics*, Amsterdam: Elsevier.
Garber, D. (1982) 'Locke, Berkeley and corpuscular scepticism', in Turbayne, ed., pp. 174–93.
Gaukroger, S. W. (2008) 'The role of natural philosophy in the development of Locke's empiricism', *British Journal for the History of Philosophy*, 17, pp. 55–83.
Gennaro, R. J. and C. Huenemann, eds (1999) *New Essays on the Rationalists*, New York: Oxford University Press.
Gibson, J. P. (1917) *Locke's Theory of Knowledge*, Cambridge: Cambridge University Press.
Glanvill, J. (1665) *Scepsis scientifica*, London.
—— (1668) *Plus ultra*, London.
Goodall, C. (1676) *The Colledge of Physicians Vindicated*, London.
Goodin, S. (1998) 'Why knowledge of the internal constitution is not the same as knowledge of the real essence and why this matters', *Southwest Philosophy Review*, 14, pp. 149–55.
—— (1999) 'Locke and Leibniz and the debate over species', in Gennaro and Huenemann, eds, pp. 163–76.
Guerrini, A. (1987) 'Archibald Pitcairne and Newtonian medicine', *Medical History*, 31, pp. 70–83.
Guyer, P. (1994) 'Locke's philosophy of language' in Chappell, ed., pp. 115–45.
Hacking, I. (1983) *Representing and Intervening: Introductory Topics in the Philosophy of Natural Science*, Cambridge: Cambridge University Press.
—— (2002) *Historical Ontology*, Cambridge MA: Harvard University Press.
Hall, A. R. (1983) *The Revolution in Science 1500–1750*, London: Longman.
Harré, R. (1964) *Matter and Method*, London: Macmillan.
Harris, J. (1697) *Remarks on some Late Papers relating to the Universal Deluge*, London.
Harris, S. and P. R. Anstey (2009) 'John Locke's seed lists: A case study in botanical exchange', *Studies in History and Philosophy of Biological and Biomedical Sciences*, 40, pp. 256–64.
Harrison, J. and P. Laslett (1971) *The Library of John Locke*, 2nd edn, Oxford: Clarendon Press.
Harrison, P. (2007) *The Fall of Man and the Foundations of Science*, Cambridge: Cambridge University Press.
Harvey, W. (1651) *Exercitationes de generatione animalium*, Amsterdam.
Helmont, J. B. van (1648) *Ortus medicinae*, Amsterdam.
Henry, J. (1986) 'Occult qualities and the experimental philosophy: Active principles in pre-Newtonian matter theory', *History of Science*, 24, pp. 335–81.
Herivel, J. (1965) *The Background to Newton's* Principia, Oxford: Clarendon Press.
Hesse, M. (1962) *Forces and Fields: The Concept of Action at a Distance in the History of Physics*, London and New York: T. Nelson.
Highmore, N. (1651) *Disquisitio anatomica*, The Hague.

Hill, J. (2004) 'Locke's account of cohesion and its philosophical significance', *British Journal for the History of Philosophy*, 12, pp. 611–30.
—— (2005) 'Was Locke an atomist?', *Locke Studies*, 5, pp. 75–101.
Hirai, H. (2005) *Le Concept de semence dans les théories de la matière à la Renaissance: De Marsile Ficin à Pierre Gassendi*, Turnhout: Brepols.
Hoffman, P., D. Owen, and G. Yaffe, eds (2008) *Contemporary Perspectives on Early Modern Philosophy: Essays in Honour of Vere Chappell*, Peterborough: Broadview Press.
Holland, A. J., ed. (1985) *Philosophy, Its History and Historiography*, Dordrecht: D. Reidel.
Hooke, R. (1665) 'A Spot in one of the Belts of Jupiter', *Philosophical Transactions*, 1, p. 3.
—— (1705) *The Posthumous Works of Robert Hooke*, London.
Hull, D. (1978) 'A matter of individuality', *Philosophy of Science*, 45, pp. 335–60.
Hume, D. (2007) *A Treatise of Human Nature*, D. F. Norton and M. J. Norton, eds, 2 vols, Oxford: Clarendon Press.
Hunter, M. (1989) *Establishing the New Science: The Experience of the Early Royal Society*, Woodbridge: Boydell Press.
—— (1994) *The Royal Society and Its Fellows 1660–1700: The Morphology of an Early Scientific Institution*, 2nd edn, Oxford: British Society for the History of Science.
—— (1995a) *Science and the Shape of Orthodoxy: Intellectual Change in Late Seventeenth-Century England*, Woodbridge: Boydell Press.
—— (1995b) 'The early Royal Society and the shape of knowledge', in Hunter 1995a, pp. 169–79.
—— (2000a) *Robert Boyle (1627–1691): Scrupulosity and Science*, Woodbridge: Boydell Press.
—— (2000b) 'Boyle versus the Galenists: A suppressed critique of seventeenth-century medical practice and its significance', in Hunter 2000a, pp. 157–201.
—— (2000c) 'Alchemy, magic and moralism in the thought of Robert Boyle', in Hunter 2000a, pp. 93–118.
—— (2007a) 'Robert Boyle and the early Royal Society: A reciprocal exchange in the making of Baconian science', *British Journal for the History of Science*, 40, pp. 1–23.
—— (2007b) *The Boyle Papers: Understanding the Manuscripts of Robert Boyle*, Aldershot: Ashgate.
Hunter, M. and L. Principe (2003) 'The lost papers of Robert Boyle', *Annals of Science*, 60, pp. 269–311. [Reprinted in Hunter 2007b, pp. 73–135.]
Hunter M. and P. Wood (1989) 'Towards Solomon's House: Rival strategies for reforming the early Royal Society', in Hunter 1989, pp. 185–244.
Hutchison, K. (1982) 'What happened to occult qualities in the Scientific Revolution?', *Isis*, 73, pp. 233–53.
Huygens, C. (1698) *Cosmotheoros*, The Hague.
—— (1888–1950) *Oeuvres complètes de Christiaan Huygens*, 22 vols, The Hague.
Jalobeanu, D. and P. R. Anstey, eds (2011) *Vanishing Matter and the Laws of Motion: Descartes and Beyond*, New York: Routledge.
Johnson, W. (1660) *Lexicon chymicum*, London.
Jolley, N. (1999) *Locke: His Philosophical Thought*, New York: Oxford University Press.
Jurin, J. (1996) *The Correspondence of James Jurin (1684–1750): Physician and Secretary to the Royal Society*, ed. A. A. Rusnock, Amsterdam: Rodophi.
Kaplan, B. B. (1993) *'Divulging of Useful Truths in Physick': The Medical Agenda of Robert Boyle*, Baltimore: Johns Hopkins University Press.

Keele, K. D. (1974) 'The Sydenham–Boyle theory of morbific particles', *Medical History*, 18, pp. 240–8.

Kieser, F. ed. (1606) *Cabala chymica*, Mülhausen.

Kim, H.-K. (2008) 'Locke and the mind–body problem: An interpetation of his agnosticism', *Philosophy*, 83, pp. 439–58.

King, Lord P. (1858) *The Life and Letters of John Locke, with Extracts from his Correspondence, Journals, and Common-Place Books*, new edn, London: Bohn.

Knight, H. and M. Hunter (2007) 'Robert Boyle's *Memoirs for the Natural History of Human Blood*: Print, manuscript and the impact of Baconianism in seventeenth-century medical science', *Medical History*, 51, pp. 145–64.

Knox, R. (1681) *An Historical Relation of the Island Celyon in the East-Indies*, London.

Kornblith, H. (1993) *Inductive Inference and its Natural Ground*, Cambridge, MA: MIT Press.

Laudan, L. (1967) 'The nature and sources of Locke's views on hypotheses', *Journal of the History of Ideas*, 28, pp. 211–23. [Reprinted with a postscript in Tipton, ed., 1977, pp. 149–62; and as chapter 5 of Laudan 1981, pp. 59–71.].

—— (1981) *Science and Hypothesis: Historical Essays on Scientific Methodology*, Dordrecht: Reidel.

Le Clerc, J. (1706) *The Life and Character of Mr. John Locke*, London.

—— (1714) 'Review of *Philosophiae Naturalis Principia Mathematica*, 2nd edn', *Bibliothèque ancienne et moderne*, 1, pp. 69–96.

Lee, H. (1702) *Anti-scepticism: or, Notes upon each chapter of Mr. Lock's Essay concerning humane understanding*, London.

Leibniz, G. W. (1996) *New Essays on Human Understanding* [1765], P. Remnant and J. Bennett, eds, Cambridge: Cambridge University Press.

Lindberg, D. C. and R. L. Numbers, eds (1986) *God and Nature: Historical Essays on the Encounter between Christianity and Science*, Berkeley: University of California Press.

Lindberg, D. C. and R. Westman, eds (1990) *Reappraisals of the Scientific Revolution*, Cambridge: Cambridge University Press.

Locke, J. (1675) 'An extract of a letter, written to the pubisher by Mr. J. L. about poisonous fish in one of the Bahama islands', *Philosophical Transactions*, 10, #114, p. 312.

—— (1686) Review of 'De specificorum remediorum cum corpusculari philosophia concordia', *Bibliothèque universelle et historique*, Tome 2, pp. 263–80.

—— (1688a) 'Extrait d'un livre Anglois qui n'est par encore publié intitulé *Essai philosophique concernant l'entendement, où l'on montre quelle est l'étendue de nos connoissances certaines, & la maniere dont nous y parvenons*. Communiqué par Monsieur Locke', *Bibliothèque universelle et historique*, Tome 8, pp. 49–142.

—— (1688b) Review of 'Philosophiae naturalis principia mathematica', *Bibliothèque universelle et historique*, Tome 8, pp. 436–50.

—— (1697) 'An account of one who had horny excrescencies or extraordinary large Nails on his Fingers and Toes', *Philosophical Transactions*, 19, #230, pp. 694[=594]–596.

—— (1705) 'A register of the weather for the year 1692, kept at Oates in Essex', *Philosophical Transactions*, 24, #298, pp. 1917–37.

—— (1720) *A Collection of Several Pieces of Mr John Locke*, ed. P. Desmaizeaux, London.

—— (1823) *The Works of John Locke*, 10 vols, ed. 12th edn, London: Thomas Tegg.

—— (1936) *An Early Draft of Locke's* Essay: *Together with Excerpts from his Journals*, ed. R. I. Aaron and J. Gibb, Oxford: Clarendon Press.

Locke, J. (1954) *Essays on the Law of Nature*, ed. and transl. by W. von Leyden, Oxford: Clarendon Press.

—— (1967) *Two Tracts on Government*, ed. P. Abrams, Cambridge: Cambridge University Press.

—— (1975) *An Essay concerning Human Understanding* [1690], 4th edn, ed. P. H. Nidditch, Oxford: Oxford University Press.

—— (1976–) *The Correspondence of John Locke*, 9 vols, ed. E. S. de Beer, Oxford: Clarendon Press.

—— (1987) *A Paraphrase and Notes on the Epistles of St Paul* [1707], 2 vols, ed. A. W. Wainwright, Oxford: Clarendon Press.

—— (1989) *Some Thoughts concerning Education* [1693], 3rd edn, ed. J. W. and J. S. Yolton, Oxford: Oxford University Press.

—— (1990) *Drafts for the* Essay concerning Human Understanding *and Other Philosophical Writings, Vol. 1: Drafts A and B*, ed. P. H. Nidditch and G. A. J. Rogers, Oxford: Clarendon Press.

—— (2006) *John Locke: An Essay Concerning Toleration: And Other Writings on Law and Politics, 1667–1683*, ed. J. R. Milton and P. Milton, Oxford: Clarendon Press.

Lough, J. (1953) *Locke's Travels in France*, Cambridge: Cambridge University Press.

Ludolf, J. (1681) *Historia Aethiopica*, Frankfurt.

Lüthy, C., J. E. Murdoch, and W. R. Newman, eds (2001) *Late Medieval and Early Modern Corpuscular Matter Theories*, Leiden: Brill.

Maclean, I. (2002) *Logic, Signs and Nature in the Renaissance: The Case of Learned Medicine*, Cambridge: Cambridge University Press.

McCann, E. (1985) 'Lockean mechanism', in Holland, ed., pp. 209–29. [Reprinted in Chappell, ed., 1998, pp. 242–60.]

—— (1994) 'Locke's philosophy of body', in Chappell, ed., pp. 56–88.

McGuire, J. E. (1970) 'Newton's "Principles of Philosophy": An intended preface for the 1704 *Opticks* and a related draft fragment', *British Journal for the History of Science*, 5, pp. 178–86.

McMullin, E. (1978) 'Structural Explanation', *American Philosophical Quarterly*, 15, pp. 139–47.

Malcolm, N. (2004) 'Robert Boyle, Georges Pierre des Clozets, and the Asterism: A new source', *Early Science and Medicine*, 9, pp. 293–306.

Mandelbaum, M. (1964) *Philosophy, Science, and Sense Perception*, Baltimore: The Johns Hopkins Press.

Mattern, R. (1981) 'Locke on power and causation: Excerpts from the 1685 draft of the *Essay*', *Philosophy Research Archives*, 7, pp. 835–995.

Mercer, C. and E. O'Neill, eds (2005) *Early Modern Philosophy: Mind, Matter, and Metaphysics*, Oxford: Oxford University Press.

Meynell, G. G. (1988) *Materials for a Biography of Dr. Thomas Sydenham*, Folkestone: Winterdown Books.

—— (2006) 'John Locke and the Preface to Thomas Sydenham's *Observationes medicae*', *Medical History*, 50, pp. 93–110.

Milton, J. R. (1985) 'Lockean mechanism, a comment', in Holland, ed., pp. 233–39.

—— (1994) 'Locke at Oxford', in Rogers, ed., pp. 29–47. [Reprinted in Anstey, ed., 2006, Vol. 4, pp. 9–25.]

—— (1998) 'The Dating of "Adversaria 1661"', *The Locke Newsletter*, 29, pp. 105–17.

—— (2001) 'Locke, medicine and the mechanical philosophy', *British Journal for the History of Philosophy*, 9, pp. 221–43. [Reprinted in Anstey, ed., 2006, Vol. 3, pp. 295–318.
—— (2006) 'Locke and the reform of the calendar', *Locke Studies*, 6, pp. 173–7.
—— (2011) 'Locke's publications in the *Bibliothèque universelle et historique*', *British Journal for the History of Philosophy*, 19, pp. 451–72.
Molyneux, W. (1685) *Sciothericum Telescopium*, Dublin.
More, H. (1653) *Conjectura cabbalistica*, London.
Morison, R. (1699) *Plantarum historiae universalis Oxoniensis pars tertia*, Oxford.
Nedham, M. (1665) *Medela medicinæ*, London.
Neményi, P. F. (1962) 'The main concepts and ideas of fluid dynamics in their historical dimensions', *Archive for History of Exact Sciences*, 2, pp. 52–86.
Newman, L., ed. (2007) *The Cambridge Companion to Locke's 'Essay concerning Human Understanding'*, Cambridge: Cambridge University Press.
Newman, W. R. (2003) *Gehennical Fire: The Lives of George Starkey, an American in the Scientific Revolution* [1994], Chicago: University of Chicago Press.
—— (2006) *Atoms and Alchemy: Chymistry and the Experimental Origins of the Scientific Revolution*, Chicago: University of Chicago Press.
Newman, W. R. and A. Grafton, eds (2001) *Secrets of Nature: Astrology and Alchemy in Early Modern Europe*, Cambridge, MA: MIT Press.
Newman, W. R. and L. M. Principe (1998) 'Alchemy vs. chemistry: The etymological origins of a historiographic mistake', *Early Science and Medicine*, 3, pp. 32–65.
—— (2001) 'Some problems in the historiography of alchemy', in Newman and Grafton, eds, pp. 385–434.
—— (2002) *Alchemy Tried in the Fire: Starkey, Boyle, and the Fate of Helmontian Chymistry*, Chicago: University of Chicago Press.
Newton, Sir I. (1687) *Philosophiae naturalis principia mathematica*, London.
—— (1959–77) *The Correspondence of Isaac Newton*, 7 vols, ed. H. W. Turnbull, J. F. Scott, A. R. Hall, and L. Tilling, Cambridge: Cambridge University Press.
—— (1989) *The Preliminary Manuscripsts for Isaac Newton's 1687 Principia 1684–1686*, ed. D. T. Whiteside, Cambridge: Cambridge University Press.
—— (1999) *The Principia: Mathematical Principles of Natural Philosophy*, ed. and transl. I. B. Cohen and A. Whitman, Berkeley: University of California Press.
Norris, J. (1692) *Cursory Reflections upon a Book call'd, An Essay concerning Human Understanding*, 2nd edn, London.
Nutton, V. (1990) 'The reception of Fracastoro's theory of contagion: The seed that fell among thorns', *Osiris*, 2nd series, 6, pp. 196–234.
Oldenburg, H. (1965–86) *The Correspondence of Henry Oldenburg*, 13 vols, ed. A. R. Hall and M. B. Hall, Madison, Milwaukee, and London: University of Wisconsin Press, Mansell, and Taylor & Francis.
Osler, M. J. (1970) 'John Locke and the changing ideal of scientific knowledge', *Journal of the History of Ideas*, 31, pp. 3–16.
Owen, D. (1991) 'Locke on real essence', *History of Philosophy Quarterly*, 8, pp. 105–18.
—— (1999) *Hume's Reason*, Oxford: Oxford University Press.
Pagel, W. (1982) *Joan Baptista Van Helmont: Reformer of Science and Medicine*, Cambridge: Cambridge University Press.

Parker, S. (1666) *A Free and Impartial Censure of the Platonick Philosophie*, Oxford.
Petty, W. (1647) *The Advice of W. P. to Mr. Samuel Hartlib*, London.
Piso, G. (1648) *Historia naturalis Brasiliae*, Amsterdam.
Porto, P. A. (2002) 'Summus atque felicissimus salium: The medical relevance of the Liquor Alkahest', *Bulletin of the History of Medicine*, 76, pp. 1–29.
Power, H. (1664) *Experimental Philosophy*, London.
Principe, L. M. (1998) *The Aspiring Adept: Robert Boyle and his Alchemical Quest*, Princeton: Princeton University Press.
—— (2004a) 'Pierre des Clozets, Robert Boyle, the alchemical Patriarch of Antioch and the reunion of Christendom: Further new sources', *Early Science and Medicine*, 9, pp. 307–20.
—— (2004b) 'Lost Newton manuscript recovered at CHF', *Chemical Heritage*, 22, pp. 6–8.
Purchas, S. (1625) *Purchas his Pilgrimes*, London.
Read, S. (1994) 'Formal and material consequence', *Journal of Philosophical Logic*, 23, pp. 247–65.
Redi, F. (1668) *Esperienze intorno alla generazione degl'insetti*, Florence.
Reid, T. (2002) *The Correspondence of Thomas Reid*, ed. P. Wood, Edinburgh: Edinburgh University Press.
Reimarus, H. S. (1766) *Vernunftlehre*, 3rd edn, Hamburg.
Roberts, R. C. and W. J. Wood (2007) *Intellectual Virtues: An Essay in Regulative Epistemology*, Oxford: Oxford University Press.
Rogers, G. A. J. (1978) 'Locke's *Essay* and Newton's *Principia*', *Journal of the History of Ideas*, 39, pp. 217–32.
—— (1979) 'The empiricism of Locke and Newton', in Brown, ed., pp. 1–30. [Revised version reprinted in Rogers, ed., 1998, pp. 133–42.]
—— (1994a) 'Introduction', in Rogers, ed., 1994b, pp. 1–27.
—— (1998) *Locke's Enlightenment: Aspects of the Origin, Nature, and Impact of his Philosophy*, Hildesheim: Olms.
—— ed. (1994b) *Locke's Philosophy: Content and Context*, Cambridge: Cambridge University Press.
Romanell, P. (1983) 'The scientific and medical genealogy of Locke's "historical, plain method"', *Transactions & Studies of the College of Physicians of Philadelphia*, Series, 5: 5, pp. 339–52.
—— (1984) *John Locke and Medicine: A New Key to Locke*, Buffalo: Prometheus Books.
Roos, A. M. (2007) *The Salt of the Earth: Natural Philosophy, Medicine, and Chymistry in England 1650–1750*, Leiden: Brill.
Rudolph, J., ed. (2006) *History and Nation*, Lewisburg, PA: Bucknell University Press.
Rycaut, Sir P. (1668) *The Present State of the Ottoman Empire*, London.
Sargent, R.-M. (1995) *The Diffident Naturalist: Robert Boyle and the Philosophy of Experiment*, Chicago: University of Chicago Press.
Schaffer, S. (1987) 'Godly men and the mechanical philosophers: Souls and spirits in Restoration natural philosophy, *Science in Context*, 1, pp. 55–85.
—— (1989) 'The Glorious Revolution and medicine in Britain and the Netherlands', *Notes and Records of the Royal Society*, 43, pp. 167–90.
Schmitt, C. (1985) 'Aristotle among the physicians', in Wear, French and Lonie, eds, pp. 1–15.
Schouls, P. (1980) *The Imposition of Method: A Study of Descartes and Locke*, Oxford: Oxford University Press.

Schuster, J. A. (2005) '"Waterworld": Descartes' vortical celestial mechanics—A gambit in the natural philosophical contest of the early seventeenth century', in Anstey and Schuster, eds, pp. 35–79.
Schuurman, P. (2004) *Ideas, Mental Faculties and Method: The Logic of Ideas of Descartes and Locke and Its Reception in the Dutch Republic, 1630–1750*, Leiden: Brill.
Sennert, D. (1656) *Opera omnia*, 4 vols, Leiden.
Sergeant, J. (1696) *The Method to Science*, London.
—— (1697) *Solid Philosophy Asserted*, London.
Shackleford, J. (2004) *A Philosophical Path for Paracelsian Medicine: The Ideas, Intellectual Context, and Influence of Petrus Severinus*, Copenhagen: Museum Tusculanum Press.
Shapiro, B. and R. G. Frank, Jr (1979) *English Scientific Virtuosi in the 16th and 17th Centuries*, Los Angeles: William Andrews Clark Library.
Sharples, R. W., ed. (2001) *Whose Aristotle? Whose Aristotelianism?* Aldershot: Ashgate.
Sharrock, R. (1660) *History of the Propagation and Improvement of Vegetables*, Oxford.
Simpson, W. (1669) *Hydrologia chymica*, London.
Soles, D. (1985) 'Locke's Empiricism and the postulation of unobservables', *Journal of the History of Philosophy*, 23, pp. 339–69.
—— (2005) 'Locke's account of natural philosophy', *Southwest Philosophy Review*, 21, pp. 1–23.
Sorell, T., G. A. J. Rogers, and J. Kraye, eds (2010) Scientia *in Early Modern Philosophy: Seventeenth-Century Thinkers on Demonstrative Knowledge from First Principles*, Dordrecht: Springer.
Spinoza, B. (1974) *The Principles of Descartes' Philosophy*, transl. H. H. Britan, La Salle, IL: Open Court.
Sprat, T. (1667) *The History of the Royal-Society of London*, London.
Stamos, D. N. (2003) *The Species Problem: Biological Species, Ontology, and the Metaphysics of Biology*, Lanham MD: Lexington Books.
Starkey, G. (1667) [Eirenaeus Philalethes, pseud.] *Introitus apertus ad occlusum regis palatium*, Amsterdam.
—— (2004) *George Starkey: Alchemical Laboratory Notebooks and Correspondence*, ed. W. R. Newman and L. M. Principe, Chicago: University of Chicago Press.
Stein, H. (2002) 'Newton's metaphysics', in Cohen and Smith, eds, pp. 256–307.
Stillingfleet, E. (1698) *The Bishop of Worcester's Answer to Mr. Locke's Second Letter*, London.
Stroup, A. (1990) *A Company of Scientists: Botany, Patronage, and Community at the Seventeenth-Century Parisian Academy of Sciences*, Berkeley: University of California Press.
Stuart, M. (1996) 'Locke's geometrical analogy', *History of Philosophy Quarterly*, 13, pp. 451–67.
—— (1998) 'Locke on superaddition and mechanism', *British Journal for the History of Philosophy*, 6, pp. 351–79. [Reprinted in Anstey, ed., 2006, Vol. 3, pp. 45–73.]
—— (1999) 'Locke on natural kinds', *History of Philosophy Quarterly*, 16, pp. 277–96.
Suchten, A. von (1575) *De secretis antimonii*, Liber unus, Basel.
—— (1604) *Mysteria gemina antimonii*, Leipzig.
—— (1606) *Concordantia chymica*, in Kieser, ed.
Swammerdam, J. (1681) *Ephemeri vita or the Natural History and Anatomy of the Ephemeron, a Fly that Lives but Five Hours* [1675], London.
Sydenham, T. (1676) *Observationes medicae Circa Morborum Acutorum Historiam et Curationem*, London.
—— (1683) *Tratactus de podogra et hydrope*, London.
—— (1686) *Schedula monitoria de novae febris ingressu*, London.

Sydenham, T. (1848) *The Works of Thomas Sydenham*, 2 vols, ed. R. G. Latham, London.
—— (1987) *Methodus curandi febres propriis observationibus superstructura* [1666; 2nd edn 1668], ed. G. G. Meynell, Folkestone: Winterdown Books.
—— (1991) *Thomas Sydenham's 'Observationes Medicae' and his 'Medical Observations'*, ed. G. G. Meynell, Folkestone: Winterdown Books.
Tachenius, O. (1668) *Hippocrates chimicus*, Brunswick.
—— (1669) *Antiquissimae Hippocraticae medicinae clavis*, Venice.
Taylor, A. (1994) 'An episode with may-dew', *History of Science*, 32, pp. 163–84.
Thévenot, J. de (1665) *Relation d'un voyage fait au Levant*, Rouen.
Thomson, George (1666) *ΛOIMOTOMIA: Or the Pest Anatomized*, London.
Tipton, I. C., ed. (1977) *Locke on Human Understanding: Selected Essays*, Oxford: Oxford University Press.
Turbayne, C. M., ed. (1982) *Berkeley: Critical and Interpretative Essays*, Minneapolis: University of Minnesota Press.
Ulman, H. L., ed. (1990) *The Minutes of the Aberdeen Philosophical Society 1758–1773*, Aberdeen: Aberdeen University Press.
Untzer, M. (1660) *Opus chymico-medicum*, Halle.
Velthuysen, L. van (1657) *Tractatus duo medico-physici*, Utrecht.
Voltaire (1994) *Letters concerning the English Nation*, ed. N. Cronk, Oxford: Oxford University Press.
Walmsley, J. C. (1998) 'John Locke's Natural Philosophy (1632–1671)', PhD thesis, King's College London.
—— (2000) 'Morbus—Locke's early essay on disease', *Early Science and Medicine*, 5, pp. 367–93.
—— (2002) '"Morbus", Locke and Boyle: A response to Peter Anstey', *Early Science and Medicine*, 7, pp. 378–97.
—— (2004) 'Locke's natural philosophy in Draft A of the *Essay*', *Journal of the History of Ideas*, 65, pp. 15–37.
—— (2006a) 'The development of Locke's mechanism in the drafts of the *Essay*', in Anstey, ed., 2006, Vol. 3, pp. 319–52. [A corrected version of the original published in *British Journal for the History of Philosophy*, 11, 2003, pp. 417–49.]
—— (2006b) 'Locke, mechanism and Draft B: A correction', *British Journal for the History of Philosophy*, 14, pp. 331–5.
—— (2007) 'John Locke on respiration', *Medical History*, 51, 453–76.
—— (2008) 'Sydenham and the development of Locke's natural philosophy', *British Journal for the History of Philosophy*, 16, pp. 65–83.
Walmsley, J. C. and E. Meyer (2009) 'John Locke's "Respirationis usus": Text and translation', *Eighteenth Century Thought*, 4, pp. 1–28.
Walmsley, J. C. and J. R. Milton (1999) 'Locke's notebook "Adversaria 4" and his early training in chemistry', *The Locke Newsletter*, 30, pp. 85–101.
Walmsley, P. (2003) *Locke's Essay and the Rhetoric of Science*, Lewisburg: Bucknell University Press.
Watts, I. (1725) *Logick: Or, the Right Use of Reason in the Enquiry after Truth, with a Variety of Rules to Guard against Error, in the Affairs of Religion and Human Life, as well as in the Sciences*, London.

Wear, A. (2000) *Knowledge and Practice in English Medicine, 1550–1680*, Cambridge: Cambridge University Press.
Wear, A., R. K. French, and I. M. Lonie eds (1985) *The Medical Renaissance of the Sixteenth Century*, Cambridge: Cambridge University Press.
Webster, C. (1965). 'Water as the ultimate principle of nature: The background to Boyle's *Sceptical Chymist*', *Ambix*, 13, pp. 96–107.
—— (2002) *The Great Instauration Science, Medicine and Reform (1626–1660)*, 2nd edn, Bern: Peter Lang.
Westfall, R. S. (1971) *The Construction of Modern Science*, Cambridge: Cambridge University Press.
Whiston, W. (1696) *New Theory of the Earth*, London.
Wilde, W. R. (1856) 'On a MS. of Dr. Willoughby's, Written in 1690, "On the Climate and Diseases of Ireland"', *Proceedings of the Royal Irish Academy*, 6 (1853–1857), pp. 399–415.
Willis, T. (1659) *Diatribae duae medico-philosophicae*, London.
—— (1681) *Dr Willis's Practice of Physic*, transl. S. Pordage, London.
Wilson, M. D. (1967) 'Leibniz and Locke on "First Truths"', *Journal of the History of Ideas*, 28, pp. 347–66. [Reprinted in M. D. Wilson 1999, pp. 353–72.]
—— (1979) 'Superadded properties: The limits of Mechanism in Locke', *American Philosophical Quarterly*, 16, pp. 143–50. [Reprinted in M. D. Wilson 1999, pp. 196–208.]
—— (1999) *Ideas and Mechanism: Essays on Early Modern Philosophy*, New Jersey: Princeton University Press.
Wilson, R. A. (1999a) 'Realism, essence, and kind: Resuscitating species essentialism?', in Wilson, ed., 1999b, pp. 187–207.
—— (2002) 'Locke's primary qualities', *Journal of the History of Philosophy*, 40, pp. 201–28.
—— ed. (1999b) *Species: New Interdisciplinary Studies*, Cambridge MA: MIT Press.
Winkler, K. (2003) 'Lockean logic', in Anstey, ed., 2003b, pp. 154–78.
—— (2008) 'Locke's defence of mathematical physics', in Hoffman et al., eds, pp. 231–52.
Winsor, M. P. (2003) 'Non-essentialist methods in pre-Darwinian taxonomy', *Biology and Philosophy*, 18, pp. 387–400.
Wolfe, C. T. (2010) 'Empiricist heresies in early modern medical thought', in Wolfe and Gal, eds, pp. 333–44.
Wolfe, C. T. and O. Gal, eds (2010) *The Body as Object and Instrument of Knowledge: Embodied Empiricism in Early Modern Science*, Dordrecht: Springer.
Wolfe, D. E. (1961) 'Sydenham and Locke on the limits of anatomy', *Bulletin of the History of Medicine*, 35, 1961, pp. 193–220.
Wolterstorff, N. (1996) *John Locke and the Ethics of Belief*, Cambridge: Cambridge University Press.
Wood, A. (1891–1900) *The Life and Times of Anthony Wood*, 5 vols, ed. A. Clark, Oxford.
Wood, N. (1975) 'The Baconian character of Locke's "Essay"', *Studies in History and Philosophy of Science*, 6, pp. 43–84.
Wood, N. (1983) *The Politics of Locke's Philosophy: A Social Study of An Essay Concerning Human Understanding*, Berkeley: University of California Press.
Woodward, J. (1695) *An Essay towards a Natural History of the Earth*, London.
—— (1696) *Brief Instructions for Makeing Observations in All Parts of the World*, London.

Woolhouse, R. S. (1970) 'Locke's idea of spatial extension', *Journal of the History of Philosophy*, 8, pp. 313–18.
—— (1971) *Locke's Philosophy of Science and Knowledge*, Oxford: Blackwell.
—— (2005) 'Locke and the nature of matter', in Mercer and O' Neill, eds, pp. 145–60.
Wotton, W. (1694) *Reflections upon Ancient and Modern Learning*, London.
Wren, C. (1750) *Parentalia*, London.
Yolton, J. S., ed. (1990) *A Locke Miscellany*, Bristol: Thoemmes.
Yolton, J. W. (1951) 'Locke's unpublished marginal replies to John Sergeant', *Journal of the History of Ideas*, 12, pp. 528–59.
—— (1969a) 'The Science of nature', in Yolton, ed., 1969b, pp. 183–93.
—— (1970) *Locke and the Compass of Human Understanding*, Cambridge: Cambridge University Press.
—— (2004) *The Two Intellectual Worlds of John Locke: Man, Person, and Spirits in the* Essay, Ithaca: Cornell University Press.
—— ed. (1969b) *John Locke: Problems and Perspectives*, Cambridge: Cambridge University Press.
Yost, R. M. (1951) 'Locke's rejection of hypotheses about sub-microscopic events', *Journal of the History of Ideas*, 12, pp. 111–30.

Index

Aaron, R. 139 n. 12
Aarsleff, H. 14 n. 6, 16
abduction 36, 76
Aberdeen Philosophical Society 131 n. 67
Académie des sciences 220
acid and alkali hypothesis 10, 83, 84–7, 88
Acosta, Joseph de 59, 60 n. 76
agreement or disagreement of ideas 71, 113, 114, 120, 132, 136–40, 142–7, 152, 222
Aiton, E. J. 91 n. 4, 93 n. 10
Aldrich, Henry 143
Alexander, P. 15, 16, 33
alkahest 11, 171, 172, 173, 175, 177–80
Amerpoel, Johannes 93
analogy 10, 32, 35, 43, 71, 73, 76–80, 83, 86–7, 89, 90, 110, 157, 158, 160, 167, 169, 191, 194, 201
  see also machine analogy
anatomy 7, 37, 39, 40, 78, 221
André, François 10, 84, 85
angels 27, 208 n. 17
  angel knowledge 125–6, 128, 133, 159
  see also spirits
animal spirits 20, 33, 183, 184
Anstey, P. R. 3 n. 7, 4 n. 10, n. 11, 6 n. 14, n. 19, 17 n. 25, 19 n. 29, 28 n. 64, 30 n. 69, 36 n. 16, 38 n. 19, 49 n. 15, 51 n. 32, 55 n. 50, 57 n. 65, 62 n. 88, 65 n. 97, 71 n. 4, 81 n. 39, 156 n. 15, 157 n. 20, 167 n. 54, 182 n. 69, 186 n. 82, 190 n. 3, 192 n. 8, 194 n. 16, 200 n. 36, 202 n. 42, 208 n. 18, 213 n. 38, 220 n. 5, 222 n. 13, 225 n. 19
Anthony, Francis 174
Arbuthnot, John 110
archetypes 34, 120, 123–4, 128, 129, 130, 132, 134, 211
archeus 178, 179, 181, 186, 190, 193, 196
Aristotelianism 4, 15, 29, 75, 160, 189
  cosmology 92
  on demonstration 137, 139, 142
  logic 137
  matter theory 84
  theory of qualities 36
Aristotle 26
  De sensu 6
  on medicine 6, 7 n. 23
  on principles of reasoning 143–4
  on *scientia* 27, 138 n. 7, 168
  on spontaneous generation 196

  on substantial forms 161
  on truth 126
Arnauld, Antoine 126 n. 55, 143 n. 28
Ashcraft, R. 59
Atherton, M. 16, 130 n. 66
atomism 14, 17, 18
  and cohesion 105
atomists: Greek 36
  on seeds 190
  see also Epicurus, Epicureanism, Epicureans
axioms 50, 74, 82, 95, 112, 115, 138, 222 n. 13
  of geometry 113, 141
  Newton on 151 n. 52, 163
Axtell, J. 90 n. 2, 152 n. 57
Ayers, M. 15, 165, 214, 215

Bacon, Francis 5, 6, 46–69 *passim*, 73 n. 7, n. 9, 76, 221
  Baconian natural history 4, 5, 6, 8, 9, 10, 14, 15 n. 9, 46–69 *passim*, 70, 81, 111, 220, 223
  induction 50, 69, 89
  in Locke's library 49, 68
  Locke's references to 48–9
Bacon, Robin 54 n. 46
Baconianism 6, 7, 39, 47, 51 n. 32, 89, 221
Barnes, J. 138 n. 7, n. 8, 139
Baron, John 3 n. 9
Barrow, Isaac 136
Bartoli, Daniello 194
Bathurst, Ralph 7
Baxter, Richard 92 n. 7
Becher, Johann Joachim 195 n. 21
Belon, Pierre 60 n. 76
Bentham, Edward 136
Berkeley, George 146
Bernoulli, Jakob 10, 74, 91, 103
  on cohesion 103–8
Blackmore, Sir Richard 88–9
Blount, Sir Thomas Pope 49 n. 15
Boas [Hall], M. 84 n. 48
Bobart, Jacob the Elder 194, 199
Bobart, Jacob the Younger 199, 213 n. 38
Bold, Samuel 49 n. 16
Bolton, M. B. 130 n. 66, 131
botany 39
  Locke's interest in 20 n. 34, 186, 193–4, 199, 200, 213
bottoming 75, 103, 148–52
Boyd, R. 209, 210 n. 23

Boyle, Robert 1–11 *passim*, 13–20 *passim*, 26, 29, 35–6, 44, 48–63 *passim*, 66, 68–9, 72, 80–6, 89, 108, 155–62, 168, 170–82, 185–6, 190–1, 194, 195, 219–23
  on acid and alcali hypothesis 84–5
  and Baconian natural history 4, 51–69 *passim*
  his books in Locke's library 49, 56, 68
  on cohesion 106
  coined the term 'corpuscularian philosophy' 18
  on relation between Experimental Philosophy and Speculative Philosophy 5, 167 n. 54
  and Familiarity Condition 77, 157–8
  instructs Locke in Helmontian chymistry 177–81, 186
  histories of the air and blood 51–8, 68
  on hypotheses in natural philosophy 29, 74 n. 13, 81–2, 89
  intelligibility arguments 160–1
  on limits of reason 21 n. 42
  and mercurialist chymistry 170–3
  on miasmic theory of disease 182
  on modes of matter 119
  on monstrous births 208 n. 18
  on nomological explanation 162
  on relation between natural philosophy and medicine 7
  calls primary qualities mechanical affections 19–20
  theory of qualities 36, 44, 156
  and queries 61–2, 66, 68
  on seminal principles 190
  on travel literature 59–60
Boyle, Robert: Works; *Certain Physiological Essays* 18 n. 27, 26, 36, 51, 52 n. 35, n. 36, 59, 195 n. 20
  Colours 51, 66 n. 101
  Defence against Linus 80 n. 33, 157
  'General Heads for a Natural History of a Countrey' 51 n. 32, 53, 60, 61, 62
  General History of the Air 48, 56–61, 68
  Human Blood 57, 58, 61
  Mechanical Origine of Qualities 84
  Observationes physicae 175
  Sceptical Chymist 192 n. 8
  Specific Medicines 2, 7, 82 n. 40, 84–5, 163 n. 41
  Spring of the Air 2, 51, 52
  1st Continuation of Spring of the Air 54
  Things Above Reason 21 n. 42, 128 n. 60
  Usefulness of Natural Philosophy 51, 53, n. 49, 81 n. 38, 175, 195 n. 20
Briot, Pierre 174
Brounower, Sylvester 104
Buchdahl, G. 71 n. 4, 77 n. 26
Buckland, John 53 n. 43
Buickerood, J. 136 n. 4, 143 n. 27

Burnet, Thomas 10, 91, 92 n. 7, 93, 97–101, 103, 188
Burrows, J. 6 n. 14, 28 n. 64, 38 n. 19, 182 n. 69, 220 n. 5
Burthogge, Richard 188–9, 193, 198, 202–3
Butler, Joseph 128
Butler, Charles 26

Campanella, Tommaso 26
Carey, D. 59, 61 n. 81
Caroline, Queen 13
Carson, E. 118 n. 37, 130–1, 133
Cartesianism 4, 9, 15, 36, 42, 72, 74, 81, 93, 97, 220
  see also vortex theory of planetary motions
Cellarius, Andreas 179
Charles II 173
Charleton, Walter 190
Charleton (Courten), William 54 n. 49
chymical physicians 8, 37–40, 170, 172–4, 181, 185, 221
  Society of 173
chymistry 7, 8, 9, 11, 25, 39, 169–87 *passim*, 188, 207, 219, 223
Cicovacki, P. 125 n. 51
Clarke, Edward 22 n. 46, 30 n. 69, 149
Clarke, Samuel 13
Clericuzio, A. 17 n. 26, 177 n. 46, 186 n. 82, 219 n. 2
Cleves, Locke's visit to 101, 173–4
Cohen, I. B. 150 n. 48, 157 n. 24, 158 n. 25
cohesion 10, 24, 30, 32, 34, 44, 74, 91, 103–8, 109, 167, 169
Colbert, Jean-Baptiste 220
Cole, William 79 n. 31
College of Physicians 8, 38, 79, 174 n. 28, 185 n. 80, 220
Colton, J. 13 n. 4
Conn, C. 214 n. 40
Contact Criterion 19, 154–5, 157, 160, 162, 167
Cook, H. 6 n. 19
Cordemoy, Gerauld de 93, 158 n. 26
Corneanu, S. 22 n. 45
corpuscular explanations 31, 36, 41, 155 n. 8, 167
  of chymical phenomena 85, 178, 180
  of disease and medicine 8, 81–2, 196
  of qualities 24
corpuscular metric 11, 144–8, 153, 165, 186, 222, 223
corpuscular pessimism 6, 10, 31–45 *passim*, 105, 222, 223
corpuscular scepticism 31, 32, 33
corpuscularianism 4–11, 14–20, 23, 24, 28, 29, 35, 45, 72, 74, 77–87, 102, 109, 155, 156, 160, 162, 167, 169, 181, 186, 223
Coste, Pierre 2, 70

Croll, Oswald 172
Cudworth, Ralph 52 n. 35, 162 n. 36, 198
Currer, William 172, 173

Darwin, C. 209 n. 21
Davidson, A. I. 15 n. 10
Dawson, E. E. 114 n. 22
de Beer, E. S. 171 n. 6
De la Bédoyère 13 n. 3
Dear, P. 91 n. 5
Deason, G. 17 n. 24
Debus, A. 6 n. 18, 170 n. 1, 174 n. 28, 184 n. 77
deluge 10, 91, 97–103, 109
demonstration 11, 33, 95, 112, 116, 136–52 passim
   Locke's theory of 132, 135, 136–52 passim, 222
   mathematical 97, 111–16, 133, 138, 139, 141, 151
   and morality 71, 125, 133, 148
   and principles 27, 152, 163
   sensory 42
   reasoning by 43, 96, 109, 130, 151, 152, 153, 169, 219
demonstrative natural philosophy 9, 81, 110, 144–7, 165–6, 168, 186, 222, 223
   see also corpuscuclar metric, *scientia*
Descartes, René 4, 17, 19, 29, 35, 91–3, 95, 97, 98, 101, 111, 190, 220, 222
   and Contact Criterion 155
   inspiration for cosmogonical genre 91
   intellibility argument 160–1
   on matter 112, 122
   and modes 119
   and qualities 19 n. 29, 44, 156
   Principles 19 n. 29, 35, 91 n. 3, 95, n. 15, 98, 158 n. 26, 160–1
   see also vortex theory of planetary motion
Dewhurst, K. 3 n. 7, 6 n. 20, 33 n. 10, 38 n. 20, n. 21, 39 n. 22, n. 24, n. 25, 40 n. 27, n. 28, 47 n. 7, 55 n. 51, n. 52, n. 53, n. 55, 63 n. 89, 64 n. 93, 84 n. 49, 171 n. 10, 173 n. 21, 174 n. 27, 182 n. 67, 194 n. 19, 201 n. 38
Digby, Sir Kenelm 190
disease 7, 8, 28, 36, 37, 38, 40, 78–9, 88, 170, 181–2
   classification of 182, 186
   epidemic constitutions 55, 182
   Galenic theory of 36, 160
   miasmic theory of 52–5
   natural history of 8, 28, 54 n. 46, 62–6, 68, 79, 87, 220
   ontological conception of 178
   seminal theories of 179–82, 188, 191, 194–5, 204
   see also physic

Dobre, M. 158 n. 26
Downing, L. 15 n. 14, 16, 17 n. 21, 19, 33–4, 41 n. 29, 105 n. 47, 154 n. 4, 155–6
Duchesneau, F. 37 n. 17, 220–1
Ducheyne, S. 96 n. 18
Duclos, Samuel Cottereau 174
Duncan, William 136
Dunton, John 3, 7 n. 25, 84 n. 47, 85 n. 52, n. 53, 163 n. 41

Ent, George 191 n. 4
Epicurus 29
Epicureanism 4, 9, 74, 190
   see also atomists
Epicureans 81
epigenesis 190
equivalence 126, 128–9, 133
   equivalence classes 189, 206, 207, 210
essence 81, 118, 120, 122–34 *passim*, 177, 178, 207
   identity of nominal and real 121, 125–6, 128–35
   nominal 123–5, 128–30, 133–4, 207–17 *passim*
   real 14, 45, 70, 71, 72, 122–3, 124–30, 133–4, 140, 145, 204, 205, 207–17 *passim*, 222
   see also nominal and real essence distinction
Evelyn, John 13, 199 n. 34
expansion, *see* extension
exantlation 178
experiments 1, 4, 7, 8, 24, 26, 28–30, 33–8, 46, 56, 71–5, 80–2, 84, 87, 93, 110, 150, 152, 157–8, 167, 222, 223, 224
   on the air 52–3, 58
   on cohesion 105, 107
   chymical 86, 174–7, 179
   on respiration 58
   on spontaneous generation 196–7
   on transfusion 57
   willow-tree experiment 186
experimental philosophers 3, 4, 5, 69 n. 111, 74, 220, 223
Experimental Philosophy 3–11 *passim*, 12, 13, 18, 24–30, 32, 37, 39, 52, 72, 75, 89, 90, 103, 109, 148, 151 n. 52, 163, 167, 180, 220–5
   mathematical form 5, 9–11, 149, 166, 223
experimental/speculative distinction 3–5, 8, 9, 10, 24–30, 32, 34, 38–9, 43, 47, 69 n. 111, 89, 90, 180, 220–3
explanation 11, 17, 18, 19, 31, 32, 36, 41, 73, 76, 77, 85, 87, 91, 106, 152, 153–68 *passim*, 169, 178, 180–1, 221
extension 44, 85, 104–8, 112–17, 119, 126, 128, 141, 145–7

Falkland, 2nd Viscount (Lucius Cary) 52 n. 36
fallen knowledge 34, 39
Farr, J. 69, 71 n. 4, 73, 151 n. 53
ferments 180, 181, 183–4, 186, 190, 191, 196
fevers 38, 63, 182
   see also disease, smallpox
Fielding, Henry 136 n. 3
Flamsteed, John 110 n. 1
Fletcher, Henry 6 n. 13
Fogel, Martin 60 n.78
form 46 n. 3, 81
   see also substantial form
Fracastoro, Girolamo 182
Frank, R. G. Jr 6. n. 19, 7 n. 21, 58 n. 69
Franklin, J. 217 n. 47
Friedman, M. 159 n. 31
Furly, Benjamen 101

Gabbay, D. M. 139 n. 14
Galenism 8, 36, 37, 39, 84, 160, 174, 178, 181, 221
Galenists 36, 37, 87, 170 n. 2, 181, 221
Galileo 48
Garber, D. 31 n. 2, n. 3, 34 n. 12
Gassendi, Pierre 75, 190
generation 11, 60 n. 78, 80, 172, 181, 183–4, 188–203 *passim*, 204, 209, 224
geometry 85, 113, 115–16, 126, 130, 132, 136, 141–2, 145, 146
   triangle example 113, 119, 121, 125, 126, 129, 130, 134, 135, 137, 140–1, 209
Gerhard, Johann Conrad 195
Gibson, J. P. 47
Girle, R. 139 n. 14
Glanvill, Joseph 13 n. 2, 74
Glauber, Johann Rudolf 171, 179
Glisson, Francis 49 n. 15
God 15, 17, 21–2, 27, 28, 33, 35, 39, 72,74, 92, 98, 100, 101, 114, 118, 154, 156, 159 n. 30, 162, 165–6, 198, 201
   see also superaddition
Goodall, Charles 54–5, 61, 182, 194
Goodin, S. 204
Graevius, Joannes G. 2 n. 4
gravity 11, 19, 100–1, 102, 103, 149, 150, 151 n. 52, 154, 158, 164–7
Gruter, Isaac 49
gry (Locke's unit of measure) 147
Guenellon, Pieter 55 n. 52, 61
Guericke, Otto von 105
Guerrini, A. 8 n. 27
Guyer, P. 204

Hacking, I. 223–4
Hall, A. R. 17
Harré, R. 13–14, 16
Harris, John 103 n. 39

Harris, S. 194 n. 16, 199, 200 n. 36, 208 n. 18, 213 n. 38
Harrison, P. 34 n. 13
Hartlib circle 177
Hartmann, Johann 172
Helmont, Francis Mercurius van 175, 177
Helmont, Joan Baptista van 4, 171, 172, 177–86 *passim*, 190, 193, 196, 223
   on ferments 180, 181, 183–4, 190
   gravimetric techniques 178, 186
   willow-tree experiment 186
Helmontian chymistry 170, 177–85
   theory of salts 172, 178–80, 182, 184
   see also alkahest, *archeus*, exantlation
Helmontian medicine 8, 11, 170, 178–81, 186
Henry VII 48
Henry, J. 17 n. 25
Herbert, Lord 111
Herivel, J. 149 n. 43, n. 44
Hesse, M. 77 n. 26
Highmore, Nathaniel 191, 195 n. 20
Hill, J. 14 n. 5, 103 n. 41, 106, 107 n. 53, 108 n. 61
Hirai, H. 179 n. 52, 190 n. 3
Hobbes, Thomas 75, 111 n. 7
homeostatic property cluster 209–10, 211 n. 27
Hooke, Robert 7, 9, 34, 58, 60 n. 78, 81, 82, 90, 182, 184, 223
Hooker, Richard 111 n. 7
Hornstein, N. 15 n. 10
Hunter, M. 1 n. 2, 4 n. 11, 5 n. 12, 6 n. 19, 7 n. 23, 51 n. 32, 54 n. 43, 57 n. 65, n. 66, 61 n. 83, 74 n. 14, 81 n. 39, 82, 170 n. 2, 172 n. 15, 176 n. 43
Hutchison, K. 158 n. 27
Huygens, Christiaan 13, 93, 219, 220
hypotheses 4, 5, 8, 10, 14, 29, 31, 32, 34, 35, 39, 42, 43, 46, 70–109 *passim*, 110, 148, 149, 157, 169
   and analogy 76–8, 87, 89, 110, 169
   meanings of the term 74
   in medicine 38, 78–9, 88–9
   and natural history 81–3, 89
   opposition to 4, 26, 28, 34, 38, 52 n. 35, 74–6, 151, 180, 220, 222–3
   speculative 26, 28, 66, 90, 102–3, 151, uses of 78–80
hypothetico-deductive method 73, 86, 89, 168

iatrochemistry 8, 169–87 *passim*, 221
   see also chymistry, chymical physicians, Helmontian medicine, physic
ideas 20, 22, 23, 32, 74, 105, 111–52 *passim*, 154, 164, 199, 205–17 *passim*, 224
   abstract (general) 34, 71, 108, 123, 125, 128, 133, 134, 187, 205–7, 211, 215
   adequate 130

clear and distinct 44, 71, 108, 113, 116, 119, 159
comparing (measuring) 112, 113, 115
complex 44, 45, 71, 118, 120, 122, 123, 125, 127, 129–31, 133, 195, 207–11, 215, 216
  homeostatic clusters of ideas 209–14
  as immediate objects of perception 31
  positive (vs negative) 114–17, 128
  real and true 122–3, 124, 126
  and resemblance 35
  simple 41, 44, 104, 108, 112–35 passim, 145, 146, 159–62, 167, 192, 205, 209, 213, 215
  theory of 33, 34, 41, 120, 124, 126, 133, 139, 160, 168, 217, 222, 224
  see also agreement or disagreement of ideas, innate ideas, intermediate ideas, modes, Simple Ideas Condition
identity 126, 128–9, 133, 147
  of principles and laws 164
  of resurrection and mortal bodies 201
  of living things over time 156–7
  see also essence (identity of nominal and real)
impenetrability 112, 163
infinity 108, 114–18, 120, 127–8
innate ideas 160
  of infinity denied 114–15
innate principles 26, 34, 41–3, 111, 148, 160
intelligibility, argument from 104, 160–2
intermediate ideas 137–9, 145, 151
  see also proofs
Ivye, Ayliffe 171, 172

Johnson, William 195 n. 21
Jolley, N. 130 n. 66
Jurin, James 75

Kames, Lord (Henry Home) 76 n. 20
Keele, K. D. 53 n. 39, 182 n. 66
Kepler, Johannes 93, 94, 97, 149
Kim, H.-K. 217 n. 47
Knight, H. 57 n. 66
Knox, Robert 60 n. 78
knowledge: 1, 2, 3, 6, 7, 10, 11, 13, 14, 20–4, 27, 29, 31–45 passim, 46, 48, 61, 70–3, 75, 76, 80, 82, 89, 103, 111, 113–15, 135, 137–52 passim, 153, 159, 161, 167, 223
  demonstrative 27, 81, 110, 112, 130, 137, 138, 222
  experimental 72, 147, 164, 165
  intuitive 137
  real 120, 121–4, 132, 133, 148
  sensitive 33, 72, 110, 165, 222
  see also fallen knowledge, maps of knowledge, scientia
Kornblith, H. 209 n. 21

Laudan, L. 14, 71, 73, 76, 78, 88
Laslett, P. 49, 59
law of nature 25
laws: area law of planetary motion 93–7, 149
  and explanation 11, 152, 162–6
  inverse square law 149, 151 n. 52
  of motion 17, 100, 102, 162
  of nature 11, 39, 152, 158
  and principles 163–6
  references to in Locke's writings 17, 162
Le Clerc, Jean 3 n. 6, 84, 90 n. 2, 110
Lee, Henry 142
Leeuwenhoek, Antony van 201 n. 38, 202 n. 43
Leibniz, Gotfried W. 142
Lilburne, Richard 60, 62
Limborch, Philipp van 2 n. 4
Lister, Martin 197
Locke, John: and anatomy 37, 39, 40, 78, 221
  and Lord Ashley's operation 40
  against Descartes' bête machine 155 n. 11
  comments on draft of Boyle's Colours 51
  involvement in Boyle's natural histories 51–9
  and calendar reform 116, 147
  offers advice for the College of Physicians 185 n. 80
  attends chymistry course 172
  and the chymical physicians 8, 37–40, 172–5, 181, 185–6, 221
  critique of Bernoulli's theory of cohesion 10, 74, 91, 103–9
  and chrysopoeia 172, 177, 185
  conventionalism about species 11, 189–90, 205–14
  and Newton on Boyle's chymistry 176
  and the deluge 10, 91, 97–103
  and division of the sciences 3, 66–8
  becomes executor of Boyle's chymical papers 176, 185
  becomes Fellow of Royal Society 1
  intellectual formation 2, 6–8, 25–6, 31–45 passim, 51–4, 140–2, 170–4, 179–83, 221
  mathematical ability 96, 109
  changes view on nature of matter 44, 104–5
  on medical reform 7–8, 26, 37–40, 63, 177
  seeks Medical Studentship 183
  practises mercurialist transmutational chymistry 8, 9, 170–7, 185, 186, 188, 223
  mismatch between theory of modes and theory of essences 133
  reaction to Newton's achievement 5, 9–11, 19, 96–7, 103, 110–11, 148–52, 153–4, 163–7, 219–23
  and natural history of disease 54–5, 62–6, 68, 79, 87, 182, 220
  has little role for nomological explanation 11, 152, 162–6

248 INDEX

Locke, John: (*cont.*)
   on observability of corpuscules 14–15, 32–4
   possibilist about uninstantiated real essences of modal ideas 127, 129, 131–2
   critique of principles and maxims 11, 34, 39, 71–3, 111, 148, 151–2, 222–3
   changes view of principles of natural philosophy 9, 11, 149–52, 163–6, 219, 223
   and queries 54–5, 61–2, 66, 68
   on the real essence of modes 124–35 *passim*
   recipe for the Sophic Mercury 173
   on respiration 3, 52, 58, 180, 183–5
   on the resurrection body 193–4, 200–3
   against Speculative Philosophy 8, 10, 26, 28–30, 34–5, 37–9, 42–3, 47, 63, 66, 74, 89, 90–1, 97, 101–3, 159, 167, 222–3
   against the syllogistic 137–44
   and Sydenham 2, 37–8, 55, 64–6, 68, 78–9, 87, 182, 219–21
   and travel literature 56, 59–61, 68
   against the vortex theory 90–7
Locke, John: Works: *Abrégé* 44, 105
   'Anatomia' 6, 33, 37, 38, 40, 41, 43, 78
   Conduct 48, 59 n. 73, 66, 69 n. 111, 73 n. 9, 86, 87, 103, 149, 150 n. 46, 151, 159, 162 n. 36, 222 n. 13
   'De arte medica' 26, 37–9, 41, 43, 49 n. 15, 63
   Draft A 10, 11, 13, 19, 20, 21, 23, 26, n. 59, 32, 33, 34, 35 n. 15, 41–5, 73 n. 9, 111–32 *passim*, 136, 140–9, 156, 159 n. 30, 160 n. 32, 186, 192, 193, 207 n. 13, 222, 224 n. 16,
   Draft B 10, 11, 13, 19, 20, 21, 23, 26, 31, 32, 33, 35 n. 15, 41–5, 104, 112–32 *passim*, 136, 141–9, 151 n. 53, 156, 159, 160 n. 32, 161, 162, 186, 192, 193, 200, 205 n. 6, 207 n. 11, n. 13, 208 n. 17, 209 n. 20, 211 n. 30, 212, 213, 215 n. 43, 222, 224 n. 16
   Draft C 104, 105
   Discourse of Miracles 162 n. 36
   Elements of Natural Philosophy 19, 52 n. 38, 93 n. 11, 150, 155, 162 n. 36, 164, 188, 193, 195, 214 n. 39
   Essay: aims of 9, 12–30 *passim*, 33
     under-labourer passage 12–13, 15–16, 19, 23, 24, 48, 219–20, 225
     a natural history of the understanding 12, 59, 223–5
   Essay concerning Toleration 25, 28
   Essays on the Law of Nature 25, 26, 43, 113 n. 19, 162 n. 36
   Examination of Malebranche 162 n. 36
   First Reply to Stillingfleet 206 n. 10, 208 n. 17, 210 n. 24, 215 n. 42

   'Morbus' 181, 191–2, 196, 198–9
   Observations upon Growth of Vines and Olives 30 n. 69
   Paraphrase and Notes on Epistles of St Paul 201 n. 38
   Principia review 2–3, 10, 90–7, 110, 149, 162–3
   'Respirationis usus' 3, 183–5
   Second Reply 48, 97 n. 21, 142–4, 148 n. 42, 154 n. 3, 162 n. 36, 163, 165 n. 50, 189 201–2
   Some Thoughts concerning Education 10, 27–30, 70 n. 2, 82, 97, 99, 101, 102, 110, n. 2, 111 n. 4, 149, 152, 155 n. 11, 162 n. 36, 166–7, 188
   Specific Medicines review 2, 7, 81–2, 84–6, 163 n. 41
Lough John 147 n. 38, 213 n. 37
Lower, Richard 6 n. 20, 7, 58
Ludolf, Job 60 n. 76
Lüthy, C. 17 n. 26

MacDonald, J. 39 n. 23
machine analogy 17, 18, 36, 155–6
Maclean, I. 6 n. 17
Malcolm, N. 175 n. 32
Mandelbaum, M. 13–14, 16, 18, 32, 33
maps of knowledge 3, 66–8
Martin, Frederique 60 n.78
Masham, Francis Cudworth 214 n. 39
Master-Builders 12–13, 16, 23–4, 28, 73, 111, 158, 219–20
material inference 139
mathematics 11, 41, 110–35 *passim*, 145, 148–52, 163, 169, 187, 223
   certainty in 112–13, 115–16, 121, 124–6, 130–2, 140–2
   in Draft A 111–15
   in Draft B 115–18
   ideas of 124–35 *passim*
   role in natural philosophy 110–35 *passim*, 148–52, 166
   see also demonstration (mathematical), Experimental Philosophy (mathematical form), geometry
matter 14, 19, 20, 27, 42, 43–5, 84–8, 102, 104–9, 112, 152, 153, 154, 155, 157, 163, 165–6, 169–86 *passim*, 188, 196, 202, 203, 224
   Cartesian theory of 42, 92, 112, 122
   corpuscular theory of 9, 18, 19, 20, 35, 45, 84, 102, 109, 156, 163, 186, 192
   divisibility of 5, 17–18, 105, 108, 128
   Draft B view underdeveloped 43–5, 104
   Draft C has mature view 104–5
   finitude of 108
   four element theory 84, 87

historiography of 17–18
homogeneity of 186
ignorance of its nature 30, 32, 35
modes of 119
and motion as principles 99–101
as subject of natural philosophy 27
tria prima of Paracelsus 84, 87
see also acid and alkali hypothesis, cohesion, gravity, impenetrability, superaddition
Mattern, R. 192 n. 11
Mayow, John 7
McCann, E. 15, 16
McGuire, J. E. 150 n. 50, 163 n. 44
McMullin, E. 156
mechanical affections 18, 19, 20, 36, 44, 84, 105, 119, 156, 178
see also primary qualities
mechanical philosophy 10, 36, 75, 92, 167, 219
and aims of the *Essay* 12–24 *passim*
definition of 'mechanism' 18
explanatory principles of 19, 154–6
and intelligibility 160–2
laws of 162 n. 36
see also machine analogy
mechanism, *see* mechanical philosophy
medicine 6–8, 36–40, 62, 66, 169–87 *passim*, 221
and chymistry 169–70, 173, 179
environmental 52–5, 182, 186
Galenic 36–7, 39, 87, 160, 173–4, 178, 181, 221
Helmontian 177–86 *passim*
medical histories 62–6
hypotheses in 78–9, 88
and natural philosophy 6–8
reform of 6–8, 26, 36–40, 63, 177–9
specific medicines 79 n. 31, 81–2, 85, 177
see also anatomy, disease, physic
Mendip hills 53
Mercurius diaphoreticus 178
mercury of antimony 172–4, 176, n. 44, 180
metrology, Locke's interest in 114, 116, 146–7
Meyer, E. 3 n. 7
Meynell, G. G. 182 n. 68, 220 n. 4
Mill, John Stuart 86
Milton, J. R. 3 n. 6, n. 7, 16, 17, 49 n. 15, 51 n. 33, 60 , 61 n. 80, 66, 67 n. 106, 90 n. 2, 147 n. 38, 172 n. 14
mind 20–3, 27, 35, 38, 73, 107, 111, 112, 115, 117, 120, 123–5, 127, 129–31, 135, 137, 146, 159, 160, 162, 205, 207, 210–11, 223–5
always thinks 83
essence of 20
as unknown as matter 35, 107
see also understanding, innate principles
modes 118–35 *passim*
mixed 118, 122–35 *passim*, 162, 210–11
simple 115, 118, 120, 122–35 *passim*, 146
Suaresian 119

Molyneux, Thomas 66, 68, 73 n. 9, 79, 80, 87
Molyneux, William 2, 6 n. 13, 56, 68, 88–9, 92 n. 7, 101–2, 110 n. 1, 111, 204, 205, 207 n. 14, 209, 218, 224 n. 17
monsters 50, 200, 208
morality 3, 23, 25, 41
demonstrative 71, 125, 148–9
mixed modes of 125, 129, 130, 132, 133,
More, Henry 93
Moray, Sir Robert 74, 220
Morison, Robert 213
Morisonian herbarium 194
Motion: conservation of 92
and heat 18, 76, 158
inertial 91
Locke's critique of 30, 32, 104, 162, 169
modes of 119, 120, 161
as primary quality 9, 17, 18, 19, 22, 23, 36, 41, 44, 85, 92, 105, 154, 155, 156, 160, 186
simple idea of 41, 104, 117
transfer of 105, 147, 154, 162, 169
see also Contact Criterion, laws of motion, matter, primary qualities

natural history 5, 7–10, 28, 35, 41, 42, 43, 45, 46–69 *passim*, 70–3, 75, 80, 81–2, 87–9, 90, 109, 110, 152, 182, 186, 213, 219, 222–4
Baconian method of 4, 5, 8, 14, 47–69 *passim*, 70, 111, 220, 221, 223
Boyle's history of the air 51–8
Boyle's history of human blood 57–8
Goodall's history of Kinkina bark 54
see also disease (natural history of)
natural kinds, *see* species
Nedham, Marchamont 7
Neményi, P. F. 96 n. 19
Newman, W. R. 9 n. 28, 17 n. 26, 18 n. 28, 170, 171 n. 9, 172 n. 11, 175 n. 31, 176 n. 44, 177 n. 44, n. 46, 178 n. 48, 180 n. 59, 181
Newton, Sir Isaac 2, 3, 5, 9–11, 13, 15, 16 n. 18, 48, 100, 109, 110, 111, 153, 162, 169, 219–23
and Burnet 99 n. 29, n. 30
and chymistry 176
on explanation 77, 157–8
on gravity 11, 19, 103, 149–51, 154, 158
on hypotheses 75–6
Principia 3, 5, 9, 10, 11, 76, 90–7, 102, 110–11, 149–52, 154, 157, 162–3, 165 n. 46, 167, 219
on principles 11, 148, 150–2, 163, 165–7, 187, 223
rules of reasoning 76, 157–8
on the vortex theory 90–9, 220
Nicole, Pierre, 143 n. 28, 180 n. 60

Nidditch, P. H. 48 n. 14
nominal and real essence distinction 32, 35, 45, 123, 134, 155, 207
  see also essence
Norris, John 219, 224
Northamptonshire 2
number 23, 27, 112–18, 120, 125–7, 145–6
  natural numbers 127, 129
  rational numbers 127
  see also infinity, primary qualities
Nuovo, V. 201 n. 38
Nutton, V. 182 n. 66

Oldenburg, Henry 46, 51 n. 32, 55 n. 54, 57, 59 n. 74, 60, 74 n. 13, 81 n. 38, 197, 220
Oliver, John 171 n. 6
opium 158
Osler, M. J. 16 n. 18
Owen, D. 138 n. 9, 214

Pagel, W. 6 n. 18, 178 n. 49
Paracelsians 181
Paracelsus 4, 6, 178, 179, 190
  matter theory 84
  sal circulatum 177, 178, 179
Parker, Samuel 75, 151 n. 53
Parmenides 48 n. 15
Paul, Saint 201, 202
Pembroke, 8th Earl of (Thomas Herbert) 13, 23
Pepys, Samuel 13
Petty, William 7 n. 23
Philosopher's Stone 8, 170, 171, 172, 173
Philosophical Mercury 8, 170–3, 176, 185
physic (curative medicine) 6, 26, 36–9, 63, 64, 66, 88, 169, 170, 173–5, 179, 182, 185, 221
  see also medicine
physiology 7, 25, 39, 170, 179, 182, 183–5, 221
Pierre, Georges 175
Piso, Gulielmus 59, 60 n. 76
Pitcairne, Archibald 8
Pitt, Robert 185 n. 80
Porto, P. A. 178 n. 47
potable gold 174–5
Power, Henry 13 n. 2, 26, 52
primary qualities 17, 19, 24, 36, 44, 105, 124, 127, 133, 134, 146, 155–6
  Aristotelian *primae qualitates* 36, 156, 178
  see also real qualities
primary and secondary quality distinction 19, 24, 32, 35, 87, 155–6, 160, 186
Prince Rupert 173 n. 21
Principe, L. M. 3 n. 7, 8 n. 26, 9 n. 28, 170 n. 2, n. 3, 171 n. 9, n. 10, 173 n. 18, 175 n. 31, n. 32, 176, 177 n. 44, n. 46, 178 n. 48, 180 n. 59, 181, 183 n. 71
principles 3, 4, 26, 34, 38, 39, 71–3, 76, 78, 83, 111, 112, 148–68 *passim*

  explanatory 11, 19, 32, 153–7, 160
  mathematical 113 n. 19, 148, 152
  metaphysical 11, 25, 34, 222
  moral 10, 23, 25–6, 71, 148
  of natural philosophy 7, 9, 11, 27, 74, 148–52, 153, 163–6, 219, 223
  Newtonian 9, 11, 97, 148, 163–6, 187, 223
  or reason 142–4
  speculative 38, 43, 148
  speculative/practical distinction 10, 25, 26
  see also acid and alkali hypothesis, innate principles, laws of nature, seminal principles
proofs 111 n. 5, 137–9, 141, 142, 149
propositions 41–3, 75, 124, 125, 130, 138–43, 148, 151, 152
  general 121, 134, 140, 165
  instructive 112, 121
  mathematical 112, 113, 121, 122, 126, 132, 135
  uninstructive (trifling) 112, 121
  universal 41, 111–13, 120–1, 141, 223
Ptolemy, Claudius 79, 92
Purchas, Samuel 60 n. 76

qualities 13, 14, 18, 19, 24, 27, 28, 30, 35–6, 44, 45, 50, 67, 71, 73, 76–8, 82, 84, 85, 86, 87, 92, 104, 105, 123, 128, 133, 155–67 *passim*, 187, 195, 206, 207, 210–13, 215–17, 222
  co-existence of 70, 71, 147
  occult 85, 97, 158
  real 124, 160
  universal 103, 158
  see also mechanical affections, primary and secondary quality distinction, primary qualities, secondary qualities, sensible qualities, superaddition
quinine (Kinkina bark) 54

Radick, G. 224 n. 15
Ray, John 197
Read, John 173
Read, S. 139 n .14
real essences of modes 124–35
realism 11, 14, 31
  about species 189
Redi, Francesco 197, 198
Reduction Principle 155–6, 157, 160, 167
Reid, Thomas 75–6
Reimarus, Hermann Samuel 136 n. 3
respiration 3, 52, 57, 58, 170, 180, 182, 183–5
resurrection 11, 189, 193, 194, 201–3
Rogers, G. A. J. 152 n. 57, 221–2
Romanell, P. 16, 47 n. 7, 54 n. 46, 65 n. 97, 78 n. 29, 79 n. 31, 81 n. 37, 85 n. 51, 182 n. 67, 194 n. 19, 221
Roos, A. M. 179 n. 51

Royal Society 1, 2, 4, 5, 6, 13, 14 n. 6, 16, 46, 47, 51, 54 n. 43, 58, 60, 61, 68, 74, 75, 82, 89, 197
Rush, Isaac 62
Rycaut, Sir Paul 60 n. 76

salt of tartar 178, 179
salts 11, 41, 85, 172, 176 n. 41, 178–80, 182, 184
Schaffer, S. 8 n. 27, 17 n. 25
Schard, Johann 173–4, 179, 180 n. 60
Schmitt, C. 6 n. 17
Schouls, P. 15 n. 9
Schuster, J. 92 n. 6, 95 n. 15
Schuurman, P. 136 n. 4
scientia 27, 110, 138, 222
  see also demonstrative natural philosophy
secondary qualities 24, 44, 122, 146, 155, 156, 161
  see also primary and secondary quality distinction, sensible qualities
seminal principles 11, 177, 179, 180, 181–2, 186, 188–96, 198–9, 201–3, 204
  see also disease (seminal theories of)
Sennert, Daniel 18, 169–70, 190, 191, 195
sensible qualities 22, 44, 85, 104, 146, 187, 207, 212, 213
  see also primary and secondary quality distinction
Sergeant, John 3, 142
Severinus, Petrus 179
Shackleford, J. 179 n. 52
Shaftesbury, 1st Earl of (Anthony Ashley Cooper) 40, 60, 174, 179
shape (figure) 9, 17, 18, 19, 22–3, 27, 36, 40, 41, 44, 85, 92, 102, 105, 119, 120, 121, 123, 125, 130, 132–5, 141, 146, 154, 155, 156, 160, 193, 195, 200, 206, 210, 212 213 n. 37
  see also primary qualities
Sharrock, Robert 199
Shaw, Peter 46 n. 3
Simple Ideas Condition 159–60, 161, 162, 167
Simpson, William 7 n. 22
Sloane, Sir Hans 2
Sluse, René 46 n. 1
smallpox 49, 64–5, 78
Smith, G. 95 n. 15
Soles, D. 15 n. 10, 71 n. 4, 73, 83 n. 45, 88 n. 58, 139 n. 12, 151 n. 52, 222 n. 13
solidity 85, 104–5, 107–8, 123, 186
Sophic Mercury, *see* Philosophical Mercury
Sorell, T. 27 n. 62
species 11, 70, 72, 121, 123, 124, 125, 129, 133–4, 140, 145, 187, 188–203 *passim*, 204–18 *passim*
  and disease 79 n. 31, 182, 186

  in Draft B 45, 205 n. 6, 208 n. 17, 209 n. 20, 212, 213
  and natural history 50–1
  nominalism about 11, 189, 205
  realism 11, 189
  see also Locke (conventionalism about species)
Speculative Philosophy 3–5, 8–11, 24, 26, 28–30, 32, 34, 38, 42, 43, 47, 66, 74, 75, 83, 97, 150, 159, 167, 188, 203, 220, 222–3
  see also hypotheses (speculative)
sperm, spermatazoa 51, 193, 200, 201 n. 38
Spinoza, Baruch 95
spirits 27, 28, 44, 68, 99, 101, 104, 126, 128, 159, 208 n. 17
  see also angels, animals spirits
spontaneous generation 191, 193, 196–8, 200
Sprat, Thomas 7 n. 23
Stahl, Peter 172
Stamos, D. 204
Starkey, George 170–80 *passim*, 185
Stein, H. 152 n. 58
Stillingfleet, Edward 34, 97, 119 n. 41, 142–4, 148, 154, 163, 165, 189, 193, 201, 206 n. 10, 207, 208 n. 17, 210 n. 24, 215 n. 42
Stove, D. 217
Stringer, Thomas 60 n. 79
Stroup, A. 220 n. 6
Stuart, M. 17, 35, 165, 209 n. 21
Suárez, Francisco 119
substantial forms 77, 160–1, 182, 206
Suchten, Alexander von 170–3, 175 n. 31, 176
superaddition 11, 15, 17, 35, 156, 165–6, 223
Swammerdam, Jan 194
Sydenham, Thomas 2, 13, 15, 24, 28, 37–8, 49, 55, 64–6, 68, 69, 78–9, 87, 182, 219–21
  Epistolary Dissertation 64 n. 95
  on fevers 38, 182
  Methodus 24 n. 52, 38, 182
  Observationes medicae 38, 65–6
  Schedula monitoria 55
  smallpox essays 49, 78
  Sydenham influence historiography 221
  Tractatus de podagra 66 n. 101
syllogistic logic 114, 137–44, 168

Tachenius, Otto 84
Telesius, Bernardino 48 n. 15
Thévenot, Jean de 60 n. 76
Thomas, David 170, 174–5, 177, 180, 208 n. 18
Thomson, George 181 n. 64
tincture of Lili 178
Tipton, I. C. 69 n. 112
Toinard, Nicolas 92, 97
transdiction 32, 43, 162, 167

transmutation 8, 9, 11, 169, 170, 176–7, 181, 184, 185, 186, 188, 191, 195, 196, 199, 207, 223
travel literature 55, 56, 59–61, 68
truthmakers 126–7, 133, 211
Tyrrell, James 23, 30, 97, 98, 99 n. 31, 177

Ulman, H. L. 131 n. 67
understanding 12, 15, 20–3, 111, 120, 151, 152, 159, 214
  functions of 142, 207
  history of 12, 45, 59, 223–5
universals 34, 123, 189, 206
Untzer, Matthias 195 n. 21

vacuum 42, 80, 112
Vanzo, A. 136 n. 3
veil of perception 31
Velthuysen, Lambert van, 191
venesection 178
Voltaire 225
vortex theory of planetary motions 4, 10, 90, 91–7, 103, 105, 109

Walmsley, J. C. 3 n. 7, 19, 37 n. 17, 38 n. 18, 41 n. 29, 49 n. 15, 51 n. 33, 62 n. 86, 172 n. 14, 183 n. 71, 192 n. 8, 199 n. 32, n. 33
Walmsley, P. 188 n. 1,
Ward, John 172
Watts, Isaac 136

Wear, A. 37 n. 17
Webster, C. 6 n. 18
Westfall, R. S. 17
Whiston, William 10, 91, 93, 97, 101–3
Wilde, W. R. 55 n. 52
Williams, Sir Thomas 173, 174
Willis, Thomas 6, 7, 63–4, 190
Willoughby, Charles 55 n. 52
Wilson, M. D. 15, 142 n. 22, 165
Wilson, R. A. 78 n. 27, 158 n. 29, 209
Winkler, K. 136 n. 4, 152 n. 57
Winsor, P. 209 n. 21
Wolfe, C. T. 221 n. 9
Wolfe, D. E. 37 n. 17, 221
Wollaston, William 13
Wolterstorff, N. 71 n. 4
Wood, Anthony 172
Wood, N. 15, 47–8
Wood, W. J. 139 n.14
Woods, J. 139 n. 14
Woodward, John 62, 101 n. 35
Woolhouse, R. S. 14, 71 n. 4, 104, 106, 133 n. 75
workmanship of the understanding thesis 205–7
Wotton, William 75, 79
Wren, Sir Christopher 31

Yolton, J. S. 16 n. 18
Yolton, J. W. 14–16, 28 n. 63, 31 n. 4, 47, 68–9, 142 n. 23, 165 n. 46
Yost, R. 14, 47, 69

The manufacturer's authorised representative in the EU for product safety is
Oxford University Press España S.A. of el Parque Empresarial San Fernando de
Henares, Avenida de Castilla, 2 – 28830 Madrid (www.oup.es/en or product.
safety@oup.com). OUP España S.A. also acts as importer into Spain of products
made by the manufacturer.

www.ingramcontent.com/pod-product-compliance
Ingram Content Group UK Ltd.
Pitfield, Milton Keynes, MK11 3LW, UK
UKHW022231230426
12048UKWH00016BA/1180